December '95

Carolyn & Mike —
this is for both of you . include
the banana & popcorn salad .
Enjoy!
        love
              Mary Elizabeth & Shari

# Fashionable Food

## Seven Decades of Food Fads

Sylvia Lovegren

**MACMILLAN • USA**

*In memory of the three beautiful McBurney girls —*
*Margaret, Grace, and Louise.*

Macmillan General Reference
A Simon & Schuster Macmillan Company
1633 Broadway
New York, NY 10019-6785

For recipe and illustration permissions acknowledgments, see Sources and Permissions, page 422.

Poem "Crumbs of Comfort," page 3, from Lovegren, W. D., *Poems & Prose*, © 1951 Mrs. W. D. Lovegren, Eugene, Oregon. Reprinted by permission of Ed Lovegren.

Excerpt on pages 130–131 reprinted by permission of the Putnam Publishing Group from Fisher, M. F. K., *With Bold Knife and Fork*. Copyright © 1969 by M. F. K. Fisher.

Recipe for 170 Degree Steak, pages 407–8, from *The 120-Year Diet,* copyright © 1986 by Roy L. Walford, Jr. M. D., Inc. Reprinted by permission of Simon & Schuster, Inc.

CERTO, MIRACLE WHIP, PHILADELPHIA BRAND CREAM CHEESE and VELVEETA are registered trademarks of Kraft General Foods, Inc. Used with permission.

Library of Congress Cataloging-in-Publication Data
Lovegren, Sylvia.
    Fashionable food/Sylvia Lovegren
    p. cm.
    Includes index.
    ISBN 0-02-575705-9
    1.Food—History—20th century. 2. Cookery, American.
  3.Cookery—United States—Social aspects. I. Title.
TX355.L88 1995
641'.09730904—dc20           94-5371
                      CIP

Manufactured in the United States of America

10 9 8 7 6 5 4 3 2

# Acknowledgments

Thanks to Harvey Levenstein and John Mariani for their readable, sound and invaluable books—without them my work would have been much harder. And thanks also to Laura Shapiro, whose wonderful *Perfection Salad* helped me to understand how much the Home Economics movement has influenced the way we eat. Thanks to everyone who allowed me the run of the amazing stacks at the Jersey City Public Library (but shame on the politicians who lined their own pockets and let the stacks be closed for lack of funds). The librarians and research staff at the New York Public Library were terrific, but even more I would like to thank the unseen helpers in the stacks and everyone in the microfilm and photocopying divisions.

Special help and encouragement were given to me by Jill Hellendale, Philip S. Brown, Marion Gorman, Libby Hillman, Gloria Bley Miller, Paul Prudhomme and his assistant Margaret Noonan Blaum, and Rulan Chao Pian. Their kindness meant more than they will ever know.

Thanks also to the staff at the James Beard Foundation, Julia Child and her staff, Jeremiah Tower and his staff, Dan Wynn, Gary Hirano at Trader Vic's, Keith Card at Benihana of Tokyo, Judith Fadden at Nabisco, Barbara Richard and Michael Greaves at Random House, Pamela Ziogas at Leo Burnett/Magic Chef, Elizabeth Adkins, Sharon Ptak-Miles and Marilyn Kruse at General Foods, Laurel Wissinger at GE, Kevin Lawry at Campbell Soup, Alissa O'Donnell at American Spoon Foods, Laurie Baker at Rival, Denise Jansen at Cuisinart, Diana Adkins at Condé Nast, Betty Boote at *House Beautiful,* Don Boden at AP/World Wide, Norman Ng at Taylor & Ng, Lisa Stone at Armstrong World Industries, Camille Appel at McCormick & Company Inc., Mary Jon Dunham at Procter & Gamble, Mrs. Bates at Putnam, Caragh Rockwood at *Gourmet,* Joe, Sr., and Joe, Jr., at Joe's Prime Meats, Louis Hernandez at Cafe Louis, and Michael Sobsey at Sobsey's.

I would also like to thank writer and friend Nancy Hathaway for her memories of LA in the 1980s; John and Paula Brecht for being (mostly) willing guinea pigs; my sister Tanya Maes for knowing an awful recipe when she found one—and for the good ones, too; Joanna Colca for all her help; Beki Petras for providing just the right artwork, testing recipes, running errands, baby-sitting and being a friend; and her husband George for not only not complaining but helping; photo researcher Gillian Speeth for her work and for keeping me calm;

my editor Pam Hoenig for knowing her job and doing it well—and gently; Justin Schwartz and Barbara Berger for their hard work; my copyeditor Candace Levy whose input was invaluable; my agent Robin Rue for persevering; my son for not complaining too much when Mommy was busy; and most of all my husband, who was always stalwart, occasionally ruthless, and ever wonderful.

# Contents

Introduction vii

1 **The Twenties** 1
Icebox Cookery and Other Modern Ideas

2 **The Thirties** 41
Comforting Food in America

3 **An Exotic Interlude, I** 85
Chinese Food in America

4 **The Forties** 114
Oh, What a Hungry War!

5 **The Fifties** 168
Fabulous Foods for the Richest Country on Earth

6 **The Sixties** 217
Nouveaux Gourmets

7 **An Exotic Interlude, II** 268
Other Oriental Foods in America

8 **The Seventies** 300
Eating Our Way to Nirvana

9 **The Eighties** 356
For Richer, for Poorer: Status Food and Comfort Food

10 **The Nineties** 415
Fin de Siècle Cooking in the Fusion Decade

Sources and Permissions 422

Index 441

# Introduction

...too many of us are addicted to fancy food—a sign that people in this country do not think critically enough about food.... I am often invited to lunch or dinner and served with fancy concoctions when I yearn for a good, plain meal.
—Cornelia Otis Skinner, actress, 1948

It has often been said that Americans don't really like to eat. In Harvey Levenstein's *Revolution at the Table* (1988), one nineteenth-century European is quoted as saying that our national motto was "Gobble, gulp, and go."

And it is true that we feel uneasy about really caring about our food—anyone who does so too openly is considered embarrassingly effete, gluttonous, or—most damning of epithets—elitist. Despite that uneasiness, we are human after all...and humans *will* enjoy their food. But to make that natural enjoyment less grossly hedonistic and more controllable, Americans have partitioned food into two categories: gourmet (which means fancy) and everyday (which means plain).

Gourmet food is allowable and even admired as a tool for social enhancement. That was obvious during the Yuppie food snobbery of the 1980s, when knowing *exactly* when green peppercorn sauce was Out and pineapple chutney was In could be a sure but subtle indicator of status. It was just as true in a genteel middle-class home in the Twenties, when a hostess might serve "Chinese" fig and cream cheese sandwiches at her mah-jongg party to impress her guests, or in the Fifties, when the host whose chafing dish specialty was beef Stroganoff made with condensed cream of mushroom soup might be admired not only for his sophistication but also for his smart modernity.

Like teenagers playing at being world-weary adults by smoking cigarettes, many of us have played at being world-wise gourmets by cooking or eating certain foods. But we never wanted to be *real* gourmets. Anyone suspected of taking eating too seriously had to admit to the occasional gorging on hamburgers or hot dogs or other all-American everyday foods to show that he or she was not really any different from the average Joe.

As we searched for the culinary magic bullet—a particular fancy recipe or ingredient—that would make us feel like gourmets without too much work and without any embarrassment, we jumped with typical American exuberance from food fad to food fad. In doing so, we created some uniquely American culinary triumphs...and some uniquely American culinary disasters as well. Those triumphs and disasters—and what led to them—are the subject of this book.

Of course, food fads are not new. Ice cream was all the rage in the late 1700s, just as lobster Newburg was in the late 1800s. But not until the twentieth century, with the coming of the automobile, telephone, radio, and finally television, did fads for certain foods sweep the entire country in a matter of weeks or months rather than years.

This book confines itself to the twentieth century, beginning with the 1920s, not just because publishing companies are oddly shy about printing two-thousand-page tomes but also because of the tremendous shifts that have occurred in the way we live and the foods we eat since the end of World War I. The vanishing of once-plentiful maids and cooks, the rise of the giant food-processing industries, the potent influence of the domestic science movement, the coming of the electric refrigerator and gas or electric ranges, and the fact that women entered the workforce in record numbers—these things in combination changed forever what was served on the American table...and how it got there.

But even with limiting myself to the last seventy-odd years of America's culinary past, I have had to leave out a great many things. In the 1920s and 1930s many of the homes of the upper crust still had French cooks. Regretfully, the sole Marguéry and other such recipes prepared by those cooks for the tables of the elite had to be pushed aside to make room for more widely popular middle-class Fancy Dishes like frozen cheese salad and pineapple upside-down cake. On the other hand, Frenchified gourmet items became fashionable with a large segment of our increasingly sophisticated population in the Fifties, and those dishes elbowed out such American standbys as tuna-noodle casserole. (But I will be glad to send my mother's recipe for the latter to anyone who requests it.) Inevitably, many readers will be shocked to find other old favorites missing: "What! No chicken croquettes? No can-can casserole? No Nesselrode pie?" The answer is no. Maybe in the next book...

Many of the once fashionable foods that did make it into these pages can be viewed only with horror and amazement (and may convince foreigners that Americans have had good reason *not* to enjoy eating). Others will elicit a fond nostalgia. Some dishes deserve to be resurrected, at least for one meal, because they were good ideas at the time...if not necessarily for all time. And some of them were, are, and always will be downright good. But for better or for worse, all of them are part of our complex, unique, and often exuberant culinary heritage.

A note on the recipes: As much as possible the recipes in this book are true to the originals. They have not been updated for modern tastes, except occasionally to reduce the amount of salt, sugar, or fat; those changes are noted. Recipes shown as "adapted" are usually combinations culled from similar-period recipes to obtain the best or most representative result. When a recipe has had to be substantially altered because the original ingredients are no longer available or for health reasons, those changes are also noted.

# 1

# The Twenties

## Icebox Cookery and Other Modern Ideas

Q: Are vegetables ever served at a buffet luncheon?
A: Yes, indeed…provided they appear in a form which will not look messy on the plate.

—A reader's query in a 1923 issue of *American Cookery* magazine,
quoted in Laura Shapiro, *Perfection Salad* (1986)

The end of World War I marked the beginning of the modern era, not only in the larger world, but in women's domain, the kitchen, as well. As America moved into the Jazz Age, gas ranges replaced wood- and coal-burning stoves in most homes, and the mechanical refrigerator began to usurp the place of the icebox. Small foods companies grew into or were swallowed up by giants like General Foods and Standard Brands, making the food-processing industry the most highly capitalized in America. Home economists continued their successful drive to modernize, economize, and desensualize the American kitchen and the American palate, using popular women's magazines and radio shows as their forum. Scientists discovered vitamins, and the food companies, home economists, and quacks were quick to claim scientific backing for their nutritional theories. And Prohibition went into effect, forever changing the way Americans would socialize. In the midst of all this, American women cut their hair, shortened their skirts, and went to work in droves.

All of these things had a profound effect on what and how Americans ate. The labor-saving devices, which must have seemed like miracles from heaven to women who had to scrub and clean the old stoves and iceboxes, did not give most women more time to cook delicious meals for their families. On the contrary, women had even less time; as many middle-class women entered the workforce, the live-in servant went the way of the dodo bird, and the maids, servants, and hired girls who had helped with the back-breaking housework preferred jobs in offices. Either way, it seemed women had more to do and less time to do it in. One Twenties cookbook, lamenting the high cost and scarcity of servants, dubbed the housewife the "modern Mrs. Three-In-One—by which is meant she must be cook, and waitress and gracious wife or hostess."

Women were looking for ways to save time in their cooking, and home economists, scientists, and the growing food-processing industry went to work to help them. As Harvey Levenstein so cogently explained in *Revolution at the Table* (1988), this meant lighter meals, with more fruits and vegetables, which were often canned.

By the 1920s, the Domestic Scientists and home economists had very nearly succeeded in their goal of making sure that American cooks were more interested in the nourishment of the human body than in the gratification of the senses. Dainty Food was winning out over real food. Hygienic canned fruits and vegetables were preferred to fresh ones, which might show evidence of real dirt and, after all, might have been picked by unknown and unwashed hands. Savory foods were masked with white sauce or mayonnaise; sweet foods—and they were legion—with mayonnaise, whipped cream, or egg custards.

## Salads in the Twenties

It was in the salad course that Domestic Scientists and other promoters of Dainty Food scored their greatest victory. Salad components, fruits and vegetables, were inherently messy. If they had to be eaten at all—and reluctantly it was concluded that they were necessary suppliers of "vitamines," "bulk," and "mineral salts"— then let them be tamed and controlled. As Laura Shapiro pointed out in *Perfection Salad*, "Salads needed to be locked into a lettuce cup, stuffed in fruit shells or banana skins," or even better, imprisoned in gelatin to be fit food for civilized beings. And if they could also be made sweet, those messy, primitive salads had indeed been tamed. Salads often became the focal point of the menu, and the flights of fancy indulged therein by home cooks and home economists would make the American salad the identifying and often ridiculous motif of American food for decades.

Salads in which the ingredients were unrecognizable, masked, or masquerading as something else were the ideal. For one popular salad, the flesh of

My great-uncle, W. D. Lovegren, obviously a food lover, wrote this poem in 1923. While I make no claims for its artistic merit, it clearly and lovingly reflects popular foods of the time. It is interesting to note how few of these things we eat anymore.

## CRUMBS OF COMFORT

*Deep-dish huckleberry pie,*
*Lobster newberg, oyster fry,*
*Shrimp croquettes and sweetbreads creamed,*
*Cocoa roll, fruit pudding steamed,*
*Cream puffs, chocolate eclairs,*
*Crabs in alligator pears,*
*Chicken in a casserole,*
*Marguéry's filets de sole,*
*Curried eggs and salmon steaks,*
*Sausages and buckwheat cakes,*
*Frogs' legs fried, Casino clams,*
*Spicy jellies, sugary jams,*
*Chicken, lobster, mayonnaise,*
*Artichokes with Hollandaise,*
*Apple fritters, cheese soufflé,*
*Spanish cream, meringue glacée,*
*Chicken livers en brochette,*
*Steak and onions, omelette,*
*Tutti-frutti, terrapin,*
*Big sweet buns with raisins in—*

♦♦♦

*Oh, my gosh, why list them more?*
*Why write them down when before*
*Me is a dough gob and some beans?*
*Cruising's pleasant, but it means*
*Sleeping on the ground and then,*
*Eating mostly mulligan.*
*But just writing down these things*
*Sort of hollow comfort brings.*

bananas was cut into balls, then placed back in the banana skin (or "shell" as it was more prettily called), so that the fruit looked like some obscenely overgrown pea pod; this was then served with French dressing. Cream cheeses, tinted pink, green, and yellow with beet juice, parsley, and hard-boiled egg yolk by the honest cook, or with vegetable dyes by the lazy one, could be rolled into balls and placed in shredded lettuce nests for bird's nest salad. In fact, this salad became so popular for luncheons on college campuses that it was renamed sorority salad.

Food processors urged the now mostly maidless housewife to just open a can to create her salads. The Association of Hawaiian Pineapple Canners solicited recipes using their product and in 1926 published this "improvement on the ever-popular pineapple-tomato combination":

## WATER LILY SALAD

6 medium tomatoes, peeled, with stem end intact
Lettuce leaves
1 (16-ounce) can crushed pineapple, drained
Mayonnaise

Cut the tomatoes in sixths, partly through to the solid part at the stem. Press gently apart until the tomato is like a water lily, about two-thirds open. Place the tomatoes on lettuce leaves and fill the centers with crushed pineapple. Garnish with mayonnaise.

MAKES 6 SERVINGS

Pineapple, asparagus (also mostly canned and promoted heavily by California growers and packers), pimiento, and cream cheese were some of the most popular ingredients in the Twenties. Miss Alice Bradley, home economist *par excellence*, food editor of *Woman's Home Companion*, and principal of Miss Farmer's Cooking School, combined them to perfection in a salad designed in response to a reader's request for easy recipes for entertaining in a small, maidless apartment.

## ALICE BRADLEY'S KITCHENETTE VALENTINE SALAD

1 head iceberg lettuce, outer leaves removed
4 slices canned pineapple
1 (4-ounce) package cream cheese, mashed until soft
1 jar guava jelly
4 stalks canned white asparagus
1 jar pimientos, drained
French dressing

Wash and shred the lettuce and place on salad plates. Cut the pineapple into heart shapes. Spread the pineapple with the softened cream cheese and place on top of the lettuce. Fill the hole with guava jelly. Place an asparagus spear through the hole so that it looks like an arrow piercing the heart. Outline the heart with pimiento strips. Pour French dressing over the salad just before serving.

**Note:** The salad may be varied for Washington's Birthday by making a pineapple/cream cheese hatchet with an asparagus handle. On the side of the plate, make pimiento circles with bits of asparagus for stems to represent cherries.

MAKES 4 SERVINGS

Miss Bradley's hearts and hatchets met their match as edible sculpture in the notorious candlestick salad—a circle of sliced canned pineapple centered with an upright banana (the candle); a pimiento piece stood in for the flame and an artful dab of mayonnaise dripped down the side of the banana to represent melted wax. Men, however, were apt to make ribald comments about the salad's likeness to more anatomical items, and candlestick salad was usually relegated to the strictly feminine luncheon.

---

## The Worst Salad of the Twenties

In a decade of truly awful salads it is difficult, but fun, to try to choose the worst. Here is my nomination.

### BANANA AND POPCORN SALAD

"Very artistic and economical," said the contributor, who, along with the famous book she contributed it to, will remain anonymous.

> 1 banana, peeled and cut in half lengthwise
> Lettuce leaf
> Popcorn
> Mayonnaise

Place the banana on the lettuce leaf. Scatter popcorn over the banana and put dabs of mayonnaise here and there.

MAKES 1 SERVING

A much simpler salad very popular in the Twenties—and not at all likely to raise eyebrows or lowbrows—was canned pear salad. A canned pear half was placed on a lettuce leaf and the center was filled with various combinations of cream cheese balls, chopped walnuts, grated cheddar, currant jelly, and so on. The pear half was then topped with a dab of mayonnaise or a splash of French dressing and served.

Another ingredient dear to the hearts of cooks in the 1920s was the pickle—and if it was sweet so much the better. Cunning cooks managed to work sweet pickles into a salad dainty enough for the ladies yet hearty enough with its leguminous ingredients for the protein-hungry men.

## Iceberg—The American Salad Basic

Salads were not very popular in America before the 1900s, and up to that point most salad greens that were eaten were grown in the home garden. But the burgeoning interest in vitamins, "roughage" (fiber), and lighter meals made salads at least a daily feature in the Twenties. And what made even a banana-popcorn-mayonnaise combination a *salad* was the lettuce leaf on which it reposed. That lettuce leaf was likely to be iceberg.

W. Atlee Burpee & Co. (Warminster, Pennsylvania) introduced iceberg lettuce in 1894. A type of heading lettuce that takes about eighty-five days from sowing to maturity (leaf lettuce averages forty-five to fifty days) and requires constant and relatively cool temperatures to form the characteristic heads, iceberg was difficult for the home gardener to grow successfully. But as demand for salad greens grew, commercial growers stepped in to pick up the profits. These new producers found that they not only could grow iceberg but they could ship its virtually indestructible heads cross-country with few casualties. Growers showed a threefold increase in lettuce shipments from 1920 to 1935, most of it in pale, crisp, and nearly tasteless iceberg.

As important as the commercial growers were to the astounding success of iceberg, Americans had long shown a preference for head lettuces over the leaf type. In 1809 founding father and gourmet Thomas Jefferson grew an early variety of head lettuce called "Tennis Ball." Burpee's 1888 seed catalog listed twenty-three head lettuces, three romaine type, and only one leaf lettuce. Iceberg lettuce, which came out six years later, would continue to be one of the only lettuces most Americans would ever know (outside of romaine, the second most popular type) until the New American Cooking brought a taste for tender young leaf lettuce in the late 1970s.

Incidentally, Burpee's 1994 seed catalog, which now includes such exotics as arugula and radicchio in its leafy offerings, lists the hundred-year-old iceberg as an heirloom variety.

## THREE P'S SALAD

Although this salad is a real period piece, the combination of peas and peanuts (sans pickles) had resurgences in the 1970s and 1980s in stylish suburban salads.

    I cup canned peas, drained
    I cup chopped sweet pickles (or substitute sweet pickle relish)
    I cup chopped peanuts
    I cup mayonnaise
    Lettuce cups

Mix all the ingredients together. Chill. Serve in lettuce cups.
MAKES 4 TO 6 SERVINGS

# Gelatin, Aspic, Jell-O and Congealed Salads

Before the turn of the century gelatins and aspics were popular—as both savories and desserts—but they were luxuries, dishes for the honored guest or the invalid. The time needed to prepare a proper jellied dish using home-prepared calf's-foot jelly was astounding and nearly impossible for the housewife with children to be fed and housework to be done. Isinglass (a gelatin made from the air bladders of fish), agar (made from algae), and various mosses were sometimes used as gelling agents, but they were not universally available. Boxed sheets of prepared gelatin made the housewife's work much easier, but the early versions of gelatin still had to be cleared by cooking the gelatin with egg whites and shells, skimming off any scum, and then dripping it through a jelly bag. Still, this was so much easier than the old method that one 1870s cookbook writer, after using the gelatin sheets, swore she would never make her own calf's-foot jelly again.

Some sources credit Charles R. Knox with first packaging gelatin sheets (after watching his wife labor over calf's-foot jelly) in the 1890s, but packaged gelatin was available long before that. It does seem likely, however, that Mr. Knox marketed one of the first commercially successful powdered gelatins in 1894.

Also in the 1890s came Jell-O. At first, sales of the presweetened, preflavored instant dessert were dismal, but by the turn of the century Jell-O was a hit. Now the homemaker could have the glamour of a shimmering gelatin almost effortlessly. When electric home refrigerators came along to make dishes that needed chilling even easier to prepare, Jell-O's popularity was boundless. By the time Postum Cereal Co. (later General Foods) took over the Jell-O Company, Inc., in 1925, Jell-O's sales made up a substantial portion of its new parent company.

Jell-O and other packaged gelatins had been intended to simplify the housewife's preparation of jellied desserts. But Domestic Scientists soon recognized the quivery stuff as the perfect place to imprison those messy fruits and vegetables Americans insisted on eating as salads. Sarah Tyson Rorer printed only one gelatin salad recipe in her 1898 *Mrs. Rorer's New Cook Book* (it was for cubed turnips in aspic). By the Jazz Age, almost one-third of the "salad" recipes in the average cookbook were gelatin based. Filled with chopped, cubed, cooked, canned, and otherwise mutilated vegetables or fruit, or with cream cheese mashed or balled, congealed salads were the "bee's knees," in the slang of the period.

Two of the most popular gelatin salads were tomato aspic (plain or studded with vegetables, hard-boiled egg slices, or chopped chicken or tongue) and perfection salad (sometimes called jellied coleslaw). But cooks realized the possibilities for this new medium were unlimited. Canned crushed pineapple was a favorite ingredient (fresh pineapple cannot be used because its enzymes break down the proteins in gelatin), as were chopped green peppers and chopped olives. Jellied cheese salads made with gelatin, grated American cheese, cottage cheese, or cream cheese could be "put in little molds and served as a cheese delicacy," according to one cookbook of the period.

*Jewel Salad*

And then there was ginger ale salad. In *Perfection Salad,* Laura Shapiro credits Fannie Farmer with its invention, but no matter who was the first to use that thoroughly modern ingredient, soda pop, in a gelatin salad, cooks took to the idea immediately. *Joy of Cooking* called its ginger ale salad one of the best molded salads ever. *Joy,* along with a number of other earlier cookbooks, included chopped candied ginger to reinforce the taste of the ginger ale.

# 1920S GINGER ALE SALAD

1 tablespoon unflavored gelatin
$^1/_4$ cup cold water
$^1/_2$ cup boiling water or fruit juice
3 tablespoons sugar
1 cup ginger ale
$^1/_4$ cup lemon juice
Pinch salt
$^1/_2$ cup chopped canned pears
$^1/_2$ cup chopped canned peaches
1 teaspoon minced candied ginger
$^1/_4$ cup canned crushed pineapple, drained
$^1/_3$ cup walnut meats, chopped
Lettuce leaves
Mayonnaise

Soak the gelatin in the cold water until soft in a large bowl. Pour the boiling water over and stir until dissolved. Stir in the sugar, then add the ginger ale, lemon juice, and salt and stir until mixed. Chill until it begins to set. Fold in the fruits, ginger, and walnuts. Turn into oiled molds and chill until firm. Serve on a lettuce leaf and top with a swirl of mayonnaise.

## Frozen Salads

If Dainty Food really came into its own in the salad course then frozen salads were the pinnacle of daintiness. Not only were potentially messy foodstuffs neatly contained in icy squares, rectangles, or—ooh la la—bombe molds, but the cold of the ingredients rendered less effective those two dangerously voluptuous senses: taste and smell. Frozen salads also had lovely snob appeal, because before the advent of electric home refrigeration they either had to be made in cumbersome ice and salt freezers or, as Domestic Scientist Ida C. Bailey Allen said, they were "rare luxuries at unusual prices" generally available only at expensive restaurants and the best hotels.

It is hard to imagine the impact of home refrigeration in these days of freezer to microwave food. In the Twenties, it meant the end of the drudgery of cleaning and maintaining the icebox. It meant controllable temperatures, in which food could be kept reliably cold for longer periods. It meant less frequent marketing and the easy reuse of leftovers. And it meant the housewife could now freeze (small) things easily at home.

# The New Home Refrigerators

It wasn't until after 1918 that mechanical refrigerators were widely available. By the mid-1920s they were still so novel that the *New Yorker* exclaimed, "Refrigerators that are small palaces of impeccably white porcelain and gleaming polished nickel are marvels of workmanship and efficiency. A little water is put in some mysterious place; a few minutes pass, a magic door opens, and a tray of small ice cubes appears before your startled eyes."

American housewives took to the mechanical refrigerator as fast as their finances would allow. By 1937 more than two million American households had the new refrigerators, and by the mid-1950s over 80 percent of the population did. (In contrast, only 8 percent of English households had refrigerators by 1956.)

Those first refrigerators were still very rudimentary. The freezing units were small, thin metal compartments inside the main cabinet of the refrigerators. Instructions were given for the woman who wanted to have ice cubes (which had to be chipped out of their trays) and a frozen dessert at the same time. For the quickest freezing, the metal freezer tray was supposed to be wet on the bottom. Unfortunately, this often made the tray itself freeze to the inside of the freezing unit. Warm cloths or steam could be applied, if necessary, to remove the tray from the freezer; using an ice pick to hack it out was specifically not recommended. If the refrigerator was not running cold enough to make ice, the housewife had to call in the dealer to lower the temperature for her.

As basic as the refrigerators were, they were a vast improvement over the old-fashioned icebox, which was, essentially, an insulated box cooled by a large chunk of ice, which was usually delivered weekly. The temperature in the icebox varied greatly, depending on how many times it was opened and the size of the piece of ice inside, and certainly nothing could be frozen in it. And the ice melted, which increased not only the temperature in the icebox but the housework involved as well. One 1929 *Collier's* article about maintaining the icebox said, "Slime accumulates in [the drainpipes] constantly and should be removed with a long-handled circular brush. If your over-flow pipe connects with an outside drain be sure there is a trap in it to prevent poisonous gases and odors flowing up it and contaminating foods in the box."

In the 1927 General Electric cookbook *Electric Refrigerator Recipes and Menus*, Miss Alice Bradley candidly admitted that refrigerators were so new that their potential was still unknown and that her recipes represented just a beginning in heretofore unknown gastronomic territory. But she urged her timid readers to "study the recipes and especially the suggestions that follow many of the recipes until you acquire the dare to make other combinations."

Although Miss Bradley gave a few refrigerator recipes, most of the book consisted of freezer recipes. And one of the most popular of these was frozen cheese salad. Here is a version from a 1924 Seattle compilation cookbook.

## FRUIT & FLOWER MISSION FROZEN CHEESE SALAD

2 (8-ounce) packages cream cheese, creamed until light
$^1/_2$ cup mayonnaise
$^1/_2$ cup heavy cream, whipped until firm
1 small jar pimientos, drained and finely chopped, about $^1/_3$ cup
1 green bell pepper, seeded and finely chopped, about 1 cup
$^1/_4$ cup chopped pecans
Salt, pepper, and paprika
Mayonnaise for serving

Mix the cream cheese with the mayonnaise and whipped cream. Stir in the pimientos, peppers, and pecans. Season to taste with salt, pepper, and paprika. Pack into a mold (note: individual serving molds are fun) and freeze until firm. Dip the mold in warm water and turn out on a platter. Serve with mayonnaise.

MAKES 6 SERVINGS

Frozen chicken, frozen asparagus, frozen celery, and frozen salmon, tuna, and crabmeat salads were all popular. Most of these salads were the perfect feminine entrée for a luncheon or light supper, and all of them were rich with mayonnaise and cream. Another popular frozen "salad" was tomato frappé, a sort of savory ice. Most recipes of the period called for tomatoes cooked with bay leaves, onions, and other flavorings to be sieved, then frozen. But in June 1929, *Pictorial Review*, in a feature about "cooking" with your refrigerator, published the following truly modern recipe.

## TOMATO FRAPPÉ, *PICTORIAL REVIEW*

This recipe has not been tested.

2 cans condensed tomato soup
Crisp lettuce

Freeze the tomato soup in a refrigerator tray for 4 hours, stirring at the end of 1 hour and every $^1/_2$ hour thereafter. Turn out onto shredded lettuce in a sherbet glass and serve with the main course.

MAKES 6 SERVINGS

Even more appealing to the home economics group and to housewives trying to prepare "company dinners" without a maid was the frozen fruit salad. It could be used, cut into squares and served on a lettuce leaf or mounded into a sherbet cup, as a first course, as a salad, or as dessert. It was white, it was creamy, and it was sweet, sweet, sweet.

Frozen fruit salad may never grace the tables of the trendy 1990s bistros, but it has been popular with American homemakers for more than sixty years. Although it may be much too sweet to take the place of radicchio dressed with extra virgin olive oil and balsamic vinegar, it is still a good, cold, creamy fruit dessert.

## FROZEN FRUIT SALAD

The *Kelvinator Book of Recipes* called this sweet treat a dessert but said, "If for salad, add one cup toasted almonds." Another popular version replaced the egg yolk mixture with one cup of mayonnaise, which did indeed make it more of a salad, but a peculiar one to modern tastes.

2 cups mixed canned fruit, well drained, and cubed, juice reserved
1 tablespoon butter
1 tablespoon flour
1/2 cup reserved fruit juice
1 egg yolk
2 teaspoons sugar
2 tablespoons lemon juice
6 large marshmallows
1 cup heavy cream, whipped until stiff peaks form
Lettuce leaves for serving

Melt the butter in the top of a double boiler, over but not in simmering water. Stir in the flour, then slowly stir in the fruit juice. When the mixture is smooth but not hot, stir in the egg yolk, sugar, and lemon juice. Cook, stirring constantly, until thick and hot. Add the marshmallows and continue stirring over low heat until they melt. Remove from the heat and cool. Stir the drained fruits into the cooled egg mixture, then fold in the whipped cream until well blended. Turn into an 8 × 11-inch pan (in the Twenties it would have been two refrigerator trays) and freeze, covered, until firm. Take out of the freezer and let sit at room temperature 10 minutes before cutting. Slice into squares and serve on crisp lettuce leaves.

MAKES 10 SERVINGS

Not all the salads popular in the Twenties were sweet, feminine fripperies, filled with pickles, pineapple, and mayonnaise. Caesar salad became popular during the Depression, and a salad dish less likely to please the Home Economists could not be thought of. With its heady aromas of garlic, olive oil, Parmesan cheese, and Worcestershire sauce; with its fresh romaine, coddled egg, and crisp croutons—this was a robust, frankly masculine salad.

Most authorities agree with John Mariani, *Dictionary of American Food and Drink*, that Caesar Cardini invented Caesar salad in the 1920s in Tijuana. Most cooks also add anchovy to the salad, which Mariani claims is heretical. But however it was first made, an "authentic" Caesar salad has as many variations as authentic bouillabaisse. And like bouillabaisse, so long as the ingredients are fresh and of high quality and so long as it is made with respect, it is very good.

## CAESAR SALAD

Unfortunately for Caesar lovers, undercooked egg nowadays may contain salmonella organisms and is no longer safe to eat. The salad may be made without the egg, but it will not have the unctuous quality that makes it so good. Pending improvement in egg quality, it is advised that this recipe is for reading purposes only.

$^3/_4$ cup extra virgin olive oil
2 garlic cloves, peeled and smashed
2 cups French or Italian bread cubes, without crusts
2 heads romaine lettuce, washed, dried, and chilled
Pinch of salt
Freshly ground black pepper
Juice of 1 lemon
$^1/_2$ teaspoon Worcestershire sauce
2 large eggs, cooked in their shells in boiling water for 1 minute
$^1/_3$ cup freshly grated best Parmesan cheese

In a heavy skillet, warm half the olive oil with the garlic cloves. When the oil is hot but not smoking, add the bread cubes and sauté over medium heat until brown. Remove the croutons from the pan and set aside.

Break the lettuce into large bite-size pieces and place them in a large bowl, preferably glass. Sprinkle the lettuce with the salt and half the remaining oil and toss it well (hands work best). Add the rest of the oil, a few grinds of fresh pepper, the lemon juice, and Worcestershire sauce. Toss the salad again. Break in the eggs and add the cheese. Toss the salad until the eggs and cheese are well blended. Top with the croutons and serve on chilled plates.

MAKES 6 TO 8 SERVINGS

# Tea Rooms

A tea-room salad that was new to me had a foundation of macaroni and celery, cut in match-like strips, mixed with Russian dressing. Each portion was garnished with a jolly red flower stamped from pimiento, with a clove stuck through as a center.

—Helena Judson, "Try These Tea-Room Touches," *Pictorial Review* (March 1926)

The Domestic Science brand of cookery—dainty, light, disguised, sweet, and creamy—found its home in the Twenties in the tea room. There could be enjoyed true Ladies' Cooking for Ladies, although men went too after Prohibition closed many of the hotel restaurants and café bars.

Across the country women by the thousands opened their cozy little restaurants, each one armed with hopes and dreams...and a pet recipe for hot rolls, graham gems, or frozen fruit salad. For, said one successful tea shop owner, "Trade Secret Number One" was to "offer one particular palate tickler that your customers cannot duplicate elsewhere." (Hers was "an old family recipe for Southern hot rolls.")

Home Economists *loved* tea rooms and frequently recommended them as the place where a hostess might find "new and superdelicious dishes for serving at her own teas and luncheons." And what were these "superdelicious" dishes? Ahh. "Novelty" cheese and vermicelli croquettes with interiors of "delicious moss-like consistency," or creamed sweetbreads in patty shells, or chicken à la king on toast points, or creamed chicken shortcake, or sausages rolled in thin pancakes "served in a prim little row with a garnish of creamed potato." But those were the hearty entrées.

Tea room salads were unrivaled in their daintiness. A salad served at the "artistic and unusual" Les Rendezvous in Philadelphia consisted of a peeled tomato stuffed with chicken salad mixed with bits of mushrooms, green pepper, and pimiento, the whole garnished with a circle of stuffed olives, a second circle of thinly sliced cucumber pickle, and dots of spiced pickled beets. Fruit salad, being sweet, was naturally the best kind of salad. In the "chatty tininess" of the Cozy-Corner Tea Shop near Washington, D.C., delicate ladies could feast on a fruit salad made with peaches, canned pineapple, banana, white grapes, dates, grapefruit, and orange; dressed with a boiled sugar, egg, and whipped cream dressing; and garnished with "lusciously plump raisins and pecan meats."

Sandwiches, of course, were on the menu at tea rooms. And for the men, the restaurants offered sliced tongue, or chopped beefsteak sandwiches with chili sauce. But to go with the sort of fruit salad described above, any lady feeling a bit peckish might want these marmalade sandwiches for an ambrosial feast.

## MARMALADE SANDWICHES FOR LADIES

Boston brown bread or whole wheat bread, thinly sliced
Butter, softened
1 (8-ounce) package cream cheese
2 tablespoons heavy cream
2 tablespoons orange marmalade
2 tablespoons finely chopped walnuts or pecans

If using whole wheat bread, remove the crusts. Butter the slices of bread generously. Mash the cream cheese until it is soft. Work in the cream, then the marmalade and nuts. If the mixture is still stiff, add more cream. Spread one slice of buttered bread with the cream cheese mixture. Top with another slice of buttered bread. Press gently, then cut into fingers or triangles.

MAKES 4 TO 6 SERVINGS

After such an ethereal luncheon, even the most delicate female would have room for dessert. In the tea rooms, icebox cakes were popular, along with the other frothy, feminine confections of the Twenties. Sponge cakes, split and filled with fruit purées and whipped cream, were a strong favorite. If appetites were very hearty, a deep-dish apple pie—with a slice of cheese alongside for the men—might be served. But sometimes ladies liked something small and neat, something that didn't have to be eaten with a fork, some perfect little bite to swallow prettily with the last cup of tea. Delicious cornflake macaroons much like those served at the "quaint and alluring" Bird in Hand Tea Shop outside Philadelphia might have been just the thing.

## TEA SHOP CORNFLAKE MACAROONS

Prepared cereals were a popular cookie ingredient in the Twenties. Don't make these on a humid day.

1/2 cup egg whites
1 cup firmly packed brown sugar
1 teaspoon vanilla
1 cup unsweetened shredded coconut
1 cup walnuts, finely chopped
1 cup cornflakes, slightly crushed

Preheat the oven to 325°F. Beat the egg whites until stiff, but not dry, peaks form. Slowly beat in the salt, sugar, and vanilla. Quickly and lightly stir in the coconut, walnuts, and cornflakes. Drop the batter by spoonfuls onto a greased and floured baking sheet. Bake until the cookies look dry and set but not brown, 10 to 12 minutes.

MAKES ABOUT 48 COOKIES

By the end of the Twenties, there was a glut of tea rooms, many of them bad. More and more people, particularly men and busy career gals, were looking for more substantial food, cooked and served more quickly, and at lower prices. Soon coffee shops and luncheonettes took a hefty share of tea room business, and most of the tea rooms closed their doors. While a few went on and even prospered through the decades, most tea room cookery survived only in better department store restaurants where ladies, looking for a gentle haven after some strenuous shopping, could find the Dainty Food needed to restore their delicate systems.

# Dainty Desserts for Ladies

Twenties' desserts often reflected Domestic Scientists' nonfood approach to food, but they also reflected the new hurry-up cooking ethic. The modern woman was probably maidless, worked in an office all day, and came home to a tiny kitchenette apartment. The age of concocted, rather than cooked, desserts had arrived.

Many of these were frothy, cloudlike, and very feminine. Whipped gelatin, whipped cream, whipped egg whites, and marshmallows were all incorporated into desserts to make them delicate, ethereal, and devastatingly rich.

## Heavenly Hash and Flapper Pudding—Pudding Desserts in the Twenties

Probably no dessert was sweeter and more concocted than heavenly hash. Nowadays what we mean by heavenly hash is usually a chocolate candy confection studded with marshmallows and nuts, but in the 1920s heavenly hash was a pudding, and an archetypal one at that. It involved no cooking, it was quick and easy, and it contained all the favorite sweet ingredients of the period.

## HEAVENLY HASH

25 marshmallows, cut into small pieces (or substitute miniature marshmallows)
$^1/_2$ cup canned small pineapple chunks, drained
$^1/_2$ cup chopped glacé cherries
$^1/_2$ cup chopped walnuts
2 cups heavy cream, whipped until soft peaks form
Ladyfingers for garnish

Fold the marshmallows, fruit, and nuts into the whipped cream. Spoon into parfait glasses and serve with ladyfingers.

**Variation:** For the pineapple and cherries, substitute 1 cup chopped dates, tossed with the juice of $^1/_2$ lemon, and 6 crushed macaroons.

MAKES 6 TO 8 SERVINGS

Something known as Flapper pudding—because it was so easy that even the modern flibbertigibbet, the Flapper, could make it—became the rage in the Twenties. A ladyfinger and pudding concoction similar to a trifle, it was also called icebox cake. These "cakes" were often flavored with lemon or chocolate, but the most popular was made with canned crushed pineapple. Their popularity lasted well into the Forties.

While icebox cakes have been out of fashion for three decades, they are certainly worth reviving. And not just for their creamy, soothing goodness. They also conjure up—for this taster anyway—the gentle world of grandmother's favorite tea room, where the old-fashioned aroma of a pineapple dessert is inextricably mixed with the comforting, feminine scents of lavender water and loose powder. Although this cake may seem positively frowzy, its similarity to charlottes, trifles, and even southern banana pudding should reassure all but the most hesitant.

## FLAPPER PUDDING (ICEBOX CAKE)

The original recipes call for uncooked beaten egg whites to be folded into a base of uncooked egg yolks creamed with butter and sugar for the filling. With the danger of salmonella poisoning present in raw eggs these days, I have adapted a recipe by using Italian meringue folded into a cooked egg yolk base. Although the modern version is similar in taste and texture to the original, it does take more time.

> 1 recipe Italian Meringue (below)
> 1 recipe Pineapple Pudding (below) or Lemon Curd (p. 73) or a basic
>  chocolate pudding
> 30 small ladyfingers
> 1 cup heavy cream
> $^1/_2$ teaspoon vanilla extract
> 2 tablespoons confectioners' sugar
> Candied or maraschino cherries for garnish (optional)

Fold the Italian Meringue into the Pineapple Pudding until well blended. Line a 10 × 6-inch pan with waxed paper (a Twenties touch—you can use plastic wrap) so that the paper comes over the sides of the pan. Line the bottom of the pan with one-third of the ladyfingers, rounded sides down. Cover with half the pineapple mixture. Top with one-third more of the ladyfingers. Cover with the rest of the filling. Put the rest of the ladyfingers over the top. Cover the pan and refrigerate for 12 hours or overnight. Whip the cream with the vanilla and sugar until soft peaks form. Unmold the cake onto a serving platter. Cover the cake with the whipped cream and garnish with the cherries.

MAKES 8 TO 10 SERVINGS

## ITALIAN MERINGUE

> 1 cup sugar
> $^1/_4$ teaspoon cream of tartar
> $^1/_4$ cup water
> 3 large egg whites, beaten until stiff but not dry

Dissolve the sugar and cream of tartar in the water in a heavy saucepan. Do not stir after this point. Bring to a slow boil over medium heat. Cover and boil 3 minutes. Take off the lid and bring slowly to the soft ball stage (238° to 240°F on a candy thermometer) when a spoonful of the syrup dropped into a cup of ice water forms a ball that flattens when you touch it. Gradually pour the hot syrup over the beaten egg whites, beating constantly until cool.

## PINEAPPLE PUDDING

1/4 cup sugar
3 tablespoons cornstarch
1/4 cup hot water
1 cup unsweetened pineapple juice
3 large egg yolks
2 tablespoons butter
1 tablespoon lemon juice
1 teaspoon grated lemon rind
1 cup canned crushed pineapple, well drained

Mix the sugar and cornstarch together in a saucepan. Slowly stir in the hot water and pineapple juice. Cook over medium heat, stirring constantly, but not vigorously, until thick; cook 1 minute more. Beat the egg yolks lightly. Beat some of the hot cornstarch mixture into the yolks to thin and warm them. Then stir the yolk mixture into the saucepan. Bring to a slow boil. Boil 1 minute, stirring constantly. Remove from the heat and stir in the butter and lemon juice and rind. Stir in the crushed pineapple. Cool before using.

Bavarian creams; pudding-filled Charlottes; and whips, sponges, and snows based on gelatin whipped just before it sets or on uncooked eggs whites beaten into gelatin or fruit mixtures were all fashionable. One of the most popular desserts in this style, however, was the no-cook, no-work, just-stir-it-up "fluff." And one of the most popular ingredients in the fluff was...canned pineapple.

## PINEAPPLE FLUFF

Don't be tempted to use miniature marshmallows—they have too much cornstarch coating, which gives an unpleasant texture. For the complete Twenties look, serve the fluff in a cut-glass bowl with pink marshmallows for garnish.

1 (16-ounce) can sweetened crushed pineapple with juice
1/2 pound marshmallows, cut into quarters
Whipped cream for garnish

Open the can of pineapple and turn it into a large bowl. Add the marshmallows. Cover and put in the refrigerator. Stir the mixture occasionally, until the marshmallows dissolve. Put in a serving bowl and serve, very cold, garnished with whipped cream.

**Variation:** Substitute canned berries (or crushed fresh berries mixed with sugar to taste and left until the juice runs) for the pineapple.

MAKES 4 SERVINGS

Just to balance the glut of pineapple desserts, here is one recipe with a banana base. (And Americans did love bananas. In desserts and in salads, bananas were second only to King Pineapple. One of the most popular songs of the Twenties was Frank Silver and Irving Cohn's "Yes! We Have No Bananas.") Obviously, other sliced or crushed fruits—even pineapple—can be substituted for the bananas in this dessert, but then it wouldn't be monkey pudding.

## MONKEY PUDDING

In the South vanilla pudding and Nilla Wafers are added to this to make banana pudding.

1 cup heavy cream
2 tablespoons confectioners' sugar
1 tablespoon vanilla extract
3 bananas, peeled

Whip the cream with the sugar and vanilla until soft peaks form. Slice the bananas. Stir them into the whipped cream. Chill and serve.

**Variation:** Mash the bananas with a little lemon juice (to prevent browning) and fold the mashed bananas into the sweetened whipped cream.

MAKES 4 SERVINGS

Pies, too, followed the ethereal fashion, and meringue pies were far and away the favorites. They came in every conceivable flavor. Nowadays we still see an occasional lemon meringue pie. In the Twenties they ate apple meringue, grapefruit meringue, orange meringue, prune meringue, apricot meringue, fig meringue, date meringue, raisin meringue, custard meringue, chocolate meringue, and…pineapple meringue.

## Let Them Eat Cake

A Betty Crocker booklet called the Twenties "the beginning of the real cake era." In looking at the cookbooks from the period you begin to see what was meant. There were spice cakes, angel cakes, devil cakes, sponge cakes, and fudge cakes. There were date cakes, nut cakes, prune cakes, and jam cakes. There were pound cakes, fairy cakes, buttermilk cakes, chocolate cakes, eggless cakes, burnt-sugar cakes, mocha cakes, sunshine cakes, maple cakes, marble cakes, and checkerboard cakes. These lush creations were stuffed, gilded, and embellished with luscious frostings, fillings, and icings opulently flavored with chocolate, coconut, marshmallow, lemon, orange, whipped cream, mocha, caramel, pineapple, maple, maraschino, and brown sugar.

Part of the reason for cake's newfound popularity was that, in those recently maidless and hurry-up days, it became fashionable to have only one dish for the dessert course. *Pictorial Review*'s April 1928 issue assured the worried hostess that her cake could be made as tall and imposing as she wished, and that by "adding story upon story to her confection…everyone who beholds it will be convinced that such a cake only, is sufficient for the complete course."

Certainly one of the most imposing cakes was the Lady Baltimore. Although this cake of Charleston, South Carolina, origin was first made in the late 1800s, it was immensely popular in the Twenties. More confection than cake, rich with butter and eggs, stuffed with nuts and fruits, and topped with a devastatingly sweet meringue frosting, Lady Baltimore was perfect Ladies' Luncheon food—and perfectly delicious.

There are as many variations of Lady Baltimore cake as there are cooks. The following one, however, is from Alicia Rhett Mayberry, a great lady of Charleston who is usually conceded to have introduced the cake. Mrs. Mayberry's recipe is made with *two* separate fillings and contains no figs or rose water, common additions in other recipes.

## LADY BALTIMORE CAKE

Although the original recipe says this will make three layers, I found it to be a two-layer, plus one very large cupcake, cake. Two layers will not make a cake as ineffably high as the standard Lady Baltimore. On the other hand, the fillings in this recipe are so achingly sweet and rich—more like divinity fudge than frosting—that two layers are already overkill. Reserve this cake only for those with a real sweet tooth.

**For the Cake**
    ¹/₂ cup (I stick) butter
    I ¹/₂ cups sugar
    2 large eggs, separated
    2 cups cake flour
    I teaspoon baking powder
    ¹/₂ teaspoon salt
    I cup milk

**For Filling I**
    I cup sugar
    ¹/₂ cup walnut meats
    ¹/₄ cup water
    I teaspoon vanilla extract
    I teaspoon almond extract

**For Filling II and Assembly**

    2 cups sugar
    ½ cup water
    2 large egg whites, beaten until stiff but not dry
    1 teaspoon vanilla extract
    1 teaspoon almond extract
    1 cup chopped raisins
    1 cup chopped walnuts
    Juice of ½ lemon

Preheat the oven to 375°F. Butter two 8-inch layer cake pans and 2 medium muffin cups. To make the cake, cream the butter and sugar together until light. Beat the egg yolks until light, then beat them into the butter mixture. Sift the dry ingredients together three times. Fold the dry ingredients into the butter mixture alternately with the milk, ending with the flour mixture. Beat the egg whites until stiff but not dry. Fold the whites into the batter. Spoon the batter into the cake and muffin cups and bake until they test done, about 25 minutes. Take out of the oven and let rest in the pans 10 minutes. Remove from the pans and cool on a wire rack. When cool, set the cupcakes aside for another use; fill and frost the cake layers as described below.

While the cakes are baking, make the fillings. For Filling I, put the sugar, walnuts, and water in a small saucepan and cook over medium heat without stirring to the very soft ball stage (232°F on a candy thermometer) when a spoonful of syrup dropped into a cup of ice water forms thick threads. Remove from the heat and let cool to 110°F. Stir in the extracts, then beat until slightly thickened. Set aside until the cake layers are cool. Spread half of Filling I over each cake layer.

For Filling II, dissolve the sugar in the water in a heavy saucepan. Do not stir after this point. Bring to a boil over medium heat. Cover and boil for 3 minutes. Remove the cover and boil over medium-low heat until the mixture reaches the firm ball stage (246°F on a candy thermometer) when a spoonful of the syrup dropped into a cup of ice water forms a ball that holds its shape unless pressed with a finger. Pour the hot syrup slowly into the beaten egg whites, beating constantly. (Be sure to add slowly or you will end up with very nasty, sticky nuggets of cooked egg.) Continue beating until cool. Quickly add the extracts, raisins, nuts, and lemon juice. Set aside until the cake layers are cooled. Spread a little of Filling II over Filling I on each layer. Stack one layer on top of the other, filling sides up. Frost the sides with the rest of Filling II.

MAKES 1 CAKE AND 2 CUPCAKES

Marshmallows were one of the most ubiquitous ingredients in the Twenties. They popped up in salads, in desserts—and in cakes as well. Although marshmallows didn't usually make it into the actual cake batter—that didn't come until the Forties—they appeared frequently in frostings, especially ones topped with coconut, to make an ethereal, delicious confection, sweet enough and dainty enough for any feminine gathering.

In the 1800s marshmallows had to be made from scratch, using gum arabic from the pharmacist. By the Twenties, commercial marshmallows and marshmallow cream were available, which made the plethora of marshmallow desserts and "salads" more understandable.

This marshmallow-coconut cake remained popular for many years. In fact it was served to President Truman on one of his trips to the Florida Keys in the early Fifties.

## MARSHMALLOW-COCONUT CAKE

Whether you use large marshmallows cut in eighths or the miniatures, be sure they are absolutely fresh and soft or they won't melt properly. If they aren't soft, put them in the top of a double boiler with a drop of water and cook over low heat for a few minutes.

> 2 cups sugar
> 1 cup water
> 2 large egg whites, beaten until stiff peaks form
> 2 cups miniature marshmallows, or large marshmallows cut in eighths
> 1 two-layer butter cake (Lady Baltimore Cake, p. 23, is fine)
> 1 cup shredded coconut (see note)

Dissolve the sugar in the water in a heavy pan. Do not stir this mixture at all after the sugar has dissolved. Bring to a boil, then cover and boil 3 minutes. Uncover and cook to the soft ball stage (238° to 240°F on a candy thermometer) when a spoonful of syrup dropped into a cup of ice water forms a ball that flattens when picked up. Slowly pour the hot syrup over the beaten egg whites, beating constantly until blended. Stir in the marshmallows and continue beating until the marshmallows have been incorporated and the mixture is cool. Spread the bottom layer of the butter cake with the frosting. Place the top layer on the frosted bottom layer. Then frost the top and sides of the cake. Sprinkle the top and sides thickly with the shredded coconut and serve.

**Note:** Freshly grated coconut is best, but if used the cake should be served at once, and any leftovers must be refrigerated. Canned coconut works well, too, and keeps better. Dry packaged coconut should be tossed with a little milk and left to sit, covered, for 1 to 2 hours. When ready to use, squeeze the coconut to rid it of excess moisture.

MAKES 1 CAKE

Chocolate cakes, especially devil's food and fudge cake, were extremely popular. In fact, Irma Rombauer in *The Joy of Cooking* said that chocolate cakes had "It" and despaired of ever serving anything else for the dessert course at parties. Devil's food (sometimes called devil cake), which appeared at least as early as Sarah Tyson Rorer's 1898 *New Cook Book*, was obviously a humorous gastronomic answer to angel food.

Exactly what made devil's food devil's food—except its chocolate flavoring—is difficult to determine, because nearly every recipe for it is different. In the early days, most devil cakes were flavored with brown sugar or molasses, but some were not. Many recipes called for a custard to be made of the sugar, milk, chocolate, and an egg; this was then beaten into the creamed butter and sugar—but some did not. Devil's food was usually frosted with a boiled white icing, sometimes embellished with nuts, but then again sometimes a fudge or buttercream frosting was used. The only consistency, it seems, in the recipes is that they all made a chocolate cake that was not too heavy and not too rich.

## MRS. FRED MENSCH'S 1910 DEVIL CAKE

The only changes made from the original 1910 recipe are that 3 ounces rather than 2 ounces of chocolate have been used and 2 tablespoons more water plus 1 tablespoon butter have been added in melting the chocolate. The cake is very tender and fragile, so use waxed paper liners in the pans and handle it very gently while frosting.

Butter and unsweetened cocoa powder for preparing the pans
1/2 cup (1 stick) plus 1 tablespoon butter, softened
1 cup firmly packed dark brown sugar
2 large eggs, separated
1 teaspoon vanilla extract
3 ounces unsweetened chocolate
1/4 cup hot water
1 teaspoon baking soda
2/3 cup milk
1 teaspoon baking powder
2 cups sifted cake flour
Fudge frosting, butter frosting (chocolate or vanilla), or (for a real old-fashioned touch) Boiled Icing for Devil Cake (below).

Preheat the oven to 375°F. Grease two 8-inch layer pans. Cut waxed paper into rounds to fit in the bottom of the pans. Grease. Sprinkle the pans with cocoa, knocking it around the pans so the sides and bottom are completely covered. Knock out any excess.

Cream all but 1 tablespoon of the butter until light. Add the sugar and continue beating until very light. Beat in the egg yolks one at a time, then the vanilla, beating hard after each addition. Melt the chocolate and the remaining 1 tablespoon butter with the hot water in the top of a double boiler over simmering water, stirring constantly. Let cool slightly, then beat into the egg mixture. Dissolve the baking soda in the milk. Sift the baking powder with the flour. Stir the flour mixture and milk mixture alternately into the batter, beginning and ending with the flour mixture. Beat the egg whites until stiff but not dry, then fold them into the batter. Scrape the batter into the pans and bake until a cake tester inserted in the center of the cake comes out clean, about 25 minutes. Let rest in the pans for 10 minutes, then carefully turn out onto cake racks, peel off the waxed paper, and let the layers cool completely. Frost.

MAKES 1 CAKE

## BOILED ICING FOR DEVIL CAKE

Use the recipe for Marshmallow-Coconut Cake (p. 25), omitting the marshmallows and coconut. After beating in the hot syrup, stir in few drops of lemon juice to stabilize the icing and keep it from becoming gritty. (If the frosting is too thin, stir in enough confectioners' sugar to bring it to the proper spreading consistency.) Fill and frost the cake, sprinkling chopped nuts between the layers and on top of the cake, if desired.

The newest and arguably the most popular cake of the Twenties did not fit the lush, many layered, frosted, iced, and stuffed style. Upside-down cake—made with that most fashionable of ingredients, pineapple—was basically an inexpensive sponge cake poured over butter, brown sugar, and fruit. It was frequently baked in the homely skillet, and can be found as skillet cake in cookbooks from the 1930s and 1940s. But in the Twenties, upside-down cake was not considered fare fit only for the family supper. It was company dinner stuff, glamorous and new.

In 1924 the cake was unfamiliar enough that Mrs. Sidney E. Goodwin gave a recipe for it titled Pineapple Glacé in a Seattle charity cookbook. The January 1928 issue of *Pictorial Review* called its Caramel Pineapple-Cake one of the best new recipes of 1927, and it, too, was pineapple upside-down cake. The cake was deservedly popular: It was easy, quick, economical...and served with sweetened whipped cream it tasted very good. It still does.

# PINEAPPLE UPSIDE-DOWN CAKE

This cake has seen a resurgence in popularity lately with the vogue for "comfort food."

⅓ cup butter
1 cup firmly packed brown sugar
7 slices canned pineapple
Maraschino cherries and walnut or pecan halves (optional)
3 large eggs
1 cup granulated sugar
6 tablespoons unsweetened pineapple juice
1 teaspoon vanilla extract
1½ cup sifted cake flour
1 teaspoon baking powder
½ teaspoon salt

Preheat the oven to 350°F. In a heavy 10-inch skillet, melt the butter. Stir in the brown sugar. Let the sugar melt into the butter for a minute, then turn off the heat. Place the pineapple slices around the bottom of the skillet. Decorate the gaps with cherries or nuts, if you like, and set aside.

Beat the eggs until thick and pale lemon-colored, about 7 minutes. Gradually beat in the granulated sugar and continue beating another 2 or 3 minutes, then beat in the juice and vanilla. Sift the flour, baking powder, and salt together. Sift again, then add all at once to the egg mixture. Beat just until blended. Pour the batter over the pineapple in the skillet. Bake until a cake tester inserted in the center of the cake comes out clean, 40 to 45 minutes. Immediately turn the cake out onto a serving platter. Hold the skillet over the cake for a minute to let all the brown sugar syrup drip out. Serve the cake warm or at room temperature with whipped cream.

**Variations:** Substitute poached or canned apricots or peaches and their juice for the pineapple and pineapple juice and use almond extract instead of vanilla. Substitute almonds for the pecans or walnuts.

MAKES 8 TO 10 SERVINGS

# Prohibition

Remedy for a dented flask, demonstrated to me when I expressed incredulity:
Fill the flask with ginger ale or carbonated water, put the stopper in, and
shake. Really!

—Lipstick (Lois Long), the *New Yorker* (June 26, 1926)

When Prohibition went into effect in America on January 16, 1920, it did more
than stop the legal sale of alcoholic beverages in our country. It also created a
ferocious underworld of rum-running crime, eroded the Bill of Rights, turned
formerly upright and temperate citizens into booze-loving law breakers, ruined a
nascent wine industry, increased the production of soft drinks, put hundreds of
restaurants and hotels out of business, spurred the growth of tea rooms and cafeterias, and destroyed the last vestiges of fine dining in the United States.

In her bitter Prohibition-era book *No Nice Girl Swears* (1933), Alice-Leone
Moats said, "No longer is drinking an art with Americans; once they drank for
the taste, but now they drink only for the effect. The more quick and fatal the
liquor, the better they like it. They are either on the wagon or else." She went on
to say, "Cocktail parties have become the line of least resistance in entertaining.
They are convenient for the person who must get fifty or sixty people off the list
of obligations and prefers to do it at one fell swoop, saving money at the same
time. It certainly isn't much trouble; all you need is a case of synthetic gin and a
tin of anchovy paste."

And the taste of that synthetic gin could be bad. Much of the liquor sold in
the United States during Prohibition was made in illegal American basement
factories from redistilled denatured alcohol flavored with extracts called "Old
Kentucky Whisky Type" to make counterfeit Old Grand-Dad or "Old Cognac
Martelli Type" to produce a VSOP French cognac. Tastes were so debased that
one gentleman, on being given a taste of authentic fine French cognac, spit it
out and demanded a glass of the "real thing"—the fake liquor he had become
used to.

Said Geoffrey Kerr in *Vanity Fair* (February 1927), "There are two kinds of
Prohibition cocktail—the gin and lemon variety, which tastes like sulphuric
acid; and what is supposed to be a dry martini, which tastes like a concentrated
solution of quinine. Either kind should be regarded as purely medicinal and
swallowed at one gulp."

Sweet cocktails also became fashionable during this period, perhaps because the sweetness killed the taste of bad alcohol, perhaps because Americans seemed to like *everything* sweet. Brandy Alexanders and drinks flavored with sweet liqueurs or orange flower water were very chic then, as were cocktails mixed with carbonated Phez brand "Applju" or Clicquot Club ginger ale ("Delightful alone…blends with friends"). Sweet cocktails became so popular that the *New Yorker* (February 20, 1926) predicted the smart set would soon be drinking "maple-nut Martinis and banana-Bronx splits."

The liking for sweet tastes passed over into nonalcoholic arenas, too. Hotels tried to reclaim some of their lost wine and spirit profits by selling candy and soda pop. The fruit cocktail cup, often garnished with marshmallows or sprinkled with powdered sugar, took the place of oysters on the half shell with champagne as a dinner party opener. One Prohibition era book, quoted in *The Good Old Days Cookbook* (Beth Tartan, 1971), suggested that before dinner, "when purple shades have fallen and the afterglow lingers touching the world with unreality, one's cocktail should reflect the purple blood of grapes, the lush richness of the raspberry, the amber of apple or ginger juice."

That "purple blood of grapes" wouldn't be from a fine bottle of wine, however. The America wine industry, unable to sell its wines legally, quickly turned its vineyards over to juice grapes. But only a small portion of the juice from the grapes was marketed as juice. Most of it was sold for home-brewed wine. Needless to say, this home brew was not usually a sophisticated viniferous product, but sales of the juice kept many of the vineyards in profits throughout Prohibition.

Prohibition also brought about "cooking wines" and artificially flavored brandy, sherry, and rum extracts. Housewives were advised to omit salt when using the cooking wines, as the wines themselves had been salted to make them undrinkable. The Virginia Dare Extract Co., Inc., promoted its Sherry-Jell ("pure sherry made semi-solid"), and Claro ("pure claret in syrup form") to give that "old-fashioned flavor" to soups, Newburgs, and sauces. Some cooks gave up on alcoholic touches, real or faux, altogether. A December 1927 *Delineator* article, called "Christmas in the Modern Manner," advised its readers to serve the traditional plum pudding without its flaming sauce.

The bad alcohol, the closing of fine restaurants, the sweet foods and drinks that took alcohol's place, the artificial flavors that were used to simulate alcohol, all these things could not help but have a deleterious effect on the American palate. Prohibition ended at last on December 5, 1933, but the "Noble Experiment"'s impact on America and American eating habits was to last far into the future.

# Foreign Intrigue—
# Foreign Cooking in
# America in the Twenties

In Jazz Age America, exotic was In. Heavy-lidded Rudolph Valentino had women swooning in the theaters. One aspiring Hollywood starlet always dressed in rich Oriental brocades festooned with precious jewels and took her two pet monkeys everywhere. Americans began to flirt with some heretofore exotic cooking, too. Up to this point, our cookery had been pretty straightforward (except some of the flights of fancy along the lines of whipped cream and violets indulged in by the Domestic Scientists), with a solid and relatively stolid English/Anglo-Saxon base. There were forays into French cooking, but this was primarily in the homes and restaurants of the elite and was regarded with suspicion by the average home cook.

But as immigrants began coming from China, Mexico, and Italy rather than from Scandinavia and Germany, and as the country started looking outside its borders in the wake of World War I, there were some tentative steps into exotic food. Much of this so-called foreign cookery would not have been recognized in the country of its presumed origin. *Good Housekeeping*'s Arabian Stew was made with pork chops, an item as forbidden to Orthodox Muslims as to Orthodox Jews. In *Perfection Salad*, Laura Shapiro described a Japanese luncheon that appeared in the *Boston Cooking School Magazine*: it featured bean sprouts with Hollandaise sauce. (See Chapters 3 and 7 for a discussion of Asian cooking in America.)

Not everyone was enthusiastic about some of these "foreign" foods. Home Economists in charge of the diets of schoolchildren often tried to get the little Antonios and Marias to give up their unhealthy pasta and garlic for muscle-building American meat and potatoes.

One form of exotic foreign cooking that became very popular in the Twenties was anything with a Spanish/Mexican slant—which meant anything containing tomatoes, hot peppers, rice, garlic, or California olives. Some of it was authentic, most of it was not—but it was different from the bland and boring food that Americans were used to eating. This was the *New Yorker*'s columnist "Lipstick" in a February 20, 1926, review of Fornos, a Spanish restaurant:

Hm, was there paprika, wit peppers, wit tabasco, wit sauces, like swallowing firecrackers!... And our little genius from Mexico ate it in spoonfuls! The specialties are Mole of Turkey Poblana, Chili Con Carne, enchilidias [*sic*], Mexican Tortillas (Mexican bread made of corn, resembling flapjacks, which are not only delicious to eat but can also be used instead of a spoon, napkin, or other utensil). Fried bananas, black beans, and so on…. For dessert, crackers, cream cheese, and Guava paste with swell coffee is the correct thing. The food really is marvelous, which is a gracious gesture in view of the fact that I, with my tender American palate, managed to order the most burning dish of the entire assemblage—Turkey Poblana.

Most Americans were content to preserve their tender palates. Although recipes for mole poblano or arroz con pollo occasionally popped up in obscure cookbooks, the two Spanish-American dishes that really took hold were the mildly spiced Spanish rice and tamale pie.

Rice cooked with tomatoes was popular in the late 1800s in America, but exactly when this turned into "Spanish" rice is hard to pinpoint. Sarah Rorer gives a recipe for Spanish rice in her 1898 *New Cook Book* (in the "Jewish Recipes" section), but her dish is more a sort of chicken paella than the spicy red rice side dish that was to become a cafeteria and lunchroom favorite. Marion Harland's 1903 *Complete Cook Book* has a Spanish rice recipe ("very nice," says she), which is the dish we would expect, although she finishes her tomatoey rice by baking it under a coating of fine crumbs until browned. By the Twenties Spanish rice was a housewife's staple and remained so until the early Sixties when it fell from favor.

## HENRY FONDA'S MOTHER'S SPANISH (MEXICAN) RICE

In his early days, actor Henry Fonda used to cook a Spanish rice on a little electric grill for a group of other struggling actors who chipped in to buy the food. The recipe was his mother's and was always a great success with his hungry friends. The original recipe called for ¹/₂ pound of bacon, which seems far too much now. It was also cooked on top of the stove, but here it is baked.

¹/₄ pound bacon
I small onion, minced
¹/₂ green bell pepper, seeded and minced
2 cups canned tomatoes, drained and chopped
4 cups cooked rice
Salt and pepper

Preheat the oven to 350°F. Fry the bacon in a heavy pan over medium heat until crisp, remove from the pan, pat the fat off with paper towels, and chop coarsely. Drain off most of the bacon fat in the pan, add the onion and pepper, and sauté over medium heat for a few minutes. Combine the onion mixture, chopped bacon, and tomatoes with the rice. Season with salt and pepper. Turn the mixture into a greased 2-quart baking dish and cover. Bake about 20 minutes. Remove the cover and bake 10 minutes more.

MAKES 6 TO 8 SERVINGS

Tamale pie, another great staple of the Twenties (and through the Fifties), is a purely American invention. It is derived from the Mexican *tamal*, an Aztec dish based on various spicy or sweet fillings stuffed into a cornmeal porridge and then steamed or boiled in corn husks. Captain John Smith is reported to have seen Indians in Virginia making tamales in the 1600s, and tamales were common throughout the Southwest in the early days of European settlement.

The American version of the Mexican *tamal*, the tamale pie, which *The Dictionary of American Food and Drink* traces to 1911, dispensed with the corn husks and the steaming. Much too pesky and time-consuming. Instead, the filling, which was usually of seasoned hamburger but sometimes of chicken, was sandwiched between two layers of cornmeal mush, then baked. By the Fifties, the bottom layer of mush was often dispensed with and the top layer was replaced by a cornbread batter. The fillings, too, became less utilitarian. As time went on, cooks added corn, olives, green pepper, cheese, and sometimes even curry powder. For those of us who have tasted these examples of casserole Disposallitis, tamale pies have a nasty ring to them. But prepared simply, the dish is surprisingly tasty.

Tamale pie was also amazingly popular. Slightly exotic, yet thoroughly American, easy to make, and amenable to sitting around in its baking dish for a good while, it was the perfect dish for luncheons, for covered-dish parties, for Sunday suppers. So popular was it by the late Forties that one cookbook gave four very different recipes for it. Unfortunately, all of them were of the tricked-out variety, departing substantially from the dish's simple beginnings.

◆◆◆

# Tamale Loaves and Timbales

Tamale pies, in their simple way, were not bad. But there was a variation on the pie, very popular in Twenties, which was *very* bad. The tamale loaf—sometimes even the tamale timbale—was an example of Domestic Scientist cookery at its highest and worst. (Timbales and loaves were favorite ways to turn humble fare into a "company" dish.) The honest tamale pie was forced into a mold with the aid of milk and eggs and studded with corn and olives. To cap it all off, with a beautiful Twenties touch, it was served with white sauce with olives scattered on top.

## 1920S TAMALE LOAF

This recipe has not been tested.

1/2 cup finely chopped salt pork
1 onion, finely chopped
1 garlic clove, minced
1 (28-ounce) can tomatoes
1 (15 1/2-ounce) can corn
1 cup pitted chopped California black olives
1 green bell pepper, seeded and chopped
1/8 teaspoon cayenne pepper, or to taste
2 cups cornmeal
1 cup milk
3 large eggs, lightly beaten
White sauce and sliced olives for garnish

Preheat the oven to 350°F. Put the salt pork in a heavy skillet and cook over low heat for a few minutes. Add the onion and garlic and sauté until the onion is soft. Stir in the tomatoes, corn, olives, bell pepper, and cayenne. Taste for seasoning. Stir the cornmeal into the milk, then beat in the eggs. Slowly add the cornmeal mixture to the salt pork mixture, stirring constantly. Bring to a slow boil, then cook over low heat for 15 minutes. Pour into greased loaf pans (or muffin pans if you want timbales) and bake 45 minutes (less for timbales). To serve, pour white sauce over each slice, scattering sliced ripe olives on top.

MAKES 8 SERVINGS

# 1920S HUMBLE TAMALE PIE

Think of this as polenta with a spicy meat sauce, and suddenly it's modern.

3 cups water
1 teaspoon salt
1 cup cornmeal
1 tablespoon butter or mild vegetable oil
1 pound ground beef
1 large onion, finely chopped
2 cups canned tomatoes, drained and chopped
2 teaspoons chili powder or to taste
Salt and pepper

Preheat the oven to 350°F. Stir 1 cup of the water and the salt into the cornmeal in a large saucepan. Bring the remaining 2 cups water to a boil and stir into the cornmeal mixture. Cook over low heat, stirring constantly, until thick. Line a buttered 9-inch-square baking dish with half of the mush.

Melt the butter in a skillet. Fry the ground beef and onion in the butter until the meat is lightly browned and the onion soft. Pour off the excess fat. Add the tomatoes and seasonings and cook for a few minutes. Taste and correct the seasoning. Pour the meat mixture over the mush, then top with the remainder of the mush. Bake until browned, 35 to 40 minutes.

MAKES 6 SERVINGS

Perhaps the most enduring of these new foreign influences was the cooking of southern Italian immigrants. What American household of the 1990s doesn't have its favorite pizza parlor and its own best recipe for spaghetti sauce? But in the Twenties, pizza had not yet been heard of in the average American home (*The Dictionary of American Food and Drink* dates the first pizzeria in the States to 1905 in New York's Little Italy). Macaroni and spaghetti were still being boiled a minimum of thirty minutes, before being dressed with butter and "served hot as a vegetable," as the Good Housekeeping Institute recommended in its *Book of Menus, Recipes and Household Discoveries* (1922). The titles of some pasta dishes that appeared in cookbooks reflected the absolute foreignness of these foods: "Wop Spaghetti" and "Dago's Delight" were two similar early-twentieth-century recipes for boiled spaghetti baked with grated cheese, onion, and canned tomatoes thickened with flour.

Yet there were glimmerings of authenticity. In New York, Chicago, and San Francisco, the immigrants from southern Italy (between 1880 and 1920 one-quarter of all immigrants to the United States were from Sicily) opened small family restaurants. Prohibition, with its tremendous impact on the eating habits of the country, also had a great deal to do with the introduction of Italian food to the masses. Mary Grosvenor Ellsworth, in *Much Depends on Dinner* (1939), said this about Prohibition and pasta: "We cooked them [pastas] too much, we dese-crated them with further additions of flour, we smothered them in baking dishes and store cheese. Prohibition changed all that. The Italians who opened up speakeasies by the thousand were our main recourse in time of trial. Whole hordes of Americans thus got exposed regularly and often to Italian food and got a taste for it. Now we know from experience that properly treated, the pasta is no insipid potato substitute."

---

## 1924 ITALIAN SPAGHETTI

This is a typical recipe from the period, which no child of Italy would recognize. It has been reorga-nized into a modern format, but the ingredients and method remain as they were. It has not been tested.

  1 pound spaghetti
  1 tablespoon butter
  1 tablespoon flour
  2 cups cold water
  2 cups sliced American cheese
  8 small garlic cloves, minced
  2 onions, sliced
  Salt and cayenne pepper
  1 cup light cream
  1 (8-ounce) can tomato sauce

Boil the spaghetti 1 hour in salted water. Strain, pour cold water over the spaghetti, then drain. Put the spaghetti in a buttered baking dish. Preheat the oven to 350°F. Melt the butter in a large saucepan. Stir in the flour and cook for 1 minute, then stir in the 2 cups cold water. Add the cheese, garlic, onions, and seasonings. Bring to a boil. Stir in the cream and tomato sauce and cook for 1 minute more but do not boil. Pour the cooked sauce over the spaghetti and bake for 20 minutes.

MAKES 8 SERVINGS

The food served in the speakeasies—with Mama doing the cooking and Papa making wine in the basement—was not quite the same as the food the Italians had eaten in the Old Country. Sicilian cooking was based on austerity, with vegetables, legumes, and starches forming the basis of the diet. Meats, seafood, and cheeses were seasonings, used sparingly. But America was a rich, and protein-rich, country, and the immigrants were happy to add these symbols of wealth to their cooking—and happy that their new American customers liked the result. Meatballs, rich meat sauces, veal cutlets cooked with Parmesan or with lemon, clams stuffed with buttered herbed crumbs, shrimp with wine and garlic, and mozzarella in huge chunks to be eaten as an appetizer were all foods of abundance, developed by Italian-Americans in the abundance of their new country.

Redoubtable Home Economist Miss Alice Bradley told her *Woman's Home Companion* (May 1926) readers how to have an Italian dinner party as it had been prepared at Fannie Farmer's School of Cookery "with recipes from a foreign chef." While this Italian dinner party menu is not particularly novel to us now, it is still pleasingly balanced, simple, and quite appetizing.

◆◆◆

## An Italian Dinner Party Menu, Circa 1926

*Antipasto of Lettuce Hearts, Tuna Fish,
and Anchovy*

*Spaghetti with Tomato Sauce and Dried
Porcini Mushrooms*

*Veal Cutlets with Escarole
Lettuce Dressed with Olive Oil
Italian Bread*

*Fresh Figs and Apricots
Black Coffee*

Miss Bradley, who, as the principal of Miss Farmer's School of Cookery and the cooking editor of *Woman's Home Companion*, should have been expected to have some degree of gastronomic sophistication, approached this Italian menu as if it were a mysterious and potentially dangerous object. She was surprised to see that the spaghetti was not broken before it was cooked, but that it gradually softened and slid down into the water. Even more strangely, the pasta was boiled less than fifteen minutes. "Italians prefer a little less cooking than Americans give it," she said. On the veal cutlet, which was lightly breaded then quickly sautéed in olive oil, she commented, "To our surprise the meat was very tender and sufficiently cooked."

Miss Bradley noted, apparently with approval, that the Italian dinner took less than two hours to prepare. This must have seemed almost revolutionary in the days when a much more typical and time-consuming American dinner party menu might have been the one Miss Bradley suggested in General Electric's 1927 *Electric Refrigerator Recipes and Menus*, all of which would have been prepared from scratch, with few packaged ingredients.

◆◆◆

# An American Dinner Party Menu, Circa 1927

*Caviar Canapé*

*Chicken Soup*
*Olives* ◆ *Dinner Rolls* ◆ *Salted Almonds*

*Roast Ham* ◆ *Frozen Crushed Pineapple*
*Southern Sweet Potatoes* ◆ *Lima Beans*

*Romaine with French Dressing* ◆ *Frozen Cheese*

*Chocolate Icebox Pudding*
*Black Coffee*

Americans liked some of the foreign dishes they were beginning to sample, but the foreignness of them was soon watered down by housewives, home economists, and restaurant cooks, who strove to make them comfortably and purely American. At the same time, French cooking was almost completely abandoned in this country, except in the highest echelons of society. The time, money, and wine and spirits necessary for good French cooking were no longer available. Under Prohibition, many of the fine restaurants that had supported French cooking on their profits from the sale of wine and liquors closed their doors completely or transformed themselves into cafeterias. French chefs in restaurants either gave up their posts and went home or Americanized their cooking. It was not until gourmet-mania began in the late Forties and early Fifties that French cooking would again be regarded with any respect.

But no one cared about any of that after the stock market crashed on October 24, 1929. The Depression marked the end of the Twenties as clearly as if a curtain had come down. When Black Thursday came and economic reality set in, Americans turned from hectic high life to quiet home life. And American home cooks turned more and more to the home economists and food-processing conglomerates for help in getting dinner on the table.

# 2

# The Thirties

## Comforting Food in America

**W**hen the Great Depression heralded the beginning of the Thirties Americans stopped dancing the Charleston and started standing on unemployment lines. Stanford graduates took jobs at fruit canneries (and felt lucky, for all that); and bread lines, soup kitchens, and apple selling became part of the American way of life. Though the Depression did not have any immediate or obvious effects on American cookery—the food sections of popular magazines never mentioned the terrible plight of many of their readers and only occasionally ran a feature on economical meals—still the effects were there, subtle but pervasive.

Had the Depression not intervened, the end of Prohibition on December 5, 1933, might have marked the beginning of a new Golden Age of fine dining. But it was not to be. Ironically, part of the pressure to end Prohibition had been economic, coming from the hotels, restaurants, and the wine and liquor industries that were hard hit by the double effects of Prohibition and Depression. But when, and if, Americans did eat out in the Thirties, it was much more likely to be at an inexpensive place, serving familiar, American food, than at a fancy restaurant. And those Americans were much more likely to order coffee or a sweet, inexpensive soft drink rather than unfamiliar and expensive wine to wash down their food.

The Depression also changed the way Americans entertained at home. Except for the upper echelons of society, most families were now maidless, which made grand, formal dinner parties impossible. Instead, hostesses gave luncheons, teas, and cozy Sunday Night Suppers around the chafing dish to satisfy their social urges and obligations. This gave rise to the hope, in some quarters anyway, that staying at home would encourage the fine art of home cooking for friends and family. An August 1932 *House & Garden* editorial, "The Return of Fine Eating," predicted, somewhat wistfully and certainly inaccurately, that Americans would "toss slap-dash meals into the same limbo whence has already gone that other American fallacy—getting rich quick."

The Thirties also ushered in an era of women's clubs—whether dedicated to charitable activities, gardening, or the fine art of bridge—perhaps as a reaction to the individualistic Twenties, perhaps as a kind of atavistic huddling together against the harsh realities of the new age. And what was eaten when the clubs got together (and eat they did) was women's food: dainty, light, frothy, sweet, creamy, and decorated. It was Home Ec cooking taken to its highest point, and this Haute Kitsch Cuisine became nearly synonymous with American food. In the March 1939 issue of *House & Garden*, an exasperated Richardson Wright, then president of the New York Wine and Food Society, said he was thrown into a "terrible temper" by the "habit some cooks have of messing up otherwise palatable dishes with marshmallows." It is unlikely that Fannie Farmer, Ida C. Bailey Allen, or Alice Bradley would have agreed with him.

## Marshmallow Madness

Marshmallows were still wildly popular in the Thirties. Fruit salads and cocktails were rife with marshmallows, and desserts, obviously, were a prime target for these soft, white blobs of gelatinized sugar. A forerunner of s'mores, called Marguerites, was one dainty sweet suitable for ladies' luncheons or teas. Although recipes varied, the basic Marguerite was a graham cracker or crisp cookie topped with a marshmallow, which was then put under the broiler for a few minutes until the marshmallow softened and browned. These were even more appealing if a bit of candied cherry was placed in the center of each as they came from the oven.

But it was the marshmallow-ized nonsweet dishes that so annoyed gourmets. One particularly popular mixture was sweet potatoes and marshmallows—served as a vegetable, not a dessert. This combination is still with us in the familiar and achingly sweet form of potatoes mixed with brown sugar under a blanket of gooey, browned marshmallows, traditional with some families at Thanksgiving as a vegetable accompaniment to the roast turkey. In the Thirties, however, a different version was fashionable—and it went along with the decade's penchant for cleverly disguising food.

# SWEET POTATO–MARSHMALLOW SURPRISES

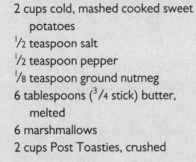

2 cups cold, mashed cooked sweet
potatoes
1/2 teaspoon salt
1/2 teaspoon pepper
1/8 teaspoon ground nutmeg
6 tablespoons (3/4 stick) butter,
melted
6 marshmallows
2 cups Post Toasties, crushed

Preheat the oven to 400°F. Mix the sweet potatoes with the salt, pepper, nutmeg, and 2 tablespoons of the melted butter. Divide the mixture into six portions and form each portion into a flat circle. Place one marshmallow in the center of each circle, then fold the potato mixture up around the marshmallows. Mix the crushed cereal with the remaining melted butter. Roll the balls in the cereal. Place the balls on a greased baking sheet. Bake until browned—but not long enough to melt the marshmallows—10 to 15 minutes. Serve hot.

MAKES 6 SERVINGS

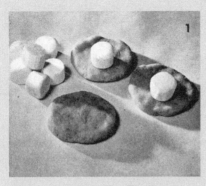

*Making Sweet Potato–Marshmallow Surprises*

But weren't many Americans starving in the Thirties? Not really. There was hunger, of course, but it was primarily concentrated in the poorest rural areas. According to Harvey Levenstein in *Revolution at the Table*, even in families earning less than two dollars per person per week, adult males averaged 2,470 calories a day. Not Lucullan perhaps, but survivable. And while Dust Bowl housewives might have had to make their bread inside a drawer to keep the drifting dust out, at least there was bread. Relief agencies and make-work jobs helped some of the worst off, and low food prices made everyone except the food companies happier. Sugar prices, too, were low, and in the Thirties Americans consumed more sugar per capita then they have done before or since. In one of the few articles to reflect the dreariness—and the high sugar content—of Depression era food, *Better Homes and Gardens* published the following "Thrifty Menus" without comment in December 1931.

◆◆◆

## Thrifty Menus for the Winter of 1931

*Turnips au Gratin*
*Tomato Jelly Salad*
*Caramel Dumplings*
◆◆◆

*Scalloped Corned Beef*
*Cinnamon Apple Salad*
*Pumpkin Pie*
◆◆◆

*Potato-Carrot Salad* ◆ *Sardines*
*Steamed Chocolate Pudding with Chocolate Sauce*
*and Apple Meringue Garnish*

# Sunday Night Supper

In the harsh world of the Depression one of most popular ways to entertain friends was the Sunday Night Supper. It was *intime* and it was inexpensive. It

**MAGIC CHEF FEATURES**

MAGIC CHEF TOP BURNER— Gives a thousand even heats. Will not clog or corrode.

MAGIC CHEF AUTOMATIC TOP BURNER LIGHTER.

SANITARY HIGH BURNER TRAY— Conceals pipes and valves, protects them against spatters and boil-overs.

RED WHEEL LORAIN OVEN REG-ULATOR—Cooks and bakes unattended. No guesswork or oven-watching.

FULLY INSULATED OVEN—Keeps kitchen cooler.

GRID-PAN BROILER—Two-piece with removable grid, porcelain enameled. Basting reservoir to catch melted fats, prevents smoking or catching fire.

GRAYSON COOKING CLOCK, TELECHRON MOTORED (Extra charge)—Self starting. Turns oven burner on and off automatically as desired.

MONEL METAL TOP—Modern, stainless, easy to clean, noiseless, durable.

**COOK WITH GAS • The Modern Fuel**
**For Speed, Safety, Comfort,**
**Cleanliness, Convenience.**

Where gas main service is not available, Pyrofax tank gas service may be obtained anywhere east of the Rockies.

*Woman's Home Companion June 1935*

also reflected an important Thirties ethos of cooperation, of sharing and togetherness, as friends were invited to become a part of the family for a few hours, in contrast to the formal division of host and guest that had been de rigueur.

The food served at these cozy little get-togethers was not the soup, fish, roast, vegetable, cheese, and sweet menu of the rich old days. In this newly poor era, one dish was likely to be the centerpiece of the meal—one that was simple, creamy, and comforting. Welsh rabbit on toast or creamed chicken on waffles soothed the family and their guests and kept the wolf from snuffling too hungrily at the door.

Table settings reflected the homey warmth of this newly casual entertaining. Instead of starched and snowy Damask, table linens sported gay prints or checks in coarse linen. Colorful pottery took the place of Limoges, and crystal was replaced by cheery mugs. And in those newly egalitarian days of more and more servantless households, guests could get a kick out of busing their own dishes to the kitchen when the meal was over.

The Sunday Night Supper often centered around the chafing dish, the waffle iron, or the toaster. But these appliances—and they were now usually electric—were no longer hidden away in the kitchen. No, they were right out on the dining table or the tea cart, and the cooking—with all its good aromas and homely mixings and stirrings—was not done by some hidden minion but by the host or hostess, or even the guests themselves. Cooking with these new electric appliances was not without its hazards in the early Thirties, however. In the January 1932 issue of *Pictorial Review*, columnist Nancy Tomlinson told of blowing all the fuses when she used her toaster, waffle iron, and percolator for a party: her house, up to that point, had only been wired to accept lamps plugged into the outlets. After rewiring, she assured her readers, she was able to use those appliances with "perfect nonchalance."

One of the most popular entrées for these cozy little suppers was Welsh rabbit (or rarebit) or one of its variants. Said Procter & Gamble's 1937 cookbook, *The Art of Cooking and Serving*:

> One nationally known literary man has made almost as much of a reputation among his intimate friends for his Welsh rarebit as for his novels of contemporary life. Almost anything is likely to go into the making of it, while his wife stands by in apprehension. But the result without fail is delightful.

The most basic, primeval recipes for a rabbit are for toasted cheese on bread; slightly later versions are the British Isles' equivalent of a Swiss fondue. Instead of Gruyère melted in white wine with garlic, the rabbit is a sharp cheddar-type cheese melted in brown ale with a little butter and a dash of cayenne or Worcestershire sauce. Sometimes an egg is stirred in at the end. The British frequently pour the rabbit over toast and brown it under the broiler.

Americans, however, almost never make a *basic* recipe. And ale, brown or otherwise, is not a common product in the American kitchen—and it would have been rarer than hen's teeth in the early Thirties before the end of Prohibition. In place of the unfamiliar ale a few misguided souls have tried to use *ginger* ale in their Welsh rabbits, but in general Americans have turned to— what else?—cream sauce.

# Entertaining Electrically

Electric gadgets were the darlings of the Thirties, evidence of the Modern Age even in the midst of Depression. Waffle irons, chafing dishes, glass "Anyheet Control" Silex coffeemakers, percolators, toasters (in one, the Toast-O-Lator, bread went in one end and toast came out the other), electric snack servers, and hot plates, all were guaranteed to "serve you with efficiency." The lucky lady who had an electric mixer could even order her own banana masher attachment from one major manufacturer.

One of the newest gadgets was the electric roaster, a free-standing portable oven. Hotpoint/General Electric made one of the biggest sellers. It was a "tireless electric servant," which doubled as a turkey roaster and a super picnic basket and was perfectly grand to "take to the lake cottage to broil crisp brown fish," according to *Better Homes and Gardens* (January 1939).

Also enthusiastic about the roaster was *Woman's Home Companion*, which in July 1939 suggested a roaster meal for "twelve hungry people." The menu was veal and ham pinwheels, succotash, and hot rolls (all cooked in the roaster), accompanied by a summer vegetable salad, ice cream and cookies, and iced tea. Said the magazine, "You start this dinner about 1½ hours before serving it. Then everyone—including hostess—goes to swim or play tennis and the roaster finishes it for you. When your party shows up ravenous on the terrace everything is ready."

## VEAL-HAM PINWHEELS FROM THE ROASTER

Although this recipe was designed for the electric roaster, an oven would do as well.

   1½ pounds ham, cut into 3 slices ¼-inch thick
   3 pounds veal, cut into 3 slices ½-inch thick
   18 slices bacon
   18 wooden skewers

Preheat roaster broiler 5 minutes. Cut ham and veal into strips 1 inch wide and 6 inches long. Lay a strip of ham on top of one of veal and roll tightly. Wrap with bacon and secure with a skewer. Repeat until all are done. Place pinwheels on roaster broiler rack and broil 2 inches from the heat for about 5 minutes on each side, until meat is lightly browned. Remove to a roaster dish and pour drippings over the pinwheels. Set roaster oven control to 350°F. Bake meat one hour. ("This is where the swim comes in," said the magazine.) Reset roaster control to 200°F so that any second servings will still be hot and serve pinwheels from the roaster.

MAKES 18 PINWHEELS

## AMERICAN WELSH RABBIT

1 tablespoon butter
1 tablespoon flour
1/2 cup half-and-half or light cream
1/2 pound snappy yellow cheese, grated
1/4 teaspoon dry mustard
1/2 teaspoon Worcestershire sauce
Few grains of cayenne pepper

Melt the butter in a heavy saucepan or chafing dish. Stir in the flour and cook over low heat for 2 or 3 minutes. Slowly add the half-and-half, stirring constantly, and cook another 5 minutes. Add the cheese and stir until melted. Add the seasonings and serve over toast.

MAKES 4 SERVINGS

## A Sunday Night Supper with Welsh Rabbit, Thirties-Style

If you want to re-create a real 1930s-style Sunday Night Supper, make Welsh rabbit in a chafing dish at the table. Also place on the table a toaster so each guest can make his or her own toast, a tray containing the bread for the toast, and bowls of pickles and California olives. Tea, coffee, or Postum (a grain-based coffee substitute developed as a health food drink in 1896) should be served throughout. Top off the meal with a sweet gelatin salad or use the peach salad receipe provided below from the 1934 *Pictorial Review Standard Cook Book* ("A Sure Guide for Every Bride").

### STUFFED PEACH SALAD

The recipe follows the original exactly, except that mayonnaise has been added.

6 canned peach halves
6 lettuce leaves
6 pitted dates
1 (4-ounce) package cream cheese, softened
Mayonnaise

For each serving, place a canned peach half on a lettuce leaf, cavity side up. In the cavity place 1 date which has been filled with cream cheese. Garnish with mayonnaise.

MAKES 6 SERVINGS

Like Procter & Gamble's nationally known literary man, Americans delighted in adding things to their rabbits and with these variations, the rabbit took on other names. For an English monkey the cheesy sauce was enhanced with bread crumbs and eggs, a pink monkey was an English monkey with tomato added, a scrappi or scrappe was cheese sauce with green onions, a pink bunny or blushing bunny was made with tomatoes, and a pink poodle (from the old San Francisco restaurant the Poodle Dog) was made with tomatoes and red wine. A woodchuck dispensed with the cream sauce and substituted tomato purée and egg, while a chilaly added green pepper and onions to the woodchuck mixture. A golden buck was cheese, white wine, lemon, and eggs; Lenox rarebit was scrambled eggs and milk with cream cheese; a Mexican rabbit was a tomato juice, green pepper, corn, and cheese mixture; and a rabbit made out of cheese, kidney beans, and green peppers was a Mt. Clemens.

But perhaps the most endearingly titled of the rabbit concoctions was something known variously as rinktum ditty, rinktum tiddy, rum tum tiddy, rinktum diddy, ring-tum-diddy, and rictim chitti—which even the cookbook that offered it admitted was absurd. *Webster's New Collegiate Dictionary* settled on rinktum ditty but professed itself unable to come up with an origin for the name.

## ABSURD RICTIM CHITTI

2 tablespoons butter
1 onion, thinly sliced
1 1/2 pounds Cheddar cheese, cut into small cubes
2 cups canned tomatoes, drained and chopped
1 teaspoon dry mustard
1/2 teaspoon paprika
1 teaspoon Worcestershire sauce
3 large eggs, slightly beaten
Salt and pepper

Melt the butter in a chafing dish or heavy saucepan. Add the onion and cook over low heat until soft. Then add the tomatoes, mustard, paprika, and Worcestershire sauce. Cook over low heat about 15 minutes. Add the cheese, stirring until it melts. Stir a little of the mixture into the eggs, then turn the warmed eggs into the saucepan and cook, stirring constantly, for 5 minutes or until the eggs thicken slightly. Correct the seasoning and serve on toasted crackers or toast.

MAKES 6 TO 8 SERVINGS

Another chafing dish Sunday Night Supper staple was creamed chipped (or dried) beef. By the end of World War II, American GIs had had their fill of this salty, creamy dish—and had invented their own rude name for it (SOS, or shit on a shingle)—but in the Thirties it was just the thing to serve over toast, split biscuits, or waffles to the gang. It wasn't elegant, but it was "grand," and men, those important arbiters of what was hearty and good, were supposed to like it.

Chipped beef has now almost vanished from supermarket shelves. But if you can come up with a jar or two of it (in some areas it's available in packets), try it. It can be surprisingly good, at least for those with a taste for it.

## CREAMED CHIPPED BEEF

Please note there is no salt in this recipe, because the beef is already very salty.

2 cups boiling water
2 cups chipped (dried) beef, chopped a little
2 tablespoons unsalted butter
2 tablespoons flour
2 cups half-and-half (it would have been called "rich milk" in the Thirties)

Pour the boiling water over the beef. Drain immediately. Melt the butter in a large skillet over medium-high heat. When it foams, stir in the beef, letting the edges frizzle a little. Stir in the flour, reduce the heat to low, and cook for about 5 minutes, stirring occasionally. Remove from the heat and slowly stir in the half-and-half. Cook over low heat, stirring occasionally, until the mixture thickens. (Don't let it boil or the half-and-half will take on a scalded taste.) Cook another 5 minutes. Serve over toast, split baking powder biscuits, or waffles.

MAKES 4 TO 6 SERVINGS

Of course, just about anything could be added to the cream sauce (with some salt and pepper) if chipped beef wasn't what the Thirties hostess had in mind. Asparagus tips (still very chic), cubed leftover chicken (with some chicken broth making up part of the cream sauce), some canned shrimps and peas (for a shrimp wiggle), or chopped hard-boiled eggs with a little riced egg yolk scattered artfully over the top (for eggs goldenrod), all made good, satisfying dishes to feed family and friends.

# Chipped Beef and the Mystery Chef

For all its popularity in the Thirties, cooks didn't do much with chipped beef except cream it, add it to a Welsh rabbit–type sauce, or scramble it with eggs. One exception to this, however, came from John MacPherson, radio's "Mystery Chef" (he called himself the Mystery Chef because his mother was embarrassed by his profession).

Housewives all over the country tuned in to their radios to learn about things to cook for their families. But while most radio cooking show hosts, like Aunt Sammy and Betty Crocker, stressed homey, feminine economy in those difficult times, the Mystery Chef was a man…and a "gourmet," who made gourmet dishes (one of which was a bouillabaisse that included curry powder, canned tomato soup, mushrooms, and sherry). He was also a Scotsman and true to his thrifty background, he strove to make his brand of gourmet cooking economical. This combination proved so successful that the Mystery Chef (who first went on the air in May 1930 in Boston) soon had *two* national radio programs, one on NBC and one on CBS.

John MacPherson's contribution to chipped beef cookery was to combine it with pineapple, which, if not as wildly popular as it had been in the Twenties, was still going strong. Perhaps the fact that chipped beef is kind of a beef "ham" inspired him to try this combination. Perhaps it was just his male gourmet imagination. But here is the recipe.

## CHIPPED BEEF AND PINEAPPLE, MYSTERY CHEF

    1 (8-ounce) can sliced pineapple
    3 tablespoons butter
    2 cups boiling water
    $^1/_2$ pound chipped beef, chopped a little

Drain the pineapple, reserving the juice. Cut the pineapple into small squares. Melt the butter in a heavy skillet. When it is foaming, add the pineapple and fry until lightly browned. Pour the boiling water over the chipped beef and drain thoroughly. Add the beef to the skillet and cook for a few minutes. Then stir in the reserved pineapple juice. Simmer 5 minutes. Serve with hot biscuits.

MAKES 6 SERVINGS

The starchy bases of the Sunday Night Suppers were an important part of their comforting nature. Toast, waffles, and biscuits were all familiar, American foods, frequently eaten for breakfast, and often the favorite foods in the nursery. Crackers were also sometimes used, but these were not the thin saltine type that we think of nowadays as crackers. An old-fashioned item called common crackers was still popular in the Thirties. These were large, thick, and crisp; they were good split, buttered and toasted, or they could be dipped in water, then put in a hot oven to puff. Common crackers are no longer common, although they are available in catalogs featuring products from New England.

Toast, of course, needs no explaining. But biscuits, once the province of every home cook, are now almost a lost American art form. Ironically, their very popularity may have hurried their demise. As Betty Fussell points out in *Masters of American Cookery*, the advent of biscuit mixes like Bisquick in the 1930s and canned biscuits in the 1940s may have turned Americans against this once basic food. A pity, as biscuits are easily and quickly made…and delicious, served hot from the oven, flaky and buttery, either with good jam or, for a Sunday Night Supper, with creamed chicken.

# Just put 'em in a pan... and Bake 'Em!

# AMERICAN BISCUITS

Although few home cooks outside the South make fresh biscuits anymore, they have enjoyed a recent vogue at trendy restaurants serving New American Cooking. Use the greater amount of butter for a richer biscuit.

2 cups all-purpose flour
1 teaspoon baking powder
1 teaspoon baking soda
1/4 teaspoon salt
2 to 6 tablespoons chilled butter, cut into pieces
3/4 to 1 cup plain yogurt thinned with a little milk, or buttermilk

Preheat the oven to 425°F. Sift the dry ingredients together into a mixing bowl. Cut in the butter with a pastry blender or two knives until the mixture resembles coarse cornmeal. Pour in 3/4 cup of the yogurt and stir it quickly with a fork, just until the mixture seems to be gathering into a mass. If the mixture seems dry, add the additional yogurt. Total stirring time shouldn't be more than 30 seconds. (If you've miscalculated and the dough is now too soft, omit the following kneading and rolling of the dough and drop the biscuits by spoonfuls onto the baking sheet. They'll still be good, just not as nicely shaped.)

Turn the dough out onto a floured board and knead lightly, no more than 10 or 12 times. Pat or roll the dough to about 3/4-inch thickness. Cut with a 2-inch biscuit cutter (or use a cookie cutter, a clean can, or a glass with a thin edge). Place on a greased baking sheet, close together if you want soft biscuits, farther apart if you like them crisp. Bake until golden brown, about 12 minutes. Serve immediately. Any not wanted right away should be kept on the baking sheet in the warm oven with the door ajar.

MAKES 8 TO 12 BISCUITS

Waffles are as American as apple pie, and like apple pie are an import. The word *waffle*, and probably the food, comes to us from the Dutch *wafel*, but the French eat them, too, calling them *gaufre* (from the Old French *wafla*). Whatever their provenance, waffles have been eaten by Americans since Pilgrim times.

Europeans eat their waffles as a sweet course, topping them with powdered sugar, whipped cream, or honey or stuffing them with icing. Americans have occasionally served waffles for dessert—perhaps a chocolate waffle with ice cream—but in general we eat them for breakfast with all-American maple syrup. At least now we do, if we eat waffles at all.

But in the Thirties, and before that, Americans ate waffles with virtually anything that could be spooned or poured over their bumpy, golden tops. And we ate them for breakfast, for luncheon, and for supper. If we served them to guests at a Sunday Night Supper, it became a waffle supper, "sure to be a party guests remember," according to the General Foods cookbook *All About Home Baking* (1933).

And we made waffles with just about everything. Cheese waffles; cornmeal waffles; coconut, pineapple, and chocolate waffles; gingerbread waffles; banana waffles; cheese and tomato, date, and peanut butter waffles; apple waffles; oatmeal waffles; and prune, bran, apricot, and even pea pulp waffles (which *Pictorial Review* featured as one of their best recipes for 1927).

Here are two waffle recipes. One is basic, to be served either with maple syrup or savory creamed things; the second is a homey dessert waffle.

## BASIC WAFFLES

Most electric waffle irons these days do not need to be greased once they have been seasoned. Check the directions for your iron.

2 cups pastry flour or 1⅞ cups all-purpose flour
1½ teaspoons baking powder
½ teaspoon baking soda
¼ teaspoon salt
3 large eggs, separated
¾ cup milk
¾ cup plain yogurt
6 tablespoons (¾ stick) butter, melted

Sift the dry ingredients together in a large bowl. Beat the egg yolks until light and add to the dry ingredients, along with the milk, yogurt, and melted butter. Beat until the batter is smooth. Beat the egg whites in a medium-size bowl until stiff peaks form. Fold the beaten egg whites into the batter.

Preheat the waffle iron. Pour or ladle about ½ cup of the batter into the iron. Close and bake until the waffle is golden brown and comes away easily from the iron, 3 to 4 minutes. Serve with butter, maple syrup, or jam, along with some sausages or crisp bacon for a satisfying breakfast or supper. The waffles may also be topped with creamed meats or vegetables and eaten whenever you please.

MAKES 6 WAFFLES

# GINGERBREAD WAFFLES

1½ cups all-purpose flour
¼ cup sugar
½ teaspoon salt
1 teaspoon baking soda
1 teaspoon baking powder
1½ teaspoons ground ginger
½ teaspoon ground cinnamon
3 large eggs, separated
½ cup unsulfured molasses
1 cup buttermilk or ½ cup regular milk and ½ cup plain yogurt
5 tablespoons butter, melted
Lemon Sauce (below)

Sift the dry ingredients together in a large bowl. In a separate bowl beat the egg yolks until light, then beat in the molasses and buttermilk. Beat this mixture into the dry ingredients. Stir in the melted butter. In a small bowl beat the egg whites until stiff peaks form, then fold in them into the batter. Preheat the waffle iron. Bake batter until golden brown and the waffle pulls away easily from the iron, 3 to 4 minutes. Serve with whipped cream or, for a homey 1930s touch, Lemon Sauce.

MAKES 6 WAFFLES

## LEMON SAUCE FOR GINGERBREAD WAFFLES

4 teaspoons cornstarch
½ cup sugar
1 cup water
Rind of 1 lemon (yellow part only), grated
3 tablespoons lemon juice
2 tablespoons butter

Mix the cornstarch and sugar together in a heavy saucepan. Add the water slowly, stirring to mix. Add the lemon rind. Bring to a boil, reduce the heat, and simmer 15 minutes, stirring occasionally. Add the lemon juice and butter. Serve the sauce over Gingerbread Waffles.

MAKES ABOUT 1 CUP

Another popular refreshment at Sunday Night Suppers was the grilled cheese sandwich, known as the "cheese dream." Men liked them. In describing her male guests' reactions to some "light wholesome" fare such as nut bread sandwiches and fruit salad, Mrs. Arthur Turner of Long Beach, California, said in a May 1938 issue of *Woman's Home Companion,*

> They merely gaze in stunned silence at the appearance of these dainty morsels and, after their lightning-like consumption, just sit there rigid and polite. The lightest thing I have been able to offer with success (by "success" I mean that placid benevolent relaxed expression that begins to steal over a man's face halfway through his meal), consists of two large slices of bread toasted on one side, topped with generous wedges of cheese, sliced tomatoes and ham or bacon strips, all placed under the broiler for six or seven minutes, served with plenty of pickles and olives and two or three cups of coffee. Many of my friends prefer topping this off with a mammoth piece of pineapple icebox cake.

---

## What Men Like

What with all the Dainty, feminine food being served up in the Thirties, women like Mrs. Arthur Turner *did* worry about what their men would eat. In a 1934 advertisement for Miracle Whip salad dressing, the Kraft-Phenix Cheese Corp. offered the following scenario, as Madge and Harry bellied up to Charlotte's buffet supper:

MADGE: *How pretty your table looks, Charlotte! You're a big brave girl, too—giving these men salad.*

CHARLOTTE: *I've got a new dressing—Miracle Whip! Men love the flavor—a combination of mayonnaise and boiled dressing.*

HARRY: *I'm after more of that gelatin stuff! Lots of dressing please! What* is *it, old dear?*

CHARLOTTE: *I say it's salad! Harry, you're converted at last. And Miracle Whip gets the credit this time!*

Exactly what went into a cheese dream depended on the cook. The most basic was a plain cheese sandwich cooked in butter in a chafing dish or heavy skillet, and this was the cheese dream *Betty Crocker's Picture Cook Book* (1950) said was "invented by boarding school girls as a chafing dish specialty...now universally popular as a main dish for light suppers and luncheons." Fannie Farmer and Irma Rombauer used an egg and cheese filling spiked with mustard or cayenne, which was then spread between slices of bread and toasted under the broiler. Slices of tomato and bacon strips were also popular additions, particularly in open-faced cheese dreams. One of the most unusual cheese dreams was one suggested in Procter & Gamble's 1937 Crisco cookbook.

## CHEESE DREAMS, PROCTER & GAMBLE

This is really a cheese dream in Monte Cristo sandwich guise.

    4 slices cheddar cheese
    Dash each of paprika and cayenne pepper
    4 thin slices firm white bread, crusts removed
    I large egg
    $^1/_2$ cup milk
    $^1/_4$ cup ($^1/_2$ stick) butter for frying (Procter & Gamble suggested Crisco)

Sprinkle the cheese with a little paprika and cayenne. Make two sandwiches out of the bread and cheese. Cut the sandwiches in half. Beat the egg in a wide, shallow bowl with the milk. Dip the sandwiches in the egg mixture. Melt the butter in a heavy skillet or chafing dish. Fry the sandwiches in the hot butter until golden on both sides. Drain on paper towels and serve hot.

MAKES 2 SANDWICHES

◆◆◆

And here is a menu for a perfect cheese dream Sunday Night Supper (sans pineapple icebox cake), suggested in General Foods *All About Home Baking* (1933):

◆◆◆

---

## Sunday Night Supper of Dreams

*Waldorf Salad*
*Cheese Dreams* ◆ *Olives*
*Summer Dessert Waffles (plain waffles with ice cream and fruit)*
*Coffee*

---

Last, but not least, another dish that was becoming popular for Sunday Night Suppers, for camp suppers, or for backyard picnics, was chili con carne. This "Mexican favorite," as most cookbooks labeled it, although it was actually from the American Southwest and supposedly detested by our south-of-the-border neighbors, first appeared in print in 1857, according to *The Dictionary of American Food and Drink*. A number of popular American cookbooks from the late 1800s included it, although it was not always recognizable. Marion Harland called it "chilli con carni" and made it with chopped steak, chili peppers, and rice. She suggested it for breakfast. Sarah Tyson Rorer identified her "chile con-cana" as a Spanish recipe and used either chicken or veal cooked in a sauce made from fresh chilies, tomatoes, and onions.

By the Thirties, the dish was essentially the spiced meat-and-bean mixture familiar today, although a few kinks were still being ironed out. John MacPherson, the Mystery Chef, included caraway seed in his recipe, presumably to replace the then foreign cumin seed that flavors many chilies. *The Worldly Modern Cook Book for the Busy Woman* (1932) included one cup of chopped celery and two cups of cooked rice in its chili, noting that it was an "excellent dish to serve as a supper for 10 people for the hostess without a maid. With a salad, jelly, radishes, dessert, and coffee it is a complete meal." (No mention was made of what was to be done with the jelly.)

Exactly why chili con carne became so popular in the Thirties is difficult to determine. Foods with a Southwest accent, no matter how Americanized—from tamale pies, to Spanish rice, to "takos," to chili—were beginning to find a home

## The Real Chili Con Carne Debate

The question of what goes into an authentic chili con carne is hotly debated in America, akin to French arguments about what constitutes a proper bouillabaisse. Whether cubed meat or ground should be used, whether onions or tomatoes should be included, whether prepared chili powder or fresh chilies or both should spice the meat, whether fresh cilantro is a proper addition—every ingredient has its avid proponents and those who would argue just as strenuously against it.

Even in the Thirties there was strong opinion on the subject. Marguerite Clark, in a November 18, 1939, article for *Collier's*, commented favorably on the "simple, old-fashioned all-American dishes" she was served from the Home Kitchen at the Waldorf-Astoria Hotel in New York. She found there, she said, instead of fancified soufflés, "Real Texas chili con carne, a blending of medium-sized cubes of succulent beef of the best cut, with small, hard, red native, Mexican beans, onions, garlic, chili powder and cumin seed, not to be confused with the peppery stew of cheap ground meat and large, soft kidney beans that some misguided folk call chili."

But what about those beans? Texas purists consider the addition of beans anathema, and most recipes before the 1930s did not include them. But by mid-decade, beans—usually pinto or kidney beans—were a common ingredient in chili, at least outside of Texas; Fannie Farmer's cookbook even suggested lima beans.

Beside beans, there are other additions to chili that would make a Texan feel faint. Cincinnati five-way chili consists of highly spiced ground meat with not only beans, onions, and tomatoes but also spaghetti and grated cheese. A Columbus, Georgia, specialty is made with chili—with beans, of course—and a chopped up hot dog, complete with bun, relish, and mustard, stirred in just before serving.

Pure, unbeaned chili con carne has lately become very fashionable in this country as part of the back-to-American-roots and Tex-Mex movements in food (although beans may be served on the side). Along with those outcast beans, hamburger is now Out and cubed beef (or venison or buffalo) is In, chili powder is Out and fresh or freshly ground dried chilies are In, tomatoes are Out and water is In. To many raised on beany, tomatoey chili like Mom (or Hormel) used to make, this revisionist style may be authentic, it may be good…but it's not chili con carne.

in this country, as the culinary guiding light of New York faded somewhat. Celebrities from all walks of public life were chili fans, perhaps because eating chili instead of poached quail eggs on toast points showed them to be down-to-earth all-Americans in those populist times. Will Rogers, Clark Gable,

Dizzy Dean, and John Garner (Franklin Roosevelt's vice president from 1933 to 1941) all ranked the "bowl of red" as one of their necessary luxuries. (In the 1960s Elizabeth Taylor's daily air-lifting of chili from Chasen's Restaurant in Los Angeles to Rome where she was filming *Cleopatra* was highly publicized—a curious case of down-to-earth meets jet-set. Chasen's also sent chili to Clark Gable when he was in the hospital: he reportedly had it for dinner the night he died.) In Los Angeles "The Biggest Meal on Earth" put on by the sheriff of Los Angeles County was an annual picnic and barbecue that fed sixty thousand people, with proceeds going to the Depression relief funds. The main dish for the picnic was chili con carne, and the recipe, recorded in *Through the Kitchen Door* by Beverly and Grace Smith and Charles M. Wilson (1939), started like this: "Take 24,000 pounds of best corn-fed Kansas City steer meat, 24 hundred pound sacks of Mexican red beans, 70 pounds of garlic, 450 pounds of salt, 3,000 pounds of onions and 50 pounds of chili powder..." The first to be served was Mae West.

It is perilous to give a recipe for chili, for more than any other American dish it will be met with howls of protest from outraged readers. But at the risk of raising great ire, here is a standard middle-American interpretation, not unsimilar to that of the Greatest Meal on Earth, noted above, except in poundage. Although many consider rice to be the proper accompaniment to chili, my own preference is for a big pan of unsweetened cornbread, some freshly made coleslaw, and of course, cold beer. In most homes in the Thirties, the beer would have been replaced with hot coffee or Coca-Cola.

## MIDDLE-AMERICAN CHILI CON CARNE

2 tablespoons bacon drippings or vegetable oil
1 pound ground beef
2 onions, chopped
2 garlic cloves, minced
2 cups canned tomatoes, chopped
3 cups cooked kidney beans, rinsed if canned
3 tablespoons chili powder
1 tablespoon cornmeal
1 teaspoon salt
3 tablespoons water
1 teaspoon dried oregano, crumbled

In a deep, heavy pan heat the drippings, then add the ground beef and onions and cook over medium heat until the beef is brown and the onions are soft. Pour off the excess fat. Add the garlic to the pan and cook over low heat for a few minutes. Stir in the tomatoes and beans and cook 10 or 15 minutes.

In a small bowl mix together the chili powder, cornmeal, and salt. Stir in the water to make a thick paste. Stir the chili paste into the beef mixture. Stir in the crumbled oregano. Cook over low heat, stirring occasionally, for 1 hour. Correct the seasonings, adding salt, oregano, garlic, or chili powder to taste. Serve hot. (If the chili is to be held overnight, check the seasonings at serving time, because the heat of the chili powder seems to dissipate on standing.)

MAKES 8 SERVINGS

# The Thirties Tea Party

For the woman without a maid no form of entertaining is more practical than the gathering together of two or three choice friends over a cup of tea. It involves no wear and tear of preparation, she can express her very innermost yearnings of daintiness and it comes at the most leisurely hour of the day.

—Procter & Gamble, *The Art of Cooking and Serving* (1937)

Teas were indeed the proper way for the 1930s hostess to express her "innermost yearnings of daintiness" or for sorority girls to "rush" freshman hopefuls. For teas were the ultimate feminine gathering. Table decorations could be as frilly and as delicate as anyone would wish, the guests could wear their floatiest and most flowered afternoon frocks, and the food... Well, nothing could be more refined and feminine than the food and drink served at tea. Occasionally men might be invited to one of these "tea fights," as irreverent males liked to call them, but in that event, noted one cookbook primly, coffee would have to be served. Most men avoided tea parties like the plague.

The insubstantial little fancies that women liked to eat and serve at tea parties centered around little sandwiches, small cakes, and dainty cookies (no large, chewy oatmeal and raisin cookies here, please). "Never serve gooey cakes which require a fork (an extra thing to clatter to the floor)," cautioned one 1933 *House & Garden* article on tea parties.

Thirties hostesses exercised all their creative urges in concocting those little sandwiches. Celery and olive, chicken and pineapple, open-faced guava jelly and cream cheese, deviled peanut, pickled walnuts and cheese, orange marmalade and pecan, apricot horseradish, tapioca coconut, curried carrot, beef and raisin, cheese and pickle, egg and olive, cream cheese and cherries—all made elegant fillings to spread on buttered bread. Needless to say, whether the breads were white, whole wheat, or nutty, they all had their crusts removed before the sandwiches were sliced into dainty fingers, diamonds, or squares.

Here are some recipes for quaint—and sometimes peculiar—tea sandwiches from the Thirties. To butter sandwiches properly, you need softened butter and *unsliced*, closely grained bread. Slice off the butt end of the bread, butter the exposed area from crust to crust, then slice off the buttered piece. Butter the next exposed section, slice off and continue.

## PEANUT BUTTER TEA SANDWICHES

1 cup natural smooth peanut butter
2 tablespoons ketchup
2 tablespoons finely chopped sweet pickles
1 loaf white bread, buttered and thinly sliced
1 head iceberg lettuce

Make a paste of the peanut butter, ketchup, and pickles. Spread on thin slices of bread. Top with a lettuce leaf and another buttered slice of bread. Cut off the crusts and slice the sandwich into three fingers.

MAKES 36 SMALL SANDWICHES

## OLIVE AND CHEESE SANDWICHES

1 (8-ounce) package cream cheese
1 tablespoon heavy cream
1/2 cup green olives stuffed with pimientos, drained and chopped
1 loaf whole wheat bread, thinly sliced

Mash the cream cheese with the cream until soft enough to spread easily. Mix in the chopped olives. Spread one slice of bread with the cheese mixture, then top with another slice of bread. Remove the crusts and slice into 3 fingers.

MAKES 36 SANDWICHES

## ROLLED SANDWICHES (DIPLOMAS)

2 (4 1/4-ounce) cans deviled ham
1 tablespoon pickle relish
1 tablespoon mayonnaise
1 loaf whole wheat bread, crusts removed
Butter
Small ribbons in pretty colors

Mix the ham, relish, and mayonnaise together. Slice and butter the bread as directed above and immediately place each slice in a lightly damp towel. Spread a slice with the ham mixture and then roll up. Place on a tray, seam side down. Tie a ribbon around each sandwich roll (be sure to coordinate the ribbon with your party color scheme!). If not to be served immediately, cover with aluminum foil or plastic wrap.

MAKES ABOUT 15 DIPLOMAS

One of the most enduringly popular of the Thirties tea sandwiches was dense, sweet fruit bread or nut bread spread with softened cream cheese. Dates and walnuts made a good combination for the bread, and a period one at that. Dates were a very common ingredient in baked goods in the early part of this century. Said *The Baker's Business Booster*, a 1922 professional baking manual, "When you mention dates it makes most everybody's mouth water, even the old folks, remembering the days when they were kiddies, and how good dates tasted."

## DATE-NUT BREAD FOR TEA SANDWICHES

To serve, slice the bread in thin slices, spread with softened cream cheese or butter, top with another slice of the bread, and cut into fingers, squares, or triangles.

    4 cups coarsely chopped pitted dates
    2 cups boiling water
    4 cups all-purpose flour
    1 teaspoon salt
    1/2 cup shortening or butter
    1 1/2 cups brown sugar, packed
    2 eggs
    2 teaspoon soda
    2 cups chopped walnuts

Preheat oven to 350°F. Put dates in a heat-proof bowl and pour boiling water over them. Sift flour and salt together. In a separate large bowl, cream together the shortening or butter and brown sugar. Add eggs one at a time to sugar mixture, beating thoroughly after each addition. Stir soda into the dates and water, then stir the date mixture and flour into the egg mixture just until blended. Stir in the nuts. Spoon batter into two greased and floured bread pans and bake 45–60 minutes, or until a toothpick inserted into the center of the loaves comes out clean. Remove from pans and cool on rack.

MAKES 2 LOAVES

In addition to the tea sandwiches, delicate cookies such as sand tarts, small cakes such as petits fours, and cinnamon or orange toast fingers were all approved nibbles for a feminine gathering. One of the most charming refreshments, however, were tiny biscuits cut from the dough with a *thimble*, and then split, buttered, and served while still hot.

Tea, of course, was the usual beverage at tea parties, poured from the hostess's best silver teapot into her finest and most fragile bone china cups. To "garnish" the tea, one magazine suggested lemon slices stuck with whole cloves,

## Taste-T Bridge Tea Sandwiches

In 1933 Kraft (then the Kraft-Phenix Cheese Corp.) put out a charming little booklet called *Kitchen Fresh Ideas*. It featured bottled mayonnaise products "made by a new and exclusive Kraft method—the Kraft Miracle Whip," which ensured "exceptional smoothness and delicacy of flavor." And, of course, these products were "kitchen-fresh."

### TASTE-T BRIDGE TEA SANDWICHES

Here are Kraft's recommendations for "taste-t" bridge tea sandwiches using their products.

    1 loaf white bread
    1 loaf whole wheat bread
    1 loaf Boston brown bread
    1 jar Kraft Ham-N-Aise Spread
    1 jar Kraft Taste-T-Spread
    1 jar Kraft Thousand Island Dressing

Use playing-card cutters in the shape of hearts, diamonds, spades, and clubs. Cut hearts and diamonds from the white bread, spades from the whole wheat, and clubs from the Boston brown. Put together in sandwiches, using Kraft Ham-N-Aise, Taste-T-Spread, and Thousand Island Dressing for fillings.

**Variation:** For pinwheel sandwiches, cut fresh white bread very thin, from the bottom of the loaf. Spread with Kraft Thousand Island Dressing or Ham-N-Aise, roll up like a jelly roll, then wrap in a napkin. When ready to serve, cut into half-inch slices.

candied ginger and orange peel, half slices of oranges garnished with rose geranium leaves, maraschino cherries threaded with sprigs of mint, and tiny gumdrops or rock candy. The modern reader has no trouble understanding the lemon slices, but were guests expected to drop minted maraschino cherries or gumdrops into their tea? Perhaps these tidbits were just nibbled daintily between sips. But the most excruciatingly dainty idea for an accompaniment to tea came from the *Boston Cooking-School Cook Book*, which recommended that food coloring be used to paint tiny flowers on the sugar cubes. In hot weather iced tea with mint sprigs might be served, but a sweet punch was also entirely proper. Here is a very simple sparkling punch, made special by tinted and flavored ice cubes.

## SPARKLING PUNCH FOR SUMMER TEA

Green food coloring and peppermint extract for ice cubes
1 quart white grape juice
1 quart soda water or seltzer
1 quart pale dry ginger ale
Fresh mint leaves for garnish

Tint the water for the ice cubes with green food coloring, stir in a small drop of peppermint extract and freeze in trays. Chill all the liquids and mix just before serving. Serve the punch in tall glasses filled with the minted ice cubes and garnish with the mint sprigs.

MAKES 10 TO 12 SERVINGS

# Club Luncheons

While an afternoon tea was the ultimate in feminine daintiness, club luncheons (or breakfasts or suppers) played an important role in women's lives in the Thirties. The woman who didn't belong to a study club, sewing club, or one of the two most important promoters of social cohesiveness—bridge and gardening clubs—was an outcast indeed. One 1934 ad for Lux soap pointed up the plight of a lonely newcomer to the neighborhood who had been asked only once to "fill in at the club, yet she loved bridge, played well, too." When she overhears a chance remark about perspiration odor in "underthings," she realizes her trouble: she smells! After she uses Lux, happiness returns. "She belongs to the bridge club now—everybody likes her," proclaimed the ad. "Now she never offends."

The advantage club get-togethers had over teas was that they afforded the ambitious woman full scope for her most creative culinary urges. Not limited to dainty sandwiches and small dessert cakes, she could go whole hog with every type of feminine frippery. Fruit cocktails, creamed meat and vegetables in patty shells or cream puffs, "surprise" sandwich loaves, molded salads, dainty desserts—and everything garnished, masked, encased, or made to look like something else.

One of the most popular luncheon *entrées*, for want of a better term, was the frosted "surprise" sandwich loaf and its variants, ribbon sandwiches and checkerboard sandwiches. These were sandwiches only in that they incorporated bread spread with various fillings, but they were strictly plate and fork affairs. The "surprise" was that these sandwich loaves looked like frosted cakes. They were sometimes called "Betty Co-eds" because they were so popular at college club meetings.

## BETTY CO-ED SURPRISE SANDWICH LOAF

Every kind of variation may be made in the fillings for a surprise loaf, of course, with the caution that the colors should contrast, while the tastes harmonize. Deviled ham, cheese spread, and grated cabbage; and chopped pimiento mixed with mayonnaise is one suggested combination of fillings; mashed sardines mixed with butter, egg salad, and shredded iceberg lettuce with mayonnaise is another.

  1 loaf firm, unsliced white bread
  1/2 cup (1 stick) butter, softened
  4 ounces pimiento cheese
  1/4 cup heavy cream
  3 hard-boiled eggs, finely chopped
  1 small green bell pepper, seeded and finely chopped
  1/2 cup plus 2 tablespoons mayonnaise
  3 (8-ounce) packages cream cheese
  1/2 pound tomatoes, peeled, seeded, and sliced
  Radish roses
  Watercress sprigs

Trim the crusts from the bread. Cut into four *lengthwise* slices. Butter each slice. Mix the pimiento cheese together with 2 tablespoons of the cream. In another bowl, mix together the eggs, bell pepper, and 2 tablespoons of the mayonnaise. In yet another bowl, cream together the cream cheese and the remaining cream.

On the first slice of bread, spread the pimiento cheese mixture; on the second slice, spread the hard-boiled egg mixture; on the third slice, place the slices of tomato spread with the remaining mayonnaise. Top with last slice of bread. Spread the top and sides of the loaf with the cream cheese mixture. Cover with plastic wrap and refrigerate for at least 2 hours. Garnish loaf with radish roses and watercress sprigs. Cut into thick slices and serve.

MAKES 12 TO 14 SLICES

**Variation:** To make Ribbon Sandwich Loaves, follow the directions for Betty Co-ed Surprise Sandwich Loaf, except that alternate slices of white bread and whole wheat bread should be used.

## CHECKERBOARD SANDWICH LOAVES

These sandwiches should be made with only one creamy and cohesive filling, such as a flavored butter or cream cheese.

    1 loaf fine-grained brown bread
    1 loaf fine-grained white bread
    2 cups softened butter- or cream cheese–based filling
    Cream cheese frosting from Betty Co-ed Surprise Sandwich Loaf (page 66)
        (optional)

Remove the crusts from both loaves of bread, then slice the loaves horizontally into ³/₄-inch slices. Cut these slices into strips ³/₄ inch wide. Put together in loaf form, alternating dark and light strips. Use softened, flavored butter or cream cheese as filling and to cement the strips together. Checkerboard sandwiches don't have to be frosted, but for maximum visual surprise, a cream cheese frosting is recommended. Chill and slice into ¹/₂-inch slices.

MAKES 2 LOAVES

The best sort of club luncheon had a theme, such as St. Valentine's Day or St. Patrick's Day, so that the table decorations and food could all be within the same color scheme. Here is a pink-and-white luncheon from the *GE Silent Hostess Treasure Book* (1932):

◆◆◆

## Valentine Pink-and-White Luncheon

*Jellied Tomato Bouillon*
*Celery Hearts* ◆ *Bread Sticks*
*Creamed Shrimps in Timbale Cases*
*Julienne Potatoes* ◆ *Baking Powder Biscuits*
*Valentine Salad (sliced beets cut in heart shapes)*
*Heart Molds of Strawberry Bavarian Cream*
*Fancy Cakes* ◆ *Heart-Shaped Candies* ◆
*Salted Nuts*
*Coffee*

## Sunbonnets and Poke Bonnets— Life in the Country

In the midst of the Depression and in the time of farm failures and the migration of the Okies (who left their homes as the fertile topsoil blew away leaving only desolate land), Americans indulged themselves in a misty-eyed nostalgia about farm life—and farm food. Della T. Lutes's *The Country Kitchen* went through nine printings between 1935 and 1937. Cora, Rose, and Bob Brown's 1937 *The Country Cookbook* ("Cooking, Canning and Preserving Victuals for Country Home, Farm, Camp and Trailer, with Notes on Rustic Hospitality") was part of the Country Series put out by the Countryman Press, Inc., and Farrar & Rinehart. Both of these books—and others like them—dwelled long and fondly on life in the country, centering around picnics, fairs, and family gatherings full of fried chicken, cream gravy, feathery baking powder biscuits, cool fresh buttermilk, rivers of melting sweet butter, rich ice cream, flaky pies bursting with sweet orchard fruits, and tender mile-high cakes. The food was lush, rich, and plentiful, and the families snug 'round the crackling fire in the winter, blessed with endless sunshine and juicy watermelons in the summer.

The poke bonnet or sunbonnet worn by old-time farm women was one symbol of the good old days that Americans were understandably yearning for in the Thirties. The canned pear poke bonnet salad was one manifestation of this. In 1933 *Good Housekeeping* gave instructions for a spring luncheon with a poke bonnet table centerpiece made out of maize-colored crepe paper with ruffles and ribbons of orchid and green, filled with individual corsages of lavender sweet peas and yellow mimosa for every feminine guest.

Dainty table favors were tiny paper poke bonnets filled with nuts. *Good Housekeeping*'s luncheon, of course, had absolutely nothing to do with the farm life symbolized by the poke bonnets. But, of course, the menu did follow the centerpiece's color scheme of maize, lavender, and green.

◆◆◆

## *Good Housekeeping's* Poke Bonnet Luncheon

*Minted Grapefruit Sections in Ginger Ale*
*Eggs à la King in Patty Shells*
*Buttered Asparagus ◆ Grape Jelly*
*Hot Baking Powder Biscuits*
*Romaine Salad ◆ French Dressing*
*Cheese Cakes*
*Apricot Sherbet ◆ Shrewsbury Rings*

Color wasn't the only consideration for the wildest sort of feminine imaginings. What Betty Fussell called in *Masters of American Cookery* "topiary" food and decoration was highly popular. Manipulating or decorating food so that it looked like something else has had a long history. From Imperial Rome's hare fitted out with wings to look like Pegasus (from Trimalchio's feast in *The Satyricon*), to Antonin Careme's fantastic eighteenth-century set pieces sculpted out of sugar to represent Turkish mosques or Chinese pavilions, the upper classes have often enjoyed playing with their food. When the banquets and feasts got to the point of overwhelming excess, of too much variety and richness, of palatal ennui, the chefs of the rich started concocting topiary food sculptures to pique the jaded senses of their gourmand clients. And the rarer the ingredients, the more fantastic and exquisite the design, the more costly the whole assemblage, the better. So what are we to make of 1930s poke bonnet salad (sometimes called sunbonnet salad) made out of a canned pear half with a face painted on with food coloring, topped with a lettuce leaf bonnet secured to the pear with cloves? From the sublime—if vulgar—to the utterly pedestrian.

In the Thirties, this topiary effect was put to best use in the salad course. Fannie Farmer's *Boston Cooking-School Cook Book* (1934) went just about everyone one better with its salad fantasies. Flavored cream cheese shaped into mushroom caps, then rolled in chopped almonds (and served on crisp wafers with orange baskets filled with currants and "a simple green salad") made a mushroom salad. Porcupine salad employed peeled tomatoes stuck with narrow pieces of celery and green pepper—"at regular intervals, allowing 7 of each to a tomato," the book advised the insufficiently artistic home cook. A salad that looked like an Indian chief's feather headdress with asparagus spears lassoed by rings of boiled beets and green and red peppers sticking out of a seeded tomato was appropriately titled Indian salad. A more complicated affair was the butterfly salad. This involved split bananas for the body; pineapple slices cut in half for the wings; ripe olives, pimiento, and capers to decorate the body and make the antenna and eyes; and finally colored mayonnaise to paint the pineapple wings. Last but not least was bunny salad, made from the standby canned pear half nestling in shredded lettuce, with blanched almonds for ears, pink candies or cloves for eyes and nose, and for the tail, what else but...a marshmallow.

But Fannie Farmer didn't stop there. If the salad itself could not be topiary, why not put the salad *in* something? Grapefruit or orange baskets were ideal, particularly if the maker tied a ribbon around the handle and inserted a sprig of flowers or mint in the knot. A head of cabbage hollowed out, its edges cut in points and then pinned with cloves, was fine, too. Cracker boxes could also be made by gluing three or four saltine crackers together with sugar syrup and then tying the resultant triangle or rectangle with a colored ribbon. This box was then filled with salad.

If the effect of all this decoration wasn't quite enough, radish roses or tulips could be added, or carrots made out of tinted cheese and a parsley sprig, or aspic cubes colored red or green. But, admonished Miss Farmer (or her subsequent editors), "Avoid overgarnishing and bad color combinations. Simplicity is safest for the inexperienced cook."

Fannie Farmer's cookbook was not the only purveyor of topiary salads, by any means. Nearly every cookbook gave a recipe for tomato rose salad, which was fashioned from a skinned tomato covered with "petals" made of softened cream cheese.

Fruit cocktails, which differed from fruit salads mostly in that they were served in sherbet cups instead of on a lettuce leaf, also offered considerable scope for ornamentation. One of the most popular was the nosegay or bouquet cocktail.

# NOSEGAY COCKTAIL

6 paper doilies

I large egg white, slightly beaten

I honeydew melon, cut into balls

2 peaches, peeled, pitted, and cubed

$^1/_2$ cup small strawberries, hulled and cut in half

$^1/_4$ cup lemon juice

$^1/_3$ cup sugar

$^1/_2$ cup ginger ale

Fresh mint sprigs and small peeled grapes tinted red with food coloring
   for garnish

For each cocktail, cut the center from a doily and make small cuts in the inner edges of the ring at $^1/_2$-inch intervals. Moisten the inside rim of a sherbet glass with the egg white and press the clipped edge of the doily around it, turning the lace out over the rim. Set aside.

Mix the fruit with the lemon juice and sugar. Pour the ginger ale over the fruit and refrigerate until thoroughly chilled. Fill the decorated sherbet cups with the drained fruit mixture, arranging the fruit to look as flowerlike as possible. Around the edges of the cup arrange mint sprigs centered with the tinted grapes to represent an old-fashioned bouquet.

MAKES 6 SERVINGS

Not all of the topiary effects popular for entertaining "the girls" were edible. *American Home* magazine ran an article on "fun and fancy" table decorations that featured amusing little people made out of colored glass bottles with kumquat or lime heads (with painted-on faces) and long, curly orange peelings for arms. They also suggested "Moses in the bulrushes," fashioned out of a wooden bowl lined with green onions; Moses himself was a light green melon with a dark green avocado head. But their most fantastic creation was the "sultan and his wives," made out of apples, a pomegranate, and an avocado with hats of turnip tops. This happy little family stood in a forest of broccoli stalks rooted in "pebbles" of dried beans.

Club luncheon desserts needed to be light, rich, sweet, feminine, and if possible, suggestive of something else. Citrus baskets filled with ice creams or sherbets were popular, as were sponge cake baskets filled with ice cream, whipped cream, or Bavarian cream and berries.

More fanciful were mock toasted marshmallows, which involved gelatin and egg white beaten to a froth and then jelled till firm. This mixture was then cut into marshmallow-shaped cubes, the cubes were rolled in crushed macaroons, and the "toasted marshmallows" were served with sugar and cream.

But one of the prettiest and certainly one of the most popular desserts of the Thirties—for Ladies' Luncheons, but also for functions when the men were invited—were meringue tortes (sometimes called meringue cakes, schaum tortes, angel pies, or meringues glacées, if they were filled with ice cream). These ethereal confections could be molded into fancy shapes, such as hearts or flowers, or baked in rounds to be sandwiched together with whipped cream or ice cream.

As Mary Grosvenor Ellsworth said in *Much Depends on Dinner* (1939), "The sweet, flattish taste of these crisp bits of fluff is particularly good with fruits of definite flavor." Strawberries, raspberries, peaches, and cherries all are good with meringue tortes, as is lemon curd or a tart orange curd. And, of course, whipped or ice cream.

## MERINGUE TORTES

8 egg whites
1 1/2 cups sugar, sifted
1/8 teaspoon salt
1 teaspoon vanilla or almond extract

Preheat the oven to 250°F. Beat the egg whites in a large bowl until thick but not stiff. Gradually beat in two-thirds of the sugar and the salt and continue beating until the mixture holds its shape. Fold in the rest of the sugar and the extract. Place baking parchment (or foil) on a large baking sheet. Shape the meringues as desired with a pastry bag for small meringues or make two large meringues, shaping them with a spoon. Bake until the meringues are crisp and just beginning to show the slightest ivory color, about 1 hour. Let sit on the baking sheet in the turned off oven with the door open for 10 minutes. Remove from the paper and put in a dry, cool spot to cool. (The centers may be removed from the meringues while they are still warm, if desired.)

**Note:** To make a large torte, sandwich 2 flat meringues together with whipped cream and serve with crushed, sugared fruits and additional whipped cream. For more serving suggestions, see text.

MAKES 8 SERVINGS

## ANGEL PIE

This is the icebox cake version of meringue torte.

> ½ recipe Meringue Tortes (p. 72), baked in a pie shell shape
> 1 recipe Lemon Curd (below)
> 1 cup heavy cream, slightly sweetened and whipped until soft peaks form
> Strawberries, candied lemon peel, candied violets, etc. for garnish

Fill the center of the baked meringue shell with the lemon curd. Cover the entire top of the torte with the whipped cream. Cover with plastic wrap and refrigerate for 3 hours or more (overnight is sometimes recommended, but the meringue may weep). Garnish with whole strawberries, strips of candied lemon peel, or candied violets.

MAKES 8 SERVINGS

## LEMON CURD

> ½ cup sugar
> 4 large egg yolks
> 2 tablespoons butter
> Juice and grated rind of 1 lemon
> Dash of salt

Combine the ingredients in the top of a double boiler. Cook over simmering water, beating constantly with a wire whip, until the mixture thickens. Cool.

# Entertaining the Gang

There were "grander" entertainments than Sunday Night Suppers or Luncheons for the Ladies, of course. But as the Depression wore on, economy and (relative) simplicity became more and more important.

Inventive hostesses circumvented tight budgets by giving Dutch treat parties—wherein the expenses and work of the party were shared by all the guests. Even relatively formal dinner parties could be handled in Dutch treat fashion, with each guest bringing one course, but informal get-togethers were more popular.

Buffet suppers, whether Dutch treat or not, were an ideal way to get the gang together and fulfill social obligations. Refreshments were simple. Said one magazine, "Long, fussy dinners are distinctly out of order; you'll want at most

only a filling buffet before the fun begins, or only a good snack after it's over."
Whether the fun was to be a costume party, barn dance, or Halloween party, you
could "trust the gang to get the others started on the games or other entertainment you have provided." Games were an important element at parties in the
Thirties: charades, limericks composed one line per guest at a time, Twenty
Questions, and other guessing games all added to a "blustering, riotous get-
together."

Here is a Halloween party buffet menu (with recipes) from *Woman's Home
Companion* that the gang could sink their teeth into both before and after the fun.

◆◆◆

# Halloween Buffet Supper

*Pastry Party Loaf* ◆ *Mushroom Sauce*
*Salad Pumpkins*
*Olives* ◆ *Celery* ◆ *Rolls*
*Spiced Cider* ◆ *Coffee*
*Fresh Jelly Doughnuts*
*Apples* ◆ *Popcorn Balls*

## PASTRY PARTY LOAF

Service of the Party Loaf is especially effective—and especially Thirties—if it is
placed on a large platter and surrounded with lettuce cups filled with individual
Salad Pumpkins. A frosted and decorated sandwich loaf could replace this Party
Loaf for easier preparation.

    6 cups small chunks cooked veal or chicken
    3 tablespoons chopped pimiento
    1 1/2 teaspoons salt
    1/8 teaspoon pepper
    1 teaspoon Worcestershire sauce
    6 tablespoons (3/4 stick) butter
    6 tablespoons flour
    1 cup chicken stock
    Standard pie pastry made with 3 cups all-purpose flour, chilled, enough
        for 3 one-crust pies
    1 large egg beaten with a little water for glaze

Combine the meat, pimiento, seasoning, and Worcestershire sauce in large bowl. Melt the butter over low heat in a small, heavy pan, then add the flour and cook, stirring, until smooth. Gradually stir in the stock. Cook, stirring constantly, until very thick. Mix the thickened stock into the meat mixture ¹/₄ cup at a time just until the mixture holds together. Taste for seasoning and correct. Spoon into a greased loaf pan and chill, covered, 3 hours or overnight.

Roll two-thirds of the chilled pastry into a large rectangle, place the loaf in the center, and fold the pastry up around the sides and ends of the loaf. Seal the corners. Roll the remaining dough into a long rectangle. Place on top of the loaf and crimp the top and side edges together. Decorate the top with scraps of pastry shaped into flower designs, leaves, etc. Chill thoroughly. Brush with the egg glaze. Bake in a preheated 425°F oven until brown, about 1 hour. Serve hot or warm with a mushroom sauce.

MAKES 12 SERVINGS

## SALAD PUMPKINS

This is similar to the golden glow salads popular in the 1930s. The "glow"—and the orange color for the "pumpkins"—comes from the carrots, orange juice, and pineapple. Please remember gelatin will not jell if fresh pineapple juice or pulp is used.

2 tablespoons unflavored gelatin
¹/₂ cup cold water
2 cups hot unsweetened canned pineapple juice
6 tablespoons lemon juice
1 cup orange juice
4 cups grated carrots
1 cup canned crushed pineapple, drained
Lettuce leaves and green bell pepper strips for garnish
Mayonnaise for serving

Sprinkle the gelatin over the cold water. Add the hot pineapple juice and stir until the gelatin dissolves. Stir in the lemon and orange juices. Set in the refrigerator to chill until the mixture begins to stiffen but is still workable. Fold in the grated carrots and crushed pineapple. Rinse small jelly glass molds (in shape of small pumpkins) or a large melon mold in cold water and fill with the gelatin mixture. Chill until firm. Unmold onto crisp lettuce leaves. Use the strips of green pepper to form pumpkin stems. Serve with a bowl of mayonnaise.

MAKES 12 SMALL MOLDS

If something a little more "sit-downish" than jelly doughnuts was wanted for dessert, cake with ice cream was always a good choice. Cake had not waned in popularity since the Twenties; if anything, it was *more* popular. And that popularity now had (pseudo)-scientific backing. A 1931 booklet from K. C. Baking Powder notes "cakes are no longer considered too rich for daily consumption; in fact, cake is now known to be an exceedingly well balanced food product."

One of the newest and most popular cakes was mystery or surprise cake—not surprising, because everyone in the Thirties seemed to love "clever" cooking. This cake was a 1925 culinary contribution from Campbell's Soup and tasted surprisingly good. "But," said *Joy of Cooking* (1964), "why shouldn't it? The deep secret is tomato, which after all is a fruit." Mystery cake was most often frosted with another brand name product—frosting made from Philadelphia brand cream cheese.

## MYSTERY CAKE, CAMPBELL'S SOUP

Cooking with condensed soups (usually Campbell's but Heinz and Hormel also were popular) had really taken hold in the 1920s, but this recipe was one of the first departures from the sauce/aspic oeuvre.

> 2 cups sifted cake flour
> 1 tablespoon baking powder
> 1/2 teaspoon baking soda
> 1/2 teaspoon ground cloves
> 1/2 teaspoon ground cinnamon or mace
> 1/2 teaspoon ground nutmeg
> 1 cup seedless raisins, coarsely chopped
> 1/2 cup vegetable shortening
> 1 cup sugar
> 2 large eggs, well beaten
> 1 (15-ounce) can condensed tomato soup
> Philly-Vanilly Frosting (below)

Preheat the oven to 375°F. Sift the flour, baking powder, baking soda, and spices together in a medium-size bowl. Toss the raisins to coat with 1/4 cup of the flour mixture. Cream the shortening in a large bowl. Add the sugar gradually to the shortening, creaming until light. Beat in the eggs until thoroughly mixed. Add the flour mixture alternately with the soup to the egg mixture. Stir until smooth. Fold in the raisins. Pour into two greased and floured 8-inch layer pans. Bake until a cake tester inserted in the center of the cake comes out clean, about 35 minutes. Frost with Philly-Vanilly Frosting.

MAKES 1 CAKE

## PHILLY-VANILLY FROSTING

1 (8-ounce) package Philadelphia brand (of course) cream cheese
4 cups confectioners' sugar
1 tablespoon butter, melted
1 teaspoon vanilla extract

Beat the cheese until soft in a large bowl. Work in the sugar, then beat in the melted butter and vanilla. Continue beating until very light.

# Dining in the Grand Manner

At the highest echelons of society formal dinners were still given, requiring maids and butlers. Admonished Leone B. Moats in "Dining in the Grand Manner" (*House & Garden*, February 1933): "You may be able to achieve smartness but never elegance by being thrifty. Unless you have an adequate staff of servants, it's better not to make an excursion into the formal. The proceedings must be conducted with silence, at a swift tempo, and must have the rhythm and swing which can be provided only by highly trained servants." She advised the aspiring elegant hostess to make no innovations in the presentation and serving of a formal dinner—too provincial—but did allow that the new fashion of using runners on a polished table instead of white Damask was acceptable. Her suggested menus were all in French and ran to the caviar, cream soup, lobster, roasted chicken, peas, lettuce salad, cheese, fruit, and baked Alaska (glacé surprise) type.

Formal dinner soups in the 1930s were basically the clear bouillons—hot in winter and jelled in warm weather (jellied madrilène "bids fair to become our national summer soup," said Mary Grosvenor Ellsworth in a 1938 issue of *House Beautiful*)—or to the light, yet rich cream soups. Vichyssoise, Chef Louis Diat of the Ritz-Carlton Hotel's creation of the 1910s, was "the last word in soups" in the summer, according to a 1939 issue of *Good Housekeeping*. Potage Saint Germain and other French-style vegetable-based cream soups were considered appropriate for the cold months.

Two soups that were very popular in the Thirties but have almost disappeared from modern menus were the similar Mongole soup (purée or cream Mongole) and boula (or boula boula).

The origins of Mongole soup are unknown. In the 1920s, Ida C. Bailey Allen gave a recipe for a soup à la Mongolese, but it was essentially a minestrone.

Mongole soup in its present incarnation of creamed split pea soup mixed with tomato appeared throughout cookbooks and magazines of the Thirties, almost always with canned soups as a base. It was served at the fashionable restaurant "21" with fresh peas, shoestring carrots, and a little onion juice stirred in. John MacPherson liked cream Mongole so much that he named his version, made without cream, Mystery Chef Soup. (And in the sinophobic Sixties, Thomas J. Lipton, Inc., gave a recipe for the soup, made with water and dried pea and tomato soup mixes, somewhat ominously called Purée of Mongole.)

## CREAM MONGOLE SOUP

Said *Joy of Cooking* (1946), "This is worth adding a fraction of a pound to your avoirdupois. Only don't fall in love with it and serve it too often."

    1 (15-ounce) can condensed tomato soup
    1 (15-ounce) can condensed pea soup
    1 soup can water
    1 soup can half-and-half or light cream
    2 tablespoons dry sherry

Combine the soups and water and stir to blend. Bring quickly to a low boil and let bubble for a few minutes. (This is done as a precaution against can-borne germs.) Remove from the heat and let cool a little. Stir in the half-and-half and heat until the mixture is hot, but do not let it boil once the cream is added. Remove from the heat. Stir in the sherry and serve in heated bowls.

**Variation:** For a noncanned version, combine homemade split pea soup (not too heavy on the ham or salt pork) with puréed tomatoes. Add cream, salt, and pepper to taste. Stir in a little sherry just before serving.

MAKES 6 SERVINGS

Boula has a more documented history than does Mongole soup. It was known in the United States as early as the 1830s and was made more recently by President Kennedy's chef, Rene Verdon. Although Verdon said that the Kennedys jokingly renamed the soup boula boula, after the Harvard song, it was frequently called that long before the 1960s. In the Thirties, boula, like Mongole, was frequently made with canned soups. Obviously it can be made from fresh ingredients…if you can come up with your own green turtle.

# BOULA

In *Much Depends on Dinner* (1939), Mary Grosvenor Ellsworth said, "M. Derouet, the maître of the Chemists' Club, told me about this one. He serves it to special stag banquets and invariably gets cheers."

1 (15-ounce) can condensed pea soup
1 (15-ounce) can condensed green turtle soup
2 soup cans water
1/4 cup dry sherry
1/2 cup heavy cream
Pinch of salt

Mix the soups and water together. Bring to a boil and let bubble for a few minutes. Remove from the heat and stir in the sherry. Pour the soup into individual ovenproof soup bowls. Whip the cream with the salt until firm peaks form. Put a blob of cream on top of each serving and brown under a hot broiler.

MAKES 6 SERVINGS

One hostess renowned for her dinner party innovations in the Thirties was designer Elsie de Wolfe. She liked to cover her table with gold lamé (confessing that she hoped it would bring back the gold standard) or with a cloth of silver lamé topped with "a lovely crystal ship, all its glass sails and its pennants set and flying and mirrored in a sheet of glass. Added to this are two rock-crystal birds and four rock-crystal candlesticks." And whether Leone B. Moats approved or not, Miss de Wolfe liked to surprise her guests with new dishes as well. Some of her favorites were duck with orange sauce, zucchini (courgettes) with tomatoes (zucchini was just starting to appear outside the Italian-American community), crêpes suzette, fruits with kirsch, and cherries jubilee. Unlike recipes from most other writers of the period, Miss de Wolfe's—which appeared in the fairly strait-laced *Ladies' Home Journal*—were liberally dosed with alcohol.

Many families could not afford Mrs. Moats's grand style of dining, nor were they equipped to emulate Elsie de Wolfe (in one article she recommended white Ming rabbits as part of an all-white winter table). Still, "company dinners," even if that just meant hubby was bringing The Boss home, had to be given.

What was the "three-in-one-hostess" to do? To help her, in March 1935 *American Home* recommended three menus that they promised could be served from "Cocktails to finger bowls with one change of plates!" They strongly suggested that the "smartest" way to serve cocktails—nonalcoholic, of course—was in the living room with the appetizers. One of their favorites was clam juice cocktail "that men particularly like." Here is one menu for the maidless family, followed by the cocktail recipe.

◆◆◆

# Maidless Dinner Menu I

*Clam Juice Cocktail*
*Ripe and Green Olives* ◆ *Cheese Wafers*
*Roast Lamb aux Poires*
*Buttered Rolls*
*French Fluffed Potatoes* ◆ *Peas Continental*
*Lettuce Salad with Fresh Tomato Mayonnaise*
*Cinnamon Candy Mousse* ◆ *Coconut Sweetmeats*
*Coffee*

## New-Fashioned Vegetables

All through the Twenties and well into the Thirties asparagus was the vegetable of choice for the smart dinner party. But the Italian immigrants' market garden was beginning to have an influence at the American table.

Zucchini, sometimes called courgette or Italian squash, became available in the Thirties. Elsie de Wolfe cooked them with tomatoes and bread crumbs but recommended cucumbers as a replacement if the hostess couldn't find squash. Cookbook writer June Platt, whom James Beard called "one of the most important gastronomic authorities this country has produced," gave a recipe for a very authentic ratatouille that called for Italian squash, "the long green ones that look like cucumbers."

Broccoli, which had been grown in America in the 1700s and then had virtually disappeared, also found a new audience in the 1930s. Far outstripping zucchini in popularity, President Bush's least favorite vegetable became nearly as acceptable on the American table in this century as peas and corn.

But perhaps the most fashionable new vegetable was the artichoke. Although it was not unknown before the Thirties, polite society was "wont to raise an eyebrow" at food that had to be "torn limb from limb" in front of others, as Jeanne Owen said in the September 1938 issue of *House & Garden*. By the end of the decade, though, white porcelain artichoke plates ($3.50 for six) were selling out at better stores, and new gourmet clubs were promoting the vegetable as haute cuisine. Jeanne Owen's recipes for them were rife with cognac, Sauternes, chestnut purée, mushrooms, shallots, and freshly grated Parmesan. And in those dark days of the Depression, one of her artichoke recipes began, "Slice two large truffles and two artichoke hearts…"

## CLAM JUICE COCKTAIL, *AMERICAN HOME*

1 bottle clam juice
Juice of 1 lemon
6 tablespoons ketchup
2 dashes Tabasco sauce
Celery salt

Mix all the ingredients together except the celery salt. Pour into a cocktail shaker with plenty of ice. Shake until well chilled. Pour into cocktail glasses and sprinkle each drink with celery salt.

MAKES 8 SERVINGS

# Dining on the Plank

One convenient way for the maidless hostess to handle a small party was with a planked dinner. Planks, which have now almost disappeared from the culinary scene, were wooden boards that could either be purchased at shops or "made at your local planing mill," as one magazine assured its readers. Small, individual planks could be used for each guest at a dinner party. The plank was heated, then partially cooked food was placed on it to be finished in the oven. Betty Crocker's 1950 *Picture Cook Book* called it a "glamorous, showy one-dish meal," and indeed the plank's advantage was that almost the entire menu could be served on it, cutting back on serving dishes. Even salads could be served on the plank, as long as they were placed at the extreme edge of the platter—and weren't too heat sensitive. Gelatin salads were definitely out.

Planked dinners were also popular in the fussy, gussied-up Thirties because many of the foods needed to be arranged or enclosed—in pepper rings; in pimiento, tomato, or onion cups; or in timbales, toast cases, or patty shells. But serving guests from the large planks wasn't always easy. Advised *American Home*, "A private rehearsal in the kitchen among the pepper cups and toast baskets may avert disaster."

Here is a typical planked dinner of the period.

◆◆◆

## Planked Dinner

*Cocktails and Tidbits in the Living Room*

**On the Plank**
*Broiled Sirloin Steak*
*Piped Mashed Potato and Turnip Rosettes*
*Candied Carrots in Orange Rings*
*Asparagus Tips in Green Pepper Rings*
*Pineapple and Cabbage Salad in Tomato Cups*
*Meringue Torte with Strawberries and Ice Cream*
*Coffee*

### DIRECTIONS FOR PLANKED STEAK

Preheat the plank (if new, season with oil, heat, wipe off the oil, then proceed). Broil the steak 6 minutes on one side. Place the steak on the plank cooked side down. Pipe the mashed potatoes (mixed with mashed turnips if desired) around the steak and brush with melted butter. Arrange the cooked vegetables decoratively in the spaces between the meat and potatoes. Place in a preheated 425°F oven until the potatoes are golden and the meat is cooked. Just before serving, put the tomato salad cups on the edges of the plank.

## Cocktail Parties

With the repeal of Prohibition on December 5, 1933, Americans could once again drink alcohol legally. The martini, that chic "silver bullet," was the drink of choice. Deco-styled chrome, aluminum, or copper cocktail shakers were fashionable, and built-in bars became a new status symbol.

But many Americans never *had* drunk, and those who hadn't certainly didn't start after Prohibition. Yet cocktail parties became popular in the Thirties, whether the tipple offered was alcoholic or not.

For nondrinkers "cocktails" were concocted from every type of juice imaginable—and some not so imaginable. Clam juice, tomato juice, minted pineapple juice, sauerkraut juice, apricot juice, raspberry juice, grape juice, and blackberry juice all could be mixed with appropriate seasonings and fixin's—even shaken in a cocktail shaker—and served over ice with a sprig of parsley or mint.

Here is one recipe for a beautiful "newly discovered bubbling purple drink" that was guaranteed to be the talk of the "dry" cocktail party—or at least so said Nell Nichols in "The Talk of the Party" in the October 1934 issue of *Woman's Home Companion*.

## BLUEBERRY FLIP

A "flip" was a common name for a cocktail. Save the juice the next time you open a can of blueberries to make a pie or muffins, advised *Woman's Home Companion*.

> ½ cup water
> ½ cup sugar
> 1 cup blueberry juice
> 1½ cups unsweetened pineapple juice
> Juice of 2 lemons
> Fresh mint sprigs

Boil the water and sugar together for 5 minutes. Combine with the other ingredients and chill. Whip with a rotary beater or shake in a cocktail shaker. Serve "at once to capture the bubbles" over chipped ice in tall glasses, garnished with a sprig of mint.

MAKES 4 SERVINGS

Cocktail nibbles and canapés also needed to be cunningly inventive to satisfy the enterprising hostess. *American Home* (October 1938) recommended spiffing up "good-but-dull" canapés by serving them in a dust pan (new, of course). Celery and olives also could be rescued from dullness by serving them in "fascinating galvanized iron chicken feeders with their neat little rows of oval holes."

If chicken feeders or dust pans were too outré, you could wrap little sausages in biscuit dough made from that new product Bisquick to make some snappy pigs in blankets. Or you could surprise your guests with that clever new treat, burning bush, made with two popular Thirties ingredients, cream cheese and chipped beef.

## BURNING BUSH

"Inserted in a polished eggplant to resemble a bush in autumn foliage, these are too attractive not to be noticed." The chipped beef is not refreshed in boiling water in this recipe. Be sure to keep this appetizer cool until serving time or the cheese—and the cheese balls—will droop.

    1 (8-ounce) package cream cheese
    1 (94-ounce) package chipped dried beef, very finely chopped
    Toothpicks
    1 large beautiful eggplant
    Crackers for serving

Make small cream cheese balls. Roll each ball in the chopped dried beef until completely covered. Put each ball on a toothpick and stick the toothpicks all over the eggplant. Serve with crisp crackers.

SERVES 6 TO 8

# The End of the Thirties

The Depression was still dragging on at the end of the Thirties. The American way of life, at least socially, had changed dramatically during that decade. Formal dinners, à la Moats, were almost nonexistent, maids were scarce or hired only for "occasions," and casual parties were the order of the day.

The gathering darkness of war in Europe was felt in a kind of uneasy and deepening dread in America. *Vanity Fair* ran a cartoon with a "touching little scene" of a European family at home together—Mom knitting, Junior playing with the dog, and Dad reading the paper—with everyone dressed in the latest style of "peace pact suits"…gas masks.

Yet American priorities were still clear. *American Home* magazine's infamous 1939 ad said, "Hitler Threatens Europe—But Betty Havens' Husband's Boss is Coming to Dinner and *That's* What *Really* Counts."

# 3

# An Exotic Interlude, I

## Chinese Food in America

I still remember the chicken chow mein I ate on my first date, hundreds of
years ago in St. Louis, in a Chinese restaurant where we were awed and
delighted by lovely hanging lamps with red silk panels that gave out little illumi-
nation, and a romantic table of black wood inlaid with bits of abalone shell or
possibly genuine mother-of-pearl. All the mysterious East was ours in
Missouri, and chow mein, too.

—Emily Hahn, *The Cooking of China* (1968)

Those marvelously strange restaurants that have become as familiar as our
own living rooms—the ones with red banquettes, dim lights, gleaming
golden idols, and odd-sounding entrées (Jade on a Bed of Coral and General
Ching's Chicken, whoever General Ching was)—were begot by a set of circumstances peculiarly American: the émigré's dream, the immigrant's reality—and a
dash of entrepreneurship.

When the first wave of Chinese immigrants left Canton province in the
mid-1800s for the Gold Mountain, as they called San Francisco, they had no idea
that they would change the course of American culinary history. They came, as
did so many others, because of the California Gold Rush. And they came with
dreams of money and a better way of life.

But the dream was a chimera for those Chinese pioneers, most of them poor
and ignorant laborers. They were hemmed in by intense racial hatreds and fears
(the dreaded "Yellow Peril"), by language barriers, and by stringent immigration
laws that kept their families in China. Many of them were even denied the right
to work the gold claims that had lured them across the treacherous sea. Some
slogged out a brutal life building the Central Pacific Railroad. (Their white
overseers felt Chinese laborers had a strong physical advantage: Chinamen, like
fish, supposedly felt less pain.) For the rest, they turned to the only ways open to

them to make a living. What was available in that woman-poor frontier was woman's work. In the Chinatowns that sprang up on the West Coast, Chinese men ran laundries, fruit stands, and tailor shops. And they became cooks, as domestic servants in wealthy California homes and, most significant, in restaurants.

At first the new restaurants catered primarily to other Chinese. Considering the difficulties of procuring some of the more exotic ingredients, the food served

## The Name Game

The Chinese penchant for the poetic naming of dishes reflects their view that cooking is an art, meant to be pleasing to all the senses. Yet some of the most picturesque—and odd—names are hidden from non-Chinese-speaking Westerners. Below are a few common dishes that may surprise you. (Before you marvel at the strange-sounding titles, consider some of our own foods: hot dogs, chocolate decadence cake, corn dodgers, baked Alaska, and blueberry slumps and grunts all sound pretty outlandish to foreign ears.)

| American Menu Name | Chinese Menu Name |
| --- | --- |
| Braised beef | Iron pounded beef—steak tenderized by pounding it with a cleaver |
| Sweet-and-sour pork | Sweet-and-sour ancient old meat |
| Marvelous taste chicken | Strange taste chicken—strange because of its sweet sauce of garlic, honey, soy sauce, ginger, and pepper |
| Chicken with eggs | Hibiscus chicken slices—the eggs puff up to look like hibiscus flowers |
| Chinese beans with beef | Bean corners beef—Chinese long beans are for some reason known as "bean corners" in China |
| Moo shu pork | Wooden whiskers pork—the crisp ingredients are all finely shredded |
| Chopped meat with bean thread noodles | Ants climbing tree—the "ants" are the bits of meat, climbing a noodle "tree" |
| Stir-fried chicken livers | Phoenix livers—the legendary phoenix, a symbol of long life and rebirth, is a popular icon in China |
| Tofu | Rotted meat—tofu is a curdled ("rotted" in Chinese) soy product that is high in protein and, therefore, considered meat |

was astonishingly authentic. In 1865 Samuel Bowles, editor of the *Springfield Republican*, attended a banquet at the Hang Hong Restaurant at 308 Dupont Street in San Francisco, where he dined on bird's nest soup, reindeer sinews, fried fungus, dried Chinese oysters, and somewhere between sixty and three hundred other such delicacies (the accounts vary). Afterward, Bowles remarked that Chinese food was "not very filling" and took himself off to an American restaurant to feast on chops, squab, fried potatoes, and champagne. This was perhaps the first inkling of the old saw "You're hungry an hour after eating Chinese food," although Bowles's appetite does seem a bit more robust than most.

As more Americans began to discover the inexpensive Cantonese restaurants—all you could eat for a dollar at the turn of the century—the enterprising Chinese began tailoring their ancient cuisine to the tastes of the New World. Those tastes were timid and the food served in the exotic new restaurants was often poorly prepared by former laborers, refugees from the gold mines and the railroad. One American gourmet mourned the fact that when a decent Chinese cook died in the States the stringent immigration laws prevented his being replaced. But most Americans didn't know what they were missing. What they did know—meat and potato eaters though they had been—was that they were eating something entirely new and strange and exciting. And they liked it.

Then came the 1920s. Jazz Age America, in the midst of a wild stock market boom, was frantically trying to forget the traumas of the War to End All Wars and the great Spanish influenza epidemic. Eager to leave behind the awful past, not anxious to think about the questionable future, what the Flappers wanted—in the present—was glamour and gaiety and excitement. And what could be more glamorous and exciting than the mysterious East? In the 1920s, America went exotic mad.

In New York the Samarkand restaurant was a popular night spot where, a contemporary advertisement coyly explained, "East Meets West" and "Omar Might Sing." Mary Pickford's dressing room at her film studio in Hollywood was decorated in exotic—and stylized—Japanese fashion. A simplified version of the Chinese game mah-jongg became very popular in the Twenties.

Meanwhile, the theater was overrun with Chinese dramas rich with unlimited golden idols, dim red lights, and burning joss sticks (incense). Dorothy Parker complained in a 1920 *Vanity Fair* review of *The Rose of China* (with lyrics by P. G. Wodehouse of "Jeeves" fame) that "just at present Chinese heroines who substitute l's for r's...have rather lost the novelty in which lay most of their appeal. Personally the rush of Chinese dramas has so affected me...I wish they'd give the whole darn country away."

Even advertisers couldn't get enough of the Eastern mystique. A lushly illustrated ad for radiator covers assured the homeowner that "Like the magic of the Orient—the ugly radiator disappears!"

## Mah-jongg Parties

Ladies were particularly fond of mah-jongg and the slap of the pretty little ivory (or Bakelite) tiles could be heard at many a feminine get-together. In 1924 Alice Bradley, then the principal of Miss Farmer's School of Cookery, suggested that mah-jongg party refreshments should be dishes from the "Celestial Kingdom," "if you are fond of eating Chinese food."

This was one of Miss Bradley's menus:

◆◆◆

# A Chinese Mah-jongg
# Party Menu, Circa 1924

*Egg Foo Yung*
*Cream Cheese and Fig Sandwiches*
*Canton Ginger with Syrup (Tongoung)*
*Litchi Nuts* ◆ *Tea*

## CREAM CHEESE AND FIG SANDWICHES

In a typical Twenties touch, Miss Bradley advised you to "garnish [the sandwiches] with bits of pimiento to resemble Mah Jung blocks."

3 canned figs
2 tablespoons blanched almonds
1 (8-ounce) package cream cheese
Salt, pepper, and soyu sauce
1 loaf of firm-textured bread, crusts removed, cut in thin slices
1 stick of butter, softened
¼ cup pimiento strips, cut in bits

Chop the figs and almonds finely and mix with the cheese. Season to taste with salt, pepper, and soyu. Butter the bread and spread the cheese mixture on one slice. Cover with another piece of buttered bread. Cut the sandwiches in fingers or triangles and garnish with bits of pimiento.

MAKES 36 FINGER SANDWICHES

Food, too, could be exotic and exciting. For all the taboos of the 1920s (apparently only high livers and Hollywood film stars enjoyed sex and alcohol), there was a craving for the sensual that, for *nice* people, was best met by eating. And eating something exotic, something Oriental, could make that gustatory act twice as thrilling.

One woman, breathlessly describing her first daring visit to a Chinese restaurant in Oakland, California, said, "We went into one of the gaudily painted Chinese houses, bright with flowers and flags, and bearing the sign, 'Chop Suey,' to find out what that might be. It is a Chinese dish made of chicken, mushrooms, and—I dare not even guess what else."

# Chop Suey and Chow Mein

"At the outset of my night club career my escort's indignant query, "Who killed that squirrel?" cured me of night club chow mein for all time."
—Lipstick (Lois Long), the *New Yorker* (April 17, 1926)

Chop suey was *the* dish that introduced most Americans to the exotic art of Chinese cookery. Yet chop suey, like spaghetti and meatballs, like goulash, was not born overseas, but was a bona fide American dish. One Chinese writer claimed to have seen a sign in Shanghai after World War II that read "Genuine American Chop Suey Served Here."

There is a story that chop suey was first made in New York City on August 29, 1896, by the Chinese ambassador's chef who was trying to soothe his boss's upset tummy, but this seems unlikely, because the concoction was mentioned in print in at least eight years before that. The dish was probably devised by one of those former railroad coolies who palmed the new dish off on hungry round-eyes eager for the taste of something new and exciting. And whatever its provenance, most Chinese were not fond of chop suey. It was, in the opinion of Sing Ching Sen, a cook at the China Garden in New York in the 1920s, "no good for China boy."

Yet despite its doubtful origins, chop suey was so popular with non-Chinese Americans in the 1920s that it was even celebrated in song. *New Yorker* columnist Lipstick recommended the Owl nightclub as a great place to hear "a fascinating high yeller girl with a guitar sing 'Who'll Chop Your Suey When I'm Gone?'" She also described the food at the Owl as "awfully good—whether you order from the Negro, Chinese, Mexican or Italian kitchens."

But what *is* chop suey, really? It depends on whom you ask—and when you ask it. As much as it can be codified, this dish of "odds and ends" (the translation of the Mandarin Chinese *tsa sui*) is basically a stew of meat (pork or chicken are the standard proteins) cut in strips or chunks, cooked with celery, bean sprouts, and sometimes mushrooms or onions. To add exotic to exotic, bamboo shoots and water chestnuts are sometimes added by cooks striving for crunch and a more "authentic" flavor, but those ingredients were not widely available until the 1950s. The melange is properly stir-fried—if anything can be said to be proper about chop suey—and then seasoned with soy sauce and served over rice.

In those days true-blue American homemakers of the heartland, whose only contact with the mysterious East might be a thrilling visit to Chinatown, also wanted to cook exotic new foods at home. Maybe the dinner guests couldn't include Rudolph Valentino in harem pants and silver bracelets or Pola Negri (whose first film role was Salome in *Slave of Sin*) or Mata Hari. Nevertheless, a demure hostess could serve her guests chop suey with "show-you sauce," (soy or shoyu sauce) and be considered worldly, sophisticated, and just a tad daring—and all without damaging her reputation.

But a typical recipe for chop suey in the 1920s was about as Oriental and daring as mashed potatoes. Ida C. Bailey Allen, one of the foremost Home Economists of the period and obviously a lady to be reckoned with judging by the expanse of both her bosom and her name, gave the following recipe for her "Chinese" version:

## MRS. ALLEN'S CHINESE CHOP SUEY

2 pounds lean pork
Salt, pepper, and flour
1 cup dried beans, sprouted
2 heads celery
1 large onion, minced
1 tablespoon Worcestershire sauce

Cut the pork into cubes, season with salt and pepper, dredge with flour, and fry in hot pork fat until brown. Have ready the young bean sprouts (Mrs. Allen then proceeds to give detailed directions for growing fresh bean sprouts). After thoroughly washing the bean sprouts and the celery, cut them into inch-long pieces and add to the minced onion. Put the pork and vegetables together in a soup kettle, cover with boiling water, and simmer on the back of the stove until tender. Just before serving add the Worcestershire sauce. Serve very hot in shallow oval-shaped dishes of Oriental china with boiled rice and black tea.

MAKES 6 TO 8 SERVINGS

There was not a drop of "bug juice," as many Americans called soy sauce, in Mrs. Allen's "Chinese" recipe. Instead, she substituted Worcestershire sauce to add flavor to vegetables boiled to death. Oddly enough, in the same volume Mrs. Allen's recipe for "Americanized Chop Suey with Fried Noodles" included soy sauce, although it was optional (a little Kitchen Bouquet could be used instead "to give a Chinese flavour"). And the vegetables were stir-fried—Mrs. Allen didn't call it that, of course, because the term *stir-fry* was not invented until the 1940s—before the broth and the meat were added. However, Mrs. Allen garnished what, to us at least, seems a much more authentically Chinese chop suey than what she called "Chinese chop suey" with shredded lettuce and hard-cooked eggs.

Mrs. Allen's recipes hewed at least to chop suey's Asian origin if not to its spirit. But once that well-known American inventiveness got hold of the dish, chop suey took on aspects undreamed of by its Chinese progenitors. When *The Handy Book of Recipes for Twenty-Five* ("A Book for Medium-Sized Groups, Fraternal Organizations, Small School Cafeterias and Tea Rooms") was published in 1931, it contained three recipes for chop suey, one of which (Chop Suey II) is recognizably the dish in question. Of the other two, Chop Suey I called for green peppers, onions, chopped beef, tomato soup, and spaghetti to be baked together and Chop Suey III called for bacon, onions, ground beef, turnips, corn, chili powder, and tomatoes! In what may be an instance of "blaming the other guy," one American food authority identified the spaghetti version as "American" chop suey, while the same dish can be found in other cookbooks under the title "Canadian" chop suey.

If chop suey was bastardized Chinese food for the American masses, chow mein was a dish for gourmets. Hard as it is to believe for those of us who have only eaten the horrid frozen or canned chow mein or the messes served under that name in doubtful greasy spoons, properly prepared chow mein can be very good indeed. To this day Trader Vic's restaurants serve the dish to loyal customers who insist that it be cooked as the Chinese do, because chow mein is authentically Chinese (the name translates as "stir-fried noodles").

The key to good chow mein is the noodles. Those nasty deep-fried things tasting of rancid fat that most Americans associate with chow mein are virtually unknown in China. Instead, the Chinese (and Trader Vic) stir-fry freshly boiled noodles in hot oil until they are crisp on the outside but still beguilingly soft in the center. The hot noodles with their contrasting crisp/soft textures are then served with a stir-fried mixture of vegetables and strips of meat.

## CHICKEN CHOW MEIN

Pork, shrimp, ham, or tofu may be substituted for the chicken. Trader Vic, like many, thickened his stir-fry mixture with cornstarch. If you want to do that, too, mix 1 tablespoon cornstarch with ¼ cup cold water and add this to the pan with the bean sprouts.

### For the Noodles
½ pound Chinese wheat noodles
¼ cup plus 1 teaspoon peanut or canola oil
Salt

### For the Chicken Mixture
2 tablespoons peanut oil
½ teaspoon salt
½ cup canned bamboo shoots, drained and sliced
½ cup canned water chestnuts, drained and sliced
1 cup sliced bok choy
½ pound fresh mushrooms, sliced
5 green onions, cut into 1½-inch-long pieces
½ pound chicken, cut into bite-size pieces
¼ cup soy sauce
1 cup chicken broth
½ teaspoon sugar
1 cup bean sprouts
Toasted slivered almonds for garnish

To make noodles, cook them in boiling salted water until just *al dente*. Drain them, toss them with 1 teaspoon of the oil and set aside until cold. Heat the remaining oil in a large skillet until very hot. Add the cold noodles and stir them gently (chopsticks or a fork work best) until heated through. Reduce the heat, stir again, cover the noodles, and let them cook about 2 minutes. Turn up the heat again, remove the cover, and turn the noodles over gently to crisp and cook on the other side. (The noodles should be crisp on the outside and hot and soft in the middle.) Salt the noodles to taste and set aside, keeping them warm.

For the chicken mixture, heat the oil in a large, heavy skillet, add ¼ teaspoon of the salt and stir, then add the bamboo shoots, water, chestnuts, bok choy, mushrooms, and onions. Stir-fry for 1 minute, just until the vegetables start to soften. Then add the chicken and stir-fry for 1 more minute. Mix the soy sauce, broth, sugar, and remaining salt together and add this mixture to the skillet. Bring to a boil, then cover and let steam about 1 minute. Add the bean sprouts and steam 1 minute. Put the warm fried noodles on a serving platter, top with the chicken mixture, and garnish with the toasted almonds. Serve immediately.

MAKES 4 TO 6 SERVINGS

In the hands of American cooks, happy to find something exotic, fun, and cheap to serve to their families, chop suey and chow mein became virtually indistinguishable. They were both dishes of meat and vegetables flavored with soy sauce—whether they were served with rice, or with fried noodles, or both, didn't really matter. In the 1940s, one midwestern hostess gave a "Chinese" dinner that consisted of orange and grapefruit salad with oil dressing, chow mein, and cheese pie. Her chow mein was served in a molded ring of buttered rice and then topped with heated "brown noodles (Chinese type)."

By the time World War II was over, chop suey and chow mein had become as American and as ubiquitous as meat loaf. An early 1950s recipe booklet put out by the First Methodist Church of East Chicago, Indiana, instructed the reader to "have the butcher cut up the meat for Chop Suey." Something known as "chop suey sauce" (soy sauce dosed with other unnamed flavors) was in the stores in the 1950s. A number of recipes enthusiastically called for both soy sauce and chop suey sauce to finish off the chow mein or chop suey.

Cans of bean sprouts and chow mein noodles lined the aisles of the A&P, as did canned Chinese vegetables and chop suey vegetables, usually a mixture of bean sprouts, celery, and sometimes water chestnuts and bamboo shoots.

And what American over the age of twenty-five hasn't at least heard of Chun King, the company started in 1947 by Jeno Paulucci? Even the *name* of the company is ersatz Chinese—it was Paulucci's version of the first Chinese city he could think of. One of his most popular products was chow mein, full of inexpensive bean sprouts and chopped celery, with a separate can of crunchy noodles attached. La Choy brand eventually surpassed Chun King in sales, but for Americans of a certain age, Chun King means canned Chinese food.

And then—again!—there was that good old American itch to improve, change, adapt. One of the best examples of the complete Americanization of Chinese food came from Reuben's restaurant (now defunct) in New York City, which was famous for its sandwiches and cheesecakes. But what's a Chinese dish doing in a cream cheese shop anyway?

## CHICKEN CHOW MEIN REUBENOLA (CIRCA 1948)

3 tablespoons butter
1 cup canned or fresh mushrooms, sliced
1 cup chopped celery
1 large Bermuda onion, sliced
1 cup canned tomatoes, drained and sliced
1 cup canned bean sprouts, drained
$1/2$ cup canned water chestnuts, drained
$1/2$ cup canned bamboo shoots, drained and sliced
2 cups sliced or diced cooked chicken
$1/2$ cup sour cream
Crisp noodles

Melt the butter in a large frying pan over medium heat; add the mushrooms and brown them lightly. Add the celery, onion, and tomatoes; cover and simmer until the onions are almost tender, about 20 minutes. Add the sprouts, water chestnuts, bamboo sprouts, and chicken; cook 10 minutes, stirring frequently. Just before serving, stir in the sour cream and heat thoroughly. Serve on a base of crisp, dry noodles. If desired, each serving may be garnished with additional slices of cooked chicken.

MAKES 6 SERVINGS

# Chinese-American Food
# After World War II

It's often hard to pinpoint exactly when a fad or fashion changes. But in the case of Chinese food in America, the end of World War II is a fairly clear dividing line between the old taste for "Chop Mein" and a growing culinary sophistication.

During World War II, China's alliance with America pretty much scotched any lingering fears of the "Yellow Peril," as personified by the evil Dr. Fu Manchu. The new popular image of the Chinese—at least as depicted in "Terry and the Pirates" in the funny papers—was of brave Chinese boys fighting shoulder to shoulder alongside American G.I.s against the Japanese during the war.

In December 1943 the Chinese Exclusion Act of 1882, which had so severely restricted Chinese immigration, was repealed. Not coincidentally, one of the prime movers behind its repeal was Richard J. Walsh, husband of Pearl S. Buck, who had done so much to change American perceptions of the Chinese with her novel *The Good Earth*. Chinese women could now join their husbands in America, and between 1945 and 1952 nearly ten thousand did so. Finally, with the establishment of the People's Republic of China in 1949, many Chinese fled the Communist mainland. And because Americans had exchanged their fear of the Yellow Peril for that of the Red Menace, these new Chinese immigrants—many of them middle-class and non-Cantonese—were welcomed with open arms.

# Some Prophets of the
# New Chinese Cooking

Like the earlier Chinese immigrants, many of the new arrivals opened restaurants. And again, they unwittingly—and mostly anonymously—contributed to a growing sophistication in the American taste for Chinese food.

Three people stand out as possibly the most influential prophets of the new Chinese cooking in this country. Two of them were women and only one of them was Chinese.

One of the most important books on Chinese cookery in the new era was Buwei Yang Chao's *How to Cook and Eat in Chinese*, first published in 1945, with

*Buwei Yang Chao*

a preface by Pearl S. Buck. Significantly, Mrs. Chao was not from Canton, but from the more northern province of Anhui. Buwei Yang Chao not only gave the West a taste of authentic Chinese home cooking, both Cantonese and northern style; she and her linguist husband Yuen Ren Chao (who translated her book into English from the Chinese) invented a number of important new culinary terms. "Red-cooking" (cooking in soy sauce) and "clear-simmering" (cooking in clear broth, without soy sauce) are attributable to the Chaos, but their most important contribution was "stir-frying," which has become standard cooking terminology.

Interestingly, a new Chin-glish verb "to chow" is replacing "to stir-fry" in some quarters—a backward step, at least linguistically. "Stir-fry" was Mr. and Mrs. Chao's rendition of the Mandarin word *ch'ao*, which means to fry in hot fat while constantly turning the ingredients. But Jeff Smith, "the Frugal Gourmet," never stir-fries—he chows.

Despite Mrs. (and Mr.) Chao's contributions to the language, the English in their book was idiosyncratic, to say the least, making it difficult to find the names of popular Chinese dishes in the text. If you wanted, say, to make stir-fried cabbage with beef, you would find it listed as "American Cabbage Stirs Meat Shreds." Plain fried rice was "Egg Stirs Rice," while pork fried rice was dubbed "Meat Shreds Stir Rice." Stuffed cucumbers were "Cucumbers Stuff Meat"; a soufflé, "Grown Eggs"; a slotted spoon, a "leaking ladle"; and chicken with oyster sauce, "Chicken Globules Oyster Sauce." The Chaos' daughter has confirmed what many readers may have suspected after reading *How to Cook and Eat in Chinese*—her parents had a lot of fun coming up with many of the recipe titles.

But if the language was charmingly convoluted, the cooking was deliciously straightforward. In *Joy of Cooking*, the Rombauers, after dismissing their own chop suey/chow mein recipe, recommended Mrs. Chao's book for "delightful" Chinese recipes. While many of Mrs. Chao's recipes used techniques unfamiliar to her Western readers, her directions were clear—if uniquely her own—and easy to follow. Nor did she include ingredients not readily available at the average American market.

## BUWEI YANG CHAO'S WINE SMOTHERS MEAT SLICES

This is a typical recipe, simply told, with simple ingredients. Mrs. Chao's directions are exactly as she gave them.

2 pounds pork chops, boned
$^1/_2$ cup sherry or $^3/_4$ cup white wine
3 tablespoons soy sauce
$^1/_2$ teaspoon salt
1 teaspoon sugar
$^1/_2$ scallion, chopped
2 slices ginger "if available"

Cut meat into $^1/_2$-in.-long and $^1/_{16}$-in.-thick slices. Mix in all the seasoning. Start with low fire and simmer $^1/_2$ hr. If you are careful to keep the lid fairly tight, the flavor will puff out impressively when served. With rice and a green, this will serve six. The juice on the rice, yes. Soy sauce on the rice, never!

MAKES 6 SERVINGS

## Helen Evans Brown

The other woman was not only not Chinese, she didn't even write Chinese cook-books. Nevertheless, Helen Brown's *West Coast Cook Book* published in 1952 was probably the first, and for many years the only, cookbook to matter-of-factly incorporate Chinese cooking into an American work, with more than forty Chinese or Chinese-inspired recipes, from don far tong soup to lichi [*sic*] nut sal-ad. Looking at Brown's light and imaginative cooking, it is hard to believe that the book was written over forty years ago. Except that some of the recipes con-tain more fat than we're used to nowadays and there isn't a kiwifruit or a rasp-berry coulis in sight, the book seems completely modern.

But Mrs. Brown's innovative Chinese cookery was not surprising given the fact that she was living and writing on the West Coast, which by 1950 contained almost one-half of the total Chinese population in the United States, including the first and third largest Chinatowns. And many of her generation had grown up with Chinese houseboys who, even if they weren't making Golden Flower Jade Tree Chicken (chicken with mustard greens and ham) for their employers, certainly influenced the way food was cooked in the West, just as African cooks had done in the South.

While the range of Chinese recipes in the *West Coast Cook Book* was impres-sive, one of Mrs. Brown's most significant contributions to the developing American cuisine was that she passed on the influence of those anonymous houseboys and incorporated Chinese techniques and ingredients into homegrown dishes. She cooked broccoli stems with soy sauce and almonds, suggested Chinese pea pods as a good accompaniment to fried chicken, and predicted that bean sprouts (which she cooked with butter, garlic, and soy sauce) would become a favorite vegetable.

## Trader Vic

And then there was Victor Bergeron, or Trader Vic, as he insisted on being known. One-legged (he did nothing to quash the rumor that he'd lost the other to a South Pacific shark, although tuberculosis was reportedly the real culprit) and enterprising, he opened the first Trader Vic's in Oakland, California, in 1938, luring his delighted customers with rum drinks and Polynesian/Oriental food. Though it is culinarily correct nowadays to dismiss his restaurants as so much kitsch, San Francisco's fashionable set thronged Trader Vic's for many years, and millions of lesser Americans enjoyed the good food, excellent service, and exotic atmosphere.

As is obvious to anyone who has dined among the flaming torches and coconut shells at a Trader Vic's, exotic atmosphere is more important than accuracy every time. The Trader thought the home cook should share this attitude. In his 1946 *Trader Vic's Book of Food and Drink*, he gave directions for creating the right setting for a Chinese dinner party at home. It was to be "not the authentic kind, but my kind," because he considered a traditional Chinese dinner, without candles and flowers, unglamorous. His instructions for decorating the table were authoritative and to the point:

> ...a simple centerpiece of lilies, chrysanthemums, or heavy-headed poppies in a flat bowl with a bit of pseudo-Chinese statuary or ceramics, and short fat candles set on teakwood or pottery pedestals. Use table mats—woven, or bright-colored linen in jade green or yellow with matching napkins.

◆◆◆

## Trader Vic's Chinese Dinner Party Menu, 1946

*Cha Sui (Sliced Barbecued Pork)*
*Batter-Fried Shrimp with Sauce*
*Mushroom Soup*
*Chow Mein or Chicken with Pineapple*
*Foo Yung*
*Chinese Peas with Water Chestnuts*
*Chinese Fried Rice*
*Sweet-Scented Tea*
*Sesame Seed Cookies* ◆ *Preserved Litchi*

The menu may sound old-fashioned and naive to us now, but in 1946 it must have seemed almost revolutionary for the home cook. Few cookbooks of the period went further out on a limb than to offer yet another recipe for chop suey. But the standard cookbooks were behind the times. Americans were being exposed to more and better Chinese food—both at Trader Vic's and at the countless new Chinese restaurants springing up.

# Popular Chinese Dishes
# in the 1940s and 1950s

A number of the dishes that Trader Vic recommended in his sample Chinese menu were wildly popular in the 1940s and early 1950s. It seemed that you could hardly turn around without being met by a plate of egg foo yung (or fu  young). The dish was a favorite with Chinese cooks, although Buwei Yang Chao distinguished between the real thing and the foo yung served in restaurants. Still, she gave recipes for both in her cookbook. Prepared for the American taste, egg foo yung is sort of an Oriental frittata of eggs cooked in lots of fat with bean sprouts, water chestnuts, green onions, and meat (shrimp, pork, or chicken) and sauced with chicken stock, cornstarch, and soy sauce. The Chinese recipe as given by Mrs. Chao is similar to a French omelet stuffed with stir-fried vegetables and meat.

Fried rice was also immensely popular, although few Americans realized that the Chinese had designed it as a way to use leftover rice. It was one of the standbys of Chinese-American restaurant cooking and a dependable plate of it could be had even in the most out-of-the-way places. One of the most fashionable dishes at the Capitol Café and Lounge in Aberdeen, South Dakota—renowned for steaks, seafood, and Chinese-style dinners—was ham fried rice.

Barbecued pork (cha sui), spareribs Chinese style, and pressed duck were all favorite dishes of Americans in the early 1950s. Cha sui was rarely made at home, even by the Chinese. Pressed duck, which involves boiling, boning, weighting, and finally browning the duck in oil before covering it with toasted chopped almonds, was really a restaurant dish. But spareribs were easy to make, and Americans made and ate them by the ton.

Sticky, messy, and delicious, Chinese-style spareribs had become so popular by the end of the 1950s that Myra Waldo gave two recipes for them in her influential *The Complete Book of Gourmet Cooking for the American Kitchen* (1960): one with pineapple (sweet and sour) and one without. But a sure sign that spareribs had really caught on was that homemakers didn't feel compelled to serve them as part of an "Oriental" meal. Helen Corbitt, the director of the Neiman-Marcus Restaurants in the 1950s, served her sweet-and-sour spareribs (with pineapple) accompanied by rice—rice mixed with Parmesan cheese and chopped spinach.

Another popular dish, which has unfortunately faded from the culinary scene, was paper-wrapped chicken. Trader Vic had a recipe for it, as did Helen Brown.

## PAPER-WRAPPED CHICKEN

Mrs. Brown said, "This is one of the most entrancing of Chinese dishes. The tender juicy chicken, the delightful seasonings, and the charm of the little paper wraps are all appealing. Though it's to be had at most Chinese restaurants, there are few homemakers who attempt it—a pity, as it's easily made." Both Mrs. Brown and Trader Vic cooked the little paper packets in hot oil, but here the paper is exchanged for aluminum foil and the packets are baked. In the frying method small packets work best, but in baking it is better to make the packets larger so they cook more evenly.

I pound chicken meat, cut into I-inch squares about $^1/_2$ inch thick
$^1/_2$ cup dry sherry
$^1/_2$ cup soy sauce100
Pinch of sugar
I clove garlic, mashed
2 slices fresh ginger, mashed
6 (12-inch) squares aluminum foil
12 sprigs cilantro (fresh coriander or Chinese parsley)

Put the chicken in a bowl and pour over it a marinade made from the sherry, soy, sugar, garlic, and ginger. Let the chicken sit, covered, in the refrigerator 2 or 3 hours. Preheat the oven to 450°F.

Drain the chicken and divide it up between the foil squares. Put the sprigs of cilantro on top of the chicken. Bring up two opposite edges of the foil and fold them together, folding them down as far as they will go. Now fold up the other edges. Place the packets in a large baking pan, folded sides *up*, and bake 6 minutes. Rush the packets to the table, open them carefully so as not to burn yourself, and serve with hot Chinese rice.

MAKES 6 APPETIZER SERVINGS

# Going Out—Chinese Style

In modern day China, it has been estimated that over half of the population of Canton eats breakfast outside the home. Shanghai alone has more than twelve thousand restaurants, and Peking offers numerous twenty-four-hour dining spots so workers on the night shift can eat out.

And in America by the late 1950s "going out for Chinese" was a popular way to entertain guests or celebrate a family event. Sharing the food from common platters, trying to eat with chopsticks, solemnly mixing soy sauce with hot mustard in the little dish provided, drinking hot green tea with the strange food, breaking open the fortune cookies (which, by the way, are a Chinese-American invention), all made for an exotic and festive meal. And always, there were the mysterious black-garbed waiters to add a piquantly romantic note.

Although there were many places in the late 1950s and early 1960s, like Douglas Lee's Restaurant in Phoenix, which served such sophisticated dishes as shrimp with black bean sauce, most neighborhood Chinese restaurants still offered complete "dinners." Easy to order and very nonthreatening to their American patrons, a typical "Number 5 Dinner—Choose 2 dishes from Column A and 2 from Column B," with all guests at the table sharing the same food, might have consisted of the following:

◆◆◆

*Won Ton Soup*
*Egg Roll*
*Almond Chicken* ◆ *Sweet and Sour Pork*
*Fried Rice*
*Fortune Cookies* ◆ *Tea*

Cosmopolitan young moderns could eat such a dinner, secure in the belief that they were getting something excitingly foreign, yet completely familiar. So familiar, in fact, that a film released in 1968 starring Doris Day and Brian Keith was titled *With Six You Get Eggroll*. The film had nothing to do with food, but it was correctly assumed by the moviemakers that the American public was so used to "going out for Chinese" that the title needed no explanation.

# The 1960s Revolution
# and Chinese Cooking

If the shift in American attitudes toward the Chinese and Chinese cooking after World War II could be called a sea change, the transformation of those attitudes in the late 1960s was a tidal wave. Along with the love-ins, be-ins, and peace marches, the flower children, psychedelic acid heads, and peaceniks turned their attention to the mysterious East. And once again, America went exotic mad.

Tiger Balm replaced Ben-Gay as the healing rub for sore muscles. Acupuncture was In and Western medicine was Out. "Throwing the Ching" (a Chinese fortune-telling device employing thrown straws or coins, which are then used to refer to a book of wisdom called the *I Ching*) became an acceptable way for trend-setting counterculturists to make decisions. And *Zen and the Art of Motorcycle Maintenance* was on everyone's bookshelf.

When the long-closed doors of the Middle Kingdom finally swung open with Nixon's historic trip to China in 1972, America's fascination with the mysterious East knew no bounds. And Chinese food was again at a peak of popularity. Moneyed sophisticates took their meals in elegant restaurants like Bill Chan's New Gold Coin in New York City, where they had their choice of dining in the Warlord Room, the Lantern Room, or the Concubine Room. For the less wellheeled, the hippies, and the artists, the undiscovered restaurant deep in the wilds of Chinatown, where most of the patrons were Cantonese Chinese, was the ticket.

## The Revolution in Cooking at Home

But Americans—hippies or not—had never been satisfied with finding their exotic gourmet food solely in restaurants. If they could "go out for Chinese" they wanted to be able to cook it at home, too. Soon everyone—everyone who knew what was what—was cooking Chinese.

The rush of new Chinese cookbooks published in the United States reflected this growing trend for exotic home cooking. One of the most popular of the new cookbooks was *The Cooking of China*, published in 1968 as part of Time-Life's Foods of the World series. Emily Hahn wrote the lucid text and Florence Lin, the well-known teacher, lecturer, and Chinese food writer, was the food consultant. As always in this seminal series, the accompanying photographs were interesting and fun. Still, the book's usefulness to the serious cook was limited by its short list of recipes—less than 130.

But the book that quickly became the bible for American cooks who wanted to prepare Chinese food in their own kitchens was Gloria Bley Miller's encyclopedic *The Thousand Recipe Chinese Cookbook*, first published in 1968 and still in print. Written by a Westerner for Westerners, the book covered nearly every aspect of Chinese cooking, from its history and traditions to the use of woks, steamers, and cleavers; from the preparation of the more familiar stir-fried dishes (such as chicken with peppers or pork with mushrooms and bamboo shoots) to more arcane and complicated dishes such as braised chicken with red dates or deep-fried fish rolls with almonds.

## STIR-FRIED BEAN CURD (TOFU) WITH PORK AND VEGETABLES

Bean curd was starting to appear in counterculture cooking in the 1970s but would not really go mainstream until the late 1980s. Chicken breast or ham may be substituted for the pork, or the meat may be omitted entirely for a vegetarian meal.

1 teaspoon cornstarch
2 teaspoons dry sherry
3 tablespoons soy sauce
1/4 pound lean pork, cut into matchstick strips
2 tablespoons peanut oil or other mild vegetable oil
1/2 pound fresh mushrooms, sliced
1/4 teaspoon salt
4 to 5 green onions, trimmed and cut into 1-inch lengths
1 pound firm tofu, drained and cut into bite-size cubes
1/4 cup chicken or pork stock

Combine the cornstarch, sherry, and 1 tablespoon of the soy sauce in a small bowl. Add the pork and toss to coat. Let stand 15 minutes, turning occasionally. In a large skillet or wok, heat the oil and cook the mushrooms over medium-high heat until they start to soften. Add the salt and green onions and stir-fry for 1 to 2 minutes. Add the pork and its marinade and stir-fry until the meat loses its pinkness, about 2 minutes, then add the tofu and stir-fry gently another 2 minutes. Pour in the remaining soy sauce and the stock, raise the heat to high so that the liquids bubble up, then lower the heat to medium, cover, and cook another 2 minutes. Taste for seasoning and serve.

MAKES 4 TO 6 SERVINGS

Although the book contained recipes from many areas of China, including Szechwan, Shantung, and Honan provinces, most of the recipes were for the more familiar Cantonese dishes, which continued to be the most popular and accessible in and out of restaurants. The book also quietly marked a maturation in the American taste for Chinese cooking: it contained only a passing mention of that now despised dish, chop suey.

The supermarket shelves reflected the growing trend toward cooking Chinese at home. No longer did canned "chow mein vegetables" and soy sauce constitute the Oriental foods section of the grocery store. Now shoppers could find hoisin sauce, plum sauce, rice noodles, and peastarch noodles, fresh ginger, Napa or Chinese cabbage, and bok choy. But one Chinese vegetable—Chinese pea pods or snow peas—took America by storm.

## Chinese Taste Powder and the Fifth Taste

Monosodium glutamate (MSG) is one of the most vilified of ingredients in Chinese restaurant cooking. Suspected of causing Chinese restaurant syndrome (headache, dizziness, chest tightness, and sweating) in some eaters and for leveling all dishes to one flavor, it fell into serious disrepute when reports came out in 1969 that it caused cancers in infant mice.

But this amino acid compound (chemically $C_5H_8O_4NaN$) has been used in China for centuries where it is known generically as "taste powder." The oldest known form of it was made in Chinese households from dried fermented wheat gluten. In the 1920s the Japanese started manufacturing their own taste powder called *ajinomoto*, "prime element of taste," from hydrolyzed gluten, followed by the Chinese with *ve-tsin*, "essence of taste." The most well-known American MSG is Accent.

Although it is true that bad or inexperienced cooks have used MSG to try to disguise the lack of flavor in inferior foods, serious Chinese cooks do not completely disdain its use. It is considered not a flavor enhancer, as it is cast by most Americans, but as a *flavor* in and of itself. In the Chinese designation of culinary enhancer, MSG falls in with other flavorers such as sesame oil and soy sauce.

Interestingly, American science is now confirming what the Chinese have known all along. The West acknowledges four basic tastes—sweet, sour, bitter, and salty. But a fifth taste, a meaty taste, called *umami* in Japan, is recognized in Asia. University of California at Davis researchers have discovered that *umami* is associated with compounds of amino acids, the building blocks of proteins. The amino acids that make up this fifth taste are found in some seaweeds, dried fish, mushrooms, and…in monosodium glutamate.

While no one wants to go back to the bad old days of the 1950s and 1960s when almost every "Chinese" recipe in American cookbooks called for at least two teaspoons of MSG, it can still be a useful addition to some foods. As Buwei Yang Chao put it, "If you use taste powder conservatively and add it only when the other ingredients are very plain, such as spinach and egg soup, then it will be a very welcome and refreshing flavor as one of many different flavors."

These Chinese peas with their edible pods seemed to turn up everywhere. Progressive markets carried the fresh vegetable, sweet and tender, at a high price. But even in the hinterlands, frozen pea pods were readily available, right next to the frozen succotash.

Snow peas got tossed into nearly all the "Oriental" recipes in that bastion of the middle-class cookery, the *Better Homes and Gardens* series of cookbooks put out in 1972. Their *Menu Cook Book* highlighted a "quick Oriental dinner" made up of cranberry pork chops (pork chops cooked with pineapple, green pepper, sweet-and-sour sauce, and cranberry sauce) and Oriental peas (frozen pea pods, water chestnuts, green onions, and soy sauce). And from *Recipes for Entertaining* came chicken Oriental with frozen snow peas, cloaked in a thick cream sauce...made with canned mushroom soup.

# Revolution to Evolution

"Wrap yourself in the beauty of the Orient," proclaimed a 1972 Sears ad for its Oriental collection of fabrics for the home seamstress. "In butterflies, plum blossoms and peonies. In mystic, far away landscape scenes. In ancient symbols of long life and love." And in that most Oriental of fabrics: 100% polyester knit.

The fad for all things Chinese was amazingly long lived—and it cut across all socioeconomic boundaries. But as the avant-garde tried valiantly to stay at least one step ahead of the teeming masses, the fad changed.

If the woman in the split-level colonial was wrapped in polyester plum blossoms, the chic woman scoured the secondhand shops for hand embroidered Chinese silk robes. If the average American was watching Bruce Lee in the theater or David Carradine on the hit television series *Kung Fu*, the fashionable were taking lessons in tai chi (a slow and deliberate form of the Chinese martial art kung fu). And if Helen Homemaker was whipping up skillet beef egg foo yung à la *Good Housekeeping* for her hungry brood, the trendsetters decided they had better find something a little bit more exotic to eat. And one of the exciting new things they found was dim sum.

## Dim Sum

*Dim sum* is a Cantonese term for "little snacks," a sort of Chinese version of hors d'oeuvres, usually eaten as a festive brunch. And regardless of the mid-1970s trendsetters' self-congratulatory opinion, dim sum was not new in America. The Chinese population here had been eating "dot hearts" (the Cantonese translation of *dim sum*) from the beginning. A number of adventurous Occidental diners, including Craig Claiborne, had enthusiastically consumed dim sum in the early 1960s and indeed before that.

But dim sum was "discovered" only in the mid-1970s. Part of its sudden popularity was due to the fact that most of the restaurants serving it were tucked away deep in Chinatown. To be able to navigate the narrow, twisting streets of Chinatown, then around a dark corner and up a rickety flight of stairs to attain one's brunch added a distinct cachet to the meal—and to the bruncher.

Dim sum also became popular because it was a delicious and unique eating experience for Westerners. Huge trays laden with little steamer baskets and small plates would be carried around the room as they came hot from the kitchen and the diner would point to the desired dish. Perhaps there might be shao mai (or shew mai), small dumplings made of wonton wrappers surrounding a pork and vegetable filling; or different kinds of bao (or pao), steamed yeast dough stuffed with pork or beef or red bean paste. There could be translucent steamed dumplings, pale pink shrimp shining through the tender skin, or succulent tiny pork spareribs. Maybe the baskets would be filled with deep-fried taro balls, the slightly sweet glutinous taro paste concealing a savory pork stuffing, or sticky rice wrapped and steamed in lotus leaves. There were even enchanting little plates of dessert dim sum to choose from: egg tarts, a sweet egg custard in a very short pastry crust; coconut pudding, a smooth cooling mixture like a softly set coconut Jell-O; or even steamed sponge cake, which was eggy and sweet and always tasted as though it had been steamed over dishwater. And all of this was washed down with endless pots of green tea—with jasmine flowers if you were In, and chrysanthemum blossoms if you were Really In. (The Chinese at these places usually drank 7UP or Coke.) Finally the waiter tallied the bill by counting up the small, medium, or large serving plates and steamer baskets left on your table—the larger the plate, the higher the charge. Eating dim sum was fun and sensual and exciting and exclusive to the avant-garde—except for the thousands of Chinese enjoying their mid-morning brunch, too.

Although a few adventurous types tried to make dim sum at home in their Occidental kitchens, these little bits were really best left to restaurants. It was more fun to eat them there anyway.

## Szechwan Cooking

The trouble with dim sum was that it wasn't *dinner*. But regular old Cantonese fare—even some of the more outré menu items—was too old hat for the fashionable set's gustation. What to do, what to do?

Reports began coming in about strange new restaurants serving strange new dishes, fiery with hot peppers and strong tastes. As word spread about this novel Chinese cooking, the trendsetters and then the not so trendy flocked to the new restaurants, which were often located outside Chinatown, the bastion until recently of the Cantonese. And what they ate, they liked.

The food the new restaurants were serving was so-called Szechwan (Sichuan) cooking—so-called because it usually encompassed dishes from Peking (Beijing) and the Honan (Henan), Hunan, and occasionally Fukien provinces as well as from Szechwan province. The dishes were hot and spicy with red chilies, Szechwan pepper, and hot soybean paste and aromatic with sesame oil and tangerine or orange peel—nothing like the bland chicken broth and soy-flavored Cantonese fare that now bored the trendsetters.

Of course, restaurants serving non-Cantonese food had existed before the 1970s in this country—particularly after the influx of Chinese immigrants following World War II. In the 1960s, one of the most popular Szechwan-style restaurants was the Mandarin in San Francisco, which claimed to have introduced smoked tea duck (duck marinated in herbs, smoked over tea leaves, steamed to render the fat, then deep fried) to the United States. In New York the most well-known non-Cantonese restaurant during the 1960s was Pearl's, which boasted an impressive clientele including Richard Rodgers, the composer; Donald Brooks, the fashion designer; and numerous Broadway luminaries. One of Pearl's most popular dishes was moo shee pork with pancakes, now better known as moo shu pork.

With Pearl's fashionable imprimatur, it was not surprising that one of the first Szechwan food crazes to attract the cognoscenti in the 1970s was moo shu pork.

## MOO SHU PORK

This is Gloria Bley Miller's version of the dish, which is actually an Honanese specialty.

$^{1}/_{4}$ cup dried lily buds
$^{1}/_{3}$ cup shredded dried cloud ear mushrooms
$^{1}/_{2}$ pound lean pork
1 tablespoon soy sauce
1 teaspoon sugar
1 green onion
1 slice fresh ginger
3 tablespoons vegetable oil
2 large eggs, beaten lightly
$^{1}/_{4}$ teaspoon salt

Soak the lily buds and cloud ear mushrooms separately in water to cover. Shred the pork and toss with the soy sauce and sugar. Drain and shred the mushrooms, removing any hard bits of stalk. Shred the green onion stalk, cutting its green leaves into 2-inch sections. Mince the ginger. In a small skillet heat half the oil, add the eggs, and scramble quickly over medium heat, but remove while still moist. Heat the remaining oil in a large skillet or wok and add the ginger; stir-fry over medium-high heat for a minute or two, then add the pork and stir-fry until it loses its pinkness. Add the salt, drained lily buds, green onion, and the shredded mushrooms to the pork. Stir-fry 1 minute, then cook, covered, 1 to 2 minutes more over medium heat. Return the scrambled eggs to the pan and stir in only to reheat. Serve at once.

MAKES 4 TO 6 SERVINGS

Moo shoo pork is usually served with Peking doilies (a kind of Chinese crêpe), which are first spread, if the diner desires, with a thick, sweet plum sauce. The doily is then rolled up and eaten out of hand—which brings up the difficulty of how to eat moo shu pork without making a mess. Buwei Yang Chao described her method in *How to Cook and Eat in Chinese*: "If you have not put too much stuff on the doily, you can now roll it up and fold up one end and bite at the other end length by length until you finish the whole doily with its juicy contents. With practice, this can be done gracefully without letting the juice trickle down your wrist." Favorite accompaniments to moo shu pork were hot-and-sour soup (spicy with vinegar and pepper) and a delicious dish known as Chinese chicken salad.

There are many different types of cold chicken salad in China, although most of them seem to originate in Szechwan. One of the most popular is pong pong (or bong bong) chicken, which is basically shredded chicken and bean sprouts dressed with a peanut butter, red pepper, and garlic sauce. But the Chinese chicken salad that was being consumed in such quantities by the fashionable set—especially among rising young record and film producers on the West Coast—probably originated in California. This version is a cold mixture of shredded iceberg lettuce, crispy fried rice noodles, and strips of roasted chicken, all tossed with a slightly sweet sesame oil–tinged dressing made sprightly with flecks of hot red peppers. There is a similar chicken salad, known as so see chicken, made popular at Johnny Kan's restaurant in San Francisco, but Kan's version omits the fried noodles. Whatever its provenance, Chinese chicken salad, which was all the rage in the mid to late 1970s, has virtually disappeared from restaurant menus.

# CHINESE CHICKEN SALAD

1 large handful Chinese rice noodles
Oil for deep frying
1 (4- to 5-pound) chicken, roasted, at room temperature
5 to 6 green onions
1 bunch cilantro (fresh coriander or Chinese parsley), stems removed
1 teaspoon salt
2 teaspoons peanut oil
2 teaspoons sesame oil
1 teaspoon fresh red chili, not too hot, finely chopped
1/2 teaspoon sugar
1/2 head iceberg lettuce, shredded

Deep-fry the noodles in 3 inches of hot oil until puffed and white, about 20 seconds. Drain on paper towels and set aside. Strip the meat from the chicken and shred it into fine pieces. Chop the white portion of the green onion and shred the stalks. Toss the shredded chicken with the green onion, cilantro, and half the salt. Heat the oils together in a small skillet and sauté the chili for 1 to 2 minutes over medium heat; then stir in the sugar and the remaining salt. Let cool to room temperature. Mix the chicken mixture, the fried noodles, and half the lettuce with the chili-oil mixture. Line a serving dish with the rest of the shredded lettuce and top with the salad.

MAKES 4 SERVINGS

Orange-peel chicken (pieces of chicken stir-fried with fragrant dried orange peel and hot peppers) was a favorite Seventies dish, as was kung pao shrimp (fried shrimp sauced with shreds of charred dried red peppers, gingerroot, garlic, and soy sauce, garnished with peanuts). Fried dumplings, similar to some of the Cantonese dim sum except that they were sautéed in oil until crisp, then served with a dipping sauce made of soy sauce, vinegar, and red-hot oil, were extremely popular as an appetizer. And the tiny ears of baby corn that cropped up in many Szechwan dishes charmed diners, and perhaps foreshadowed the late 1980s fad for mini-vegetables. Sizzling rice (so-called because of the impressive fuming and hissing the deep-fried rice makes when it hits hot liquid) was particularly popular, although a great deal of its popularity probably came from the great show put on by the waiters tableside.

Chinese food, especially Szechwan Chinese food, was so widely fashionable in the late 1970s that a book was published—devoid of recipes—instructing eager eaters on the art of ordering properly in Chinese restaurants. Dorothy Farris Lapidus's *The Scrutable Feast—A Guide to Eating Authentically in Chinese*

*Restaurants* (1977) had pages of sample Cantonese and Szechwan menus—rated from "curious" to "knowledgeable" to "adventurous"—in both English and Chinese, along with an explanation of the dishes. The diner was expected to take the book to the restaurant and point out an appropriate menu to the waiter.

# The End of an Era

But once books were being printed on how to order knowledgeably or curiously or adventurously in Chinese restaurants, anyone could do it. The cachet of "eating Chinese" was gone—perhaps irrevocably.

A brief fad for "Mongolian barbecue" did appear in the mid-1980s. Diners could choose their own mixtures of shredded meats and vegetables and spicy (or not) sauces, and then the whole mess was cooked before their eyes on a huge blazing hot griddlelike affair. But Mongolian barbecue didn't offer enough variety to really become a lasting or serious food fad.

## Tibetan Food—A Mystery Solved?

Tibetan food may indeed be one of the last truly exotic cuisines, but most people will probably never sample it outside Tibet's mountain fastness. According to *Food in Tibetan Life* by Rinjing Dorje (1985), most Tibetans are Buddhist and consequently don't eat meat—except when the animal is killed by another animal or accidentally falls from a cliff. Some favorite Tibetan party delicacies (postaccident, presumably) are listed below.

◆◆◆

*Lowa—stuffed sheep lung*
*Luggo—stewed sheep's head*
*Sho—yogurt (which is reportedly a favorite party*
*snack)*
*Sengong—a kind of pancake used to sop up savory*
*sauces.*

Of sengong pancakes, Dorje says, "As for this Sherpa-style cake, Tibetans never chew it—they just swallow chunks whole."

About the only area of China that hadn't been examined for its culinary merits was Tibet: whether the fault lay with Tibetan food or whether there just weren't enough Tibetans in the United States opening restaurants is unclear. An unhappy customer's comment, upon emerging from one of the few Tibetan restaurants in the United States in New York City, that the food was "absolutely awful" might be an indication of the problem.

And finally by the late 1970s, early 1980s, the craze for China—its cuisine and its culture—was over. The avant-garde had moved on, abandoning the dim sum parlors for sushi bars (see Chapter 7). The average American had eaten enough mediocre Cantonese food to be tired of it. And Szechwan cooking? Well, a lot of Americans weren't really that fond of hot peppers and soy jam anyway.

Another potent reason for the death of the myth of the fabulous Orient was the acculturation of the Chinese in this country. In the early years of the Chinese settlement in America the émigrés, numbering less than 100,000, were a small, clannish—and hence, exotic—group. But by 1960, half of the nearly 240,000-strong Chinese-American population was native born, and the émigré Chinese nationalists formed a growing middle class that disassociated itself from Chinatown. By 1980, there were more than 800,000 Chinese-Americans, and although many of them were new immigrants, there was a large segment of the population that was third- or even fourth-generation American. As the Chinese became a large, acculturated group, exoticness disappeared. And while Chinatown still exists, it has become a cultural relic, like Little Italy in New York, or the Scandinavian festivals in the Northwest.

Of course, many good restaurants—both Cantonese and otherwise—survive and continue to serve loyal customers. And plenty of bad little corner places still exist to serve the hungry passerby some chow mein or barbecued pork: the Chinese-American equivalent of McDonald's.

## The Top Ten—Plus One—Chinese Restaurants in the United States

## (Listed Alphabetically)

1. Chin Chin, New York City

   Some may consider it chichi, but Chin Chin's stylish cooking makes it one of the tops in New York. *Specialties:* steamed salmon with black beans, three glass chicken (a casserole with water, soy sauce, and rice glass noodles), and Grand Marnier shrimp—their best-seller.

2. Formosa Café, Los Angeles

Although this Hollywood hangout has terrible food, its tacky but clubby atmosphere, stiff drinks, and cheap prices have made it a favorite of movie-industry types for decades. Terrific for people-watching or tête-à-têtes. *Specialties:* "Forget the menu. Stick to the Scotch," advises *L.A. Access.*

3. Golden Dragon, Honolulu

In business for more than thirty years, Chef Dai Hoi Chang is still serving some of the most innovative Chinese food in Hawaii. *Specialties:* stir-fried lobster with walnuts and Szechwan beef.

4. Harbor Village, San Francisco

This four-hundred-seat branch of a Hong Kong restaurant is famous for its opulence and delicate Cantonese cooking. *Specialties:* dim sum and oyster sauce chicken.

5. Ho Yeun Ting, Boston

A hole-in-the-wall with what some consider the best Chinese food in Boston. *Specialties:* whole crisp fish with vegetables and clams with black bean sauce.

6. House of Hunan, Chicago

This large, elegant dining room serves up outstanding Mandarin, Hunan, Szechwan, and Cantonese food. *Specialties:* pot stickers (sautéed dumplings) and moo shu pork.

7. Lotus Restaurant, Los Angeles

Some consider this the best Mandarin cooking outside Taipei. *Specialties:* shanghai vegetarian goose (stuffed tofu skin), jellyfish with candied pine nuts, and pork fillet in lotus leaves.

8. The Mandarin, San Francisco

One of the first major Szechwan-style restaurants in the country, the Mandarin is still rated one of the best after three decades. *Specialties:* smoked tea duck and Mongolian fire pot (meat and vegetables cooked in broth at the table).

9. Shun Lee Palace, New York City

Popular since the 1970s, this elegant restaurant has some of the best Chinese food in New York. *Specialties:* Peking duck and orange peel beef.

10. Tai Tung, Seattle

This dark, dingy restaurant is still serving excellent Cantonese food after forty years (but ignore the American menu). *Specialties:* whole Dungeness crab with black bean sauce and chicken with cloud ear fungus.

11. Trader Vic's, major cities in the United States

Purists will scream bloody murder, but the Trader did more than anyone else to bring good Cantonese food to the masses and deserves credit for it. *Specialties:* pepper beef, pineapple duck, and sweet-and-sour pork.

# The Forties

## Oh, What a Hungry War!

The health of the nation is one of the most important forces in our National Defense. Build strong bodies with the right food—this is a challenge to all Homemakers.

—Elaine Allen, *Watkins Household Hints* (1941)

This week we queue up for the first Federal ration books that Americans have ever possessed—somewhat ominously entitled War Ration Book No. 1.

—*New York Times* (May 3, 1942)

Food shortages in the United States are so acute that in some states we are already eating horse meat, and in Oklahoma a state official urges that we eat crows, which he says, taste like roast duck.

—Clarence Birdseye, *American Magazine* (July 1943)

Don't squander drippings—pour every dinky dab into a covered dish, store in refrigerator. Use for seasoning and shortening in muffins, spice cookies, gingerbreads, corn bread, and meat-pie toppers. Can't use it all? Strain it—pass it on for ammunition.

—*Better Homes and Gardens* (November 1943)

As the Forties dawned, America was still not in the war in Europe or the Pacific, but we were already profoundly affected. The growing defense effort, both in preparedness for the likelihood of the United States entering the battle and in our support of Britain under Lend-Lease, revitalized the depressed American economy and put the unemployed back to work. Restaurants raised prices to cover the rising costs of food and labor being siphoned off by defense. The price of a hot meat sandwich rose from fifteen to seventeen cents, causing problems for many restaurants—not so much from patrons, who were getting used to rising prices, but from cash registers that couldn't handle denominations smaller than a nickel.

*Portrait
of a Patriot*
SUMMER 1944

FOOD
FIGHTS
for freedom

She'll have Jams and Jellies to serve
next winter—made the fruit-saving
certain way . . . with Certo

## The FNB, the RDA, and the Basic Seven

Vitamins and nutrition had real Sex Appeal in the Forties, although many people were still not sure exactly what vitamins were or how to get them. To help them— and to make sure that the U.S. fighting machine, consisting of soldiers, defense workers, and the home front housewife, was in prime condition for the war effort—the government issued Recommended Daily Allowances (RDAs) for basic nutrients in 1941. When these proved perplexing to the cook trying to figure out how to get enough of the mysterious but essential thiamin or riboflavin into every meal, the Food and Nutrition Board (FNB), under the new Office of Defense Health and Welfare Services, came up with the Seven Basic Food Groups.

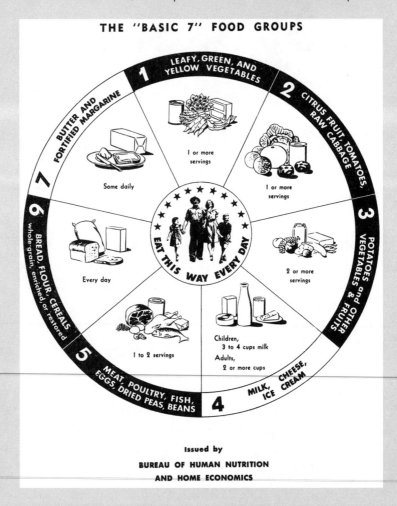

THE "BASIC 7" FOOD GROUPS

1 LEAFY, GREEN, AND YELLOW VEGETABLES — 1 or more servings

2 CITRUS FRUIT, TOMATOES, RAW CABBAGE — 1 or more servings

3 POTATOES and OTHER VEGETABLES & FRUITS — 2 or more servings

4 MILK, CHEESE, ICE CREAM — Children, 3 to 4 cups milk; Adults, 2 or more cups

5 MEAT, POULTRY, FISH, EGGS, DRIED PEAS, BEANS — 1 to 2 servings

6 BREAD, FLOUR, CEREALS whole grain, enriched, or restored — Every day

7 BUTTER AND FORTIFIED MARGARINE — Some daily

EAT THIS WAY EVERY DAY

Issued by

BUREAU OF HUMAN NUTRITION

AND HOME ECONOMICS

Illustrated with charts, graphs, and pie slices, the Basic Seven appeared in magazines and cookbooks alongside daily menus designed to provide servings from each food group—within the strictures of rationing and shortages. The housewife was urged to take a copy of the Basic Seven with her when she went to the market, and to plan weekly menus with the charts alongside her list of available ration points and her budget. Little wonder that many women felt confused and intimidated by the task of feeding their loved ones.

Food producers and advertisers quickly jumped on the nutrition bandwagon. Sealtest ice cream was "mobilized for your protection" and contained "natural vitamin A and calcium and the other vital elements of fresh milk." Welch's Grapelade was "high in energy value" and, said the company, "it doesn't take a single ration point to serve this delicious, energizing treat." Blood donors for the war effort were urged by the American Meat Institute to eat meat because "The proteins of meat are of highest quality, of the RIGHT KIND not only for blood regeneration but also for every other protein need."

The Basic Seven would continue to plague housewives and high school Home Ec students for years, until it was finally simplified to the Basic Four (protein, carbohydrates, fruits and vegetables, milk products). Recently the Basic Four was deemed too full of proteins and fats and was replaced by the Food Pyramid.

Shortages due to stoppage of foreign imports were beginning to make themselves felt, too. By the spring of 1941, sage, picked by Greek and Yugoslav goatherders, had nearly disappeared from the market, as had thyme (from France), paprika (from Hungary and Spain), and saffron (from Spain). Cinnamon and the other warm spices still reached the United States, but only in occasional dribs and drabs. Stockpiles of East Indian peppercorns were expected to last until at least 1943, but after that no one could predict. Coconut was scarce and olive oil was selling for nine to eleven dollars a gallon.

As war approached, what had been a lamented trend in the Twenties and Thirties became an accepted reality in the Forties: Servants, except in the highest reaches of society, were a thing of the past. The cook, the kitchen maid, the butler, the second man, and the upstairs girl were much more likely to be wielding a blowtorch in a munitions factory than a saucepan or a dustpan in someone else's home.

War would bring a New America, an America richer and more powerful than ever before—and in the things people did and the things people ate in their daily lives, an America more alike from coast to coast, more egalitarian than ever before.

# Mummy Foods for Victory

You can order a whole dinner dehydrated. Get a packet of soup powder, one of dried egg yolks, a vegetable, a fruit, and the dried whole milk. Slip the grocery assortment in your pocketbook and be your own delivery boy.

—Clementine Paddleford, "What War Has Done to Life in the Kitchen,"
*House Beautiful* (September 1942)

Dehydrated foods were going to be the great technological breakthrough that would help feed the world, win the war, and change the way we shopped and cooked forever. Needless to say, the dried food idea was pretty much of a bust.

The idea of processed food had long been acceptable in America, with canned foods making up the bulk of the processed food we ate, and frozen foods not far behind. But with war came shortages of packaging materials, along with the need to ship thousands of tons of food overseas to the Boys and our allies. Light in weight and small in size, dehydrated food sounded like the perfect solution.

By far the most popular dehydrated item was soup—American housewives bought it at the rate of one hundred million packages a year during the war. Dried potato flakes, which could be used to turn out "a fluffy bowl of mashed potatoes in seven minutes flat," also found a ready market. But just about everything you could think of was also being dried. Clam powder pressed into "pennies" ("take two pennies, add hot water, it's a bowl of clam bouillon"); dried tomato juice cocktail; dried spinach, beets, and sweet potatoes (all of which, unfortunately, took twenty to thirty minutes of boiling to be edible); powdered eggs for scrambling or cooking; and even tiny shreds of dried meat (which could be used to make stews, soups, or hamburgers) were being produced by food processors who sensed gold in the dehydration business. Researchers were also working on drying whole steaks and roasts that would also be precooked before dehydration.

Dehydrating seemed like the next logical step for the modern postwar world. In "'Mummy' Foods for Victory," *Popular Mechanics* predicted in February 1943 that "it's only a question of time" until dehydrated dinners were available in handy packages. And in typical *PM* fashion, they offered their readers complete instructions for building their own home-food dehydrators using a wooden cabinet and an oil stove.

But the American housewife didn't go for it. Dried soups, instant mashed potatoes, and dried pudding mixes retained some popularity (Tumbo was one brand of war-era pudding mix that didn't survive), but most dried foods found what little market they would get in the restaurant and commercial foods industries.

It wasn't until the back-to-the-land camping and hiking fad in the late Sixties and the full acceptance of microwaveable instafood in the 1990s that dehydrated foods became part of the American way of life.

But before the war, few people realized the enormity of the change that would occur. In 1940 the American Friends of France published the cookbook *Spécialités de la Maison*, the proceeds of sale of which were to "go to help those who are fighting for civilization and in civilization the art of cooking holds a high place." Recipes were contributed by such luminaries as Katharine Hepburn, Pearl Buck, Vivien Leigh, Oscar of the Waldorf, Mrs. William Randolph Hearst, Mrs. William H. Vanderbilt (Newport, Rhode Island), and Mrs. Franklin Delano Roosevelt (The White House, Washington, D.C.). One recipe in particular, from Mrs. Douglas Ives (New York City), reflected a prewar way of life, one that would soon be gone.

### PREWAR BANANAS FLAMBÉS KIRSCH

2 bananas (split lengthwise)
1 teaspoon sweet butter
1 teaspoon sugar
1/2 cocktail glass kirsch

When you sit down to luncheon, have cook put bananas in copper saucepan in which there is butter. Sprinkle sugar, cover, and let simmer over a very *low* fire while lunch is being served. When plates are changed, cook must throw kirsch over bananas and set it on fire, shake pan until fire dies out, repeat, and serve.

MAKES 2 SERVINGS

# Keeping the Home Fires Burning—Food Rationing and the War

Q: How can I best budget my points?
A: One way to do it is to figure out your family's approximate weekly point allowance. Each person is allowed forty-eight points a rationing period, which means that, if your family consists of two, you have approximately twenty-four points a week to spend. Then list the point-rationed foods and the quantities you expect to buy for the week, jotting down the point value beside each item. Add up the points and compare the sum with your family's point allowance for the week.

Jane Holt, "The ABC of Point Rationing," *New York Times Magazine*
(February 21, 1943)

When war finally came to the United States at the end of 1941, Americans were told that food shortages "approaching famine" might occur. But although meat and butter almost disappeared from the shelves for a few months in the spring of 1942, Americans ate more food during the war, in total and per capita, than they ever had before.

The food they ate, however, wasn't necessarily the food they had grown accustomed to. Commercially canned goods were restricted, but home-canned fruits and vegetables weren't, so Americans started Victory Gardens—more than twenty-five million of them—and put up their own produce or ate it fresh. Juicy cuts of beef, veal, pork, lamb, and mutton were restricted or rationed, but poultry, fish, "innards," and offals (things like feet, heads, and tails) weren't. Fats of all types were expensive or rationed, particularly olive oil and butter, but margarine and "salad oils" made from American-grown seeds and grains like corn and sunflower seeds were cheaper and more widely available. Sugar was rationed, except for home-canning use, but honey, corn syrup, and molasses weren't. (The streetwise homemaker could get around sugar and fat shortages by buying cake, muffin, or biscuit mixes that already contained precious sugar and shortening and weren't rationed.) Flour was plentiful, but the government and Women in National Service (WINS) urged everyone to use whole wheat flour for its health-building properties or, at the very least, enriched flour. "Your family needs the extra vitamins and minerals enriched flour provides," said a WINS spokeswoman in the October 1943 issue of *Ladies' Home Journal*.

So what was the home cook to serve her family in those parlous times? Clarence Birdseye (the father of "frosted" foods) recommended suckling seal, squirrel, prairie dog, muskrat, lynx (to be soaked in wine for one month before cooking), and starling as possible main dishes. Unfortunately, the shortage of ammunition on the home front made his suggestions difficult to accomplish. Some less outlandish ideas came from *Ladies' Home Journal* in September 1943.

◆◆◆

# No Ration-Point Menu for a Monday, 1943

### Breakfast
*Sliced Oranges*
*Oatmeal with Milk*
*Unbuttered Sweet Rolls (from the bakery)*
*Coffee or Cereal Beverage (Postum)*

### Lunch
*Vegetable Soup (made from dehydrated mix)*
*Cottage Cheese and Tomato Sandwiches*
*Carrot Sticks*
*Baked Apple with Honey or Maple Syrup* ◆ *Milk*

### Dinner
*Chicken Giblets and Mushroom Gravy on*
*Brown Rice*
*Green Beans Creole* ◆ *Rye Wafers*
*Maple Custard* ◆ *Coffee*

Making a little look like a lot—particularly when it came to meat—was the homemaker's rallying cry. Said Betty Crocker's wartime pamphlet *Your Share*:

Make the most of meat: Use small left-over bits, diced or ground, in scrambled eggs, omelets, souffles, hash. Simmer bones or trimmings an hour or two; use stock in soup, gravies, meat sauces. Fry out fat, render it and save for cooking.

And while one pound of juicy, rich porterhouse steak cost twelve rationing points in 1943, one pound of that newly popular standby, ground beef, cost seven points. The homemaker who knew what was what might use the ground beef for spaghetti and meatballs, or tamale pie, or meat loaf (extended with bread crumbs), or stuffed peppers. One simple way to s-t-r-e-t-c-h the hamburger was to make a meat roll.

# PATRIOTIC PINWHEEL MEAT ROLL

Served with sour cream, or low-fat yogurt for a 1990s touch, this meat roll is
very much like large Russian piroshki.

$^3/_4$ pound ground beef, veal, or lamb
2 large onions, chopped
1 large egg
$^1/_2$ cup bread crumbs
$^1/_2$ teaspoon salt
$^1/_4$ teaspoon black pepper
$^1/_2$ teaspoon dried thyme
Biscuit dough made with 2 cups all-purpose flour (or use Bisquick if you've
    spent all your shortening ration points)

Preheat the oven to 450°F. Brown the meat in a large heavy skillet over
medium heat. Remove the meat to a bowl. Pour off (and save, of course) all but 1
tablespoon of fat in the pan. Sauté the onions in the fat over low heat until soft.
Add the onions to the meat in the bowl. Mix in the egg, bread crumbs, and seasonings. Cook 1 teaspoon of the mixture in the pan and taste for seasonings.
Correct the seasonings.

Roll out the biscuit dough to a 6 × 12-inch rectangle. Spread the dough
with the meat mixture, leaving at least $^3/_4$ inch clear at the edges. Roll the
dough lengthwise like a jelly roll. Pinch the seam to seal. Put the roll seam side
down on a baking sheet or in loaf pan. Bake until golden brown, 20 to 25 minutes. Cut into thick slices and if you wish, serve with cream gravy made from
leftover drippings, flour, and milk.

MAKES 6 TO 8 SERVINGS

Americans' meat craving was prodigious. And while meat was expensive,
both in dollars and in ration points, it was mostly readily available, except when
distribution problems caused temporary shortages in the stores. In fact, while
meat was one of the most heavily rationed foods, annual per capita meat
consumption in this country never fell below 139 pounds, compared with the
prewar figure of 126 pounds. Americans were allowed an average of roughly six
ounces each per *day* during the war, in contrast to the English allowance of sixteen ounces each per week.

If the family's demand for a roast or T-bone steak couldn't be met through
normal channels, there was always "Mr. Black." There are no figures for the
number of people who used the black market or the amount of food that was sold
under the table, but black marketeering was serious enough during the war for
an October 1943 *Ladies' Home Journal* article, "Let's Face the Facts About Food,"
to say sternly,

a lot of people don't play fair—to put it gently. Let's get over the black market quickly—it's like sniping our fighting men from behind. If you don't know what it is…the black market is quite clearly you who buy what you know you aren't entitled to.

For the homemaker who wanted to play fair and still give her family hearty, meaty dishes, cookbooks and magazines offered such recipes as tripe and onion casserole with potato dumplings, hog jowls with turnip greens, stuffed heart with apples, and scrambled eggs with ground tongue. While M. F. K. Fisher may have rightly advised us to "savor to the fullest the beasts we have killed" in *How to Cook a Wolf*, most Americans were none too sanguine about eating the funny parts of those beasts. One hearty low-point meat dish that could be served to the family without qualms—at least so long as the squeamish ones didn't know what was in it—was the following casserole made with lamb necks. And it was ideal "when your family sets up a howl for ration restricted dishes."

## WHITE MARKET LAMB NECK CASSEROLE

A delicious, inexpensive cool-weather dish, rich with meaty lamb flavor. Dry red or white wine may be substituted for the water or stock, the vegetables may be varied by adding onions, garlic, omitting the green beans, etc. Carrots and potatoes are basic to the dish, however. Herbs such as oregano or thyme may also be added to gild this sturdy lily.

    4 ($^3$/4- to 1-inch-thick) lamb neck slices
    2 tablespoons flour
    2 tablespoons fat (bacon drippings are especially good)
    Salt and pepper
    1 cup water, stock, or wine
    4 carrots, cut into 1-inch pieces
    2$^1$/2 cups green beans, blanched in boiling water for 5 minutes and cut into
        1-inch pieces
    3 potatoes, peeled and cut into 1-inch chunks

Dredge the lamb slices in the flour. Heat the fat in a large heavy skillet and brown the lamb in the hot fat over medium heat. Season with salt and pepper. Add the water and bring to a slow boil. Cover, reduce the heat to a bare simmer, and cook 1 hour. Preheat the oven to 300°F. Put the vegetables in a greased casserole dish. Season with salt and pepper. Place the lamb neck slices on top. Remove the fat from the lamb cooking liquid and pour it into the casserole. Cover and cook until the vegetables are tender, about 30 minutes.

MAKES 4 SERVINGS

Still, there were times when even the most meat-hungry Americans had to do without. Whether the family's meat points had already been spent, whether it was "Meatless Tuesday" (a not very successful campaign to stop Americans from eating meat one day a week—Catholics complained because they were already forgoing meat on Fridays), or whether the budget just wouldn't stretch any further, we did occasionally try to eat something beside red meat.

One of the most popular ways to make a red meat–less meal seem more substantial was to serve the main course in a ring—perhaps of noodles, or of rice, or other acceptable starches. Creamed chicken in a rice or noodle ring was always good, and unrationed, but unfortunately chicken was expensive. Shrimp Newburg in noodle nests was a frequent Meatless Tuesday suggestion—although the eggs, butter, and cream needed for a good Newburg were also expensive and not always readily available. (Undeterred, Americans substituted flour, margarine, and milk.)

## What the Boys Liked

Although the American soldiers have firm food habits and decided likes and dislikes, they are making the best of the food they get—and they get along all right!

—*New York Times* (June 6, 1943)

Our Boys in the Armed Forces were eating better than they had ever done as civilians—better, in fact, than almost anyone had eaten in the history of humankind. According to Harvey Levenstein in *Paradox of Plenty* (1993), the average American soldier in 1942 was allotted 360 pounds of meat per year, most of it beef, while the average male civilian was allotted 125 pounds. Paradoxically perhaps, given this gargantuan allotment, a *Ladies' Home Journal* article from 1942 pointed out that too many of our Boys went into the services eating only meat, gravy, potatoes, and pastries—and Uncle Sam wasn't happy about that. Fresh fruits and vegetables, cereals, and fresh milk were considered important for their health-building, hence fight-building, properties, so the Boys got them in abundance, too.

And while local foods such as couscous and baby artichokes (North Africa), gazelle (African interior), breadfruit and soursop (South Pacific), and haunch of reindeer or caribou (Greenland and Alaska) might be used to supplement meals in the Mess occasionally, the armed services overwhelmingly favored middle-American foods. Southern boys may have longed for pot likker and cornbread, Easterners may have craved clam chowder and fresh shad, boys from the Southwest may have hankered after chili and tamales, and boys from ethnic backgrounds may have liked to find gefilte fish or spaghetti with garlic and oil on the table, but what they were fed mostly was midwestern farm food. And in that great homogenizing machine that was the American war effort, they mostly learned to like it.

Here is a sample of what the Army was serving the Boys on a Monday in March 1942 (fresh fruits were to be added as available locally):

◆◆◆

# A Monday in the Army, 1942

### Breakfast
*Stewed Prunes*
*Oatmeal*
*Eggs*
*Hominy*
*Bread* ◆ *Toast* ◆ *Butter*
*Coffee* ◆ *Milk*

### Lunch
*Split Pea Soup*
*Roast Pork* ◆ *Applesauce*
*Sweet Potatoes*
*String Beans with Cream Sauce*
*Raw Vegetable Salad* ◆ *Eggless Dressing*
*Bread* ◆ *Hot Rolls* ◆ *Butter*
*Cherry Pie* ◆ *Coffee*

### Dinner
*Beef Liver*
*Sautéed Potatoes* ◆ *Creamed Onions*
*Carrot and Cabbage Salad*
*Eggless Dressing*
*Bread* ◆ *Butter*
*Cottage Pudding* ◆ *Coffee*

## What the Boys Didn't Like

In 1942, the K Ration largely replaced the earlier C Ration, which, the men complained, was too heavy and likely to hurt if they fell on it while parachuting or hurling themselves to the ground to avoid bomb blasts. The new ration, which was dubbed K because that letter was unlikely to be mistaken over a field telephone, consisted of three small packets for one three-thousand-calorie day, done up in a weatherproof, gasproof, brown paper package weighing two pounds and measuring $6 \times 4 \times 2$ inches.

Each breakfast, lunch, or dinner packet contained the following items for "the most scientific diet ever devised in a laboratory," according to Helena Huntington Smith ("Food That Fights," *Collier's*, August 7, 1943):

1. Small tin of meat, eggs, or soft cheese; the tin could be heated over direct flame, on the motor of a tank or jeep, or eaten cold.
2. Small cellophane envelopes containing coffee powder, bouillon powder, and lemonade powder with vitamin C.
3. Fruit bar.
4. Malted-milk tablets.
5. Nonmelting chocolate bar, fortified with thiamin, which could be boiled with water to make cocoa; oat flour was added to the chocolate to keep it from melting.
6. "Defense biscuits," an enriched graham cracker–like affair.
7. Chewing gum.
8. Cigarettes.
9. Brown toilet paper (white was too visible from the air).

Although the meat and sweet packets were relatively popular with the G.I.s, there was almost universal dislike of the "lemonade," which had a peculiar taste, and the graham crackers, which were extremely hard. But after a steady diet of K rations, even the least discerning soldier craved fresh meat, fresh vegetables, fresh milk, and fresh coffee.

Creamed fish served in a ring made economic sense, because it was low in both dollar and ration point costs—but it was low because Americans didn't like fish very much. In a March 5, 1945 Collier's article, "You'd Better Like Fish," Chef Louis Diat of the Ritz-Carlton felt compelled to admonish housewives to try it, saying, "It is not only good for them, but now it is patriotic, too.... And, the ladies should like fish, it is so good for the slender, willowy figure." One cookbook suggested fish and sweet pickles in cream sauce to be served in a baked hominy grits ring. Such a combination was not likely to encourage nonfish eaters to change their minds. A more appealing possibility was the following noodle ring with halibut in a rich, cheesy sauce.

# HOME FRONT RING OF PLENTY WITH CHEESY HALIBUT SAUCE

"A tonic for budget troubles…yet it reflects bounty," said Betty Crocker of her noodle ring.

**For the Noodle Ring**

1 (8-ounce) package noodles or macaroni, cooked in boiling salted water until tender but not limp, and drained

1 tablespoon fat

2 cups hot milk

2 cups soft bread crumbs

2 large egg yolks, well beaten

1 teaspoon salt

¼ teaspoon pepper

2 large egg whites, beaten until stiff peaks form

**For the Cheesy Halibut Sauce**

1 (1-pound) fresh halibut

2 tablespoons fat

2 tablespoons flour

2 cups hot milk

¼ teaspoon salt

1 cup grated American cheese

½ teaspoon Worcestershire sauce

2 teaspoons lemon juice

¼ teaspoon pepper

Preheat the oven to 325°F. Combine the noodle ring ingredients, folding in the egg whites last. Pour into a greased 10-inch ring mold set in a pan filled with water that comes halfway up the sides of the mold. Bake 30 minutes or until set.

While the noodle ring is cooking, poach the halibut 15 minutes in barely simmering water. Remove the skin and bones, and flake. Set aside. Melt the fat in a large heavy saucepan. Stir in the flour and cook 5 minutes, stirring constantly. Gradually whisk in the milk. Cook, stirring constantly, until the mixture is thick and smooth. Stir in the salt, cheese, and seasonings and cook over very low heat until the cheese is melted, stirring constantly. Add the flaked fish and cook over very low heat for just a few minutes, until the fish is heated through. Turn the noodle ring onto a serving dish. Pour the sauce into the center of the ring and serve.

MAKES 8 SERVINGS

Last but not least of the troubles plaguing the housewife trying to win the war on the home front were budget troubles. While unemployment virtually disappeared during the war, food and fuel prices went up in a seemingly endless spiral. Food prices alone rose 44 percent during the war years. At the end of the month, with most ration points spent and only a few pennies in the piggybank, what was the beleaguered homemaker to do? M. F. K. Fisher had one answer in her famous "Sludge" (p. 131), although most families shied away from anything so stark. But beans and nuts, inexpensive, unrationed, filling, and high in protein, could be made into something the family *might* eat…and then again, might not.

Soybean casseroles, nut burgers, and nut loaves—served with thick white sauce—were popular meat substitutes, at least in the pages of wartime cookbooks and magazines. Whether they were as popular at home as thick steaks and chops was another story. One hearty recipe that combined nuts *and* beans, cost very little in points or cash, used Victory Garden vegetables, and was served in a ring could be considered the archetypal patriotic main dish.

## RED, WHITE, AND BLUE CARROT-NUT RING WITH LIMA BEANS

This is strangely good…if you like this sort of thing.

4 eggs, beaten until thick and lemon-colored
2 cups milk
1/4 teaspoon pepper
1 teaspoon salt
1 teaspoon honey
1 tablespoon lemon juice
1 cup slivered blanched almonds
5 cups grated carrots, steamed until tender
2 cups cooked seasoned baby lima beans, kept hot

Preheat the oven to 325°F. Mix the first six ingredients together. Stir in the almonds and carrots. Pour into a greased 9-inch ring mold set in a pan filled with water that comes halfway up the sides of the mold. Bake about 40 minutes. Unmold on a platter and fill the center with the limas. The lima beans may be tossed with a little butter—if there is any—or other compatible fat before being sent to the table.

MAKES 4 SERVINGS

# Entertaining in Wartime

For a first course our hostess has planned a caviar mousse. Don't say it isn't true. A peek at the Ridder storeroom shelves would show you that caviar, which, after all, is not one of those things necessary to the war effort, is there in abundance.

—Virginia Safford, ed., *Food of My Friends* (1944)

At the beginning of the war entertaining seemed downright unpatriotic. Many people felt uneasy about getting friends together to have *fun* while our Boys—husbands and sons—were fighting and dying. Entertaining posed another problem beside the moral one: Where were the precious points and money to feed friends to come from? But as the war ground on, people realized that getting together to eat, to share food and good times in tough times, was a home front spiritual necessity.

Yet entertaining in the old, grand, prewar fashion was out of the question. Servants were practically nonexistent and virtually no one had the time or the money—or the points—to provide a fancy spread, which seemed a little unpatriotic anyway. An April 1944 *Better Homes and Gardens* article, "Let's Have Folks In," had this to say about wartime entertaining:

> Don't apologize when you serve fish or the less classy meat cuts. We're at war, everybody is afflicted with point or budget trouble, or both. Hospitality is more prized than ever before. More credit to you if you extend it with grace and humor!

Humor and informality were the keys to successful wartime entertaining. Betty Crocker's pamphlet *Your Share* suggested a Hobo Party "for an evening of fun." Guests were to be supplied with bandanna knapsacks filled with pigs in blankets, peanut butter sandwiches, potato salad in little paper cups (with covers), pickles, cookies, and a piece of fruit. As a centerpiece, a stewing kettle was to be placed over an artificial fire made using crumpled red paper hiding a light bulb. Patched tablecloths and napkins, and tin plates and cups, completed the hobo effect. To complete the hilarity Betty suggested, "After supper all sit around open fire…tell stories and sing old-time songs."

Barbecues were popular, with every guest bringing his (or more likely her) own hamburger or wienies to roast over the coals. Potluck suppers with those in points providing meat or butter or sugar were also a wartime vogue. Another way to get together while still minimizing time and expense for the hostess was the neighborhood Victory Garden supper, with each family bringing the fruits of its harvest as a contribution to the community pot.

Service wives often shared housing while their husbands were away. For the gals left behind, a May 1944 *House Beautiful* article suggested an after-church lunch with a "stop-em-dead menu that two working wives can manage." After all, the writer of the article said somewhat defensively, "living in a cocoon for the duration isn't what Jim wants for me." Because making drinks was usually the prerogative of the mostly absent husbands, the article suggested a big bowl of May wine punch as the solution to the problem of bartending for the service wife. This menu also would have made an ideal spread for a Red Cross luncheon.

◆◆◆

## Stop-em-dead Low-point After-Church Lunch

*May Wine Bowl*
*Cream of Mushroom Soup*
*Sliced Tongue with Mustard*
*Mustard Spinach with Nutmeg and Lemon*
*Baked Sherried Sweet Potatoes*
*Spring Salad with Mustard French Dressing*
*Soy Baking Powder Biscuits*
*Lime Sherbet*
*Coffee*

## Cooking Your Own Wolf: M. F. Fisher

It was a nice piece of toast, with butter on it. You sat in the sun under the pantry window, and the little boy gave you a bite, and for both of you the smell of nasturtiums warming in the April air would be mixed forever with the savor between your teeth of melted butter and toasted bread, and the knowledge that although there might not be any more, you had shared that piece with full consciousness on both sides, instead of a shy awkward pretense of not being hungry.

—M. F. K. Fisher, *How to Cook a Wolf* (1942)

Mary Frances Kennedy Fisher's third "cookbook," *How to Cook a Wolf*—with its dreamlike, sinuous prose and its wartime prescriptions for living on weeds, or wolves, or toast, or air—was a gentle, yet shocking thing when it appeared. In a time when magazines told the housewife to keep a chart of essential foods pinned to the curtain of the kitchen window, in a time of menus full of soya chili con carne and sugarless cottage pudding, her strange book reminded people of their real hungers. For her, eating was a spiritual as well as a sensual necessity. And food, as well as those to be fed, were to be treated with love and respect. Fisher was not of the "food as fuel" school.

When, whether out of poverty or other wartime necessities, food *had* to be fuel, Fisher got down to business with hard-headed grace. For those times "when helpful hints about turning off the gas when not in use are foolish, because the gas has been turned off permanently," Mrs. Fisher came up with her famous recipe, if recipe it is, for Sludge.

## SLUDGE, OR HOW TO KEEP ALIVE

**Essential Equipment**
> 50¢ (in 1942 money)
> Borrowed stove
> Food grinder
> Big kettle

**Ingredients**
> 1 bunch carrots
> 2 onions
> Some celery
> Small head cabbage
> With left-over cash: zucchini, tomatoes, beans, garlic (if you like it), etc.
> 15¢ worth ground beef
> 10¢ worth ground whole-grain cereal

Grind the vegetables and put in the kettle. Break up the meat and add to the vegetables. Cover with too much water. Bring to a boil and let simmer 1 hour. Add the ground cereal. Mix thoroughly and cook slowly 2 or more hours. Let cool and keep in a cold place (the cellar if you can't borrow an icebox). Eat it cold (sludge is not *served*) or reheat when wanted. Sludge can also be sliced and fried like scrapple, but "of course that takes it into the luxury class, what with the fat you'd need, and the fire."

Chicken fat and margarine, not butter, were the solid fats used in this menu; Wesson oil, not olive oil, was used in the salad; the shortening in the biscuits was stretched by using soy flour (which also upped the protein content); and the sherbet could be made with less sugar by using presweetened Jell-O.

# Boiled Tongue

Well, we're going to have red meat. Don't get excited. And I have no intention of black-marketing. Our meat is of the low-point variety—a smoked beef tongue.

—Florence Paine, "Don't Stop Entertaining Just Because He's Away," *House Beautiful*,
(May 1944)

Tongue was a popular meat in the Forties, and the fact that it was readily available during the war only boosted its popularity. In our more squeamish age, tongue is almost impossible to find outside ethnic markets or German restaurants. A pity, as this fine-grained, low-fat meat is cheap and delicious.

## BOILED TONGUE

1 (3-pound) beef tongue (smoked, if you can find it)
2 teaspoons salt (only if tongue is fresh, not smoked)
2 bay leaves
1 onion, chopped
2 celery ribs, chopped
2 carrots, chopped
1 lemon, sliced

Wash the tongue thoroughly. Place in a large kettle and cover with cold water. Add salt if using it and the rest of the ingredients. Bring to a simmer, cover the pot, and let the tongue cook until tender, about 3 hours (tongue takes approximately 1 hour per pound to cook). Let cool in the cooking water. When cool enough to handle, remove the skin and any small bones or connective tissue. Slice crosswise against the grain. Serve with mustard or a mustardy mayonnaise.

MAKES 6 SERVINGS

There were other tricks, too, to getting around wartime food restrictions while still providing an impressive spread for your guests. Virginia Safford, in *Food of My Friends*, told of one hostess who saved up all her butter ration points and, "after buying the butter, patted and carved it into a family of graceful, long-necked swans with black clove eyes. It was a profitable investment of time and talent, because no guest had the heart to touch the adorable little creatures." A more common and less risky way to stretch the butter supply was to mix the

# Entertaining in Wartime—Progressively

One type of dinner party that swept the country during wartime and then almost completely disappeared was the Progressive Dinner. Going house to house "like a brush man, only not to sell anything but to eat" was an easy and hilarious way to pool the work, the rationed resources, and the fun.

Here is Ann Batchelder's prescription for a good time, from the *Ladies' Home Journal* of February 1943. Needless to say, after the dessert is consumed, the evening should be wound up with dancing and a few rubbers of bridge.

◆◆◆

# Progressive Dinner

### Soup with Bill and Babs
"Something different you know…. It's really a swell soup."

*Avocado and Chicken Soup*

### Nell and Madge Ganged Up for the Main Course
"Progressing to our next meeting…what did we find but a buffet, boasting a 'frosted' meat loaf? Don't raise an eyebrow—just give it a whirl yourself."

*Relishes*
*Mashed Potato Frosted Meat Loaf with Gravy*
*Buttered Peas ◆ Corn*
*Buttermilk Rolls*

### Salad at the Bob Pattons'
"You could hear the salad fairly crackle, it was so cold and crisp."

*Green Salad with Bleu Cheese*
*Cauliflower and Red Apple Slices*
*Pretzel Sticks*

### Sadie Did Herself Proud with the Dessert
"The boys fell in love with this cooky shell idea, and so did the girls, too."

*Cherry Ice Cream in Sugar Cooky Shells with*
*Hot Cherry Sauce*
*Coffee*

butter with gelatin. Many homemakers gave up butter altogether and turned to margarine (still called "oleo" in those days), even though, because of dairy industry pressure, it came in unappetizing white chunks with a packet of yellow coloring to be stirred in at home.

© 1947 by Magic Chef.

## has everything a woman wants to make cooking *easier – faster – better*

# Dessert Parties: Johnny We Hardly Knew Ye

For hostesses who had the urge, but not the points, to entertain often, coffee and dessert parties were the ticket. "They'll just love it!" said Jean Freeman in an April 1944 *Better Homes and Gardens* article. "It's a crackerjack of an idea if you happen to be a pie wizard or if you've a telling way with rice pudding, apple Betty, or banana fritters."

Because sugar and butter were scarce and expensive, smart cooks cut back on these precious items by substituting mixes, margarine, soy flour (high in fat), peanut butter, honey, corn syrup, maple syrup, and molasses. If the desserts were highly flavored with spices, molasses, or chocolate, chicken fat or even strained bacon grease could be used as a shortening.

Chocolate was sometimes in short supply during the war because of the vagaries of shipping. The clever homemaker made the most of what chocolate she might have by swirling chocolate through part of her cake batter to make old-fashioned marble cake, by offering hot fudge as a sauce for starchy puddings, or using chocolate frosting only on the tops of her cakes. Sweetened chocolate, when available, was often called for in recipes to get around sugar rationing. When the wartime cook found herself with plenty of chocolate, she might have surprised the family with these cupcakelike cookies.

---

## Melts in Your Mouth, Not on Your Rifle

M&Ms, those milk chocolate candies with the colorful, brittle sugar shells, were a product of the Forties. Company executives Forest Mars and Bruce Murrie lent their initials to M&Ms when the Newark, New Jersey, producer developed the candy in 1941. According to *Panati's Parade of Fads, Follies and Manias*, the crunchy little morsels became an immediate hit with soldiers who didn't want to worry about sticky chocolatey fingers on their rifle butts or grenade pins.

It wasn't until 1954 that M&Ms peanut candies appeared, and though they were popular, the peanut variety never took hold of young America's imagination like the original did. More than fifty years after the introduction of M&Ms, children were still trying to decide which color tasted best (although the candies all have the same formula, save the dyes). In informal playground polls, the elusive red M&Ms won out as the most desirable.

---

# CHOCOLATE DROP COOKIES WITH NO-SUGAR CHOCOLATE ICING

"Send some of THESE to a Boy in Service!" said the newspaper clipping. This unattributed wartime recipe was found pasted inside an old cookbook. The no-sugar icing was sweetened with unrationed marshmallows.

$1/2$ cup vegetable shortening or margarine
$1/4$ cup sugar
$3/4$ cup dark corn syrup
I large egg, well beaten
2 ounces unsweetened chocolate, melted
$1^3/4$ cups sifted enriched flour
$1/2$ teaspoon salt
$1/2$ teaspoon baking soda
$1/2$ cup buttermilk
I cup nuts, coarsely chopped
No-sugar Chocolate Icing (below)

Cream the shortening. Add the sugar gradually, creaming well. Add the corn syrup gradually, beating well. Then slowly beat in the egg and chocolate. Sift the dry ingredients together. Blend into the shortening mixture alternately with the buttermilk. Blend in the nuts with the last of the flour mixture. Chill the dough for 1 hour. Preheat the oven to 375°F. Drop the dough by teaspoons about 2 inches apart on a greased baking sheet. Bake until the cookies look dry, 10 to 12 minutes. Cool on a rack. When cool, frost with No-Sugar Chocolate Icing.

MAKES ABOUT 48 COOKIES

## NO-SUGAR CHOCOLATE ICING

12 ounces marshmallows, cut into quarters (or substitute minis)
3 ounces unsweetened chocolate
6 tablespoons evaporated milk

Combine the ingredients in a heavy saucepan. Cook over low heat, stirring constantly, until the chocolate and marshmallows are melted and blended. Remove from the heat and let cool until of spreading consistency.

Angel food cake, long a symbol of hospitality and proof of a cook's abilities, was a rare treat in wartime, eggs being expensive and sugar dear. But it was possible to make angel food with honey or syrup (although Betty Crocker advised against it). And if the cake was a small one, because you cut back on the number of egg whites, and wasn't iced or was iced only on the top, no one could call it an unpatriotic luxury. With coffee, this cake was a real treat for sugar-hungry guests.

## ALL-AMERICAN MAPLE-NUT ANGEL FOOD CAKE

This cake and frosting were made with maple syrup, which was unrationed, plentiful, and inexpensive…then.

   1 cup sifted cake flour
   ½ cup confectioners' sugar
   1 cup pure Vermont maple syrup
   1 cup large egg whites (about 8)
   ¼ teaspoon salt
   1 teaspoon cream of tartar
   ½ cup chopped California walnuts
   Maple-Nut Cream Filling (below)

---

### Spare the Sweets

These were the sugar-saving tips from Betty Crocker's *Your Share* (1943).
Here's the way we save our sugar when we must.
Salt brings out sweet flavor of fruits and cooked foods. Add a pinch.
Use Bisquick for shortcakes, fruit rolls, cobblers. It contains sugar.
Get prepared milk powders. No sugar is needed.
After dinner, serve jam with cheese and crackers.
Reduce tartness of sour fruits by combining with dried fruits.
Serve fruits and vegetables naturally rich in sugar.
Add sugar last when cooking dried fruits. Takes less.
Vary cereals with brown sugar, honey, syrup, dried and sweet fruits.
Include tapioca in fruit pies to cut tartness.
Never throw away canned fruit syrup. Use for beverages, jellied salad, etc.
Get into the habit of serving coffee cakes and sweet rolls for dessert.
Thoroughly dissolve sugar in beverages. Don't leave in bottom of cup.
Instead of sugar, use corn syrup for beverages, fruits, sugar-water syrups.
Plan to serve desserts with no sugar (fruit cups, fruit gelatin, etc.)
Serve ripe fruits. They need little or no sugar.
When ample amounts of sugar are available, it is preferable for best baking results.

---

Preheat the oven to 300°F. Sift the flour and sugar together four times. Bring the maple syrup to a boil in a small heavy saucepan and cook without stirring until it reaches the soft-ball stage (232°F on a candy thermometer), when a little syrup dropped into a cup of ice water forms a soft ball that flattens when you try to pick it up. Let syrup cool to 180°F. Beat the egg whites until frothy. Add the salt and cream of tartar and beat the whites until stiff but not dry. Pour the syrup in a thin stream over the egg whites, beating constantly. Sift the flour-and-sugar mixture over the whites in small amounts; sprinkle the nuts over the top and fold them in carefully. Push the batter into an ungreased 9-inch tube pan. Gently pull a knife through the batter to break air bubbles. Bake 1 hour. Let cool inverted in the pan. The cake may be dusted with confectioners' sugar or for a luxurious treat, split and filled, with the Maple-Nut Cream Filling.

MAKES 1 CAKE

## MAPLE-NUT CREAM FILLING

To save sugar during the war, cakes put on battle dress by being iced only on top, not the sides. If the cake were filled, icing was omitted entirely. Many wartime frostings and icings were based on beaten uncooked egg whites mixed with honey or jam. This filling gets around the modern health problems of uncooked eggs, uses some of the egg yolks left over from the cake, and is patriotically based on American maple syrup.

6 tablespoons pure Vermont maple syrup
1/4 cup sugar
3 large egg yolks
2 tablespoons butter (or "oleo")
1/4 cup milk
1/3 cup chopped California walnuts

Put all ingredients except the walnuts in the top of a double boiler. Stir constantly over simmering water until the mixture is thick and hot, about 10 minutes. Remove from the heat and stir in the walnuts. Let cool.

MAKES 3/4 CUP

Last, but not least, in the list of entertaining headaches for hostesses, was the wartime wedding. Often short-notice (because the groom was about to disappear into the war effort), wartime weddings called for quick, easy, and low-point refreshments. A simple cake and a punch bowl could be all that was offered wedding guests, without embarrassment on anyone's part. "For more elaborate refreshment," said Betty Crocker in *Your Share*, "finger or heart-shaped chicken sandwiches, or chicken salad in tiny popover or cream puff cases or bite-size enriched rolls, and salted nuts may be added."

The last word on wartime etiquette for weddings came from the June 1943 issue of *Harper's Bazaar*: "Shower no rice on this year's honeymooners. You can't waste a good starch on sentiment."

# After the War: An Orgy of Eating

When the war finally ended in 1945, Americans turned their attention homeward. The Depression was resoundingly over, factories were humming, five million new homes were being built (including the first Levittown, on Long Island, in 1947), and new stoves, refrigerators, washing machines, and lawn mowers were being bought to make those new homes the best the world had ever seen. America found itself a world power, young, strong, rich, and bursting with can-do spirit.

This New America seemed unstoppable. And its citizens' appetites, for food as well as goods, seemed unstoppable, too. The deprivations of the Depression and the war with its shortages and rationing—although, as was pointed out, Americans ate more food during the war than they had before 1941—were followed by an orgy of eating. The rest of the world, still reeling from the horrors of war, its industrial base shattered, its farmland untended or blown to bits, could only sit back in amazement and watch. Americans didn't mind: They had enough of everything for everyone.

And what Americans wanted to eat was meat. Our Victory Gardens went to seed or were turned into suburban lawns, our home-canning pressure cookers and jars were put in the basement, we turned our backs on carrot-nut rings, and went for the steaks, chops, and roasts that we felt we had been denied so long.

Everywhere the cry was for meat, meat, and more meat. In 1947, Americans ate 155 pounds per person—a forty-year record. Farmers depleted their grain stockpiles to fatten their hogs and cattle and slaughtered their breeding stock to meet the voracious craving. But rising demand for meat, coupled with rising incomes, sent meat prices soaring. Housewives, irate at $1.10 a pound for sirloin, revolted. The president of the Dallas Women's Chamber of Commerce, Mrs. R. D. Vaughn, started a nationwide boycott of butcher shops, with the result that sales dropped as much as 20 percent in 1948. Some butchers even closed their doors temporarily, to wait for calmer times.

## Pre-postwar Parties

Here is your bid to our Postwar Party,
But you don't have to be an intelligent smarty.
With thinking and hokum and much jollity,
We'll consider the world as we'd like it to be.
> —From Clifford Parcher, "Post War Party," *The American Home*
> (March 1944)

With the end of the war in sight in 1944 Americans began looking ahead to peace, and what better way to celebrate the future than with a party? A short-lived fad, Postwar Parties were popular through 1944 to August 1945, when Japan at last surrendered.

Two suggested parties to celebrate the New World Order were prophetic of the powerful New America. The first was the Ground-breaking Party, as Americans geared up to build thousands of new homes come the peace. A summer barbecue on the new home site with bring-your-own meats for the grill, iced tea, and "more coffee than possibly could be used" set the scene for the festivities. Clifford Parcher's postwar party had a political theme. Guests could play "European Boundaries," in which each was given a map of Europe and instructed to carve up the Continent into new countries. This was followed by "World Balance," a relay race in which competing players carried globes across the room balanced on plates. Unlucky guests whose globes lost balance had to start over from the beginning. The menu for the party was international.

◆◆◆

# Carving-up-the-world Postwar Party Menu

*Creamed Turkey*
*English Muffins* ◆ *Danish Pastries*
*Java*

Ground beef, inexpensive and infinitely stretchable, had become a staple during the war. Afterward, with meat prices spiraling, it stayed popular. And meat loaf, America's own pâté de campagne, was one of the favorite ways to serve ground beef.

## POSTWAR MEAT LOAF

Despised as utterly pedestrian in the chic Seventies, meat loaf reappeared on the menus of down-home (and upscale) American restaurants in the late 1980s. Served hot with mashed potatoes and gravy, or cold on homemade bread as one of the best sandwiches ever, the humble but delectable meat loaf is once again in fashion.

1 1/2 pounds ground beef (or use 1 pound beef and 1/2 pound ground pork)
1 cup soft bread crumbs
1 large egg, lightly beaten
3/4 cup milk
1 1/2 teaspoons salt
1/4 teaspoon black pepper
2 tablespoons minced onion
1/4 teaspoon dried thyme
3 pieces good bacon or 1/3 cup ketchup

Preheat the oven to 350°F. In a large bowl mix together the ground meat(s), crumbs, egg, and milk. The most efficient way to mix it is with your hands, but mix gently or the loaf will be dense and heavy. Then mix in the seasonings. Pack the mixture into a greased 9 × 5 × 3-inch pan. Lay the bacon slices over the top (or spread with the ketchup). Bake until brown and pulling away from the sides of the pan, about 1 1/2 hours, pouring off the grease that accumulates in the pan 2 or 3 times during the baking. Serve hot or cold.

MAKES 6 TO 8 SERVINGS

When ground beef palled and sirloin steak or standing rib roast were out of reach for the postwar pocketbook, Swiss steak was an inexpensive, hearty substitute. According to John Mariani in *The Dictionary of American Food and Drink*, the title of this dish came not from any such pot roast made in Switzerland, but from the English term *swissing*, which describes a method of rolling and pounding cloth flat. Who, exactly, invented Swiss steak is a mystery. The name first appeared in print in America in 1924, but the dish was not common in cookbooks until the Forties. The method of pounding the meat with flour and then braising it would seem to point to Pennsylvania Dutch origins, but there is no hard evidence of this. Cora, Rose, and Bob Brown identified it in the Forties as a Wyoming specialty, while Clementine Paddleford spotted it in Indiana. James Beard's 1949 *The Fireside Cookbook* identifies it simply as braised beefsteak, "sometimes called Swiss Steak."

## SWISS STEAK

The tougher round, chuck, or shoulder cuts that should be used in Swiss steak are tenderized three ways: by pounding to break down the meat fibers before cooking, by long, slow braising, and by being cooked with acid tomatoes that form the basis of the braising liquid. The meat may be pounded with a meat pounder, a potato masher, or the edge of a strong plate.

> $1/2$ cup all-purpose flour
> 1 teaspoon salt
> $1/8$ teaspoon pepper
> 2 pounds boneless beef (round, chuck, or shoulder), 1 inch thick, in one piece
> 2 tablespoons rendered beef fat, butter, or bacon drippings
> 2 medium onions, sliced
> 1 bay leaf
> $1/2$ cup liquid (water, stock, or wine)
> 1 cup canned tomatoes, chopped

Mix the flour with the salt and pepper. Pound part of the flour into both sides of the beef. Continue adding the flour mixture and pounding it in until the meat will accept no more. Brown the beef in the hot fat in a heavy frying pan or Dutch oven. Remove the meat from the pan and stir in the onions, cooking them until lightly browned. Return the meat to the pan, add the rest of the ingredients, and cover tightly. Simmer over low heat (or bake in a preheated 300°F oven) until the meat is very tender, about 2 hours. Uncover and cook another $1/2$ hour until the juices are thick. Put the steak on a large heated platter and keep it warm while you degrease the pan juices. Pour the gravy over the meat and serve with buttered noodles or mashed potatoes.

MAKES 4 SERVINGS

Veal had never been an American meat staple. Mary J. Lincoln in her 1904 *Boston Cook Book* expressed the Anglo-Saxon horror of eating baby cows when she said, "At its lowest price veal is never a cheap food when we take into consideration the small amount of nutriment it contains, the large amount of fuel required to cook it, and the danger of being made ill by its use." And though the amount of veal we did eat fell off after the war, it was used occasionally (except by immigrants who *liked* it) as an inexpensive substitute for the desirable high-priced chicken or turkey, which were not yet being raised in huge numbers by poultry factories.

## MOCK DRUMSTICKS

Considering the reversal of prices since the 1940s, a thrifty cook now would be much more likely to use chicken or turkey to make mock veal.

1/2 teaspoon salt
Black pepper
1 pound veal steak, cut into 2 × 3-inch strips
4 wooden skewers
1/2 cup plus 2 tablespoons flour
1 large egg, beaten slightly
1/2 cup dry bread or cracker crumbs
3 tablespoons bacon drippings, butter, or chicken fat
1 1/2 cups milk or milk and stock mixed

Preheat the oven to 325°F. Salt and pepper the veal. Arrange the strips on the skewers, pressing firmly in the shape of a turkey drumstick. Dip the veal in 1/2 cup of the flour, then in the egg, and finally in the crumbs. Let stand about 1/2 hour to help the crumbs adhere better. Heat the fat in a heavy frying pan until very hot but not smoking. Brown the veal on all sides and remove to a baking pan. Stir the remaining flour into the frying pan over low heat, scraping up all the brown bits. Gradually stir in the milk and cook until the cream sauce is hot and thick. Pour the sauce over the veal drumsticks and bake, covered, until tender, about 1 1/2 hours.

MAKES 4 DRUMSTICKS

Meat wasn't the only thing Americans were eating a lot more of after the war. Milk and cream consumption was up, as was that of cheese, eggs, and canned and frozen fruits and vegetables. Butter consumption was down, but that was more than made up for in the quantity of margarine Americans ate. The foods that we didn't eat as much of after the war were breads and cereals, potatoes, peanuts, and dried beans. Americans were rich, and we were damned if we were going to eat the staple foods that had sustained poor people for generations.

In addition to the large quantities of food we were eating, that food also became much more standardized from coast to coast. Through the war years, soldiers of all ranks—from enlisted men to officers, from Arkansans to Alaskans—had been fed the same food: the food of the American Midwest. Soldiers brought home that taste for plain cooking, and what had been a regional style became the American style. They also came home to wives who had learned to cook not from their mothers but from radio shows and magazines; who had been taught to find nutritionally "balanced" meals more important than aesthetically balanced menus; who had come to prefer the time-saving value of cans and mixes to the taste-saving value of "from scratch" cooking; and who had learned to prefer margarine to butter, Wesson oil to olive oil, Crisco to lard, and canned and frozen fruits and vegetables to the hard-won fresh article harvested from Victory Gardens.

Coffee drinking peaked during the war—coffee was considered essential for morale when it was rationed in 1942-43—then fell off drastically. Though the coffee companies argue the causes, the fact that before the war most of the coffee for the U.S. market was made from the expensive, aromatic, and delicious arabica beans but that after the war more of the cheap, harsh robusta beans were used may have had a great deal to do with the decline. Coffee really *didn't* taste as good as it used to. Many Americans, looking for the pause that refreshes, turned to soft drinks instead.

## Likker Is Quicker—The Cocktail Party

Cocktail parties were going strong in the Forties. Even Fannie Farmer gave directions for successful cocktail parties with hot and cold appetizers (including one of the first mentions of potato chips with dips), although her "cocktail" recipes were all nonalcoholic. *Joy of Cooking* (1946) provided some boozy recipes, but, said Irma Rombauer,

> To give this book the impression of sobriety and stability it deserves, the alcoholic cocktails have been relegated to the chapter on Beverages. There they may blush unseen by those who disapprove of them and they may be readily found in the company of many other good drinks by those who do not.

No such delicacy was necessary for James Beard, whose first book, published in 1940, was *Hors d'Oeuvre and Canapés* ("With a Key to the Cocktail Party"). Beard's book eschewed "doots" (fussy, feminine canapés and knickknack food) and was full of recipes for strongly flavored tidbits. Drinks recipes were few but classic, along the lines of sours, sidecars, old-fashioneds, and the martini, still the most popular cocktail in America. There was, as yet, no sign of the margarita, the tequila-based cocktail that was taking Los Angeles by storm and was a specialty of the Tail of the Cock restaurant there.

Another very masculine guide to drinking (and some eating) was the 1949 *Esquire's Handbook for Hosts*. "You won't find doily tearoom fare here: no radish roses, no menus designed for their calorie content," said *Esquire*. "Esky has concentrated on food of, for and by MEN." (The food, of course, with the exception of the recipes for such things as marinated bear paws, was of the "gourmet" genre.) The drinks, too, were for MEN, although *Esquire* admitted that there were times when the host would have to mix up those "fluffy, multi-colored abominations which…the 'ladies' insist upon downing." Those drinks—brandy flips, alexanders, pink ladies, and sloe gin fizzes—were relegated to a section titled "Something for the Girls." The book also included "pick-me-up" recipes for the "really first-rate hangover—one with long, matted hair and a guttural voice." Here is one of those.

## SEA CAPTAIN'S SPECIAL

"Distilled dynamite which may beg the question by putting your hangover off—until tomorrow." It is no longer legal in the United States to sell absinthe that contains wormwood, because the herb destroys brain cells. Pernod or absinthe flavored with anise may be substituted.

$\frac{1}{2}$ lump sugar
Few drops Angostura
1$\frac{1}{2}$ jiggers rye
Ice
Champagne
2 dashes absinthe

Put sugar in old-fashioned glass. Douse it with Angostura. Add rye and 1 lump of ice. Fill the glass with champagne and top it off with the absinthe.

Interestingly, the consumption of sugar also peaked during the war, and then declined consistently. Though sugar had been rationed during the war, candy had not and American civilians and soldiers, who were issued candy bars in their field rations, ate huge quantities. After the war, candy consumption fell off and food processors started using corn syrups instead of granulated sugar in their products.

But we hadn't lost our sweet tooth. Icebox cakes or puddings (no longer called Flapper puddings) were still very much in vogue, as were meringue tortes and upside-down cakes. Four sugary, all-American delights that were invented and/or wildly popular in the Forties were chocolate chip cookies, pudding cake, chiffon pie, and chiffon cake.

While the popularity of the other desserts has waned, chocolate chip cookies are as dear to the hearts of Americans now as they were in the Forties. And probably no other warm-from-the-oven food says "home" as much as these buttery, brown-sugary treats studded with meltingly luscious chocolate bits.

## CHOCOLATE CHIP COOKIES

Created by Ruth Wakefield of the Toll House Inn in Whitman, Massachusetts, in 1930, this sweet American staple was little known until Betty Crocker publicized it in her radio series on "Famous Foods from Famous Eating Places" in 1939. By the early 1940s, *Joy of Cooking* contained a recipe for chocolate chip drops, and Fannie Farmer had a similar chocolate crunch cookie. These early recipes called for chipping up a bar of semisweet chocolate, but the cookies' popularity soon induced manufacturers to sell bags of chocolate morsels or chips. This recipe makes the classic flat, soft, rich, and buttery cookie chock-full of chips. Some cooks substitute shortening for the butter, which admittedly makes a softer cookie, but only butter delivers the right taste.

1 cup (2 sticks) butter (no substitute)
3/4 cup granulated sugar
3/4 cup firmly packed dark brown sugar
2 large eggs
2 1/4 cups all-purpose flour, sifted
1 teaspoon salt
1 teaspoon baking soda dissolved in 2 tablespoons water
2 teaspoons vanilla extract
2 cups semisweet chocolate chips
1 cup walnuts, coarsely chopped

Preheat the oven to 350°F. In a large bowl, cream the butter, then cream in both sugars until the mixture is light and smooth. Beat in the eggs. Sift the flour and salt together, and stir into the creamed mixture, beating well. Stir in the soda water and vanilla. Stir in the chips and nuts. Drop by teaspoonfuls 2 inches apart on a greased cookie sheet. Bake until golden, 10 to 12 minutes.

MAKES ABOUT 5 DOZEN COOKIES

## Pudding Cakes

With a soft cakelike top, and moist goozly bottom, these pudding cakes seemed to spring up all over the country in the Forties. Lemon and chocolate were the two favorite flavorings, although Betty Crocker's 1950 cookbook also gave recipes for lime, orange, and pineapple. The puddings have a comforting, old-fashioned air that kept them popular into the Fifties, but doomed them in the Go-Go Sixties.

### HOT FUDGE PUDDING CAKE

The soft cake rises through the rich sauce. It is best eaten the day it is made—no problem if you have friends or family with a fondness for chocolatey nursery food!

1 cup sifted all-purpose flour
2 teaspoons baking powder
1/4 teaspoon salt
3/4 cup granulated sugar
1/4 cup plus 2 tablespoons unsweetened
    cocoa powder
1/2 cup milk
2 tablespoons butter, melted
3/4 cup chopped walnuts
1 cup firmly packed brown sugar
1 3/4 cups hot water

Preheat the oven to 350°F. Sift the flour, baking powder, salt, granulated sugar, and 2 tablespoons of the cocoa into a large bowl. Stir in the milk and melted butter, then the nuts. Spread in a greased 9-inch-square pan. Mix the remaining cocoa with the brown sugar. Stir in the hot water. Pour the brown sugar mixture over the batter. Bake until a knife inserted in the top half of the batter comes out clean, about 45 minutes. Spoon into bowls, ladling some of the sauce over each portion. Whipped cream or ice cream is a nice extra.

MAKES 8 SERVINGS

## SHEILA HIBBEN'S ORANGE-LEMON PUDDING CAKE
## FROM FLORIDA

This pudding doesn't make a sauce like the chocolate version, but has a cakey bottom and a quivery top. The plain lemon variety was sometimes baked in a pie crust in the Thirties. In the Eighties, Deborah Madison made a similar pudding at San Francisco's fashionable Greens restaurant and served it with fresh berries, a fine idea.

2 tablespoons butter
³/₄ cup sugar
2 large eggs, separated
2 tablespoons flour
Grated rind of 1 orange
Grated rind of ¹/₂ lemon
Juice of 1 lemon
³/₄ cup plus 1 tablespoon milk
Whipped cream flavored with vanilla extract for topping

Preheat the oven to 300°F. Cream the butter and sugar together until light. Beat the egg yolks together well, then add them, along with the flour, grated rinds, lemon juice, and milk to the butter mixture. Mix thoroughly. Beat the egg whites until stiff, then fold them into the butter mixture. Pour into a buttered 1-quart baking dish or 6 custard cups. Set in a pan filled with hot water that comes halfway up the sides of the dish or cups and bake until a knife inserted into the cake topping comes out clean, about 50 minutes. Serve hot or warm with the whipped cream.

MAKES 6 SERVINGS

# Chiffon Pie

According to the *Gold Medal Jubilee* recipe pamphlet (1955), light and airy chiffon pies were popular under the name of "sissy pies" in the early 1900s. These sissy pies—also called fairy tarts or fluff, sponge, or soufflé pies—were based on variously flavored puddings, lightened with beaten egg whites, that were then baked in a pastry crust. They contained no gelatin, the common ingredient in the modern unbaked chiffon pie. The first mention I have been able to find of a chiffon pie as we know it, made with gelatin and uncooked beaten egg whites, appears under the name of coffee soufflé pie in *Good Housekeeping's Book of Menus, Recipes, and Household Discoveries* from 1922.

Gelatin and egg white–lightened chiffon pies—which were basically old-fashioned gelatin sponges or "snows" served in a crust—became all the rage in the Forties. They were so popular that they rated a separate section in the 1943 edition of *Joy of Cooking*. Raspberry, strawberry, loganberry, pineapple, apricot, coffee, pumpkin, rum, lemon, lime, and orange—virtually any flavor you could come up with—went into these confections. Chiffon pie also helped usher in the era of the crumb pie shell based on crushed graham crackers or breakfast cereal.

## EGGNOG CHIFFON PIE

Essential to chiffon pie's light, ethereal texture are the uncooked beaten egg whites folded in at the last. Again, with the problem of salmonella poisoning present nowadays, this recipe is *not recommended* for eating, and is presented for historical reasons only. Perhaps when our hens and the eggs they lay are healthy and disease free, we will once again be able to sample a dessert that was fashionable fifty years ago and remained so for more than two decades.

I tablespoon unflavored gelatin
$^1/_4$ cup cold water
4 egg yolks
I cup sugar
$^1/_2$ teaspoon salt
$^1/_2$ cup hot water
3 tablespoons rum or brandy
I teaspoon ground nutmeg
4 egg whites
One 9-inch graham cracker crust (below), baked
Additional nutmeg for garnish

Dissolve the gelatin in the cold water. Place the egg yolks, $^1/_2$ cup of the sugar, the salt, and hot water in the top of a double boiler. Beat until light over simmering water. Continue beating and cooking until the mixture is the consistency of thick cream. Remove from the heat, stir in the dissolved gelatin, and let cool. Stir in the rum and nutmeg. Beat the egg whites until foamy, then beat in the remaining sugar until stiff. Fold the egg whites into the egg yolk mixture. Pour the mixture into the crust and chill. Sprinkle with additional nutmeg before serving.

MAKES I (9-INCH) PIE

## Sheila Hibben—The New American
## Cook of the Forties

Sheila Hibben wasn't as famous as M. F. K. Fisher, but she was one of Mrs. Fisher's favorite food writers. Like Mrs. Fisher, Mrs. Hibben wrote on food often during the Forties for *House Beautiful* and was also a frequent contributor to the *New Yorker*—in fact, she originated the latter's "Restaurants" column. Among her books were *The National Cook Book*, published in the 1930s, and *A Kitchen Manual* and *American Regional Cookery*, published in the 1940s.

Unlike Mrs. Fisher, however, whose focus was often on French cooking, Sheila Hibben was interested in American cooking: the American cooking she was afraid was vanishing in the aftermath of the war. Said she in *American Regional Cookery*:

*Sheila Hibben*

If the changing world is not to be flavored by the dreary synthetic foods which manufacturers have thought up with, I suspect, less interest in our survival than in their own, our palates must be awakened to old and simple pleasures.

She urged home cooks to forget about crêpes suzette until they had mastered the art of a well-made strawberry shortcake. She thought that the small-town Illinois woman who could cut into a pound cake and tell what was wrong (or right) with it was just as much a connoisseur as the New Yorker who could criticize a pheasant flambé.

Mrs. Hibben thought that if we could teach ourselves again to taste food with honesty and pleasure and forgo the "graceless routine of eating out of packages and cans," then (and here she sounded much like M. F. K. Fisher, or perhaps Mrs. Fisher sounded much like her), "…hunger will truly be fed, and women—and maybe men, too—will know the satisfaction of nourishing with their own strength and skill those whom they love."

Here is Sheila Hibben's dyed-in-the-wool-American menu, from the March 1942 *House Beautiful*, for the woman (or man) who understood the difference between careful cooking and elaborate cooking. Except that it contains no items from the Southwest, her menu would fit right in at the trendiest modern bistro.

◆◆◆

# Sheila Hibben's Thoroughly American Dinner Menu

*New England Clam Chowder*
*Pan-broiled Chicken*
*Southern String Beans* ◆ *Nebraska Corn*
*Pudding*
*Alabama Methodist Buttermilk Biscuits*
*Tomato, Green Pepper, and Scallion Salad with*
*French Dressing*
*Rhode Island Apple Pan Dowdy with Cream*
*Vermont Cheddar Cheese*
*Black Coffee*

*Lemon Chiffon Pie*

## GRAHAM CRACKER PIE SHELL

The origins of crumb pie shells are unknown but are undoubtedly related to promotions by the major cracker and cereal companies. The 1938 *Watkins Cook Book* contains one of the first mentions of both graham cracker and corn flake "pastry."

    1 cup graham cracker crumbs
    2 tablespoons confectioners' sugar or to taste
    6 tablespoons (³/4 stick) butter, melted
    ½ teaspoon ground nutmeg (optional)

Preheat the oven to 375°F. Mix all the ingredients together and press into a 9-inch pie plate with your hands. Bake 15 minutes. Cool and fill.

MAKES 1 (9-INCH) PIE SHELL

## Alternative Chiffon Pies

The problem with raw eggs in chiffon pies can be, and has been, gotten around in a number of ways. The first, obviously, is to substitute an Italian meringue. The second is to omit the gelatin in the basic recipe, fold the beaten egg whites into the egg yolk mixture, pour the batter into an unbaked shell, and bake until set. In the 1960s, some homemakers substituted whipped chilled evaporated milk. In the 1970s, ultramodern Cool Whip took the place of the egg whites.

## 1960S EVAPORATED MILK CHOCOLATE CHIFFON PIE

1 envelope unflavored gelatin
$^3/_4$ cup sugar
$^1/_8$ teaspoon salt
1 large egg yolk
$^3/_4$ cup milk
3 ounces unsweetened chocolate
1 teaspoon vanilla extract
1 cup evaporated milk
1 (10-inch) pie shell, baked
1 cup heavy cream, whipped until soft peaks form
Chocolate curls for garnish

Combine the gelatin, sugar, and salt in a small bowl. In the top of a double boiler over simmering water, beat the egg yolk and milk until thick and hot. Beat in the gelatin mixture, stirring for 1 minute. Add the chocolate and cook, stirring constantly, until the chocolate is melted. Remove from the heat. Beat with an egg beater or whisk until smooth. Chill until the mixture forms soft mounds when dropped from a spoon. Stir the vanilla into the chocolate mixture. Chill the evaporated milk in a metal bowl or tray until ice crystals form around the edges. Beat with an egg beater or mixer until stiff. Fold the chocolate mixture into the beaten milk. Pour into the pie shell and chill until set. Serve with the whipped cream and chocolate curls.

MAKES 1 PIE

# Chiffon Cake

"The first really new cake in 100 years!" trumpeted *Better Homes and Gardens*, which introduced the cake in its May 1948 issue. Neither a sponge cake nor a butter cake, chiffon cake used the newly popular salad oil and was beaten rather than creamed. The cake was invented by a California salesman named Harry Baker in 1927. Although he kept the recipe a secret for many years, the cake became famous in Hollywood where Mr. Baker made it for celebrity parties. He finally sold the recipe to General Mills in 1947—which posted gains of 20 percent on sales of cake flour after the recipe was published.

Just about every flavor possible was popular in chiffon cakes, with lemon and orange leading the pack. Other candidates were maple-pecan, chocolate, chocolate chip, peppermint chip (crushed peppermint sticks were folded into the batter), spice, mocha, coffee, pineapple, banana, and cherry nut. Here is an unusual coconut variety.

## SPICE ISLANDS COCONUT CHIFFON CAKE

2¼ cups sifted cake flour
1½ cups sugar
3 teaspoons baking powder
1 teaspoon salt
½ teaspoon ground nutmeg
½ teaspoon ground cloves
½ cup vegetable oil
5 large egg yolks, at room temperature
½ cup canned unsweetened coconut cream
¼ cup cold water
1 cup egg whites (about 8), at room temperature
½ teaspoon cream of tartar

Preheat the oven to 325°F. Sift the dry ingredients together into a large mixing bowl. Make a well in the dry ingredients. Add the oil, egg yolks, coconut cream, and water and beat with a spoon until very smooth. Beat the egg whites with the cream of tartar in a large bowl until they hold very stiff peaks and the whites are almost dry. Underbeating will result in a tough, heavy cake. Fold the egg yolk mixture gradually and gently into the egg whites. Pour the mixture into an ungreased 10-inch tube pan and bake until the top springs back when touched, 65 to 70 minutes. Immediately invert the pan and let the cake hang on a funnel or bottle neck until cool. May be served un-iced, or frosted with a vanilla buttercream and topped with shredded coconut.

MAKES 1 CAKE

# American Gourmet

"I can spot a goormy right off. Moment he sits down he wants to know do we have any boolybooze!"

"Bouillabaisse," said Mr. Flood.

"Yes," said Mr. Murchison, "and I tell him, 'Quit showing off! We don't carry no boolybooze. Never did. There's a time and a place for everything. If you was to go into a restaurant in France,' I ask him, 'would you call for some Daniel Webster fish chowder? I love a hearty eater, but I do despise a goormy!'"

—Quoted by Lillian Bueno McCue and Carol Truax, *The 60 Minute Chef* (1947)

Along with the standardization and lower standards of postwar American food came the revolt against standardization and lower standards. To most Americans who cared, that meant gourmet food—and gourmet usually meant foreign.

Although such authorities as James Beard have said that U.S. soldiers came home from the war with a taste for foreign foods, there is little evidence to support that idea. But with or without gourmet soldiers, the foreign/gourmet trend had been developing in this country since the Thirties. Writers such as Mary Grosvenor Ellsworth, June Platt, Richardson Wright, and M. F. K. Fisher all brought to their writing an awareness of the sensuous foods and wines available abroad and a horror of the home economists' marshmallow–canned pineapple–gelatin concoctions that passed as American food. Americans were also forming "Gourmet Clubs" to get together to cook and sample mostly French dishes. Some of these clubs took themselves extremely seriously, notably Les Amis d'Escoffier, whose chairman told G. Selmer Fougner (*Gourmet Dinners*, 1941) it would become "the high authority and final arbiter in all matters epicurean."

In 1939, at the New York World's Fair, Americans were able to eat Albanian, Czech, Italian, Cuban, Chinese, Brazilian, Swiss, and English foods prepared by natives of those countries with native ingredients. At the fair they were also able to taste French haute cuisine at Le Restaurant du Pavillon de France.

Le Restaurant was run by Henri Soulé and was phenomenally successful. In its short existence from May 9 to October 31, 1939, it served a total of 136,261 meals to ecstatic crowds. Americans went wild for Soulé's coq au vin ($1.60), suprême de barbue Mornay ($1.50), and soufflé palmier ($0.90), accompanied by Perrier-Jouët champagne ($6.00), Château Margaux 1929 ($4.50), and Château Beychevelle 1924 ($3.00).

When the fair was over, Soulé, out of work and unhappy about returning to German-occupied France, decided to open a restaurant in New York. That restaurant was Le Pavillon. It opened on October 15, 1941, with no advance publicity, and its 112 seats were sold out. This was the menu.

◆◆◆

---

# Opening Night Menu, Le Pavillon, October 15, 1941

*Beluga Caviar*
*Sole Bonne Femme*
*Poulet Braisé with Champagne*
*Cheese*
*Dessert*

---

Under Soulé's guiding and demanding hand Le Pavillon was to be the leading light of French haute cuisine in America for the next twenty years. The cooks (including one-time head chef Pierre Franey), the waiters, and the wine stewards who worked there would go on to open other restaurants or otherwise influence cooking in America. But in the Forties, Le Pavillon was to be the highest symbol of the gourmet food that was beginning to intrigue even those practitioners of the Gelatin Salad School of Cookery.

All-American cookbooks like *The Herald Tribune Home Institute Cook Book* (1947) offered a "Foreign Recipes" section, along with a few pages on cooking with wine, which had heretofore been ignored. *The American Woman's Cookbook* (1945) assured its readers, "The secret of French cooking (except for sweets) is the use of a whiff of garlic. Even when it does not appear in the recipe, the bowl, baking dish or food is usually rubbed with it," and gave the following in its "French Recipes" section.

## FRENCH CASSEROLE OF SAUSAGE AND CORN

Perhaps the "French" part of the recipe was that it was baked in a casserole, a popular new way of doing things in the American kitchen. There was no garlic.

7 Vienna sausages, cut into short lengths
1 (no. 2) can whole grain corn, drained
½ green pepper, seeded and chopped
1½ cups cracker crumbs
2 cups medium white sauce
2 tablespoons butter

Preheat the oven to 350°F. Mix the sausages, corn, and green pepper together. In a greased baking dish place layers of the crumbs, corn mixture, and sauce, finishing with layer of crumbs dotted with the butter. Bake until browned and bubbly, about 20 minutes.

MAKES 5 SERVINGS

Even high-toned French restaurants palmed off dishes that would make a discriminating palate shudder. New York's Restaurant Voisin, a pricey and fashionable *palace de cuisine*, offered its patrons zucchini gratin, which consisted of boiled Italian squash covered with white sauce and grated cheese.

Of course, many of the French, Frenchified, and/or foreign recipes that became popular in the America of the Forties bore no resemblance to that sausage and corn casserole. Bouillabaisse was a favorite of the ambitious home cook, as was lobster thermidor, minestrone, beef stroganoff, chicken cacciatore, duck à l'orange, fillet of sole Marguéry, and Louis Diat's creation, vichyssoise.

In the hands of the instant haute cuisiniers of the Fifties and Sixties, vichyssoise would become a horrible thing made from dried onion powders and canned potatoes. But in the Forties, this delicious soup was still (mostly) the pure and simple dish it was meant to be—although one future-seeing cook was not averse to adding curry powder to a can of vichyssoise and then topping her "gourmet" concoction off with sprigs of lemon balm!

## CRÈME VICHYSSOISE, GENERAL ELECTRIC INSTITUTE

In the introduction to its "Food for the Gourmet" section, the GE cooking pamphlet *The New Art of Simplified Cooking* (1940) said, "The recipes on the next few pages are designed to please the fastidious taste of the gourmet—the person who appreciates piquant flavors and delicate seasonings in food." (Presumably the average American preferred dull flavors and harsh seasonings.) "The recipes in this section are not designed for everyday use, but for special occasions and when 'something different' is desired."

1/4 cup (1/2 stick) butter
4 leeks, white part only, or 3 medium onions, sliced
2 cups chicken broth
2 cups light cream or half-and-half
2 teaspoons salt
1/4 teaspoon white pepper
2 1/2 cups peeled and diced potatoes
1 cup heavy cream
2 tablespoons minced fresh chives
Paprika for garnish

Melt the butter in a large saucepan, then cook the leeks over low heat until soft and lightly browned. Stir in the broth, light cream, salt, pepper, and potatoes, bring to a simmer, then lower heat and cook over low heat until the potatoes are very soft, about 30 minutes. Mash through a fine sieve. Stir in the heavy cream. Serve hot or cold, sprinkled with the chives and paprika. ("An excellent flavor is obtained by adding $1/2$ cup rum to the soup before serving.")

MAKES 8 SERVINGS

Another milestone along the road to the American fascination with gourmet food was the publication in January 1941 of the new magazine *Gourmet*. Dedicated to "good food, good drink, fine living," *Gourmet* was full of the symbols of the sybaritic life, sometimes to its readers' wrath during the years of rationing. Writers and gastronomes such as M. F. K. Fisher, James Beard, Lucius Beebe, and Samuel Chamberlain (a.k.a. Phineas Beck) set the high (and sometimes high-falutin') tone of the magazine, much as Andre Simon was doing in England with *Wine and Food*, the magazine of the English Wine and Food Society.

While M. F. K. Fisher was yearning after baby peas cooked à point on a Swiss hillside, and Samuel Chamberlain was writing poignantly of the cooking of Burgundy (*Clementine in the Kitchen,* published in 1943, was his charming fictionalized account of a Burgundian cook's odyssey), and Lucius Beebe was gushing over any sort of fancy cooking, James Beard was writing of gourmet foods with a masculine, American hand. His 1940 *Hors d'Oeuvre and Canapés* was full of strongly flavored cocktail food, like beef tartare and lamb kidney barquettes, food that would make the ladies of the home economist brigade wrinkle their delicate noses. In 1949 he published *The Fireside Cook Book.* Though the book had a definite gourmet slant, with dishes like chicken marengo (a popular Forties item) and mussels marinières, the recipes were accessible to the timid American cook. Caneton aux cerises was called duck with black cherries, quiche (an early example) was called Swiss cheese tart, navarin was braised lamb, and crêpes were French pancakes. Nor did Beard forgo American food. Recipes for fried chicken, corn on the cob, chicken shortcake, broiled tenderloin steaks, corn muffins, and snickerdoodles were presented right alongside the celeriac vinaigrette and côte de porc charcutière.

One of Beard's recipes was for crêpes suzette (typically, it was listed under "Pancakes" in the index). These dessert crêpes, a restaurant specialty in the Thirties, became the *sine qua non* of chic desserts in the Forties. Although crêpes suzette were simple to make, they were so French, so *alchemical* with their blue haze of fire, that they *looked* difficult to the uninitiated. Any host or hostess who could prepare the dish with savoir faire was automatically a gourmet. One brash Forties socialite even used the dish to crash a private dinner being given for the renowned acting team of Alfred Lunt and Lynn Fontanne: she assured her unwilling host that if she were allowed to attend, she would prepare crêpes suzette for the guests of honor.

This poem in honor of crêpes suzette appeared in *Gourmet* in February 1943:

> *No food is quite so debonair,*
> *Nor so imbedded with savoir-faire.*
> *It goes with pearls 'round swan-like necks,*
> *With limousines, five-figure checks.*
> *It matches coats of mink and sable,*
> *And priceless silver on the table.*
> *And yet, withal its rich appeal,*
> *So fitting for a prince's meal,*
> *The fact remains—and what a shame!—It's only*
> *pancakes set aflame.*

---

The flames that most people associate with crêpes suzette are a late, and possibly American, addition. Escoffier's recipe for them is not flamed, nor is the recipe in *Larousse Gastronomique. Larousse* also says somewhat sniffily that while Henri Charpentier "who was Rockefeller's cook in the United States" claims to have invented crêpes suzette in 1896, he couldn't possibly have been old enough at that time to have done so. But they do allow that Charpentier introduced the fashion for *flaming* crêpes suzette in America. However, Charpentier says in his autobiography that he invented the dish when he was a teenage kitchen boy. Another source credits Jean Reboux, author of *Parfait Confiturier*, with inventing crêpes suzette in 1667, decidedly before Charpentier.

Most French recipes are tangerine- and curaçao-based, while most American recipes use orange or orange and lemon, along with cognac, curaçao, and sometimes rum. (Craig Claiborne and Henri Charpentier add kirsch and maraschino to the orange- and curaçao-flavored sauce.) And then there is the 1947 Herald Tribune Institute's recipe for waffles suzette, with a sauce flavored with curaçao, orange, and instant coffee.

## SEMICLASSIC CRÊPES SUZETTE

"This very famous but really very simple dessert is not difficult. A more awe-inspiring recipe for the crêpes is common at many great Parisian restaurants, but this is excellent and simple," said *The American Woman's Cookbook* (1945). It would be fun to know what that "awe-inspiring" recipe was.

**For the Crêpes**

    1 cup sifted all-purpose flour
    $1/4$ teaspoon salt
    3 large eggs, beaten slightly
    1 cup milk
    Juice of 1 tangerine
    1 tablespoon curaçao
    2 tablespoons olive oil
    Butter for cooking the crêpes

**For the Suzette Sauce**

    6 tablespoons ($3/4$ stick) unsalted butter
    6 tablespoons confectioners' sugar
    Juice and grated rind of 1 tangerine
    $1/4$ cup plus 2 tablespoons curaçao
    $1/4$ cup cognac

To make the crêpes, sift the flour and salt together into a mixing bowl. Beat the rest of the ingredients, except the butter, into the flour mixture, using a rotary beater, whisk, or spoon. Beat until smooth, then cover and let stand in a cool place for at least 2 hours.

Melt a tablespoon of the butter for cooking over medium heat in a 7-inch skillet. Pour in just enough batter to cover the bottom of the pan. Immediately tilt the skillet back and forth to spread the batter evenly and thinly. Cook the crêpe on one side until lightly browned, then turn the crêpe and let it brown lightly on the second side. Remove to a plate. Continue cooking each crêpe in the same way, adding butter to the skillet as necessary. If the crêpes are not to be used immediately, you may separate them with waxed paper and cover them to keep them from drying out. Unused crêpes may be frozen if tightly covered. Bring to room temperature before using the frozen crêpes (they'll keep for up to 1 month).

For the sauce, cream the butter and sugar together until light. Work in the tangerine juice and rind and 2 tablespoons of the curaçao. In a chafing dish or large skillet melt the butter mixture. Add the cognac and remaining curaçao. Avert your face and ignite the liqueurs with a long match. As the flames die down, add the crêpes one at a time, turning them in the sauce, then folding them into quarters. Serve hot. Allow 2 to 3 crêpes per serving.

MAKES 16 TO 18 CRÊPES

*Making Crêpes*
*Suzette*

Zabaglione was another extremely popular gourmet dessert in the Forties. The actress Joan Fontaine was known to stir up the wine-and-egg concoction personally for her guests while the dinner plates were being cleared. In an April 1949 article on the perfect dinner for *House Beautiful*, M. F. K. Fisher chose zabaglione as the perfect dessert to make for herself when she dined alone—and, typically, she chose to put it in the icebox uneaten and go to bed.

Zabaglione was a particularly favorite ending for Italian Spaghetti Suppers, one of the international gourmet theme parties that were an important social event in the Forties. One Minneapolis hostess hired a famous local chef to come to her house to make the zabaglione for her Venetian party. "I can just hear him now," she said, "clattering up the back stairs with his pots and pans, and I can also hear Delia throwing him back down again with the remark, 'I guess I can make anything that's made in this house!' And that was that."

Although the ingredients (egg yolks, sugar, and wine or spirits) and the method (beat in a double boiler until thick and frothy) are both extremely simple, zabaglione nevertheless requires complete attention, as the eggs can easily scramble before the proper consistency is reached. Said *Esquire's Handbook for Hosts* (1949), "This is darned hard to make and takes much patience and slow cooking—which is probably one of the reasons it's so expensive in restaurants."

## ZABAGLIONE

"Tricky. Delicious, if successful," said *The American Hostess* (1948).

2 large egg yolks
1 tablespoon sugar
1 tablespoon Marsala or other fortified wine, rum, brandy, etc.

Beat the egg yolks with the sugar until thick and lemon colored. Put the mixture in the top of a double boiler (the thicker-bottomed the better) over simmering water. Beat in the wine with a whisk or electric beater, beating until the mixture holds its shape and is thick, hot, and foamy. Serve in sherbet glasses or as a sauce. May be sprinkled with cinnamon if desired. The glasses may be frosted by dipping the rims first in the wine used, then in sugar.

MAKES 1 SERVING

Mrs. Julia Cooley Altrocchi (who contributed the zabaglione recipe above) also contributed a menu for a formal dinner, circa 1948, to *The American Hostess*. The menu was purportedly Italian, but exhibited the period's schizophrenic food attitudes of Ladies Luncheon versus Gourmet. According to *The American Hostess*, Mrs. Altrocchi was a Methodist and a Republican and was married to a professor of Italian literature, so perhaps this explains something.

◆◆◆

## Mrs. Altrocchi's Savory and Exotic Italian Formal Dinner

*Frozen Tomato Salad*
*Crackers*
*Pollo alla Cacciatora*
*Burgundy*
*Rounds of Cranberry Jelly on Orange Slices*
*Artichoke Hearts Fried in Olive Oil*
*Wild Rice with Mushrooms*
*Slices of French Bread*
*Zabaglione*
*Cupcakes*
*Coffee* ◆ *Candies*

Another dessert that was all the rage was strawberries Romanoff ("We're having a run on that dessert, you know," said Virginia Safford in *Food of My Friends* in 1944). This classic dish of orange- and curaçao-flavored strawberries topped with sweetened whipped cream was often served at the great Carlton Hotel in London when Auguste Escoffier reigned over its kitchens. But in America the dish became the signature of "Prince" Mike Romanoff, the flamboyant owner of Romanoff's restaurant in Los Angeles. The Prince, to enhance the glamour of the restaurant where Hollywood's most famous loved to meet and eat (the young and unfamous Julia Child was also an occasional guest and eater of strawberries Romanoff), claimed to be descended from the Russian royal family. No one believed him, but in the land of make-believe, a make-believe prince was at least as good as a real one…and maybe better.

Romanoff's restaurant wasn't the only famous eatery claiming strawberries Romanoff as its own. The Palace Hotel in San Francisco featured the dessert, although their very unorthodox version included ice cream, maraschino, and anisette. The Biltmore Hotel in Los Angeles made strawberries Romanoff with ice cream, too, but called its version—what else—strawberries Biltmore. Most American cookbooks included ice cream as standard in the dish. But as James Beard said in *Theory and Practice of Good Cooking* (1977) "If there is one satisfactory version of strawberries Romanoff, there are twenty-five." (In the Sixties, one gourmet cookbook gave a recipe for strawberry pie Romanoff, which was strawberry ice cream in a graham cracker crust [of course], topped with liqueur-enhanced whipped cream. A few fresh strawberries made an appearance as the garnish for this classic Sixties gourmet pie.)

## STRAWBERRIES ROMANOFF À LA MODE AMERICAINE

This version combines the features of many American recipes of the Forties and Fifties. If you would prefer to try Escoffier's classic, omit the liqueur-flavored ice cream and top the strawberries with whipped cream flavored with a little vanilla sugar.

> I quart fresh strawberries, hulled
> Confectioners' sugar to taste, if necessary
> I cup freshly squeezed orange juice
> 1/3 cup curaçao, Cointreau, or Grand Marnier

### For the Topping
> 1/4 cup curaçao, Cointreau, or Grand Marnier
> I pint vanilla ice cream
> I cup heavy cream, whipped until firm peaks form

Put the strawberries in a large bowl and add sugar if necessary. Pour over them the orange juice and the 1/3 cup of curaçao and let them soak for at least 1 hour. Drain the strawberries of most of their liquid and place them in a chilled, pretty serving bowl. Work the 1/4 cup curaçao into the ice cream (the liqueur will soften the ice cream considerably). Fold the whipped cream into the ice cream and pour the mixture over the strawberries. Serve at once.

VARIATION: The strawberries may be crushed slightly after their maceration and then folded into the ice cream along with the whipped cream, to make a sort of luxurious fool.

MAKES 4 SERVINGS

Americans were beginning to like the "gourmet" foreign foods they were eating at fancy restaurants and, more and more, trying to make them at home. And when they found their pockets full of cash, Americans were likely to cross the Atlantic on the fast new airliners, where they "fell in love with France at first bite," as Betty Fussell did.

When they came back to America, they found the recipes for the French dishes they had sampled in *The Cordon Bleu Cook Book*, first published in 1949. The author of the book, Dione Lucas, was an Englishwoman who had given up the cello to study cooking at l'École du Cordon Bleu in Paris, had opened Le Petit Cordon Bleu in London with another English student, and finally had arrived in New York in 1940 to open the Cordon Bleu Restaurant and Cooking School. Lunch was the only public meal served at the Cordon Bleu, which was more cooking school than restaurant. Mrs. Lucas's luncheon specialty was the omelet. In a typical, somewhat forbidding aside, she said, "All these omelets I make in my special pan, which has not been used for anything else in the sixteen years I have owned it. Neither has it ever been washed, for water would cause the omelets to stick to the pan."

In that small comment on her omelet pan lay the difficulty many Americans had with French cooking. The average American homemaker would consider the idea of cluttering up the kitchen with a pan used for only one thing—and that thing an *egg* dish for goodness sake—frivolous and uneconomical. And then never to wash that pan with good hot water and soap? Disgusting! The result was that Americans were intimidated by a simple dish like an omelet, what with needing an otherwise useless, unwashed pan around, and rarely made the silly, extravagant thing. Much better to leave omelets and such to connoisseurs, snobs, gourmets, and other effete types.

Mrs. Lucas also had a television cooking show on CBS and ABC for a short time, followed by a show that appeared in local markets. With her somewhat reserved personality, Dione Lucas was not Julia Child, and she did not set the American cooking world on its head as Mrs. Child was to do a decade later. Lucas's half-page recipes made good cooking sound like *work* ("Cooking cannot be relegated to the same category as dishwashing or making beds," she said sternly. "Preparation of good food requires time, skill and patience."), whereas Child's eight-page recipes made cooking sound like fun. But in her quiet, somewhat austere way, Lucas set the stage for the coming gourmet revolution. And her *Cordon Bleu Cook Book* was, for many years, the bible for American cooks struggling to reproduce French dishes.

# POULET SAUTÉ AU CITRON
# (CHICKEN WITH LEMON CREAM SAUCE)

This is very easy and very good. The original recipe called for ½ cup butter, which has been reduced here, and a little grated cheese, which is omitted. I have also upped the lemon content slightly.

2 tablespoons butter
1 (4-pound) chicken, cut into serving pieces, rinsed, and patted dry
Salt and pepper
2 tablespoons dry sherry
Grated rind of 1 lemon
Grated rind of 1 small orange
3 tablespoons fresh lemon juice
1 cup light cream
Bits of butter
Thin slices of lemon for garnish

In a large, heavy, nonaluminum skillet, melt the butter over medium heat. When the butter is foaming, add the chicken, season it with salt and pepper, and cook on both sides until golden brown. Reduce the heat to low, cover the skillet, and continue cooking, turning occasionally, until the juices run clear with no trace of pink, about 30 minutes. Remove the chicken from the pan and pour off all but 1 tablespoon of the fat. Over low heat stir in the sherry, the grated rinds, and the lemon juice, scraping up any brown bits. Raise the heat to medium and stir in the cream slowly. Taste for seasoning and correct. When the cream is just starting to simmer, put the chicken back in the pan and let it warm up in the cream, turning it a few times.

Preheat the broiler. Put the chicken in an ovenproof serving dish and pour the sauce over it. Dot the top with the bits of butter. Put under the broiler until just starting to brown, 4 to 5 minutes. Garnish with the lemon slices and serve.

MAKES 4 TO 6 SERVINGS

By the end of the Forties, cookery in America was breaking down into two separate camps. There was "home" cooking, full of meat and potatoes and ersatz, processed, and instant ingredients (canned soup, a roast with boiled or mashed potatoes, canned vegetable with margarine, gelatin fruit salad, cake from a mix with ice cream, washed down with milk, water, and coffee); and there was "gourmet" cooking, full of wine, garlic, liqueurs, and exotic and expensive ingredients (caviar, roast Guinea hen with wine sauce, wild rice, braised artichoke hearts, endive salad, cold apple mousse with calvados and apricots, accompanied by champagne, wine, and demitasse).

America's home cooking had been debased by the effects of Prohibition, followed by the Depression, followed by the war. Gourmet cooking was snob cooking for fancy dinner parties, not designed for everyday use. The twain could *not* meet in any logical gastronomical way. But gastronomical logic was not something most American cooks were thinking about at the end of the Forties. Instead, they marched into the brave new culinary world of the Fifties armed with a can opener in one hand and a recipe for bouillabaisse or tomato aspic in the other.

# 5

# The Fifties

## Fabulous Foods for the Richest Country on Earth

America was a rich country in the Fifties. The middle class was growing rapidly, unemployment was low, and real incomes were rising. New homes, with the help of low-interest federal mortgages, were built at the rate of one million a year throughout the decade, most of them in suburbia.

Now that the men were home from the war and were driving off to work in one of the more than twenty-one million cars that Americans bought in the late Forties, the new suburban kitchen—filled, of course, with every modern appliance imaginable—was women's place. And women seemed happy in their newly exalted realm after the independence, the loneliness, and the hardships of war.

If women *weren't* happy, it was obviously their own fault. The drudgery of housework was gone, thanks to all those new appliances and the new open-plan houses. Mom had the choice of cooking from the huge array of convenience foods that were appearing in all the new suburban supermarkets or of cooking like a gourmet from scratch. She had the time, and she had the money. And she was just as likely to whip up a six-can casserole for the family on the nights that the P.T.A. kept her busy, as she was to labor over boeuf bourguignon and Grand Marnier soufflé when Dad was bringing The Boss home for dinner.

## Campfire Cookery in the Wilds of Suburbia

We have...definite opinions about charcoal cookery. We believe that it is primarily a man's job and that a woman, if she's smart, will keep it that way.

Men love it, for it gives them a chance to prove that they are, indeed, fine cooks. The ladies can do the planning and the marketing, the preparation and the hostessing, but the man will do the actual cooking over the coals.

—James A. Beard and Helen Evans Brown,
*The Complete Book of Outdoor Cookery* (1955)

Both tin-can casserole cookery and gourmet cookery were imports to suburbia. But suburbia did have its own native cookery: the backyard barbecue. With its sweeping lawns, patios, and decks, the suburban home could be almost self-sufficient, the place that had everything. Why bother to lug a picnic basket to an urban park, a campground, or even the woods, when all the family had to do to get away from it all was to step out into its own backyard?

The backyard cookout—on the built-in barbecue, the rotisserie, or the portable grill—became popular in the West where outdoor living was fitted to the mild climate. This casual way of doing things also fit postwar America to a tee. By the mid-Fifties, sales of outdoor cooking equipment were reaching thirty million dollars a year.

Cooking on the barbecue, with its primitive echoes of cavemen around the fire—or, at least, of cowboys cooking their grub around the campfire, and cowboys were a very strong Fifties leitmotif—was a man's job. Slapping a well-aged raw hunk of steak on the grill was about as primitively He-Man as you could get in the suburban Fifties. For those men who were still afraid of putting on a barbecue apron, even one with a funny slogan, Victor Bergeron (Trader Vic) had these reassuringly fightin' words in the July 1952 *House Beautiful*: "You can take my word for it that a yen to cook is in the same rugged tradition as jousting or going on a crusade to fight the Saracens."

Here is a recipe for charcoal-grilled steaks from southern Californian Arthur Froehlich, who, while not off fighting the Saracens, was an architect featured in *Celebrity Recipes* (1958). Mr. Froehlich cooked the steaks on a barbecue pit of his own design, another manly fillip.

## STEAKS RANCHERO, ARTHUR FROEHLICH

6 steaks, 1 ½ to 2 inches thick
½ cup (1 stick) butter
3 tablespoons dry mustard
¼ cup Worcestershire sauce

Grill the steaks on a hot charcoal fire 4 inches from the coals. Turn the steaks to sear each side, then allow to cook as desired. (About 5 minutes per side gives a very rare steak with a charcoal crust.) Melt the butter with the mustard and Worcestershire sauce in a large, shallow pan on the side of the barbecue. When the steaks are done, remove from the fire and "swish" both sides of the steaks through the butter sauce. Serve hot.

MAKES 6 SERVINGS

The only problem with barbecuing steaks was that there wasn't much room for creativity. So barbecue sauces—either to use as a marinade, to brush on during grilling, or to top the meat when it was done—became the new secret of good, manly cooking. Sauce recipes were jealously guarded, or exchanged over a friendly martini in a sort of manly version of the distaff gelatin salad recipe exchange over a nice cup of tea. The style of the sauce marked the style of the man. A fiery chili-based sauce reflected a rough-ridin', straight-shootin', cowboy-type He-Man, while a garlic- and herb-based sauce reflected a suave, international gourmet-type He-Man—John Wayne versus James Bond.

## COWBOY-TYPE SPICY BARBECUE SAUCE

Although it is possible to use this sauce on a steak, it is better on ribs or chicken. This recipe comes from a spice and herb manufacturer. Can you tell?

3 (8-ounce) cans tomato purée
3 (8-ounce) cans water
$\frac{1}{4}$ cup vinegar
3 tablespoons butter
3 tablespoons Worcestershire sauce
2 tablespoons onion flakes or grated fresh onion
2 tablespoons celery flakes or $\frac{1}{4}$ cup chopped fresh
1 teaspoon pepper
$\frac{1}{2}$ teaspoon ground allspice
$\frac{1}{2}$ teaspoon chili powder
$\frac{1}{2}$ teaspoon ground cinnamon
1 teaspoon paprika
1 teaspoon dry mustard
$\frac{1}{2}$ teaspoon ground nutmeg
2 teaspoons McCormick-Schilling Season-All
2 teaspoons McCormick-Schilling Barbecue Spice
$\frac{1}{2}$ teaspoon garlic salt or 1 fresh clove, minced
$\frac{1}{4}$ teaspoon cayenne pepper

Combine all the ingredients in a deep saucepan. Bring to a slow boil, stirring occasionally. Reduce the heat and let simmer at least 1 hour, more if possible. Cool and use to baste meats while they are grilling. May be made ahead of time and refrigerated or frozen.

MAKES ABOUT 1 QUART

## GOURMET-TYPE BARBECUE SAUCE

This recipe, also from *Celebrity Recipes* (1958), was from Armand Hammer, the long-lived international businessman and man about town. He put it on steaks cut from the blue-ribbon Aberdeen Angus cattle he raised in New Jersey, but it works equally well on chicken or burgers. The herbs were key to gourmet cookery, and it was rightly assumed that any self-respecting manly gourmet would have his own favorite.

4 cloves garlic, peeled
1 teaspoon salt
2 teaspoons dry mustard
$^1/_2$ teaspoon freshly ground black pepper
1 teaspoon dried basil, tarragon, or savory (or "your favorite herb")
$^1/_4$ cup ($^1/_2$ stick) butter

Crush the garlic in a mortar or a heavy bowl with the salt. Blend in the mustard, pepper, and herb of your choice. Spread the mixture on both sides of the steaks (or other meats) and let sit, covered, in the refrigerator for 2 hours. Let the meat come to room temperature, then grill to proper doneness. Remove to a warm platter and place a tablespoon of the butter on top of each steak.

MAKES ENOUGH FOR 4 STEAKS

Steak might be the ideal manly meat for outdoor cookery, but, even with various sauces, steak could pall—and it was expensive. Hamburgers and chicken were other favorite grilling items, and so were hot dogs. A new possibility when steak wasn't on the agenda was suggested in a Crisco cookbook titled *Praise for the Cook* put out in the late Fifties. In the "Cookery for Men" section, there appeared a recipe for barbecued bologna. Whether men actually grilled whole bologna sausages or not is hard to tell, but the idea popped up in a number of cookbooks and magazines of the period.

## BARBECUED BOLOGNA FOR MEN À LA CRISCO

$^3/_4$ cup Crisco vegetable shortening
2 tablespoons Kitchen Bouquet
2–3 pounds whole bologna sausage

Mix the Crisco and Kitchen Bouquet together. Spread over the sausage. Grill the bologna over hot coals, or spit roast the bologna until it is browned and hot through. Cut into thick slices and serve on rye bread or toasted hamburger buns.

MAKES 8 TO 10 SERVINGS

The "go-withs" of barbecuing were as important as the proteinaceous dishes sizzling on the grill. One of the most popular go-withs, and one most typical of the Fifties, was garlic bread. The long loaf, laved with butter (or margarine) and garlic (or garlic powder) and wrapped in foil, was a "he-man favorite," according to the *Better Homes and Gardens Barbecue Book*.

Garlic bread seems to be an American variation on Italian bruschetta and the Spanish peasant dish of bread rubbed with olive oil and garlic. The first mention of it I found, under the name Austrian savory bread, was in a 1938 cookbook put out by the International Institute of Lowell, Massachusetts. Garlic bread was an important adjunct to Spaghetti Suppers in the Forties, but only in the Fifties did it come into its proper and very popular role as a barbecue side dish.

As time passed, people grew bored with garlic and substituted other flavorings, particularly dill, for this foil-toasted bread. But garlic remains the classic flavoring—and the best.

## The Protein Age

A major factor in the mania for barbecuing was the new wealth that allowed Americans to buy large chunks of tender meats. The February 9, 1954, issue of *Look* magazine dubbed the era the Protein Age. Americans were happy to be convinced that the best way to build strong, and svelte, bodies was to eat protein. Dieters should cut back on starches, but to lose weight successfully, said the April 1954 issue of *McCall's*, they had to eat meat (no one was worried about fat grams and cholesterol *then*). And eat meat Americans did. About 150 pounds each every year in the Fifties, most of which were beef (74 pounds) and pork (63 pounds).

In addition to the hamburgers, steaks, chops, and roasts that Americans were expected to eat daily, these massive quantities of protein were to be supplemented with dried beans, cheese, peanut butter, and three or four glasses of milk per day. *Look* suggested upping the family's protein intake by serving desserts packed with milk or nuts. Even *Look*'s Welsh rabbit recipe, for its budget conscious readers, was fortified with leftover meat or fish.

Roasts of any kind were popular, pork chops were purchased mainly by lower-income families (although double-cut chops, suitable for stuffing, were considered upper-class fare), and hamburger and bacon were two of the most popular meats in all income classes. But as incomes rose, steak, especially sirloin steak, was the protein of choice.

Succulent, tender, high in well-marbled fat, and full of protein, beefsteak in the 1950s came to epitomize American cooking and eating. Pork could be raised from economically scrap-fed pigs, even roast beef was relatively economical when the leftover possibilities were taken into consideration. But steak was luxurious, expensive, and wasteful, a mammoth single serving of high-quality, high-fat protein cut from an expensively grain-fed steer.

Steak was manly, too, and manliness—in food anyway—was important in the Fifties. The He-Men home from the war were not about to put up with any sissy stuff. Not for them the creamed chicken in a noodle ring beloved by the home economists. Real men wanted MEAT, and real meat was steak.

# The Barbecue as Architectural Statement

For Americans in the Fifties, the choice of barbecue equipment was not just the basic grill, on wheels or not, picked up at the local home-improvement store. Certainly many did buy the basic portable grill, but other options were legion.

One of the most popular was the home-built outdoor brick fireplace. Ricky and Lucy Ricardo built one at their Connecticut home in one of their mid-1950s shows, and James Beard gave complete instructions for building one in both his 1952 *Argosy Barbecue Book* and in his 1955 *The Complete Book of Outdoor Cookery* written with Helen Evans Brown. Even the *New York Times* in its June 22, 1952, edition showed its readers how to construct a simple homemade grill from cinder blocks, pipe, and wire mesh, with a method developed by the University of Connecticut. (Barbecuing was so popular that both Cornell University and the University of Connecticut worked out barbecue recipes and instructions for building grills.)

Not all home-built grills were made out of bricks and mortar. One ingenious Mississippian wrote to *Look* (November 30, 1954) with his description of how he constructed a barbecue pit from an old refrigerator. Although his directions were pretty specific, he did not mention what he did with the freon.

Many of the grills, home built or not, had attached rotisserie spits. Spit cooking was fashionable enough that *House Beautiful*'s 1953 Pace-Setter Kitchen contained a vertical-fire rotisserie that could be moved off the kitchen counter onto a rolling cart "to go out to the terrace or porch." (The kitchen also contained a built-in charcoal grill, another Fifties architectural fad, although there was no discussion of the potentially dangerous fumes.) The January 1954 *Vogue* recommended an "effortless meal cooked in a Rotiss-O-Mat" for elegant dining indoors or out.

The barbecue fad met the Oriental food fad in the hibachi in the mid-Fifties. Said James Beard in *The Complete Book of Outdoor Cooking* (1955), "It has captured the fancy of the American hostess, and hibachis are everywhere." Hibachis could be used as small outdoor barbecues for the small family, but its most fashionable use was indoors. Said *Vogue* in May 1954, "As a party asset, an hibachi table…is better than drink or a dancing poodle…guests like to skewer their own bits of beef or chicken, or toast their *canapes*." But, again, no mention was made of venting the dangerous fumes.

# FOIL-WRAPPED GARLIC BREAD

Foil cooking was a real fad in the Fifties, although everything ended up tasting steamed. But it was *modern*—and there was no messy pan to wash. For the most authentic steamed and squishy result, the bread should be thoroughly saturated with the butter or oil. Margarine may be substituted for a true Fifties touch, but butter tastes better.

I loaf good Italian or French bread
$^1/_2$ cup (I stick) butter (or use $^1/_4$ cup butter and $^1/_4$ cup olive oil)
I medium garlic clove

Slice the bread on the diagonal into even $1^1/_2$-inch slices, but don't cut all the way through. Melt the butter over low heat. Mash the garlic clove thoroughly. Mix the garlic into the butter and let sit 10 minutes for the butter to absorb the garlic flavor. Using a pastry brush, brush the butter mixture on all sides of the cut slices. Any leftover butter may be brushed over the top. Wrap loaf tightly in aluminum foil and place on the grill. Cook 30 to 40 minutes, turning occasionally. (The loaf may be baked in a 350°F oven for 35 to 40 minutes.)

**Variation:** Slice the bread all the way through and proceed with the recipe. After the bread is hot, remove from the foil wrapping. Grill each piece over a hot fire just until browned and crunchy. Delicious.

MAKES I LOAF

Potatoes were another likely barbecue go-with, and foil-wrapped potatoes baked in the coals were popular and easy. But in the mid-Fifties a peculiar method of cooking potatoes in rosin, an idea that developed in Florida, became a fad. Potatoes cooked this way apparently developed a very earthy taste and mealy texture, but their popularity was mostly attributable to their novelty. The fad was short-lived, however, because rosin (a chemical by-product of pine used to make varnish and ink, which had to be ordered from varnish and ink factories) was difficult to come by, not to mention highly flammable.

◆◆◆

## ROSIN BAKED POTATOES

This recipe, which appeared in a 1955 *Look* article, "America is Bit by the Barbecue Bug," has not been tested and is presented for historical purposes only. It is NOT recommended for eating.

Large bucket
15 pounds lump rosin
6 large baking potatoes
6 squares aluminum foil
Butter, salt, and pepper

Fill a large bucket two-thirds full with rosin. Melt the rosin over a charcoal fire until bubbling hot. Carefully (rosin burns if it splashes) drop in the potatoes. Cook until they rise to the surface, about 40 minutes. Remove with a slotted spoon or tongs and immediately wrap each potato in a square of foil. To serve, cut through the foil and potato skin. Pinch to open the potato. Season to taste with butter, salt, and freshly ground pepper.

MAKES 6 SERVINGS

Gelatin salads were generally banished from outdoor barbecue menus. Not manly enough, and besides, they tended to melt in the summer heat. The men were usually happy with a tossed green salad with tomatoes, or perhaps a lazy Susan relish tray filled with green onions, radishes, pickles, olives, cucumber sticks, and cherry tomatoes. But because women were pretty well forbidden from cooking on the barbecue pit, their creativity needed an outlet, and the salad department was it. Potato salad was always popular, but a little old-fashioned and dull, not to mention how hot the kitchen got cooking up a big pot of potatoes. And certainly no one was likely to ask for the potato salad recipe because every family was presumed to have its own favorite. But composed salads made from mostly canned ingredients were ideal.

That standby of potluck suppers, three-bean salad, was the perfect composed salad barbecue go-with. It tasted better if made ahead of time, it involved little or no cooking (assuming canned beans were used), it held up well even on the hottest day, and the female guests were sure to ask the hostess for the recipe.

The history of three-bean salad is undocumented, although many recipes exist prior to the Fifties for various bean salads dressed with either mayonnaise or vinaigrette. Wax bean salads with a sweet-and-sour dressing are typical in the German settled areas of the United States and may have been the precursors. Ceil Dyer's *Best Recipes from the Backs of Boxes, Bottles, Cans and Jars* (1992) credits Stokely-Van Camp with one of the first of the three-bean salads, and indeed, the following recipe is adapted from a Stokely-Van Camp mid-Fifties recipe.

## THREE-BEAN SALAD

"The salad *men* love!" said the advertisers' pamphlet *Let's Eat Outdoors.*

1 (15½-ounce) can red kidney beans, drained and rinsed
1 (15½-ounce) can cut yellow wax beans, drained and rinsed
1 (15½-ounce) can cut green beans, drained and rinsed
½ cup diced celery
3 tablespoons sweet pickle relish
4 green onions, chopped
¼ teaspoon salt, or to taste
Few grinds of black pepper
3 tablespoons olive oil (or salad oil)
3 tablespoons cider vinegar
Red onion rings, chopped green onion, or green bell pepper rings for garnish

Combine all the ingredients except the garnish and toss lightly together. Chill well. Heap in a chilled bowl and garnish as desired. "Hurry to that outdoor meal."

MAKES 10 SERVINGS

---

In the 1950s, most black pepper was sold preground and with as much flavor as day-old dust. If the hostess was hoity-toity, she might buy Spice Islands cracked pepper. But if she really wanted to climb the ladder of culinary status, she could, said *Better Homes and Gardens*, "go gourmet—by adding freshly ground pepper" from her own pepper grinder.

---

Beans were also likely to appear at a barbecue in the guise of baked beans. Although a few traditionalists still made their own, most women were happy to let Hormel or Van Camp do the cooking, and were content to stir in a little molasses, ketchup, and mustard to ease their culinary consciences. Corn on the cob was, and still is, another necessary barbecue adjunct, the fresh corn either being roasted in the husk, in foil, or brought, piping hot, from its boiling water bath on the kitchen stove.

The electric skillet, that archetypal piece of Fifties kitchen equipment, also found its way to the barbecue. With an outlet near the grill, Mom could fry up some chicken, heat up the canned baked beans, or whip up an exotic ratatouille, while Dad was busy wielding the barbecue tongs.

# Kebabs

Along with standard barbecue fare, skewer cookery was a huge fad in the Fifties. According to Betty Fussell in *Masters of American Cookery,* James Beard traced the shish kebab craze to Russian immigrants who settled both coasts after World War I, and Craig Claiborne claimed that after World War II the "shish kebab craze was second only to the national rage for pizza."

Virtually anything that could be strung on a skewer was barbecued in the Fifties. The most traditional kebab cookout was marinated chunks of lamb (or steak) grilled on one skewer, while tomatoes, onions, green peppers, and mushrooms grilled alongside on their own skewers. (The vegetables and meat could then be grilled according to their own cooking times, without the problem of ending up with overdone tomatoes and raw lamb.) But as good as traditional shish kebab was, American creativity demanded more. Here is a variation on a 1956 *Better Homes and Gardens* recipe for "a gay party kebab" for a company cookout.

## PARTY KEBABS

"Cut ham cubes to suit your appetite—ladylike tidbits or he-man size," said the *Better Homes and Gardens Barbecue Book* (1956). The original recipe called for canned, spiced crabapples, which are not generally available anymore.

Chunk of suet or ham fat
2 pounds cooked or canned ham, cut into 1- to 1½-inch cubes
1 (20-ounce) can pineapple chunks, drained and the syrup reserved
2 large cooked sweet potatoes, cut into chunks roughly the same size as the
     ham cubes
¼ cup (½ stick) butter
2 tablespoons soy sauce
¼ cup firmly packed brown sugar
¼ cup maple syrup

Run skewers through the suet. String the ham cubes on skewers interspersed with the chunks of pineapple and sweet potatoes. Melt the butter in a deep-sided saucepan. Add the soy sauce, brown sugar, and syrups. Bring to a boil, then remove from the heat and set aside to cool. Brush the filled skewers with the brown sugar glaze, then cook 4 to 5 inches from the heat until warmed through and golden brown, about 30 minutes, turning occasionally and brushing with the glaze.

Makes 6 to 8 servings

*Better Homes and Gardens* also recommended no-cook kebabs, consisting of skewered salami, pickled onions, green pepper strips, and tomato quarters. This "easy-does-it family supper" was accompanied by hollowed out muffins filled with baked beans.

But kebab possibilities were unlimited. Tropical kebabs could be made from Spam with pineapple and banana chunks, California kebabs were chunks of hot dogs, bacon, and pitted ripe olives. Marinated shrimps and scallops made ideal seafood kebabs, eggplant and zucchini were great for Middle Eastern kebabs, kidneys and mushrooms with bacon made English kebabs. But even dessert could be cooked on a skewer kebab-style.

## CARAMEL APPLE KEBABS

Other firm, tart fruits, such as pineapples or peaches, are delicious this way too.

    1 (24-inch-long) piece heavy-duty aluminum foil
    1/2 pound caramel candy
    2 tablespoons water
    6 tart apples, cored and cut into quarters

Fold the foil lengthwise and then fold up the sides of the double-thickness foil to make a disposable pan. Place the caramels and water in the foil pan and set on the grill. Stir occasionally until melted. Skewer the apple quarters. Each guest toasts his apple over the grill until the apple starts to soften, then twirls the apple in the melted caramel. Let cool and eat from the stick.

MAKES 6 SERVINGS

Kebabs appealed to the child in adults who had delighted in toasting their very own wienies and marshmallows over the campfire. But they also had glamour and style, inherent in their exotic Middle Eastern origins. The best complement for glamorous kebabs was a bed of rice or, even better, wild rice. As Betty Fussell pointed out in *Masters of American Cookery* (1983), after World War II newly wealthy Americans turned their backs on corn—that most pedestrian American grain—and substituted the more exotic Far Eastern grain rice. Also fashionable were bulgur wheat, brown rice, and kasha. Wild rice, which is not truly a rice but the grain of a marsh grass, was most appealing because it was the most expensive grain.

And the best way to serve these exotic grains with kebabs was in a pilaf. Here is an archetypal Fifties menu for a company kebab dinner from Margo Rieman in *Twelve Company Dinners* (1957).

◆◆◆

# Kebab Company Dinner
# with Pilaf

*Brandied Liver Pâté*
*Cheese Balls Stuffed with Deviled Ham*
*Dark Rye Bread*
*Lamb Shish Kebab with Eggplant, Onions, Tomatoes,*
*and Green Pepper*
*Kasha Pilaf*
*Hot Rolls*
*Green Salad with Anchovies and Grated Cheese*
*Chocolate Rum Roll*

This being the Fifties, the kebabs, the pilaf, and the dessert were made from scratch, but the pâté was doctored canned liver pâté, the cheese balls were based on a jar of processed cheese food, and the hot rolls were from a Betty Crocker mix.

## BROWN RICE PILAF

Although the original recipe called for kasha, brown rice is more readily available and easier to work with.

6 tablespoons ($3/4$ stick) butter
1 $1/2$ cups brown rice
1 teaspoon salt (use less if using canned broth)
3 cups chicken broth (if using canned, use $1/2$ canned broth and $1/2$ water)
$1/2$ cup slivered almonds

Preheat the oven to 350°F. Melt $1/4$ cup of the butter in an ovenproof casserole. Sauté the rice in the butter until it is hot and begins to look pale. Add the salt and chicken broth and stir with a fork to combine. Bake, covered, until the liquid is absorbed and the rice is fluffy and dry, about 1$1/2$ hours. Melt the remaining butter in a small sauté pan. Add the almonds and toss in the hot butter until they are just lightly browned and smell toasted. Distribute the almonds over the rice and serve.

MAKES 6 SERVINGS

# The Modern Epicure

This new epicureanism has an Alice-in-Wonderland aspect. Even though you may have avoided any connection with matters culinary in your life, now *you can start at the top*. You don't have to do simple dishes first. When you put your dependence upon a chocolate pudding mix, for instance, a *soufflé au rhum* is a good deal easier than a regular pie. A miraculously dark, glossy, beer-rich, beef *flambé* leaps in less than fifteen minutes from a tin of beef stew and a can of onion soup.

—Poppy Cannon, "How to be a Pace-Setting Gourmet," *House Beautiful* (May 1953)

In the ultramodern, ultrarich, and ultraclean America of the Fifties, starting at the top was all. With all the modern conveniences—shining new stoves and ranges, dishwashers, even garbage disposals, not to mention all the modern processed foods available—the Fifties homemaker (no longer a housewife) was expected to be an artist in the kitchen. Cooking the old-fashioned way was dirty drudgery. But cooking the new way, with all the preparation done by the unseen minions at the processing companies, was a creative work. And because the homemaker now had the time, her creative work was expected to match that of the haute cuisine—without the benefit of either labor or experience.

There was no need for the homemaker to go to any trouble to make a soufflé de tomates à la Napolitaine. Not for her the freshly cooked macaroni, the stiff béchamel, the fresh tomato purée, and the clouds of freshly grated Parmesan that Escoffier directed. Instead, she could find all the work done for her with a can of Heinz's cooked macaroni in cream sauce with cheese and a can of Campbell's condensed tomato soup. Her artistry came in adding a Spice Islands bay leaf, a sprig of thyme, and a couple of chicken bouillon cubes to the can of soup. And the epicurean dish would be done without a drop of sweat bedewing her untroubled brow, without a sink full of dirty dishes, without the heat and the smell of cooking disturbing the immaculate kitchen—and without the taste of an honest bite of food. But not too many were troubled about *that*. At least not yet.

There have been many theories propounded about the peculiar Fifties penchant for instant haute cuisine. Certainly the food companies had a great deal to gain by promoting their processed products, while assuring the housewife that her role in the kitchen was still key. Certainly many young women learned cooking not from their mothers and grandmothers, but from magazines and cooking shows, and were, therefore, intimidated by the prospect of making a stew from scratch, let alone a carbonnade flamande. Certainly, with all their modern conveniences, women in the Fifties seemed to have less time to spend in the kitchen, what with organizing their Welcome Wagon clubs and chauffeuring Johnny to Little League and Janie to ballet class. And certainly the idea of the good life for many people in the Fifties was that everything that was modern, new, and improved was desirable, and that everything old was not.

What it all boiled down to was there was no reason for the modern homemaker to be anything so unappealing as a plain old *cook*, when she could be a *Chef*.

---

### A Loaf of Bread, A Can of Soup, and Thou

"Dear Carol," wrote Carol's sister, the novelist Rhoda Truax, "If you are collecting gourmet recipes, here is a delicious one. It is so simple and not at all expensive. You buy 29 cents worth of haddock. Then you open a can of mushroom soup, pour it over, and pop it in the oven.

"Here is Carol's recipe for fish with mushroom soup: Poach fillets of sole in white wine. Open a can of mushroom soup. Throw the soup out the window and serve the sole with sauce Meunière."

—Lillian Bueno McCue and Carol Truax, *The 60 Minute Chef* (1947)

When the Campbell Soup Co. started selling its canned soup in 1897, it met with such success that sales increased from five hundred thousand cans a year in 1900 to eighteen million cans a week in the early 1920s. For the first few years these canned soups were eaten, not surprisingly, as soups. But housewives soon discovered how much easier it was to just open a can of tomato soup (Campbell's first and most popular variety) than to chop up fresh or even canned tomatoes for their tamale pies and other tomato-based casseroles.

By the late Twenties, when canned foods in general were popular with the hurry-up homemaker, the idea of canned soup as a sauce or base became widely accepted. In November 1927 *Delineator* magazine published an article, "When the Cooking is Done in the Can," that recommended some of the following dishes for "the bachelor husband's summer meals," unexpected guests, and "many other culinary crises":

- Spaghetti and cheese with condensed beef soup
- Tuna fish mixed with condensed asparagus soup with mushrooms, pimientos, or peas
- Salmon in condensed tomato soup with green pepper
- Tuna fish and olives in diluted tomato soup
- Shrimp and peas in condensed celery soup
- Condensed vegetable soup baked au gratin with cheese
- Ham baked with condensed pea soup
- Ragout of canned beef, vegetable, and tomato soup

In the Thirties both the Campbell Soup Co. and their closest competitor, the H. J. Heinz Co., came out with cream of mushroom soup. Quick-cook artists immediately recognized its value. In May 1934 *Good Housekeeping* proposed a dinner featuring canned tomato juice, canned shrimp in condensed cream of mushroom soup to be served on toast, canned peas, and canned pineapple slices, and said with evident pride, "This menu is built around a main dish of creamed fish for which no sauce has to be made!"

By the Fifties, canned condensed cream soups, with their salty and peculiarly metallic taste, had become our *fond de cuisine*. Cooking with canned soup was not only acceptable, it was chic and terribly modern. One magazine assured its readers that a sauce made with soup was "in real gourmet class, often fully as good as the time-consuming kinds based on venerable recipes." Poppy Cannon, the queen of Can-Opener Gourmets, agreed. Her recipe for béchamel sauce, "one of the classic sauces of the great French cuisine," was this: one can condensed cream of chicken soup mixed in the top of a double boiler with one-quarter to one-half a can of water or milk. "Strain if you wish, though actually it isn't necessary."

By using packaged foods and prepared mixes, said Helen Bryson, in an article titled "A French Chef in Your Kitchen?" in a 1954 issue of *Vogue*, "a memorable and delicious meal can be produced with a minimum of time and expense, and with only a basic knowledge of cooking."

◆◆◆

# Menu for a Modern Epicure

*Baby Borscht*
*Velvety Crab and Cheese Soufflé*
*Uncanny Salmi of Duck with Wild Rice*
*Working-gal Tomato Aspic Rounds*
*with Hearts of Celery*
*Extra-fresh Apricot-Orange Parfait Pie*

## BABY BORSCHT

Puréed baby food was a hot item for making jiffy gourmet dishes for adults in the Fifties. After all, wasn't baby food made from the best and freshest ingredients? Soups, soufflés, tea breads, jellied salads, and creamy desserts were the usual recipients of a jar of strained junior food. (This recipe is reprinted with permission of *House Beautiful*, copyright © April 1952. The Hearst Corporation. All rights reserved.)

> 2 (4³/₄-ounce) jars strained beets
> 1 (4³/₄-ounce) jar strained carrots
> 2 cups canned beef bouillon
> 1 tablespoon lemon juice
> Salt and pepper
> Sour cream and chopped fresh chives for garnish

Combine the first four ingredients in a saucepan and bring to a simmer. Season with salt and pepper. Serve in soup cups garnished with a blob of sour cream and a sprinkling of chopped chives.

MAKES 4 SERVINGS

# VELVETY CRAB AND CHEESE SOUFFLÉ

Velveeta was a kitchen staple in the Fifties, especially good in hot dishes where its disinclination to curdle was very much appreciated. In making this sturdy and surprisingly good soufflé the Fifties homemaker might very well have used a can of Sardi's Jiffy Sauce, rather than go to all the trouble of making her own béchamel.

6 tablespoons (³/₄ stick) butter
¹/₂ cup all-purpose flour
1¹/₂ cups milk, hot but not boiled
¹/₄ teaspoon salt
Pepper and a pinch of ground nutmeg
1¹/₃ cups grated Velveeta cheese
4 eggs, separated
1¹/₂ cups crabmeat (about 1¹/₂ pounds), picked over for cartilage
6 slices canned pineapple, drained

Preheat the oven to 325°F. Melt ¹/₄ cup of the butter in a heavy saucepan over low heat. Stir the flour into the butter and cook slowly, stirring constantly, until well blended and frothy, about 3 minutes. Take the saucepan off the burner and gradually stir in the hot milk, stirring vigorously to prevent lumping. Return to medium heat and cook, stirring constantly, until the sauce is smooth, thick, and hot. Season with the salt and a pinch of pepper and nutmeg. Remove from the heat and stir in the grated cheese all at once. Continue stirring until the cheese is melted. Beat the egg yolks until thick and lemon colored in a large bowl. Slowly pour the cheese mixture into the egg yolks, stirring vigorously. Stir in the crabmeat. Beat the egg whites in a large bowl until stiff but not dry. Gently spread the cheese mixture over the egg whites and fold in until blended (a few lumps of egg white here and there are okay). Pour into a buttered 6-cup soufflé dish. Place in a pan filled with hot water that comes halfway up the sides of the soufflé dish and bake until browned and a knife inserted gently near the center comes out clean, 45 to 55 minutes. While the soufflé is cooking, melt the remaining butter in a heavy skillet over high heat. Add the pineapple slices and sauté on both sides until golden brown. To serve, place a pineapple slice on each plate and top with a serving of the soufflé.

MAKES 6 SERVINGS

# Tomato Aspic

A formula for a really well-flavored tomato aspic will be as useful to you as that other basic—the simple black dress.
—Jean Harris, "Gelatine—Escalator to Cooking Freedom," *House Beautiful*
(June 1951)

Marian Burros drew fire—and laughs—in a 1985 *De Gustibus* column when she reported on a retro-food dinner party she had attended wherein "it was universally decided that our palates had progressed past the point at which we could tolerate tomato aspic." Some people wrote to her to say that they *still* served tomato aspic to "universal acclaim," while another reader said that her family had decided it was "icky" in the Forties.

Tomato aspic has had a long, if not necessarily honorable, history in the United States. Mary J. Lincoln, Marion Harland, and Sarah Tyson Rorer all included recipes for jellied tomato salads in their turn-of-the-century cookbooks. The salad gained popularity in the Twenties and Thirties with the rise of packaged gelatin. It was a particular favorite for Ladies' Luncheons—especially when made in heart-shaped molds for Valentines' Day soirees. By the Forties, it had become a staple of refined dinner parties, while continuing its role as a favorite at ladies' gatherings (where the guests were sure to ask the hostess for the recipe).

Tomato aspic reached its peak of popularity in the Fifties, appeared occasionally in the Sixties, and then disappeared almost completely. Here is a classic recipe from Stokely-Van Camp from 1947.

## FINEST TOMATO ASPIC

"To be your family's prime flavor favorite, this enticing aspic must be bursting with rich tomato zip and zing!" said Stokely-Van Camp's ad in *American Home* (September 1947). Many variations were possible on this aspic theme. In the Fifties and Sixties, canned tomato soup was often a base. Marian Burros added zip and zing to her tomato aspic with raspberry-flavored gelatin and horseradish.

1 bay leaf
Few drops of Tabasco sauce
Few drops Worcestershire sauce
5 onion slices
1 celery stalk, coarsely chopped
$^1/_2$ teaspoon salt
$3^3/_4$ cups tomato juice
2 tablespoons unflavored gelatin
$^2/_3$ cup cold water
2 tablespoons tarragon vinegar
Few drops lemon juice
Lettuce leaves and mayonnaise for garnish

Add the bay leaf, Tabasco and Worcestershire sauces, onion, celery, and salt to the tomato juice in a medium saucepan. Simmer for 10 minutes. Soften the gelatin in the cold water. Dissolve the softened gelatin in the hot juice mixture. Stir in the vinegar. Taste for seasoning, adding lemon juice if desired. Strain through a sieve. Pour into an oiled 9-inch ring mold and chill until firm. Unmold on lettuce leaves and top with mayonnaise.

MAKES 8 SERVINGS

## UNCANNY SALMI OF DUCK WITH WILD RICE

A historical curiosity as canned duck and canned wild rice are no longer on the market shelves. This recipe appeared in a February 1953 *House & Garden* article, "20th Century Short Cuts to Old-Fashioned Dishes."

3 shallots, minced
2 tablespoons butter
2 thin slices ham, minced
1 heaping tablespoon Italian tomato paste
$^1/_2$ cup Burgundy
1 canned duck, drained and juices reserved
1 can pitted black olives, drained
1 can wild rice

In a large skillet sauté the shallots in the butter until soft. Add the ham and cook until the ham curls and crisps slightly. Blend in the tomato paste, wine, and juices from the canned duck and bring to a simmer. While the sauce is heating, carve the bird into serving pieces and add to the pan with the black olives. Heat the wild rice. Serve the duck very hot with the hot rice, with the sauce spooned over the top.

MAKES 4 SERVINGS

## WORKING-GAL TOMATO ASPIC ROUNDS WITH HEARTS OF CELERY SALAD

Another curiosity, because tomato aspic *never* comes in cans these days and hearts of celery almost never. Trader Vic thought this salad, put together by "one busy working gal" of his acquaintance, genuinely good.

I can celery hearts
1/2 cup store-bought French dressing (not the tomatoey one)
I can tomato aspic, well chilled
Crisp lettuce

Drain the celery hearts, toss with the French dressing, and let stand in the refrigerator at least 1 hour. Slice the aspic. Place a lettuce leaf on each plate (which should be chilled). Alternate aspic slices and celery hearts on the lettuce. Dribble any leftover dressing over each serving.

MAKES 4 SERVINGS

## EXTRA-FRESH APRICOT-ORANGE PARFAIT PIE

Parfait Pie was a 1952 *Better Homes and Gardens* introduction and one of their most requested recipes ("ice-cream and gelatin filling sets up extra fast, tastes extra fresh"). Strawberry and raspberry were favorite flavorings. Here BH&G's Parfait Pie has been melded with an apricot-orange pie idea from one of their competitors. The pie has an old-fashioned nursery food flavor—probably because, even with the intensity of the apricots, the taste of the packaged gelatin shines through. But it's good, in a school-cafeteria-meets-gourmet kind of way.

1 (9-inch) frozen pie shell, thawed
5 to 6 ounces dried apricots (half an 11-ounce box)
2 cups water
1 (3-ounce) box orange-flavored gelatin
1/2 cup sugar
1/2 cup cold orange juice
1 pint vanilla ice cream, cut into chunks
1/2 cup heavy cream flavored with 2 tablespoons sugar and 1 tablespoon
    Cointreau or other orange-flavored liqueur, whipped until soft peaks form

Preheat the oven to 450°F. Bake the pie shell until golden brown, 7 to 10 minutes (or as directed on the package). Cool. Cook the apricots with the water over medium heat until tender, about 20 minutes. Drain the apricots and reserve 1 cup of the cooking liquid. Purée the apricots in a blender, reserving a few whole ones for garnish. Heat the reserved apricot liquid to the boiling point. Pour over the gelatin in a large bowl and stir until dissolved. Add the sugar and apricot purée and stir until the sugar dissolves. Add the orange juice and ice cream. Stir until the ice cream melts. Chill in the refrigerator until the mixture is very thick but still soft, 20 to 30 minutes. Pour into the baked pie shell and chill in the refrigerator until firm. Cover the pie with the whipped cream and garnish with the sliced reserved apricots.

MAKES 1 (9-INCH) PIE; 6 SERVINGS

Not all quick-cooking was start-at-the-top-gourmet-chef stuff. The lower rungs of the cooking ladder were also rife with canned and processed ingredients and two of the most popular of these were fruit cocktail and Spam.

Fruit cocktail appeared in coleslaws, in pork chops Hawaiian (pork chops with a soy-fruit cocktail sauce), in muffins, in frozen fruit salads, in upside-down cakes, in a sauce for duckling, and disguised as fresh fruit. Said *American Home* in August 1957, "[fruit cocktail] straight from the can when fresh fruits are in season? Why not? This is the very time of year when you should save yourself the hot, bothersome task of buying and preparing umpteen different fruits. For fresh fruit flavor, add frozen juice." It was an ingredient in a gloppy-textured cake (Fruit Cocktail Cake, p. 255), a precursor to Carrot Cake (p. 338), and it appeared straight, in little glass bowls, as the first course at hundreds of rubber-chicken dinners.

Spam was first marketed by Hormel in 1936, five years before America got into World War II. It quickly became *the* economy meat par excellence, beloved of Depression-hardened and point-rationing housewives—if despised by soldiers who ate it too often. A few years after the birth pangs of Spam, Armour ground out its own "luncheon meat," which it called Treet. Both Treet and Spam claimed to be made with a "blend of fine ham and choice pork shoulder" and both came in almost identical square cans. But Spam's prior entry into the market, its use by the armed services, and perhaps its more meaty sounding name made it the winner in the battle of the brands.

After the war, Spam was still popular with economy-minded housewives. It found its way into macaroni and cheese dishes, it was studded with cloves and baked whole like a ham, and it was fried and served up as Spam 'n' Eggs. It could even be made glamorous if it was served encased in aspic.

For all-out glamour, here is a party loaf that combines fruit cocktail *and* Spam with gelatin, Miracle Whip, and paprika for the ultimate in decadent, yet proper, Fifties food.

## FRUIT COCKTAIL-SPAM BUFFET PARTY LOAF

1 (no. 2½) can Del Monte fruit cocktail, drained (reserve syrup)
2 tablespoons unflavored gelatin
2 tablespoons vinegar
½ teaspoon ground cinnamon
⅛ teaspoon ground cloves
2 (12-ounce) cans Spam, very finely chopped
½ cup very finely chopped celery
¼ cup green olives, very finely chopped
½ cup Miracle Whip
1 teaspoon prepared mustard
½ teaspoon salt

**For Garnish**
5 lemons
Paprika
Additional Miracle Whip

Arrange the drained fruit cocktail in a 9 × 5 × 3-inch loaf pan. In the top of a double boiler, mix the reserved syrup with the gelatin, vinegar, cinnamon, and cloves. Place over hot water and stir until the gelatin dissolves. Carefully pour ½ cup of the gelatin mixture over the fruit. Place the pan in the refrigerator and chill until the gelatin has thickened but is not set. Mix the Spam with the celery and olives. Mix the Miracle Whip with the mustard, salt, and the remaining gelatin mixture. Add the Spam mixture to the Miracle Whip mixture and blend well. Spread over the fruit cocktail. Chill until firm, at least 4 hours.

For garnish, make lemon cups by halving the lemons, slicing off the pointy ends (so the lemons will stand up), and scooping out the pulp. Dip the cut edges of the lemons in paprika. Fill the cups with Miracle Whip and sprinkle lightly with additional paprika. To serve, unmold the loaf onto a large platter and surround with the lemon cups.

MAKES 8 TO 10 SERVINGS

Spam and fruit cocktail also appeared together in a menu for a quick-cook Fifties dinner from the July 1956 *Good Housekeeping*. Such a menu makes understandable the vehemence of the Sixties health food movement.

♦♦♦

## Spam Quick-cook Stove-top Special

*Sautéed Spam*
*Instant Mashed Potatoes*
*Frozen Buttered Peas and Zucchini*
*Fruit Trifle (made with canned fruit cocktail, sponge cake, and instant vanilla pudding)*

## The Modern Epicure's Top Three Favorites

Three elegant dishes that were particularly popular with the Modern Epicure were beef stroganoff, chicken divan, and lobster thermidor. They were all gourmet restaurant dishes, they were rich and creamy (an important factor in making them gourmet), and they were easy to make using convenience foods.

### Beef Stroganoff

Beef stroganoff is indeed a Russian dish and has been known, in some form or other, since the eighteenth century, according to *Larousse Gastronomique*. Chef Charles Brière, who was working in St. Petersburg at the time, contributed a classic recipe for it to the French publication *L'Art Culinaire*, in 1891. Mary J. Lincoln included a bowdlerized version (using boiled beef that was then sliced and cooked in butter) under the name of beef à la Russegue in her 1904 cookbook.

But beef stroganoff didn't really become a common American party dish until the 1940s. By the 1950s, nearly every cookbook with any pretensions to gourmet cookery contained a recipe. And nearly every recipe was different. Some cooked the beef with mushrooms and onions, others garnished the finished dish with these vegetables. Some added a dab of tomato paste (as Brière had), while others omitted it. Some sautéed the beef quickly in hot butter, while others baked it "until tender" in its sauce and, said a disgusted James Beard in the *Theory and Practice of Good Cooking* (1977), "bastardized [it] into a stew, which it was never meant to be." Beard had no comment on those, like President Kennedy's chef, René Verdon, who used canned cream soup for their sauce.

## A CLASSIC BEEF STROGANOFF

"A good he-man dish," said *Esquire's Handbook for Hosts*. This recipe is not *the* classic recipe, as there doesn't seem to be one, but it is good, quick, and easy and respects the basics of the dish.

1 ½ pounds fillet of beef
¼ cup (½ stick) butter
½ cup baby white onions, peeled and cored
½ pound mushrooms, sliced
½ cup fresh beef broth, or water
Salt and ground nutmeg
1 cup sour cream, at room temperature

Slice the fillet into paper-thin slices against the grain. (This is most easily done if the meat is slightly frozen.) Melt half the butter in a large, heavy skillet until hot and foaming. Add the beef slices and cook quickly, turning to brown all sides, about 5 minutes. Remove the beef from the pan. Add the rest of the butter and the onions. Cook the onions over medium heat until softened and starting to brown. Add the mushrooms to the onions and sauté until the mushrooms are soft and just starting to reabsorb their moisture. Stir in the broth (or water) and bring to a simmer. Return the beef to the pan and season with a little salt and nutmeg. Stir in the sour cream and heat, but do not let the sauce boil or it will curdle. Serve at once with buttered noodles, pilaf (p. 180), or for a more Russian touch, with crisp shoestring potatoes.

Makes 6 to 8 servings

# HAMBURGER STROGANOFF

While you have might supposed that this very American variation dated from the "Hamburger Helper" era, Betty Crocker weighed in with her hamburger and canned soup recipe in 1954. But then it was considered fancy enough to grace a buffet dinner party. (By the Sixties, Betty called this recipe "No Fuss Stroganoff" and offered a classical "Stroganoff Superb" for a buffet dinner.) Betty didn't add white wine to her stroganoff, but other recipes of the period did.

2 tablespoons butter
$^1/_2$ cup finely chopped onion
$1^1/_2$ pounds ground beef
2 tablespoons flour
$^1/_4$ teaspoon paprika
$1^1/_2$ teaspoons salt
8 ounces canned mushrooms, drained and sliced (Broiled-in-Butter style canned mushrooms were considered the most "gourmet" in the Fifties)
1 can condensed cream of mushroom soup, undiluted
1 cup sour cream
2 tablespoons white wine

Melt the butter in a large, heavy skillet. Sauté the onion in the butter until soft. Add the beef and brown. Pour off most of the accumulated fat. Add the flour, seasonings, and mushrooms and cook for a few minutes. Stir in the soup. Cook slowly, uncovered, for 15 minutes, stirring occasionally. Stir in the sour cream and wine and heat but do not boil. Serve with buttered noodles.

MAKES 8 SERVINGS

## Chicken Divan

While beef stroganoff was an old European gourmet specialty, chicken Divan belonged to twentieth-century America, having been created at New York's Divan Parisien restaurant. And, at its best, it was a restaurant dish, involving as it did a freshly poached chicken, freshly cooked broccoli, béchamel sauce, hollandaise sauce, freshly grated Parmesan—not to mention mounds of pots and pans.

At its worst, chicken Divan was Instant Gourmet Heaven. Canned chicken or deli chicken slices, frozen broccoli, canned hollandaise, or (even lower on the culinary scale) canned soup could be called into play for the benighted dish. Poppy Cannon, the Alice-in-Wonderland of the new epicurianism, dispensed with the hollandaise altogether and substituted mayonnaise mixed with beaten egg whites; Myra Waldo, who could sometimes be a *real* gourmet cook, recommended a packet of cheese sauce mix.

A good chicken Divan was time-consuming to make at home, and bad chicken Divan wasn't worth making. By the Sixties, this gourmet specialty had all but disappeared.

There are many recipes for chicken Divan, but because the Divan's chef refused to cook and tell, no one knows which is authentic. Two 1950s Peter Pauper Press cookbooks, Edna Beilenson's *Simple French Cookery* (1958) and *The ABC of Gourmet Cookery* (1956), contain recipes that are almost identical to Craig Claiborne's in *The New York Times Cook Book* (1961 edition). The Semi-Authentic Chicken Divan (below) is similar to Claiborne's except that the final sauce omits $^1/_2$ cup heavy cream, whipped, for those of you counting fat grams.

## SEMI-AUTHENTIC CHICKEN DIVAN

This recipe is based on a "hint" given by the maître d'hôtel at the Divan Parisien to Peggy Harvey, who wrote about it in her book *When the Cook's Away* (1952).

$^3/_4$ cup plus 2 tablespoons ($1^3/_4$ sticks) butter
2 tablespoons flour
$1^1/_2$ cups milk, warmed
Pinch ground nutmeg
$^1/_2$ teaspoon salt
$1^1/_2$ tablespoons lemon juice
3 large egg yolks
$^1/_4$ cup boiling water
1 large bunch broccoli
$^1/_2$ cup grated Parmesan cheese
3 large chicken breasts, poached in chicken broth until tender

Melt 2 tablespoons of the butter in a heavy saucepan. When it foams, stir in the flour and cook over low heat, stirring frequently, for 5 minutes. Remove from the heat and gradually stir in the warm milk. Return to low heat and continue cooking and stirring until the sauce is thick and smooth. Season with the nutmeg and $^1/_4$ teaspoon of the salt and set aside.

Make the hollandaise by melting $^1/_2$ cup of the butter and keeping it warm. Warm the lemon juice at the same time. Put the egg yolks in the top of a double boiler over simmering water. Beat the yolks with a wire whisk until they begin to thicken. Add 1 tablespoon of the boiling water, beat until thick, and continue adding the boiling water and beating until it is all used. Then beat in the warm lemon juice. Add the melted butter slowly while beating constantly. Beat in the remaining salt. Cover the hollandaise and keep it warm while the broccoli is cooking.

Cut the broccoli into spears and cook in boiling salted water until tender but not soft. Drain. Arrange the broccoli in a buttered shallow casserole. Dot the broccoli with some of the butter and sprinkle half the Parmesan over it. Slice the chicken breasts and arrange them over the broccoli. Pour the hollandaise slowly into the white sauce, mix lightly, and pour over the chicken. Dot with the remaining butter and sprinkle with the rest of the cheese. Broil in a preheated broiler until the sauce is browned and bubbly.

MAKES 6 TO 8 SERVINGS

## CHICKEN DIVAN CONTINENTAL

"Diamonds or no, a gal's best friend can be a can of soup," said the October 1952 *American Home*, which estimated that preparation of their version of chicken Divan would take only 15 minutes.

1 package frozen broccoli, cooked according to directions
2 cans condensed cream of mushroom soup, undiluted
$\frac{1}{2}$ cup milk
1 teaspoon Worcestershire sauce
1 (6-ounce) can chicken or $1\frac{1}{4}$ cups sliced cooked chicken
$\frac{1}{4}$ cup grated Parmesan cheese

Arrange the broccoli in a shallow baking dish. Combine the soup, milk, and Worcestershire sauce. Pour half the soup mixture over the broccoli. Sprinkle with half the cheese. Top with the chicken and the remaining soup mixture and cheese. Broil until hot and lightly browned.

MAKES 4 SERVINGS

### Lobster Thermidor

Lobster thermidor is another rich dish, this time of lobster sauced with cream and sometimes mushrooms or truffles. Whether it was first made for Napoleon during the month of "Thermidor" (part of the First Republic's new calendar), as Jane and Michael Stern report in *American Gourmet* (1991), or for the premiere of Victorien Sardou's play *Thermidor* in January 1894 at Maire's Restaurant in Paris, as *Larousse Gastronomique* says, lobster thermidor is undoubtedly a French creation.

Everyone does agree, however, that it had snob appeal. It was served at Sardi's and at the Waldorf-Astoria, and it was the second course at a formal dinner for eighty-three people given for Chief Justice Warren at the White House in 1957.

# White House Menu for Chief Justice Warren, January 29, 1957

This menu is typical of fancy Fifties entertaining with its mix of sophisticated French components, such as pâté de foie gras and lobster thermidor, and of simpler American fare, like hot tomato juice, brown bread sandwiches, and pickled beets. Wild rice is there, as is a different bready item for every course. The menu also includes that newly fashionable item, rock Cornish game hens. And it concludes with cigars and cigarettes, unthinkable in our puritanical age.

*Hot Tomato Juice with Whipped Cream*
*Fairy Toast*
*Hearts of Celery* ◆ *Assorted Olives*
◆◆◆
*Lobster Thermidor*
*Sliced Cucumbers Marinated in French*
*Dressing*
*Boston Brown Bread Sandwiches*
◆◆◆
*Roast Rock Cornish Game Hen*
*Pâté de Foie Gras* ◆ *Wild Rice Dressing*
*Crabapple and Watercress Garnish*
*Creamed Zucchini*
*Sliced Pickled Beets*
*Bread Sticks*
◆◆◆
*Tossed Bibb Lettuce in Blue Cheese Dressing*
*Toasted Club Crackers*
◆◆◆
*Frozen Rum Pudding* ◆ *Melon Mold*
*Butterscotch Sauce*
*Ladyfingers*
◆◆◆
*Assorted Nuts* ◆ *Candies*
*Coffee*
*Cigars* ◆ *Cigarettes*
*Liqueurs*

## LOBSTER THERMIDOR CLASSIQUE

The only agreement on the classic recipe seems to be that there must be lobsters in cream sauce flavored with a soupçon of mustard, and that it must be browned slightly under the broiler before being served. Most U.S. recipes include mushrooms (the Waldorf said truffles) and Parmesan.

4 (1-pound) lobsters, cooked in court bouillon, removed from the shell, meat
    cut into bite-size chunks, and shells reserved
2 cups béchamel made with heavy cream and lobster stock and flavored with
    $^1\!/_2$ teaspoon dry English mustard
$^1\!/_2$ pound small whole mushrooms, sautéed in butter
$^1\!/_2$ cup freshly grated Parmesan cheese

Preheat the broiler. Mix the lobster meat, béchamel, and mushrooms together in a large heavy saucepan and heat slightly. Pile the lobster mixture into the reserved shells. Sprinkle with the Parmesan cheese and put under the broiler until lightly browned, about 3 minutes.

MAKES 4 SERVINGS

## LOBSTER THERMIDOR, CAN-OPENER GOURMET-STYLE

It seems a terrible crime to sauce beautiful, expensive lobster with canned soup, but many fashionable cooks had no qualms about doing just that in the Fifties.

1 (15-ounce) can condensed cream of mushroom soup
$^1\!/_4$ soup can water
1 tablespoon lemon juice
$^1\!/_4$ cup grated Parmesan or Romano cheese
$^1\!/_2$ teaspoon prepared mustard
3 cups frozen cooked lobster meat, thawed and cut into chunks

Preheat the oven to 450°F. Mix the soup, water, lemon juice, half of the cheese, and the mustard in the top of a double boiler. Add the lobster chunks and heat (do not boil) over simmering water. Pour into a buttered shallow baking dish or into lobster shells. Sprinkle with the rest of the cheese. Place in the oven until the cheese is browned, about 15 minutes.

MAKES 6 SERVINGS

Last but not least, to top off a rich meal featuring any of the three preceding dishes, was the dessert sensation of the Fifties. It didn't have a name and recipes weren't usually given for it, but it was chic, quick, easy, and very refreshing. And the use of the liqueur guaranteed its (and the homemaker's) gourmet status.

## LEMON SHERBET WITH CRÈME DE MENTHE

**For each serving:**
Scoop of lemon sherbet
Dollop of crème de menthe

Put the sherbet in a cup. Pour the crème de menthe over it. Serve.

# Gourmets—International and Otherwise

From the home base of an American kitchen, you can eat your way around the world. You can lunch in Mexico, dine in Italy.… Or journey still farther to the steamy forests of Equatorial Africa, and contemplate the delicious mysteries of peanut-coated Congo Chicken with blackened peppers.

—Lesley Blanch, "Food for Americans from Around the World," *Look*
(September 20, 1955)

With their new wealth and leisure, the number of Americans venturing abroad increased dramatically in the Fifties. Not surprisingly, their interest in the delights of European cookery increased dramatically as well. This growing fascination with foreign foods was encouraged by writers and cooks like James Beard, M. F. K. Fisher, and Dione Lucas, who had first gained recognition in the Forties, as well as by *Gourmet* magazine, which devoted itself almost exclusively to international cooking.

Influential new writers appeared, too, like Myra Waldo and Poppy Cannon, both of whom alternated between classic "from scratch" Euro-style cooking and instant-gourmet-from-cans cookery. Myra Waldo's 1956 *Complete Round-the-World Cookbook* ("Recipes gathered by Pan American World Airways from the 84 countries they serve") assured readers that the "exotic and delicious dishes" from Bulgaria to the Lesser Antilles would "amaze and delight" their friends. Even some of the old-school Home Economists got into the international gourmet act. Ida C. Bailey Allen, whose cookbooks in the Twenties and Thirties were rife with gelatin and marshmallows, invited her readers to "Join me in a new and exciting adventure in the realm of connoisseur foods," in her 1958 *Gastronomique*. And Chicago's Culinary Arts Institute, that now-defunct bastion of Home Economists, put out booklets on French cooking and "gourmet foods," alongside pamphlets like 250 *Ways of Serving Potatoes*.

The hautest gourmet cooking, of course, was French. In its April 16, 1950, edition, the *New York Times* delighted in reporting the menus for dinners served by Les Chevaliers du Tastevin and Les Amis d'Escoffier in New York. (Interestingly, both menus included Guinea hens Souvaroff—rife with foie gras and truffles—and ham in aspic.) The *Times* conceded that the food was too elaborate to offer much to home cooks, but said that the menus were of "general gastronomic interest, not only in point of food served but also wine." In other words, they had snob appeal.

But while snob appeal was inherent in French cooking for Americans, most writers tried to ease the home cook's fears of difficult, time-consuming, and expensive dishes. Said Ruth Rosen, the author of *Pardon My Foie Gras* (1956), "Once you have mastered the sauces on which the success of many recipes depends and have learned the art of seasoning and tasting for flavor, you can gradually build up a repertoire of fine French dishes, without loss of time, temper or tears."

Rather than Guinea hens Souvaroff, magazines and cookbooks gave recipes for boeuf bourguignon, soupe à l'oignon, blanquette de veau, and poulet sauté à la marengo. If the home cook was especially daring, she might try sautéed frogs' legs, but her daring came more from the shock value of eating amphibian appendages rather than from any difficulty of execution (the frogs may have disagreed).

*American Home* magazine (March 1959) gave its readers a list of basic French culinary terms ("Chateaubriand: thick slices of filet of beef; *à la Duchesse*: containing mashed potatoes") so that they would not be intimidated when going to a French restaurant. Should the reader be unable to memorize the list, the magazine said reassuringly, "just ask the waiter, they're usually very understanding and will gladly help."

Here is a menu for a French Peasant Supper based reassuringly on "homey, comfortable dishes" from a February 1950 *Good Housekeeping*.

◆◆◆

# Three-Course French Peasant Supper

*Hors d'Oeuvres*
*Hard-cooked Eggs Stuffed with Crab ◆ Buttered Radishes*
*Bread Sticks ◆ Sliced Salami ◆ Tiny Pickled Beets*
*French Potage ◆ (Split Pea-Spinach Soup with Frankfurters)*
*Salad Niçoise with French Vinaigrette*
*Toasted Garlic-Cheese Bread*
*Grape Juice or Cider*
*Baked Norvégienne*
*Coffee*

Baked Norvegienne, or baked Alaska, was a favorite gourmet dish in the Fifties. It appealed on a number of levels: (1) it tasted good; (2) it was easy to make (at least so long as it was made quickly); (3) it looked as though as it *must* be difficult; (4) with its simple meringue, ice cream, and cake base it was a safe dessert to serve to even the stodgiest guests; and (5) it was both festive and fancy.

Everyone seems to agree that a dish something like baked Alaska appeared in France in the mid-1800s. Whether it was invented earlier by an American scientist named Benjamin Thompson (1753–1814) who was experimenting with the insulating properties of egg whites or by a Chinese chef in Paris who baked ice cream in an insulating pastry shell in the 1860s is debated. Personally, I prefer John Mariani's explanation that Dr. Thompson's experiments resulted in a dessert called "Alaska-Florida" that was popular at the famous Delmonico's restaurant in New York in the 1800s. For all its French pretensions, baked Alaska has always seemed like an American dish.

The French name *omelette à la Norvégienne* refers to the fact that the cake base is traditionally cut into an omelet shape. Presumably *Norvégienne* alludes to its chilly interior, although François Rysavy, President Eisenhower's chef, said that baked Alaska is a "Scandinavian delicacy." There seems to be no evidence for his statement, however.

## BAKED ALASKA

Said *641 Tested Recipes from the Sealtest Kitchens* (1954), "Elegant, glamorous Baked Alaska is simple as ABC if you'll rigidly follow these 3 musts: a. the ice cream must be very hard; b. the ice cream must be sealed in with a fluffy egg meringue; c. the oven must be piping hot. The result—out of this world eating!" You may increase the egg whites to five and the sugar to eight tablespoons and pipe pretty designs over the top of the meringue just before baking. But only attempt this if you are expert—this is no time to experiment while the ice cream melts.

    4 egg whites
    6 tablespoons sugar
    ¼ teaspoon salt
    ½ teaspoon vanilla extract
    1 (9-inch) layer sponge cake or genoise, about 1 inch thick
    ½ cup currant jelly
    1 quart hard strawberry ice cream
    2 large eggshell halves, with neat edges, washed and dried
    3 tablespoons brandy, heated just before using

Preheat the oven to 450°F. Beat the egg whites until stiff but not dry. Beat in the sugar and salt, adding them gradually but quickly, until the meringue is thick and glossy. Beat in the vanilla.

Cover a bread board with baking parchment. Place the cake on the board and spread the jelly on the cake. Mound the ice cream on the cake, keeping $^1/_2$- to 1-inch edge clear on the cake. Frost with the meringue, working quickly. Be sure every bit of the ice cream is covered for best insulation. Nestle the eggshell halves open side up on top of the meringue. Pop the cake into the oven until the meringue has just browned slightly, 3 to 5 minutes. Quickly slip the Baked Alaska onto a chilled platter. Fill the eggshells with the heated brandy, set alight, and rush the baked Alaska to the table.

**Note:** For tender Fifties sophisticates who didn't use likker, sugar cubes soaked in lemon extract replaced the eggshells and brandy.

MAKES 10 TO 12 SERVINGS

The Chinese chef who may have invented baked Alaska (but probably didn't) baked his ice cream in pastry shells. That idea was also a popular one in the Fifties. Ice cream pies were very chic then, and a baked Alaska ice cream pie was too *soigné* for words. To make a baked Alaska pie, fill a baked nine-inch pie shell with ice cream and freeze until hard. Frost with the meringue (using the recipe above), making sure that crust and ice cream are completely covered, then brown in a hot oven.

A knowledge of wine—French wine, of course—was considered essential for the Fifties gourmet. Books and magazines frequently printed charts showing vintages and comments on each year. Assiduous gourmets collected wine labels in little books and talked knowledgeably and mysteriously of nose and finish. For baked Alaska (although *Good Housekeeping* saw fit to serve it with coffee), Vincent Sardi, Jr., of Sardi's Restaurant fame, suggested Bollinger Champagne, Brut 1945.

Cooking with wine was a sure passport to sophistication, hence the popularity of dishes like boeuf bourguignon and coq au vin. While many people still thought of wine cookery as extravagant, it wasn't, assured James Beard in *House & Garden* (December 1959). "Cooking with wine is not fancy cooking," he said, "just good cooking." Americans stubbornly disagreed.

Another French restaurant or party dish Americans considered very haute cuisine was tournedos. These small pieces of beef cut from the heart of the filet, wrapped in fat, tied, and sautéd in butter were glamorous, but very easy to prepare. Once cooked, tournedos could be garnished with mushrooms, béarnaise sauce, artichoke hearts, wine sauce, or other symbols of gourmandise. One of the most popular preparations, because it was the most extraordinarily costly and the most extraordinarily French, was tournedos Rossini.

## TOURNEDOS ROSSINI

"Suitable for the finest occasion," said the Culinary Arts Institute of Chicago. Because the tournedos are small, plan on two for each guest. And then throw away your checkbook.

12 slices fine unsweetened white bread, cut into rounds the size of the
   tournedos
10 tablespoons (1 ¼ sticks) butter
12 (3-ounce) tournedos (have your butcher prepare them)
Salt and pepper
12 small slices foie gras, dusted with flour
12 small slices black truffle
³/₄ cup demi-glace sauce
2 tablespoons Madeira

Melt ¼ cup of the butter in a large skillet. Sauté the bread on both sides in the melted butter until golden brown. Place the bread croutons on a heated platter and keep warm. Season the tournedos with salt and pepper. Melt the remaining butter in a heavy skillet. Add the tournedos and cook about 5 minutes per side. Remove the tournedos from the pan, place on the croutons, and keep warm. Quickly heat the foie gras and truffle slices in the pan juices. Top each tournedos with a slice of the foie gras and crown with a truffle. Put the demi-glace sauce and Madeira in the pan and bring to a boil, scraping up all the brown bits stuck to the pan. Pour the sauce over the tournedos and serve immediately.

MAKES 6 SERVINGS

While French cooking carried the most cachet (and was considered the most difficult), Scandinavian cookery—to go with the plethora of blond Danish Modern furniture and bright-colored Dansk pots decorating the chicest homes—was In, In, In. And though Scandinavian restaurants were popular (yes, they did exist then, outside of Minnesota), Scandinavian food was most often found at buffet parties. For what could be more modern, more chic, more fun, and easier, than a smorgasbord at a party? Said *House & Garden* (November 1959), "As a good delicatessen can supply the bulk of the fish appetizers, cold cuts, Scandinavian cheeses and breads, you can afford to spend time making salads and hot foods and preparing and garnishing one or two spectacular dishes such as a Swedish salmon in aspic."

Decorations for a smorgasbord were easy, too. All the hostess needed were a few Swedish straw stars, some slim white candles, and the food, arrayed on teak trays, Swedish crystal bowls, and gleaming chafing dishes. To go with the food: beer and aquavit ("frosted fire in its ice-encased bottle") and pots of strong, hot coffee.

Scandinavian food is not very popular these days. The hot, spicy flavors of warm climate countries are preferred to the cool and salty flavors of the chilly north. And besides, Americans now don't like strongly fishy tastes as they did in the Fifties. But a traditional smorgasbord would make an exciting and original party, *if* you number among yourself and your friends those who will eat pickled herring.

◆◆◆

## Smorgasbord Buffet

*Pickled Herring* ◆ *Herring Salad*
*Stuffed Eggs with Anchovy*
*Pickled Beet Salad with Mayonnaise*
*Assorted Cheeses and Cold Cuts*
*Radishes* ◆ *Tomatoes* ◆ *Cucumber Pickles*
*Pumpernickel* ◆ *Swedish Rye* ◆ *Hardtack*
*Poached Salmon in Aspic, Garnished with Shrimp,*
*Eggs, and Tomatoes*
*Köttbuller (Swedish Meatballs) from the*
*Chafing Dish*
*Fish Rolls Poached in Court Bouillon with*
*Egg-Lemon Sauce from the Chafing Dish*
*Plattar (Tiny Crêpes) with Lingonberries*
*(Scandinavian Cranberries)*

Salmon in aspic never caught on big as a party dish, but Swedish meatballs became an American standard both for home eating and for buffets. They were simple and good, whether served up with their sauce on potatoes or noodles, or as a nibble on the end of a cocktail toothpick. And they could stay warm for hours in the chafing dish, so long as a cover was provided to keep them from drying out.

They are no longer fashionable, but then lots of good things aren't—and people *will* go on serving them anyway.

## SWEDISH MEATBALLS (KÖTTBULLER)

My grandmother's cousin Elaine Bechtel was a staff home economist at the Culinary Arts Institute in Chicago, and a more Home Economical maiden lady there never was. But she could turn out a boeuf bourguignon, a cheese soufflé, or some köttbuller with the same skill that she conjured up a tuna salad mold. This recipe was adapted from one that she helped test in the 1950s.

¼ cup (½ stick) butter
3 tablespoons minced onion
½ cup soft bread crumbs
¼ cup water
¼ cup light cream
½ pound ground beef
¼ pound ground veal
¼ pound ground pork
1 large egg
1 teaspoon salt
⅛ teaspoon pepper
½ teaspoon ground nutmeg
½ teaspoon sugar
1 tablespoon flour
½ cup warm beef stock
1 cup warm milk or light cream

Melt 1 tablespoon of the butter in a small skillet, then sauté the onion in it until soft. In a large bowl, mix together the bread crumbs, water, and cream. Add the meats, egg, cooked onion, seasonings, and sugar and mix thoroughly (your hands are the best mixers here). Form the meat mixture into small balls. Melt the remaining butter in a large skillet, then brown the meatballs. Remove the meatballs from the pan as they brown and place them in another large skillet or in a chafing dish. Pour off all but 3 tablespoons of the fat from the skillet. Add the flour and stir until it is mixed with the fat. Remove the pan from the heat and stir in the stock and milk, scraping up all the brown bits. Cook, stirring constantly, until the gravy is smooth and has thickened slightly; it should be thin. Pour the gravy over the meatballs and let simmer partly covered over very low heat 30 minutes to 1 hour. Thin the gravy with stock or milk if necessary.

MAKES ABOUT **48** SMALL MEATBALLS

## Glamour Foods from the Chafing Dish

You couldn't ask for a more charming way to entertain than with a chafing dish supper. The flame that does the cooking or keeps the foods warm adds its friendly flow to the candlelight. You serve casually in the living room. And if you wish, you can cook before guests with all the fanfare of a magician.

—*Better Homes and Gardens* (February 1953)

The chafing dish's history goes back at least as far as Roman times when portable coal-burning braziers were used to warm rooms and cook simple meals. It is Frenchman Alexis Soyer who is generally credited with inventing, in the early 1800s, the modern form of the chafing dish, complete with spirit lamp-heated blazer pan for cooking and a water-filled pan below for moderating the heat.

By the 1890s the growing shortage of domestic servants and the fact that the famous Waldorf-Astoria was renowned for serving after-theater chafing dish suppers to the likes of J. P. Morgan and Lillian Russell helped make the chafing dish a middle- and upper-class fad. The chafing dish was so fashionable that special sets of napkins and tablecloths embroidered with a rabbit (symbolizing Welsh rabbit, the most popular chafing dish item) were considered the ultimate supper accessory.

After the Gay Nineties, the chafing dish quickly lost its cachet. But in the 1940s and early 1950s it became almost as popular as it had been sixty years before. And the reasons were probably the same: a lack of household help; the rise of informal entertaining; and the wish to add charm, glamour, and intimacy to simple meals. Many of the favorite Gay Nineties chafing dish entrées such as Welsh rabbit, chicken à la king, and lobster Newburg were still popular as well. But there were plenty of new or newly fashionable dishes like cheese fondue, beef stroganoff, Swedish meatballs, sukiyaki, crêpes suzette, and cherries jubilee that were perfect for (or at least often prepared in) the chafing dish. And if they could be flamed, so much the better.

In the ultramodern and sophisticated 1950s, the chafing dish was also a way to turn canned sows' ears into gourmet silk purses. *Good Housekeeping* (March 1952) suggested an elegant chafing dish buffet brunch featuring an "Old-Dutch Style" entrée. This European chafing dish classic was constructed from canned luncheon meat in a sauce made of canned apple wedges ("in syrup"), lemon juice, nutmeg, and onion.

# Entertaining in the Fifties

## The Cocktail Party

I presume that the way to shorten the duration of a cocktail party is to starve your guests. Hunger might make them go. However, your pride as a hostess does not permit you to be ungenerous. I don't know which is worse. I've attended cocktail parties where the food consisted of potato chips, mucilaginous olives, and peanuts. I have been to others where hors d'oeuvres rich enough for Chateaubriand or Honoré Balzac were served: smoked turkey, Nova Scotia salmon, caviar (though mostly red caviar), water chestnuts wrapped in bacon, meatballs, shrimps Orleans, piroshki, and petit saucissons (hot dogs). At the first party I ate stuff I detest because I didn't have anything else to do. At the second party I ate too much. In either case, I get no place.

—Richard Williams, "Never Again!" *House Beautiful* (October 1951)

The chicest thing to do about cocktail parties in the Fifties was to detest them—or to spoof them. The fat man spilling a daiquiri into the baby grand piano, the host with the lamp shade on his head, the cigarette butts encircling the potted plants, were all grist for the "I Hate Cocktail Parties" mill. The *New York Times* (January 21, 1951) even printed an article filled with supposedly highbrow cocktail party phrases that its readers might inject into conversations while "wearing a small smile on your face or a look of intense absorption."

But the reason cocktail parties were so easy to detest was that they were an inescapable way of entertaining. Everyone who was anyone either went to one or gave one. And the poor hostesses, as pointed out by Richard Williams (above), had to feed the hordes.

Although some tried to plump for the sit-down party, cocktail parties by their nature were usually stand-up affairs. The difficulty for guest and hostess was how to juggle a drink, a cigarette (didn't everyone smoke in those days?), and something to eat. Beware to the hostess who served her guests anything requiring a plate and utensils, for, the laws of physics being what they are, something was certain to end up on the rug or the couch.

Cocktail canapés were still going strong, although there was a strong backlash against soggy bits of bread or cracker topped with unidentifiable glop. Organized hostesses, with capacious freezers or "help," might try for hot nibbles like cheese puffs, quiche tartlets, or stuffed mushrooms. Swedish meatballs, kept hot in the chafing dish and served with toothpick "stabbers," were popular (although prone to leaving drips of gravy across the damask tablecloth). But for many, the new idea of *dips*, which had gotten a start in the Forties, was the easiest way to go.

Dips in the Fifties hadn't yet taken on the colorful and polyingredient guise that they were to do in the Sixties. They tended to be based on sour cream, thinned cream cheese, or mayonnaise mixed with a single flavoring ingredient, such as chives, Roquefort, deviled ham, or...clams.

When the recipe for clam dip first appeared on the *Kraft Music Hall* television show in the early Fifties, New York City sold out of canned clams within 24 hours. The mania for clam dip continued through the Sixties (by then, premade clam dip could be found in the refrigerator section of the supermarket). Although dips per se are no longer In, having been replaced by salsas, clam dip is an American classic, worthy of an appearance at your next cocktail party.

## *KRAFT MUSIC HALL* CLAM APPETIZER DIP

1 garlic clove, cut in half
1 (8-ounce) can minced clams, drained and ¼ of their liquid reserved
1 (8-ounce) package Philadelphia brand cream cheese, softened
2 teaspoons lemon juice
1½ teaspoons Worcestershire sauce
½ teaspoon salt
Dash of pepper

Rub a mixing bowl with the garlic halves. Combine the remaining ingredients, mixing until well blended. Chill. Serve with chips, crackers, or raw vegetables as dippers.

MAKES 1⅔ CUPS

"There is nothing that adds more to the sophisticated look of the kitchen," said Helen Corbitt in *Helen Corbitt's Cookbook* (1957), "than an herb chest or racks filled with different herbs." And no herbs were more sophisticated than the expensive and high-quality Spice Islands brand. Here is another typically Fifties dip, employing cream cheese and herbs, those symbols of the gourmet.

## GOURMET HERB DIP

If Beau Monde Seasoning, which is an herb-and-garlic-seasoned salt, is not available in your area, add $^1/_2$ teaspoon salt (or to taste) and a very small bit of crushed garlic. This is a very pleasant dip or spread, not unlike one served with fresh whole-grain bread at San Francisco's Greens restaurant.

    1 (8-ounce) package cream cheese, softened
    $^1/_4$ to $^1/_2$ cup light cream
    2 teaspoons Spice Islands Beau Monde Seasoning
    $^1/_2$ teaspoon dried thyme
    $^1/_2$ teaspoon dried marjoram
    $^1/_2$ teaspoon dried summer savory
    1 teaspoon black pepper
    2 tablespoons finely chopped fresh parsley

Several hours before serving time, mash cream cheese with the cream until soft and "dippable," adding more cream if necessary to get the right consistency. Mix in the herbs and seasonings. Chill. Serve with crackers, chips, breadsticks, or raw vegetables.

MAKES 1 $^1/_2$ CUPS

To go along with the dips and dunks, the hostess who wasn't up for much in the way of cooking could offer smoked salmon, smoked turkey, or ham, all cut into thin slices and ready to go onto pumpernickel or French bread. A smoked ham pâté or a pâté de foie gras was a good spreadable for crisp crackers or bread, too. But perhaps the most popular spreadable of all was the cheese ball.

It is unknown who first had the idea of making a gigantic ball of soft cheese covered with nuts to serve as a sort of cheese pâté. Small cheese balls as an adjunct to Ladies' Luncheon salads had been popular since the turn of the century. By the Forties, walnut-size balls of cheese, rolled in nuts, parsley, or chipped beef (see Burning Bush, p. 84), were a common cocktail party tidbit. The first mention I have been able to find of the large cheese ball was in Virginia Safford's *Food of My Friends* (1944), where it was listed as the specialty of the house of a Mrs. Selmer F. Ellertson of Minneapolis.

"Nippy" process cheese spreads, mixed with cream cheese, were at the heart of the Fifties cheese ball. Roquefort often played a role, too, along with Worcestershire sauce, onion, mustard, horseradish, lemon juice, and other sharp seasonings. The balls were usually rolled in pecans, the rich, sweet nuts adding an unctuous crunch to the cheese. Parsley was often added to the nuts for color, as was paprika. Helen Corbitt suggested finely chopped pickled beets, although she said, "If you think the pinkness of the beets will annoy you, leave them out, but I like the added flavor." Her idea did not catch on in a big way.

Cheese balls are no longer fashionable, although they are certainly still served. Their biggest disadvantage is their tendency to look very messy after the guests have been at them, with the nut coating mashed unappetizingly into the cheese mixture. Try the mixture instead rolled into small balls, served on toothpicks as small, nippy bites.

## NIPPY CHEESE BALL

The cheeses may be mixed in a blender or a food processor.

$\frac{1}{2}$ pound Roquefort cheese, softened
$\frac{1}{2}$ pound sharp processed cheese spread, softened
1 (8-ounce) package cream cheese, softened
6 tablespoons ($\frac{3}{4}$ stick) butter, softened
$\frac{1}{2}$ teaspoon Worcestershire sauce
$\frac{1}{2}$ teaspoon Tabasco sauce
2 tablespoons brandy
$\frac{1}{2}$ cup pecans, chopped

Mash the cheeses and butter together, then beat very hard with a spoon until fluffy. If the mixture is too stiff, beat in a little cream or milk to soften it. Beat in the Worcestershire sauce, Tabasco sauce, and brandy. Shape into a ball and roll in the pecans. Chill several hours. Let come to room temperature before serving. Serve with crisp crackers.

MAKES 1 LARGE CHEESE BALL

There were two other no-cook but fancy-looking appetizers that were sure to make an appearance at many a Fifties cocktail party.

## WEDGIES A.K.A. BOLOGNA PIE

1 (8-ounce) package cream cheese
Cream or milk to moisten
2 tablespoons chopped fresh chives
1 teaspoon prepared mustard
1 pound bologna, casing removed and sliced into 12 rounds

Mash the cream cheese and moisten with enough cream so the cheese is soft and spreadable. Season with the chives and mustard. Place a circle of bologna on a plate. Spread with the cream cheese mixture. Top with another slice of bologna spread with cream cheese. Continue stacking and spreading until 6 slices of bologna have been used, but leave the top slice unspread. Repeat with the remaining ingredients. Cover and chill at least 2 hours. Cut into small wedge-shaped pieces. Secure each piece with a toothpick.

MAKES 2 WEDGIE PIES

## COCKTAIL LILIES

I pound bologna, salami, etc., casings removed, cut into thin slices
2 carrots cut into 2- to 3-inch-long very thin sticks
2–3 pickles cut into 2- to 3-inch-long very thin sticks
Toothpicks

Fold the meat slices into cornucopias. Push carrot or pickle sticks into the center of the cornucopias (to make "stamens"). Run a toothpick through the end of the cornucopia to secure the stamen to the sausage. Arrange the lilies on a platter, stamens out—especially colorful if you alternate carrot and pickle stamens.

MAKES ABOUT 20 LILIES

The other most popular item at cocktail parties was...the cocktail. Daiquiris (frozen or not), Manhattans, old-fashioneds, and whiskey sours were standard and reliable cocktail drinks. But the most ubiquitous drink at a cocktail party, or indeed anywhere then, was the martini.

The martini's uncertain history may have begun in the 1860s in San Francisco as the "Martinez," although that drink was notably sweet. By 1894 Hublein was advertising its premixed Club Cocktail Martini as the way to keep your man at home and away from the bars. President Franklin D. Roosevelt, who liked to gather his staff every night for cocktails, is said to have mixed the first "legal" martini at the end of Prohibition. Such was his regard for the nightly martini ritual that his silver cocktail cups are now on display at the Franklin D. Roosevelt Library at Hyde Park, New York.

As the martini grew in popularity (from the 1930s through the 1960s nearly three hundred martinis per day were served at the bar at the St. Regis Hotel in San Francisco), the cult of the Perfect Dry Martini began. A vermouth atomizer was marketed in the Fifties that blew a mist of vermouth over the martini glass. Even more serious techniques to attain dryness were attempted, as

reported in Lowell Edmunds's *The Silver Bullet* (1981), an entertaining and infor-
mative book about the national cocktail:

1. Turn the bottle of vermouth so that the label is exposed to the gin for a
   minute or two.

2. Keep the bottle of vermouth in the cupboard. Whisper the word "vermouth" over the gin.

3. Don't bother with vermouth at all, but salute in the direction of France.

And in the atomic Sixties, according to Mr. Edmunds, "The conceit was carried a
step further by Mr. Paul A. Pollock of Lowell, Massachusetts, who wrote that, at
the time of the first atomic explosion at White Sands, New Mexico, a bottle of
vermouth was secreted in the device and thus subjected to fission. Thereafter,
Mr. Pollock and his friends could add vermouth to their Martinis simply by
holding their glasses out the window. This was the 'Fissionable Martini.'"

The martini was considered an adult drink, sophisticated, tough, upper
class, and urbane. In the Fifties, it was the drink a visitor to New York City
could order without marking himself as a rube from the sticks. At a cocktail party, the urbane host was expected to take charge of the arcane and manly art of
drink making while his wife fussed over the canapé trays.

## URBANE COCKTAIL PARTY MARTINIS

According to Mr. Edmunds, the drink should be served in a chilled glass and
should be no bigger than 2$\frac{1}{2}$ ounces so it will stay cold. But "seconds are
welcome."

> 4 quart bottles gin, chilled
> $\frac{1}{2}$ quart bottle dry vermouth
> Ice cubes made from spring water
> Small strips of lemon peel

Mix the gin and vermouth together and keep in a decanter in the refrigerator. At serving time, pour the gin mixture over ice, stir, and strain into glasses.
Twist a lemon strip over each glass to release its oil, then throw out the rind.

MAKES APPROXIMATELY 20 MARTINIS

## Electronic Entertainments

Television and the high fidelity record player (hi-fi) were *the* electronic home gadgets of the Fifties. Both TV and record players had been around before, but it wasn't until the Fifties that they were as affordable, as high quality, and in the case of television, that there was as many shows to watch. These two items brought about a small revolution in home entertainment—and indeed in home design.

No longer was the dining *room* to be the center of family meals. In its September 1, 1957, issue, *Vogue* gave directions for creating an open-plan living room that contained a dining *area* so that family and guests could eat and watch TV or listen to the hi-fi unimpeded. *Vogue* even gave a series of recipes that could be prepared ahead of time and wouldn't "collapse if they wait around, *in situ*, for the denouement of a television thriller." Now, attention was not focused on the people or the food during dinner, but on the expensive electronic box.

At first a certain prestige attached to having guests over to watch the tube. (In 1957 nine million U.S. families still didn't have a television.) The After-Theater Supper had long been a fashionable late-night gathering for the chic to eat. With the advent of television, the elegant and intellectual could watch one of the new TV drama "playhouses," then discuss the show around the cozy glow of the chafing dish. Here is a menu for just such a night, as suggested by the Sardi's Restaurant cookbook, *Curtain Up at Sardi's* (1957).

◆◆◆

# After-Television Intellectual Supper

*Pâté Maison*
*Lobster Newburg en Chafing Dish*
*Rice Pilaf*
*Sliced Tomatoes with French Dressing*
*Almond Tart*
*Coffee*

Of course, not all TV parties were so highbrow. Football games offered a great way to get the gang together for a food-fest and some fun. But lobster Newburg and pâté were not what the gang wanted to chow down on while they were watching the two-point conversion. After all, the food was secondary while dining with one eye on the screen. *Sunset* magazine (October 1953) came to the hostess's rescue with one of the first TV tray menus. The main-dish casserole, prepared by the hostess, was frozen in individual foil dishes, then popped in the oven a half-hour before kickoff. At serving time, a lap tray for each guest was set with an individual foiled casserole, dip and dippers, bread, and coffee. And before the meal, guests could nibble on TV mix.

♦♦♦

## TV Football Party Menu

*TV Mix* ♦ *Cold Beverages*
*Chicken Noodle Casserole with Potato Chip*
*au Gratin*
*Carrots, Celery, and Radishes with Bleu Cheese Dip*
*Brown 'n' Serve Rolls*
*Ice Cream Pie*
*Coffee*

TV mix, also called party mix, nibblers, and nuts and bolts (the latter was made with pretzels and Cheerios), seems to have been the inspired invention of breakfast cereal manufacturers. This snack mix was the perfect thing to have in bowls around the living room, because a TV watcher could grab a handful without missing a second of the show. Betty Crocker gave an early recipe in her *Picture Cook Book* (1950) that featured Kix cereal baked with garlic salt and butter. In 1952 the Ralston Purina Company's Checkerboard Kitchens came up with their version, which, of course, was made with their Chex line of cereals. But the charm of this snack rested in the different sizes and shapes in the bowl and the most popular recipes included products from a number of different manufacturers.

# TV MIX—NUTS AND BOLTS STYLE

TV Mix usually incorporated those two favorite 1950s flavoring powders, garlic salt and Accent (MSG). With the salt already in the cereals and nuts and the added table salt, this made a very high-sodium snack, but who was counting? A pinch of chili or curry powder may be added to the mix for extra zip.

$^1/_2$ cup (1 stick) butter, melted
$^3/_4$ teaspoon Worcestershire sauce
$^3/_4$ teaspoon salt
$^3/_4$ teaspoon garlic salt
$^1/_2$ teaspoon Accent
$2^3/_4$ cups Cheerios
2 cups Rice Chex
$1^1/_2$ cups pretzel sticks
$^3/_4$ cup salted peanuts

Preheat the oven to 250°F. Mix the melted butter with the seasonings. Mix the cereals, pretzels, and nuts in a large bowl. Pour over the seasoned butter and toss lightly to coat. Spread the cereal mixture in a 15 × 10-inch baking dish. Bake for 2 hours, stirring gently every now and then.

MAKES 7 CUPS

Hi-fi was nearly as important as TV in the Fifties, although its impact on American eating habits was smaller. Music was there to set the mood, to be the background for dining, not the focus. (And, of course, the choice of hi-fi equipment and records showed off the hosts' sophistication quite nicely.) By the late Fifties, albums of "mood music" were popular as stage setters for parties.

In August 1950 *House Beautiful*'s Virginia Stanton suggested a musical dinner around the hi-fi with Eddie Duchin records during the cocktail hour, Fred Waring and Andre Kostelanetz ("with 'Star Dust' included") for the main course, and with coffee, Guy Lombardo and his orchestra. After the coffee, "If your guests wish to sit cozily around the fire and chat, then soft melodious music is in order." But if your guests were feeling madly gay, said Stanton, "more spicy music such as rumbas by Henry King, Jose Cortez, and of course, Xavier Cugat are good, interlarded with a few records of Louis Armstrong."

And if the essence of TV dining was the easy gulp and gobble with one eye on the screen, the essence of hi-fi dining was sophistication.

◆◆◆

# Fifties Sophisticates' Hi-fi Dinner

*Martinis (Clam and Tomato Cocktails for*
*nondrinkers)*
*Celery Stuffed with Cream Cheese and Red Caviar*
*Olives Broiled in Bacon Strips*
*Cheese Straws* ◆ *Salted Nuts*

◆◆◆

*Boeuf Bourguignon*
*Garlic French Bread*

◆◆◆

*Endive and Artichoke Heart Salad*

◆◆◆

*Grilled Pineapple and Apricot Kebabs with*
*Brown Sugar and Butter Sauce*
*Vanilla Ice Cream*
*Coffee*

It is difficult to tell whether Americans in the 1950s really were as optimistic, as full of can-do spirit, as sophisticated (yet so innocent) as they seem to us now from the vantage point of the jaded and dispirited 1990s. But looking back, what comes through across the years is that Americans then were convinced that their way of life was absolutely the most modern, the most desirable, the most sophisticated—*the best*—that the world had ever seen. They also seemed utterly sure that that best would only get better.

In the same way, American cooks in the Fifties seemed convinced that whatever they did in the kitchen—whether concocting a gourmet meal from cans or painstakingly making a fresh boeuf bourguignon—was also the most modern and the best the world had ever seen. They, too, seemed utterly sure that, with just a *few* more tricks to learn from a European chef or two, their best would only get better.

The Sixties would bring plenty of surprises.

# The Sixties

## Nouveaux Gourmets

O.K., Baby. It's Foodsville.

—*Esquire* (May 1963)

I remember how frustrated I felt one day when the chef [at the Cordon Bleu School] was doing poulet à l'estragon, chicken breasts in a creamy tarragon-flavored sauce. It took that skillful man one hour and a dozen pots to make his chicken gravy. I was awed even before I tasted it. And it was good. But as I sampled it, I realized with a jolt that it tasted just like a good canned gravy I'd bought from time to time back home. It's just one ingredient in a complex recipe, I thought, I could use that canned gravy and no one would ever know.

—Esther Riva Solomon, *Instant Haute Cuisine* (1963)

It's not nice to fool Mother Nature.

—Advertisement for margarine (mid-1960s)

The Sixties were the high point of instant food, quick food, space age food. In that age of astronauts and plastic go-go boots it was not only practical to eat instant food, it was chic. Instant food was not what we now call fast food—Twinkies, Tastykakes, and McDonald's were still for kids. But consenting adults ate instant gourmet food because their lives were so fast, so racy, so *modern*. And, after all, even the very chic Kennedys' White House French chef used canned mushroom soup in his beef stroganoff.

For people who had learned in the Forties and Fifties to eat Spam with mustard-currant sauce, instant mashed potatoes, and trifle made with canned fruit cocktail and instant pudding, this instant gourmet food was not only edible, it was sophisticated. *Potage Sénégalese, jambon en croûte, carottes à la poulette, gâteau chocolat au rhum?* Now that's gourmet. It was irrelevant that these dishes were, in order, canned cream of chicken soup with curry powder, canned ham wrapped in frozen pie dough, canned carrots in canned chicken gravy (garnished with canned truffles, to be sure), and devil's food cake made from a mix with a jar of rum sauce. Appearance was all and reality was the cook's own little secret.

## CHICKEN BREASTS WITH TARRAGON, *INSTANT HAUTE CUISINE*

3 chicken breasts, boned, skinned, and cut in half
2 cans chicken broth
1 sprig fresh tarragon
1 (8-ounce) can chicken pâté, minced
1¼ cups canned chicken gravy
1 tablespoon chopped fresh or 1 teaspoon dried tarragon

Poach the chicken breasts in the broth with the tarragon sprig at a low simmer until tender and done. Remove the chicken. Cut a pocket in each breast and insert 1 tablespoon of the pâté. Heat the gravy. Add the chopped tarragon and the stuffed breasts. Heat just until the breasts are hot. Serve at once.

MAKES 6 SERVINGS

We Americans were rich, enthusiastic, and very sure of our ourselves in the Sixties. In a January 11, 1966, article, "Is the American Woman the World's Best Cook?" *Look* said, "...she may be naive enough to think that she is as good as that chef at the Ritz. But isn't it positive thinking that counts?"

Many disagreed. Food writer and gourmet Joseph Wechsberg complained in the October 1961 *Esquire* that, "The same people who wouldn't dream of attempting a Chopin concerto after five piano lessons are confident to turn out 'gourmet food' after reading five non-cookbooks." *Newsweek* (July 17, 1961) said, "There is no mystery about the reasons for the poor state of American gastronomy. The principal villain is the refrigerator-freezer." (The magazine also blamed the dieting fad, the working woman, and the high cost of labor for the bad food we were eating.) In the October 3, 1964, *Saturday Evening Post*, writer John MacPhee said he burned all the "junk cookbooks" he could find—and used the heat from their fire to make a fresh pot-au-feu. He also suggested that some cookbook writers used so much canned food that they obviously were practicing for life in a bomb shelter.

John MacPhee had plenty of choices for his fireplace. In the early Sixties, the United States was rife with new cookbooks, many of them in the hurry-up vein, and they were selling like hotcakes. Among them were *What Cooks in*

## Food for a Nuclear Winter

Not all the instant food being served up carried fancy French names. This "party-pretty dessert" could be made ahead (weeks probably) to save "hostessing time," according to the *Better Homes and Gardens Guide to Entertaining* (1969).

## BOMB SHELTER CHOCOLATE-CHERRY DELIGHT CAKE

1 (18¼-ounce) package devil's food cake mix
1 (20-ounce) can cherry pie filling, undrained
1 (3.9-ounce) package instant chocolate pudding mix
2 tablespoons unsweetened cocoa powder
1 package dessert topping mix (or use Cool Whip), enough to make 2 cups
    whipped topping
Maraschino cherries for garnish

Prepare and bake two 8- or 9-inch layers from the cake mix according to the package directions; cool. Whirl the pie filling in a blender for a few seconds, just until the cherries are chopped. Stir the pudding mix and cocoa into the pie filling. Prepare the dessert topping according to the package directions; fold into the cherry mixture. Spread about ½ cup of the cherry mixture on the bottom cake layer; top with the second layer. Spread the rest of the cherry mixture on the top and sides of the cake. Garnish with maraschino cherries. Chill until serving time.

MAKES 1 CAKE

*Suburbia* (with a recipe for tuna tetrazzini); *The Instant Epicure* (with lobster Landeck—frozen lobster sauced with chili sauce, mayonnaise, A.1., and tomato paste); *Eating European Abroad and at Home* (baked fillet of sole with shrimp sauce—made from canned cream of shrimp soup); *The Madison Avenue Cookbook* (leek transit Gloria); *Easy Gourmet Cooking* (one man's poisson); *Gourmet Meals for Easy Entertaining* (V-8 aspic); *The Second Chafing Dish Cookbook* (tuna crunch); *Mary Meade's Magic Recipes for the Electric Blender* (blended veal birds—"The birds don't sing but you will"); *365 Ways to Cook Hamburger* (hamburger gumbo); *The Chinese-Kosher Cookbook* (bubuhluh won ton soup); *The Fast Gourmet Cookbook* (chicken moutarde with grapes—made from canned chicken, canned gravy, and canned grapes); and *Cooking from the Pantry Shelf* (beef stroganoff—with canned roast beef, canned gravy, canned mushrooms, and instant minced onions).

The supermarkets, too, were filling up with items for the nouveau gourmet. In 1964 Safeway opened its first "international" supermarket, although it emphasized that it catered to the average American who had been abroad, not to gourmets. "You say 'gourmet' and people think of some kind of kook or oddball," said a Safeway spokeswoman. "We don't carry chocolate-covered ants or fried grasshoppers." But they did sell canned kangaroo steaks ($3.75), and heat-and-serve halibut à la Parisienne ($0.59 for a four-ounce serving).

Perhaps Nika Hazelton summed up the new gour-mania best when she said in a February 1, 1966, *National Review* article:

> Americans may be taking an increasing interest in their vittles, but it strikes me that this interest, in spite of all the huffing and puffing, is largely theoretical because, at the same time, the standard of the food, of the cookbooks and of the restaurants, has deteriorated beyond belief.... What our nouveaux gourmets apparently don't know or don't care about is that the secret of good food is its utter freshness, both as a produce and in cooking.

# The Flaming Feast—In Which Cooking Goes to Blazes

Liqueur in (and after) the food was a serious gourmet item in the Sixties, and putting on a fancy show one of the prerequisites for being considered a culinary sophisticate. Combine these two notions and what do you get? Flambéed food, one of the hottest trends in nouveau gourmet cooking.

The realization that virtually anything *could* be flamed (and thus lent incredible elegance), guaranteed that virtually everything *would* be flamed in that era of exuberant culinary excess. Cocktails were set on fire, meats incinerated, omelets scorched, and every dessert imaginable wreathed in flames. One hostess even figured out a way to set her soups on fire, although she never divulged her secret. About the only things that weren't flamed were salads but, presumably, it wasn't for lack of trying.

No restaurant could be deemed fancy unless it flambéed: The larger the number of flambé trolleys in a restaurant, the larger the check was sure to be. The Pump Room in Chicago was renowned for its luxury, its elegance, its prices ("liable to be mistaken for the annual report of General Motors"), and its flaming

# Joy of Cooking

Smack in the middle of the deluge of gourmet, instant gourmet, and "hate to cook" cookbooks came the 1964 edition of *Joy of Cooking*. By 1969, this bible of basic American cooking had sold more than eight million copies in the twelve revisions it had gone through since it was first written by Irma S. Rombauer in 1931. One story has it that a young bride who had eloped to England sent her family the following telegram: AM MARRIED. ORDER ANNOUNCEMENTS. SEND ME ROMBAUER COOKBOOK AT ONCE.

The phenomenal popularity of *Joy* was partially explained by its encyclopedic nature, with its recipes, tips, and explanations for everything from akee (puréed) to zwieback. Yet other cookbooks, like *The Boston School Cooking Book, The Settlement Cook Book*, and the *Better Homes and Gardens Cook Book,* were nearly as comprehensive. What set Mrs. Rombauer's book apart was her very personal and chatty way of doing things. Here is *Joy* on frog legs:

> Through an experiment with a twitching frog leg, Galvani discovered the electric current that bears his name. Should you prefer keeping your kitchen and your scientific activities separate and distinct, chill the frog legs in advance.

And on breadfruit:

> If ever your fate is that of Robinson Crusoe, remember that you can eat raw any breadfruit that has seeds.

Irma Rombauer was the novice cook's wise and friendly guide, standing at our shoulders like an *in situ* mother or grandmother, teaching us our kitchen letters with concise directions seasoned with amusing anecdotes and family lore. It might have been Rombauer family lore, but we were all made to feel like her welcome children.

As American cooks gained in knowledge, they went on from *Joy* to learn more sophisticated kitchen lore from Julia Child, Elizabeth David, Robert Carrier, and Richard Olney. But *Joy* still had an honored place on their shelves, and was constantly turned to for reliable information on everything from skinning a squirrel to making almond milk to concocting a soufflé. Said one 1960s review, the "recipes are safe, true and occasionally outstanding. Even highly sophisticated cooks value some of them."

Irma S. Rombauer died in October 1962 (the 1964 edition of *Joy* was revised by her daughter, Marion Rombauer Becker). *Time* said in her obituary that she left behind "two children, two grandchildren and legions of cooks to whom her book was—and is—the kitchen bible."

food—usually served up on swords. Owner Ernest Byfield was quoted as saying, "We serve almost anything flambé in that room. It doesn't hurt the food much." According to John Mariani in *America Eats Out* (1991), one group of Pump Room diners was served hot dogs on flaming swords and another twelve, ripe olives on individual swords brought in by twelve waiters.

There were a few who had a jaundiced eye for all the flaming display going on. Food writer and gourmet Roy Andries de Groot applied what he called his "fire-and-ice test" to judging restaurants. If they had too much of either, in the form of fleets of wagons bearing flambé equipment or miniature icebergs, he assumed that the service and the prices would be fancy...and the food bad. In *Esquire* (January 1969) he described a trip to the Pump Room in the late Sixties:

> At the table to the left, a dish of Crabs Casanova was blazing mightily. To the right, a roast guinea hen was afire from stem to stern. In front, a burnt offering of Crêpes Suzette. Behind, bacon-wrapped oysters glowing on a sword. And in all directions, flaming cups of Café Diable. The captain now approached, bowing as if he were trying to kiss my feet. In his tailcoat of midnight blue, I mistook him, at first glance, for the Earl of Snowdon.... Almost kneeling, they begged me to begin with the Grande Spécialité de la Maison: a salad of hearts of palm, Chinese water chestnuts, capers and bananas, with an Oriental Spice Dressing. My order taken, the captain and his escort backed off, bowing at each retreating step. As they neared a table engulfed in sheets of flame, I feared that they would all be incinerated.

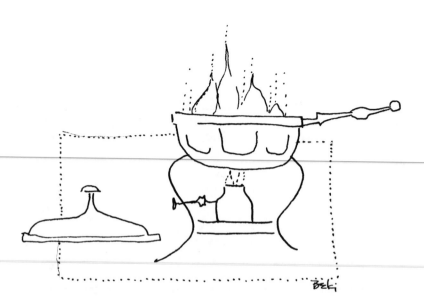

But for most people, flames were an exciting yet fairly easy way to turn everyday fare into a feast for the connoisseur. Some of the most popular flamed foods were cherries jubilee (the *Pyromaniac's Cookbook* [1968] listed eight different recipes), crêpes suzette (Poppy Cannon flamed canned crêpes), café brûlot, steak Diane, coq au vin, and bananas Foster. But as was pointed out earlier, there was no reason to stop there.

**Note:** To ensure safety when flambéing, always be sure that long hair, floppy sleeves, etc., are out of the way. Use a long match to ignite the liquor, and avert your face. When ladling flaming sauces over something else, use a long-handled heatproof spoon or ladle, again making sure that anything flammable—like hair, sleeves, or paper towels—is out of the way. And it's a good idea to have a fire extinguisher or at least a box of baking soda handy to control any accidents.

## BAKED BEANS AU GLOW-GLOW

Why anyone would want to flame something as pedestrian and homey as baked beans is beyond me, but John J. Poister thought it gave the beans a tinge of glamour. Perhaps they could be served as an accompaniment to flaming hot dogs en brochette à la Pump Room. And the rum does add a certain something.

> 4 cups canned baked beans
> 1/4 cup molasses
> 1/4 cup ketchup
> 1 tablespoon yellow table mustard
> 4 slices bacon, cut in half
> 1/2 cup dark rum

Preheat the oven to 350°F. Combine all the ingredients except bacon and rum in a large ovenproof casserole. Cover the beans with the bacon slices and bake until the bacon is done, about 2 hours. Warm the rum in a small saucepan, ignite the rum, and spoon it over the hot beans.

MAKES 4 TO 6 SERVINGS

◆◆◆

## LOBSTER IN PINEAPPLE BOATS FLAMBÉ

This is an archetypal Sixties recipe, all fancy fillips combined in one awful—but expensive—dish. It is from *Conversation-Piece Recipes*, an amazing cookbook, filled with plenty of flaming dishes, and recipes for elegant things like tasty tato puffs and crème de menthe en gelée aux fruits. If you want to amaze your friends (I didn't say delight), try serving this at your next dinner party.

> 2 pineapples, cored, halved, and diced, shells intact
> 1 cup sweet white wine
> 2 tablespoons butter
> 2 cups diced cooked lobster meat
> 2 tablespoons minced green onion
> $1/4$ cup sherry
> 1 cup condensed cream of mushroom soup
> 1 teaspoon dry mustard
> 1 cup hollandaise sauce (canned is fine)
> Truffles, thinly sliced, for garnish (canned, please)
> $1/2$ cup white rum, warmed

Preheat the broiler. Put the pineapple dice and wine in a saucepan and cook over low heat for about 5 minutes. Melt the butter in a large skillet, then sauté the lobster meat in it until hot. Add the onion, sherry, mushroom soup, and mustard, stirring and cooking over low heat until the mixture is smooth. Add the hot pineapple. Pile the pineapple-lobster mixture into the pineapple shells and spoon the hollandaise over the top. Broil until golden brown and bubbly, 3 to 5 minutes. Garnish with truffle slices. Ignite the rum and ladle, flaming, over each pineapple boat (this should be done at the table in front of the eager guests).

MAKES 4 SERVINGS

## FLAMING BLUE ICEBERG

This is another conversation-piece recipe, all flash and no substance, but lots of fun. And it utterly fails Mr. de Groots's fire-and-ice test.

Water and blue food coloring
Deep metal mixing bowl
1 empty juice can (cut to the same depth as the mixing bowl)
Various fruits: preserved kumquats, preserved cherries, fresh pineapple chunks,
    fresh strawberries, melon chunks, etc.
Colored cocktail picks
Wreath of vines for garnish
$1/4$ cup white rum
$1/4$ cup blue curaçao

The day before the party, fill 3 ice cube trays with water tinted light blue with a few drops of food coloring. When the cubes are frozen, crush them fine and pack the crushed ice into a deep metal mixing bowl. Place the empty juice can in the middle of the bowl so that the open end is down and the bottom is flush with the ice. Place the bowl in the freezer until the "iceberg" is firm. At serving time unmold the iceberg onto a large crystal or silver platter. Garnish the iceberg with a wreath of vines. Spear the fruits on colored toothpicks and insert the picks all around the iceberg. Combine the liqueurs, warm them slightly, and pour into the empty juice can. "Light with a match and serve to your enchanted guests."

MAKES 1 ICEBERG

# The French Chef and Really, Truly From-Scratch Gourmet Cooking

Into the exuberant Sixties cooking revival galloped one of the most exuberant cooks Americans had ever seen: Julia Child. American cooks, and many non-cooks, welcomed her appearance on the culinary scene with open arms. (The British public, however, complained about that "mad, drunken American woman" on their television screens.) American cooking was never the same.

Fashionable
Food

*Julia Child*

In 1961 Julia Child, along with Simone Beck and Louisette Bertholle, published *Mastering the Art of French Cooking*, which by 1964 had sold more than one hundred thousand copies at $10 each. But even more than Mrs. Child's first and extensive cookbook, her televised cooking show turned this six-foot galloping gourmet into a runaway success. Beginning in 1962 at Cambridge, Massachusetts, public station WGBH, *The French Chef* was soon broadcast on more than sixty educational channels.

At first some viewers assumed that Julia, as she would soon fondly be known, was parodying the traditional cooking show. But even when they realized the show was entirely serious, viewers watched her shenanigans with enthusiasm. Mrs. Child huffed, puffed, and galumphed across the screen, her high-pitched voice cracking like an adolescent schoolboy's, and she was famous for dropping things and demonstrating cuts of meat using her own body. All of this enchanted viewers and assured them that if this seemingly average American woman could cook French food, then so could they.

Her recipes were thorough (her recipe for French bread ran to twelve pages), and virtually foolproof. If they tended to be rich with butter, cream, and eggs, they were also made using ingredients available in the average American supermarket. She didn't go in for showy gewgaws in her cooking, but stuck to basic and relatively simple classic French cooking.

And because of Julia Child's popularity, cooking schools and cooking equipment stores blossomed almost overnight. Fish poachers, charlotte molds, chefs' knives, and copper beating bowls became best-sellers. Wire whisks sold out in Pittsburgh after one of her shows. A butcher who usually sold seven geese a year reported selling sixty-five after Julia cooked a goose on television. Everyone seemed to be in the kitchen with Julia in the Sixties.

Some naysayers sniffed that Mrs. Child's training was scanty (she didn't start cooking until after her marriage to Paul Child in her thirties), that her technique was sloppy to nonexistent, and that she relied entirely too much on flour to thicken her sauces. But for the majority of American cooks, Julia Child was a wonder, and the food she cooked a revelation. Unlike that other Cordon Bleu alumna Esther Riva Solomon, Mrs. Child didn't think she could slip canned chicken gravy past her unsuspecting guests. And if her velouté sauce was thickened with flour, it was still made from fresh ingredients—and not from a can of Campbell's.

Some of her favorite dishes became America's favorite dishes, too. Chocolate mousse, Grand Marnier soufflé, coq au vin, and boeuf bourguignon, all became standard dinner party fare, thanks in great part to Mrs. Child.

Veal Orloff was another dish that Child prepared on *The French Chef* television show (the eightieth). It was developed by French chef Urbain Dubois while he was in the service of the Russian Prince Orloff in the 1800s. Veal Orloff was elegant, delicious, rich, expensive, and time-consuming to prepare, which made it just right as an impressive entrée, but, said Julia Child, "It makes a perfect party dish as all but the final browning in the oven may be readied in advance."

## VEAL ORLOFF

Julia Child baked her veal roast but here it is braised. For real budget-busting show-off cookery, the slices of veal may be layered with pâté de foie gras and truffles along with the mushroom-onion stuffing. Veal Orloff should be the centerpiece of an otherwise simple and uncomplicated meal. A first course of buttered asparagus tips and artichoke hearts, an accompaniment of tiny carrots and potatoes, a salad of young, tender lettuce leaves, and a dessert of fresh strawberries in orange liqueur would cut the delicious richness of the veal.

**For the Veal**
1/4 cup (1/2 stick) butter
2 slices bacon, blanched in boiling water for 3 minutes
Veal bones
1 (4-pound) boneless loin of veal, tied (ask the butcher to do this)
1 carrot, sliced
1 small onion, sliced
1/2 teaspoon salt
3 cups water
1 bouquet garni, consisting of 2 celery stalks, 1 bay leaf, 4 parsley sprigs, and
    2 thyme sprigs

**For the Stuffing**
5 tablespoons butter
3 cups chopped onions
1/2 cup veal cooking liquid
2 cups chopped mushrooms
2 tablespoons flour
1/2 teaspoon salt
1 cup heavy cream
Few grinds of black pepper
Pinch of freshly grated nutmeg

**For the Masking Sauce and Assembling the Orloff**
1 cup thick béchamel made with heavy cream and the veal braising liquid
2 tablespoons butter, melted
¹/₂ cup grated Parmesan cheese

To make the veal, melt the butter in a large, heavy casserole. Brown the bacon in the butter, add the veal bones, and then add the veal, browning it on all sides. As you turn the veal to brown the last side, add the vegetables, stirring them around in the fat. Do not let them get too brown; they should only cook a little. Add the salt, water, and bouquet garni. Cover the pot and simmer over low heat—the water should just bubble occasionally—until the meat juices run clear with no trace of pink, about 1 hour and 20 minutes. Remove the veal to a large platter and cover loosely with aluminum foil. Strain the cooking liquid and degrease it.

To make the stuffing, melt 3 tablespoons of the butter in a medium skillet and sauté the onions in it over medium heat until soft. Add the veal liquid and bring it to a boil. Reduce heat to low, cover the pan, and let the onions cook until they are almost dissolved, 20 to 25 minutes. In the meantime, melt the remaining butter in another medium skillet and sauté the mushrooms over medium heat until they have given up their moisture. Stir the flour and salt into the mushrooms and let them cook about 10 minutes. Stir half the onions into the mushrooms, add the cream, bring to a simmer, and cook until the sauce has reduced by about half and is thick enough to stay put when spread on the veal. Stir in the pepper and nutmeg. Taste for seasoning and correct.

Preheat the oven to 350°F. Combine the béchamel and remaining onions and purée in a food mill or blender. The sauce should be thick enough to coat a spoon. If too thick, thin with cream. If too thin, cook down. Taste for seasoning and correct.

Remove the ties from the veal roast and slice it like a loaf of bread into serving pieces about ³/₈ inch thick. Butter an ovenproof serving platter. Lay the first slice of veal at the end of the platter and spread with the stuffing. Lap the next piece of veal over the first and spread with stuffing. Continue layering veal and stuffing, finishing with a layer of meat, adjusting the layers so that they form an attractive shape on the platter. Spoon the sauce over the veal, pour the melted butter over the top, and sprinkle with the cheese. (The veal Orloff may be refrigerated at this point.) Put the veal into the upper third of the hot oven until the sauce is bubbling hot and the top is browned, about 30 minutes.

MAKES 6 TO 8 SERVINGS

# If Dave Brubeck Is On the Hi-fi
# We Must Be Having a Dinner Party—
# Entertaining, Sixties-Style

| **Serve One** | **Serve All Three** | **Serve One** |
| --- | --- | --- |
| Beef Wellington | Tomato Aspic | Cherries Jubilee |
| Duckling à l'Orange | Green Beans Amandine | Grand Marnier Soufflé |
| Coq au Vin | Wild Rice with Canned Mushrooms | Chocolate Mousse |
| Steak au Poivre | | |
| Veal Orloff | | |
| Chicken Kiev | | |

Earnest gourmets, whisks and copper bowls in hand, painstakingly prepared their (mostly) French entrées and desserts. But when it came to the side dishes, they faltered. The three vegetable accompaniments listed above, while they might not have been included in any of Julia Child's meals, showed up at nearly every dinner party in America in the early Sixties. Tomato aspic (p. 186), still going strong from the Fifties, seemed an essential adjunct to any "serious" meal, as did that gourmet item, wild rice, usually served tossed with canned "broiled-in-butter" mushrooms. Green beans amandine was another standby.

## GREEN BEANS AMANDINE

Almonds were a gourmet cliché in the Sixties and appeared as a garnish on everything from soup to...dessert. For an authentic period touch, use frozen green beans. For good taste, use fresh.

3 cups green beans, snapped and any strings removed
2 tablespoons butter
1/2 cup sliced almonds

Cook the green beans in boiling salted water until tender, but still slightly crisp. Drain. Melt the butter in a medium skillet, add the almonds, and toast them slightly over low heat, being careful they don't burn. Add the beans to the hot butter and almonds and toss them to coat. Serve in a hot dish.

MAKES 6 SERVINGS

# Betty Crocker's Extra-Special Dinner Party Starring Beef Wellington

Here is a menu that very clearly stars a spectacular entree. Dramatic, delicious Beef Wellington demands all the cook's time and talent, so everything that goes with it is as super-simplified as planning and convenience foods can make it. A smart hostessing trick!… This stunning main dish is accompanied by canned and frozen vegetables chosen to ease the preparation and to color complement the meat. The quick-mix dessert is glamorously garnished and can be served flaming, if you like.

—*Betty Crocker's Hostess Cookbook* (1967)

*Canned Beef Consommé and Tomato Juice*

*Daisys™ (a General Mills snack cracker)*

*Tenderloin of Beef Wellington*
*Canned Potatoes Parmesan*
*Frozen Carrot Nuggets with Brown Sugar*
*Frozen Green Peas and Onions with Butter Sauce*

*Spinach-Apple Salad with Mayonnaise-Frozen Orange Juice Dressing*

*Lemon Cake with Lemon Frosting (from mixes),*
*Garnished with Chopped Green Grapes and Pistachios*
*(optional flaming sugar cubes atop)*

# Beef Wellington—The Stunning Main Dish

Beef Wellington was the premier party dish of the 1960s. Even more than coq au vin, veal Orloff, beef stroganoff, steak Diane, steak au poivre, or duckling à l'orange, it was rich, dramatic, expensive, and seemed difficult and time-consuming to prepare. In short, it was everything a gourmet dish should be.

In *Masters of American Cookery*, Betty Fussell credited beef Wellington's phenomenal popularity in the Sixties to "the discovery that anybody, with a little care, could make an edible crust." Given the fact that the dish has virtually sunk without a trace—try finding a recipe for it in a contemporary cookbook—beef Wellington's appeal for Americans seems to have been just about pure food snobbery.

Exactly who invented beef Wellington is not known, but there is a long Anglo-Irish-French tradition of meat cooked in pastry. Undoubtedly what we in the United States call beef Wellington is based on the Wellington steak of England and the *steig* Wellington of Ireland. Said to have been a favorite of the duke of Wellington, the Anglo-Irish version consists of a two- to six-pound fillet sautéed rare, wrapped in puff pastry, and then baked. Sometimes mushrooms or pâté are laid over the fillet before it is wrapped in its pastry blanket. In France the dish is known as filet de boeuf en croûte, but whether it originated on the west or the east side of the English Channel is unknown.

*Vogue* (September 15, 1954) published one of the first post–World War II recipes for beef Wellington, although they used the French title filet de boeuf en croûte. Exactly why it was called filet de boeuf is unclear as ground top round was substituted for the expensive filet. However, the writer assured us that the ground beef could be sliced "in the same way as the *filet*, and closely approximates its flavour and texture." In addition to the ground beef, *Vogue*'s 1954 version called for pie crust mix, bacon to be baked with the beef (the bacon could "be used later in a sandwich for lunch"), and canned pâté, all sauced with undiluted canned cream of mushroom soup mixed with ketchup. To quote the magazine again, "a memorable and delicious meal can be produced with a minimum of time and expense, and with only a basic knowledge of cooking."

## BEEF WELLINGTON WITH MADEIRA SAUCE

"Time-consuming and budget-wrecking but worth it," according to Marian Tracy in *Parties from the Freezer* (1962). The key to a rare roast and pastry that is not too soggy is to cool the beef after its initial roasting and to chill the pastry-wrapped beef before its final baking.

1 (3½- to 4-pound) beef tenderloin
2 tablespoons butter
½ pound mushrooms, minced
Salt and pepper
5 ounces pâté de foie gras, at room temperature
1¼ pounds frozen puff pastry, thawed, or enough pie pastry for
     3 one-crust pies
1 large egg white, lightly beaten
1 large egg yolk mixed with 1 teaspoon water
Madeira Sauce (below)

Preheat the oven to 425°F. On a rack in a roasting pan, roast the beef until the meat thermometer reaches 120°F, about 30 minutes. Cool the meat completely. Degrease and reserve the pan drippings.

Melt the butter in a large skillet, then sauté the mushrooms over low heat until they absorb all the liquid they give off. Season to taste with salt and pepper, then cool. Mash the foie gras into the mushrooms.

Roll out the pastry to make a rectangle about 14 × 12 inches, or enough to completely wrap the beef. Cover the center of the pastry with one third of the mushroom mixture. Place the roast on the center of the pastry. Coat the top of the beef with the rest of the mushroom mixture.

Fold up the long sides of the pastry to cover the beef, sealing the edges with the beaten egg white. Fold up the ends of the dough, brush with the egg white, and seal. Place on a greased baking pan, seam side down. Roll out the excess pastry and make cutouts—rosettes, leaves, etc. Brush the wrapped beef with some of the egg yolk wash. Decorate with the pastry cutouts and brush the cutouts with the wash. Cover and refrigerate the roast for 1 hour.

Preheat the oven to 400°F. Bake the fillet until a meat thermometer registers 130°F, about 40 minutes. Let the fillet stand 20 minutes while you make the Madeira Sauce. Cut into ¾-inch slices and serve with a spoonful of sauce on each portion.

## MADEIRA SAUCE

This is not a true *sauce Périgueux*, the classic French accompaniment to beef Wellington, in that a starch-thickened beef broth (*jus lié*) is used rather than brown sauce. For those of you willing to go the extra mile in an already lengthy recipe, by all means substitute classic French brown sauce (to be found in any basic French cookbook) for the beef broth and cornstarch. When making a cornstarch-thickened sauce, remember not to stir too vigorously or the thickening power of the starch may break down.

1 tablespoon cornstarch dissolved in 1 tablespoon cold water
Reserved pan juices from the roast
1/2 cup Madeira wine
1 1/2 cups beef broth
2 tablespoons finely chopped black truffles
Salt and pepper to taste

In a saucepan stir the cornstarch mixture into the pan juices, then stir in the wine and beef broth. Bring the mixture to a boil, then lower the heat to a simmer, stirring occasionally until the sauce has thickened. Stir in the truffles, then simmer another 10 minutes, stirring occasionally. Taste and correct the seasonings.

MAKES 8 TO 10 SERVINGS

## The Beef Wellington Era

One of the first American recipes for beef Wellington as beef Wellington appeared in 1957 in *The Gourmet Cookbook, Vol. II*. But après *Gourmet*, the flood. While the Kennedys dined on classic beef Wellington prepared by White House chef René Verdon, elegant and expensive restaurants in New York served their own versions (stuffed with chopped veal, ham, and chicken at the Colony; with minced sweet-breads, veal, and mushrooms at Pierre's). Ethnic restaurants put beef Wellington on their menus right next to the prosciutto or feijoada. Some Greek restaurants even dubbed their lamb baked in phyllo pastry "beef Wellington, Greek style." By the mid-1960s recipes for the dish were appearing in magazines ranging from *Esquire* to *Farm Journal. Gourmet* magazine proclaimed it the "beef Wellington era."

Even advertisers used beef Wellington as an indicator of their elegance: "In the mood for gourmet beef?" asked American Express in an ad that listed restaurants serving beef Wellington (and accepted American Express cards, naturally). Pepperidge Farm asked, "When is a Pepperidge Farm Patty Shell not a patty shell? When it's Beef Wellington." And Italian Line cruises showed a satisfied customer saying "I asked for a Beef Wellington. It wasn't on the menu, but I got it. Marvelous."

Did beef Wellington taste good? There was—and is—considerable debate. *New York Times* writer Marian Burros came to the conclusion that, whatever the recipe, it was not possible to produce both rare beef and flaky pastry. (That was in the Eighties. In the Sixties, it seems, Ms. Burros was serving beef Wellington with frozen green beans amandine just like everyone else.) Other gourmets and gourmands complained that not only was the beef overdone by the time the pastry had cooked but it developed a steamed taste inside its cloak. It has even been suggested that the dish was named Wellington not because it was the duke's favorite dish, but because it resembled the boots he wore. Yet many disagreed. In a September 1978 interview in *Bon Appétit*, Julia Child maintained that while beef Wellington was indeed Out, it could be delicious if prepared properly. And more recently, Jane and Michael Stern waxed rhapsodic about it in *American Gourmet* (1991), calling it "a melt-in-the-mouth, lardaceous dish that is rich beyond reason and the height of sybaritism." And it is still standard dinner party fare in England.

Beef Wellington did not give as much scope to "creative" cooks as many other dishes had. Consequently, even the worst recipes for it were relatively tame, only substituting frozen pie dough, then available in stick form, for good pastry and liverwurst sausage for the pâté de foie gras. But sometimes creativity could be astounding in its starkness.

# HAM WELLINGTON

This recipe appeared in a gas company booklet in the mid-Sixties.

I stick pie crust
I (1½-pound) canned ham
I large egg yolk, beaten

Preheat the oven to 425°F. Prepare the pastry for a 1-crust pie and roll it into a 12 × 8-inch rectangle. Place the ham in the center; overlap the pastry ends to cover the ham. Moisten the seam and ends with water; seal securely. Place the ham seam side down in the pan; brush with the egg yolk. Bake until browned, about 30 minutes.

MAKES 6 TO 8 SERVINGS

# Grand Grand Marnier

Grand Marnier soufflé was probably about the most elegant and gourmet dessert that could be served in the Sixties, even surpassing chocolate mousse. A soufflé seemed trickier and more French than a mousse—and Grand Marnier was chic, chic, chic, both in and out of food.

But not all Grand Marnier desserts were soufflés. That golden liqueur lent its silky, orange flavor to any number of sweet concoctions, including this cake.

## GRAND MARNIER TORTE

Writer and cooking school owner Libby Hillman, whose recipe this is, liked the torte so much that it appeared in her first book, *Lessons in Gourmet Cooking* (1963), and in her most recent book, *The Best From Libby Hillman's Kitchen* (1993).

I cup (2 sticks) unsalted butter
1¼ cups sugar
4 eggs
I cup cornstarch, sifted
I cup all-purpose flour, sifted
I teaspoon baking powder
2 teaspoons vanilla extract
2 tablespoons Grand Marnier
Grated rind of I orange (without the white pith)
Grand Marnier Chocolate Sauce (below)
Candied orange peel for garnish, optional

Preheat the oven to 375°F. Grease a 1½-quart turk's-head mold or kugel-hopf pan. Cream the butter and sugar together until light and fluffy, about 10 minutes. Beat in 1 of the eggs. Add half of the cornstarch and blend well. Beat in the second egg. Add half of the flour and blend well. Beat in the third egg. Add the rest of the cornstarch and blend well. Beat in the fourth egg. Add the rest of the flour mixed with the baking powder. Blend well. Stir in the flavorings. Bake until a cake tester inserted into the center of the cake comes out clean and the cake is starting to pull away from the sides of the pan, 40 to 50 minutes. Cool in the pan. Remove from the pan and dust with confectioners' sugar or drizzle with the Grand Marnier Chocolate Sauce. Strips of candied orange peel would be festive scattered over the chocolate sauce.

### GRAND MARNIER CHOCOLATE SAUCE

> 4 ounces semisweet chocolate
> 3 tablespoons light cream or half-and-half
> 1 teaspoon Grand Marnier

Melt the chocolate in the cream over low heat, stirring until smooth. Remove from the heat and stir in the Grand Marnier. Drizzle the sauce over the cooled cake.

Makes 1 cake

# Fondue—Gourmet Fun in a Space Capsule

Want to entertain in a way that is different, fun, and amazingly easy to do? Borrow from the Swiss and have a Fondue Party. The novelty of cooking at the table turns it into the evening's entertainment as well.
—*Better Homes and Gardens* (November 1965)

In the early Sixties, Americans were enamored of international gourmet cooking, of casual but chic entertaining, of foods dipped or dunked, and of the Space Age. And nothing fit that gastronomic bill quite as well as Swiss fondue.

Foreign, sophisticated, easy, and fun, fondue was served in a gleaming pot, which in its streamlined beauty bristling with long-handled dipping forks resembled nothing so much as the space-age satellites circling Earth's atmosphere. It was the perfect dish of a snowy evening for young moderns to serve by the chalet fire après-ski, or for sophisticates with glittering penthouse city views to serve après-theater.

The word *fondue* itself is from the French verb *fondre* ("to melt"); hence cheese melted in wine. The thrifty Swiss mountain folk who invented fondue as a way to use up their hard cheese and stale bread would have been astounded at the glamour invested in their simple dish.

There are as many "classic" cheese fondue recipes as there are Swiss cantons. The cheese to be melted can be Emmentaler, Gruyère, Beaufort, Comte, or Fribourg or a mixture thereof, and it can be grated or sliced. Some recipes use a stabilizer such as cornstarch, flour, potato starch, or grated potato to thicken the melted cheese, while others use none. Most recipes direct that the cheese be melted in a dry white wine, but fondue Fribourgeoise uses only a little hot water and no wine. Kirsch is frequently added to the melted cheese, but in some recipes the kirsch is withheld and bread cubes are dipped in the liqueur before being swirled in the fondue. And finally, some fondues are flavored with a garlic clove, others with pepper or nutmeg. Given all the variations possible, here is a "classic" cheese fondue for two.

## CHEESE FONDUE VAUDOISE

1 garlic clove, cut
1 tablespoon unsalted butter
2 cups grated Gruyère cheese
1 teaspoon flour
⅓ cup dry white wine
Pepper, salt, or ground nutmeg
1 jigger kirsch
French bread

Rub the saucepan interior with the garlic and butter. Toss the cheese with the flour. Place the saucepan over low heat, then add the cheese and wine. Mix well with a fork while the cheese melts. Add the seasonings, and at the moment of serving, the kirsch. The mixture should be light with a creamy consistency. Serve with chunks of French bread, with a section of crust on each chunk, for dipping.

MAKES 2 SERVINGS

Cheese fondue can be made, or kept hot, in a fondue pot or chafing dish. To serve, each diner spears a piece of good bread through the crust and dips the bread in the melted cheese. Because each diner shares responsibility for keeping the fondue au point, everyone is urged to swirl the bread in a figure-eight pattern through the cheese mixture (simply dunking the bread or stirring it through the cheese is incorrect form). The cheesy crust that forms on the bottom of the pot is considered a delicacy, although some cynics claim the notion is just an easy way for the hostess to get the pot cleaned. Cold drinks, including wine, are not to be drunk with fondue (Swiss old wives say it makes the cheese hard to digest), but kirsch or hot tea is acceptable. Finally, tradition has it that any man who loses his bread in the cheese must buy drinks for all the diners, while a woman who loses her dipper must kiss her neighbors on the left and right.

Many other dishes have gone and still do go by the name of fondue, most of them not at all like the classic Swiss version except that they involve melted cheese. A common recipe found in most American cookbooks before the 1950s was basically a rich, savory pudding of buttered bread, cheese, milk, and eggs. And in classic French cooking the name *fondue* is given to a preparation of vegetables such as tomatoes, onions, and celery that have been cooked to a pulp—or melted—over very low heat, usually in butter.

The fondue that took America by storm in the late 1950s and 1960s was the classic Swiss cheese fondue. Although Swiss fondue was written about in popular magazines as early as the 1920s in America, its very informality made it strictly a family supper affair. One January 1939 *House & Garden* article called it delicious for "those who wish to experiment in regional cooking." But they noted archly, "We are afraid this is not a *party* dish." After World War II, when only the wealthiest homes had "help" and formal, seven-course, sit-down dinners had pretty much gone the way of the dodo bird, the American hostess decided that fondue was just the easy, but glamorous, dish to entertain her dazzled guests.

Americans, of course, couldn't leave such a simple dish alone. The first aspect to be tinkered with was the speed and ease of preparation. Although fondue is a quickly made dish, for the incautious or inexperienced cook, overheated cheese *will* get stringy and rubbery. That tireless short-cut artist Poppy Cannon came to the rescue in *The Can-Opener Cook Book* (1952) with directions for a fondue "without fuss" using processed Swiss cheese. By the Sixties, cooks could even do without Mrs. Cannon's little foil-wrapped squares of processed cheese and buy premade fondue in cans or packets. At least nine different brands were on the market by the end of the decade.

But fondues made with processed Gruyère or a package of mix were still basically mixtures of cheese and wine with seasonings. Creative cooks couldn't resist the urge to fancy things up. In the 1960s, the logical and American thing to do was to dispense with the wine and substitute milk and soup base—canned, frozen, or dried. One recipe contributed by V. R. Atherton of California to the February 1962 issue of *Sunset* combined two cans of shrimp soup with one cup of milk and four cups of shredded Swiss cheese. This could be served as a dip for chunks of bread, raw vegetables, or cooked shrimp. For those who found dipping too messy and earthy, the shrimp-cheese sauce could be served, sprinkled with paprika, over rice, toast, or English muffins.

With as much fun as everyone was having around the fondue pot, fondue mania could not be confined to even nominally cheese-flavored hot dips. When in 1956 Konrad Egli, the chef-owner of New York's Chalet Suisse restaurant, who had done much to popularize cheese fondue, introduced fondue bourguignonne, it was an overnight sensation. Soon every restaurant worth its salt—and every hostess—was serving cubes of raw beef to be dunked in boiling oil by enthralled guests. A mid-Sixties *Glamour* cookbook suggested a "Gourmet Gangfest Buffet XI" centered around fondue sans fromage (beef fondue).

While fondue bourguignonne is not a true fondue—in that nothing is melted—it obviously fits the fondue mold.

## BASIC FONDUE BOURGUIGNONNE

In November 1965 *Better Homes and Gardens* said, "Go Elegant with Beef Fondue...and every guest becomes an epicure! It's fun to spear a cube of beef tenderloin with a fondue fork, and hold it in bubbling cooking oil till it's nicely browned on the outside, done just to your taste. (Doesn't take long!)" The only quarrel among cooks in the preparation of this simplest of dishes is whether the cooking medium should be oil, which allows the flavor of the meat to shine through, or clarified butter, which adds its own delicious flavor. An occasional recipe comes along that uses chunks of chicken or chicken livers, but beef is the flesh of choice. Where the fun comes in is with the dips and condiments meant to accompany the cooked meat.

>Mild vegetable oil or clarified butter
>Bread cubes
>2 pounds best beef tenderloin, cut into bite-size cubes

Fill a metal fondue pot with the oil or butter to a depth of 1½ inches and heat on the stove until it will brown a bread cube in 1 minute. Put the pot on a fondue stand and light the fuel burner. Each guest spears cubes of meat with a long-handled fork and cooks them in the hot oil to his or her taste. Serve a variety of well-seasoned sauces alongside for dipping the finished product.

Makes 4 to 6 servings

◆◆◆

---

## Some Suggested Sauces

- Hollandaise sauce
- Béarnaise sauce
- Sour cream–blue cheese sauce
- Sour cream–horseradish sauce
- Anchovy butter
- Garlic butter
- Caper butter
- Mustard sauce
- Sauce rémoulade
- Curried fruit sauce (Betty Crocker)
- Pungent peach sauce (*American Home Magazine*)
- Red pepper relish
- Curried mayonnaise
- Garlic mayonnaise
- Chutney sauce
- Sweet-and-sour sauce
- Barbecue sauce
- Bordelaise sauce

---

If beef tenderloin was too expensive, dollar-conscious revelers might make do with meatballs cooked in oil. One cookbook's prescription for "budget-wise fondue" was to cook teriyaki-flavored meatballs or "jazzy beef bites" (ground beef mixed with ketchup and horseradish rolled around cheddar cubes) fondue-style and then dip them in ketchup, mustard, or mayonnaise mixed with dill pickle. Hold the béarnaise sauce.

Fondue Orientale or Mongolian hot pot also became popular in the late 1950s and early 1960s. Again, Konrad Egli was credited with its popularization. In this variation on fondue bourguignonne the meat (often seafood, chicken, pork, or veal as well as beef) is cooked in a hot broth, rather than in oil. Dipping sauces are provided each diner, but they are frequently soy- or sake-based to emphasize the Oriental aspect of this "fondue." After the meat is served, the broth may be served as a soup or soaked up with bread or rice.

Last of the fondues au courant in the 1960s was chocolate fondue. It was not only popularized by Konrad Egli, it was invented by him in conjunction with the canny folks at Toblerone Chocolate. *Look* called it the "New Hip Dip."

# HIP DIP CHOCOLATE FONDUE

Said *Look* in its February 7, 1967, issue: "Youth '67, get set to flip over a new crowd pleaser: chocolate fondue. What began as a publicity gimmick (to sell more chocolate, what else?) has taken off like a space dish." As a variation, three tablespoons of Kahlúa, brandy, or Cointreau may be stirred in just before serving or the amount of cream may be reduced and ½ cup strong coffee added.

4 (3-ounce) bars Toblerone chocolate with honey and nuts
1 cup heavy cream

Break the chocolate into pieces and place in a heavy saucepan. Add the cream and stir over low heat until the chocolate is melted and the mixture smooth. Transfer to a fondue pot over a medium flame. Do not let the chocolate boil. Serve with marshmallows, squares of pound or sponge cake, ladyfingers, strawberries, chunks of pineapple or banana, etc.

MAKES 4 SERVINGS

Toblerone chocolate was the original chocolate in dessert fondue, but it wasn't long before anything went. Other chocolate candies such as Mounds bars or peanut butter cups could be used, along with plain old chocolate chips. Once the idea of fondue as last course had caught on, cooks were quick to try hot strawberry, lemon, or butterscotch sauces—sans chocolate—as dipping media for chunks of fruit, marshmallows, cakes, or cookies.

By the early 1970s fondue mania had peaked (although newlyweds were still getting multiple fondue pots as wedding gifts in the 1970s). A multitude of cookbooks devoted to fondue in all its permutations had been published. Recipes for Italian cheese fondue (with ground beef, spaghetti sauce mix, mozzarella cheese, and Chianti) and dippity frosting fondue (made with melted margarine, canned chocolate frosting, and miniature marshmallows) explored the outer limits of taste and fashion. Over thirty-seven brands of fondue pots were available in the United States, ranging from Alexander's Department Stores' enamel-aluminum pot with burner and tray, on sale for $3.77, to Copco's porcelain-on-cast iron set with forks, cover, and stand for $52. And the East New York Savings Bank offered a free heavy-gauge aluminum fondue set with enamel finish if you opened a new savings account of $500 or more.

Although fondue faded quickly in the 1970s after its fifteen-year fashionable run, it has recently been rehabilitated as entertaining fare. A few years ago *Bon Appétit* magazine announced the return of the fondue party—with a typical 1990s twist. Their Tex-Mex cheese fondue included Monterey Jack cheese, tequila, and the seasonings of the Nineties: chilies and cilantro.

# A Rare and Excellent Soup

With all the gour-mania going on, there was one small dish that was as fashionable as all get out, yet virtually unknown. That dish was billi-bi, a mussel and cream soup, and it usually could be found only in the poshest big-city restaurants, or in the summer homes of America's oldest and richest families.

Billi-bi was created in France sometime in the early part of this century. But whether it was first made and named at Maxim's for American tycoon William Bateman Leeds, Sr.; at Maxim's for William Brand, another American; or at Ciro's restaurant for that same William Brand, is a matter of debate.

J.F.K.'s French chef served billi-bi at the White House, but he left the mussels in the soup, Normandy fashion. In a true billi-bi the mussels are strained out before serving.

## BILLI-BI

"A fine, high-toned soup. Only the fanciest eaters will know what they're getting," said George Bradshaw and Ruth Norman in *Cook Until Done* (1962). Some recipes thicken the soup at the end with egg yolk. This one doesn't.

18 mussels, well scrubbed and beards removed
$^1/_4$ cup chopped onions
3 tablespoons chopped shallots
1 bay leaf
2 cups dry white wine
Salt, pepper, and dash of cayenne pepper
3 cups heavy cream

Put the mussels, onions, shallots, bay leaf, and wine in a large nonaluminum or non–cast-iron soup kettle. Cover, bring to a boil, then lower the heat and simmer until the mussels have opened, about 10 minutes. Discard any mussels that do not open. Strain the broth through a sieve lined with cheesecloth. Rinse out the kettle and return the broth to the kettle and season with the salt, pepper, and cayenne. Add the cream and bring the soup to a boil. Lower the heat and simmer, uncovered, 2 to 3 minutes. Taste for seasoning and serve. The soup may also be served very cold, with a few grindings of black pepper for garnish.

MAKES 5 TO 6 SERVINGS

# Parties a Go-Go! The International Gourmet

Want to entertain for friends planning far-flung trips? Or give your gourmet club a special treat? Then try these tables with foreign-flair.

—"Parties A Go-Go!" *Better Homes and Gardens* (July 1967)

Although the cooking revolution in the Sixties centered around French cooking, Americans were also eager to learn about the foods from other countries. While anything young and chic was "a go-go" in those days, a foreign-themed party was especially so. "Pick the country—and have a party! You'll like the excitement of these international-style parties, the new taste experiences, the chances for creative table settings," said *Better Homes and Gardens. Today's Health* (February 1962) said, "American Cooking is Going International." And *Parents' Magazine* (October 1968) chimed in with "Foreign Foods aren't Foreign Anymore."

In the late Sixties, Time-Life Books began its influential Foods of the World series. With writers and consultants like Joseph Wechsberg, Nika Standen Hazelton, Waverley Root, M. F. K. Fisher, James Beard, Julia Child, and Michael Field, the books were beautiful enough to grace any coffee table, well and often wittily written, and full of clear and (mostly) accurate recipes for everything from French aioli to Ethiopian zilzil alecha.

One of the most popular of the foreign influences, in both foods and decor, was Spanish Mediterranean. Smart homemakers redecorated their dining rooms with white plaster walls hung with Spanish bullfighting posters, dark beams on the ceiling, and heavy Spanish-style dining tables with matching carved chairs. Smart hostesses served up Spanish dishes like gazpacho and paella, accompanied by a festive pitcher of sangria…with Miles Davis's *Sketches of Spain* album on the stereo, of course.

As a side note, there is a strange and interesting little book that was published in 1960 called *Bull Cook and Authentic Historical Recipes and Practices*, by George Leonard Herter and Berthe E. Herter. The Herters ran a store in Wisconsin, sort of a Midwestern version of L.L. Bean. In their book there are recipes for Swedish muskrat, gazelle escalopes rhazes, and crème de menthe gelatine, directions for "The Only Correct Way to Cut Up Venison," and helpful hints for surviving an atom bomb attack ("stay in a cave for 3 days to avoid radiation fall out"). The Herters emphatically state (although I suspect it was mostly George Leonard talking) that gazpacho was "invented by a poor Andalusia farmer in Spain named Xavier Fernandez in 1861." How they came by this remarkable piece of information is not explained, and I leave it to you to judge its veracity.

Paella was one of Craig Claiborne's most requested recipes from his *New York Times* column in the Sixties. So ubiquitous and fashionable was this Spanish dish that Julia Child included a version in her *French Chef* cookbook.

Gazpacho, that cold and refreshing "salad soup," had gained quite a following in the Fifties and even before. In *With Bold Knife and Fork* (1968), M. F. K. Fisher gave a "freak" recipe for something called "guzpatchee" made with hardtack, mayonnaise, tomatoes, and vegetables, which was popular in military circles in Florida in the late Forties. With the fashionable rise of Spanish food in the Sixties and the fascination with the blender, gazpacho was a sure-fire hit.

## SPLIT-SECOND GOURMET WITH A BLENDER GAZPACHO

"A perfect summer soup, tantalizingly fresh, and faintly perverse as are all primitive dishes eaten by too-worldly people," said M. F. K. Fisher. Many recipes use beef broth as the liquid for this soup, but purists insist on plain water.

 2 pounds ripe tomatoes, peeled and seeded
 1 cup Italian or French bread crumbs
 1 large onion, halved
 2 garlic cloves, peeled
 1 large cucumber, peeled and cut into large chunks
 $1/2$ cup red wine vinegar
 $1/2$ cup olive oil
 2 cups cold water
 $1/2$ teaspoon salt, or to taste
 Freshly ground pepper
 Ice cubes

 **For garnish:**
 $1/2$ cup seeded and chopped green bell pepper
 $1/2$ cup chopped fresh tomatoes
 $1/2$ cup peeled and chopped cucumbers
 $1/2$ cup chopped mild onions
 1 cup French or Italian bread croutons sautéed in olive oil

Put the tomatoes, crumbs, onion, garlic, and cucumber in a blender or food processor and whirl them until smooth. (You may also mash them together in a mortar the old-fashioned way.) Stir in the vinegar, oil, water, salt, and pepper. Cover and refrigerate at least 4 hours. Serve in individual bowls with an ice cube or two in each bowl. Pass separate bowls of the garnishes so that each guest may add them as wished.

MAKES 6 SERVINGS

## JELLIED GAZPACHO

"Along with castles, olives and sherry, Spain has its beloved cold soup, gazpacho, doubly delicious jellied," said a 1962 Knox Gelatine booklet. Gelatin-based foods were still popular in the Sixties. Here, the Home Economists attempted to jump on the International food bandwagon.

I envelope unflavored gelatin
1 1/2 cups water
I bouillon cube
1/3 cup red wine vinegar
I teaspoon salt
I teaspoon paprika
1/2 teaspoon dried basil
1/4 teaspoon ground cloves
1/8 teaspoon Tabasco sauce
I garlic clove, minced (optional)
2 tablespoons finely chopped onion
1/4 cup finely chopped celery
1/2 cup seeded and finely chopped green bell pepper
1 1/2 cups finely chopped fresh tomatoes
Sour cream for garnish

In a small saucepan sprinkle the gelatin on 1/2 cup of the water to soften it. Place over low heat and stir until the gelatin is dissolved. Remove from the heat and stir in the bouillon cube. Add the remaining water, the vinegar, and seasonings. Mix well. Chill in the refrigerator until the gelatin is the consistency of egg whites. Fold in the garlic, onion, celery, green pepper, and tomatoes. Cover and chill at least 1 hour. Serve garnished with sour cream in soup cups.

MAKES 8 SERVINGS

# Entertaining the Middle-
# Brow Gourmet Way

Not everyone wanted to cook the French Chef way, whisk and copper bowl in hand. At least not all the time. The great divide in Middle American cookery between high-brow-from-scratch gourmets and hard-core-jiffy cooks was beginning. But in the Sixties, many cooks still felt perfectly at ease serving beef Wellington to guests one night and jiffy crab casserole the next.

## Soup Is Good Food

For a great many people condensed soup had become the American fond de cuisine by the Fifties. In the next decade, dried soup mixes also became a staple. Lipton's onion soup mix was one of the most popular, but Knorr's line of fancy dried soups was more expensive and considered more gourmet. Dried onion soup was so accepted in culinary circles that Julia Child recommended making "your own" soupe à l'oignon by gussying up dried onion soup with wine and herbs.

Aside from its use in sour cream dips, onion soup mix's other star turn was in a foil-wrapped pot roast, a dish that became a dinnertime cliché in the late Fifties and early Sixties. It was extremely easy, it dirtied no pots or pans, it made its own gravy, the soup mix provided an appetizing brown color to otherwise gray steamed meat, and it was very tasty (if your taste ran to salt). *Joy of Cooking* (1964) recommended it for informal dinner parties, when the guests' appetites would be whetted as the foil-wrapping was opened—letting out the aromatic smells of beef, onions, and monosodium glutamate.

Peg Bracken, who called this pot roast "sweep steak" because of the way the recipe swept the country, wrote *The I Hate to Cook Book* (first published in 1960 and still going strong), one of those "junk cookbooks" that John MacPhee decided to burn (p. 218). The book was full of cutesy names (beetniks, idiot onions) and some pretty awful dishes based on various canned soups. But it was also honest: Bracken didn't pretend a can of gravy was a velouté sauce, as did Esther Riva Solomon. Hers was a book written by a woman who didn't particularly enjoy cooking, but found herself having to cook day-in and day-out nonetheless. Her amusing book told how she—and probably thousands of other busy American noncooks—coped.

## POT ROAST À L'OIGNON—A.K.A. SWEEP STEAK

If you want to make this extra-special, put the meat on top of the onion soup mix and spread a can of cream of mushroom soup over the top of the roast.

    1 (3-pound) round steak or pot roast
    1 package dry onion soup mix

Preheat the oven to 300°F. Put the meat on a sheet of aluminum foil large enough to wrap it in. Sprinkle the onion soup mix on top, fold the foil airtight around it, and put it in a baking pan. Bake for 3 hours.

MAKES 6 TO 8 SERVINGS

As popular as this pot roast was, however, it was still *pot roast* and not really suitable for a truly elegant dinner party. The following casserole, however, was as elegant as all get-out. It was perfect for a dinner party, and even more perfect for a special luncheon dish. And any hostess smart enough to make this simple, but expensive, dish was sure to get plenty of requests for the recipe.

## CRAB AND ARTICHOKE CASSEROLE

You *could* omit the canned soup and substitute a béchamel sauce, but on the other hand you could not make the thing at all.

1 (14-ounce) can artichoke hearts (or substitute frozen hearts, cooked according to package directions)
$^3/_4$ pound crabmeat (canned may be used), picked over for cartilage
2 tablespoons butter
1 (2-ounce) can sliced mushrooms
1 tablespoon sherry
$^1/_4$ cup heavy cream
$^1/_2$ cup condensed cream of mushroom soup
$^1/_4$ cup grated Parmesan cheese

Preheat the oven to 375°F. Drain the artichoke hearts and arrange in a buttered shallow casserole. Arrange the crabmeat over the artichokes. Melt the butter, then drain the mushrooms and sauté them in the butter about 5 minutes. Sprinkle the mushrooms over the crab. Mix the sherry, cream, and soup together and stir until smooth. Pour the soup mixture over the casserole. Top with the grated cheese and bake until browned and bubbly, about 20 minutes.

MAKES 4 TO 6 SERVINGS

Gourmet with a capital "G" cooks turned up their noses at condensed soup. But in the late Sixties when Campbell's soup came out with its new Golden Mushroom soup, even Gourmets turned to it with enthusiasm.

## GOLDEN GOURMET CHICKEN

"Soup with the Midas touch—Turns everything it touches to gold," said Campbell's in 1969.

2 tablespoons butter
6 chicken legs or thighs
$^1/_2$ cup dry white wine
$^1/_2$ cup chicken broth or water
1 can Campbell's condensed Golden Mushroom soup
$^1/_2$ cup sour cream

Melt the butter in a large, heavy skillet. Brown the chicken on all sides in the hot butter and remove to a plate. Pour the wine and broth or water into the skillet, stirring and scraping up all the brown bits. Return the chicken to the skillet and pour the soup over the top. Stir gently to blend. Cover the skillet and cook until the chicken is tender, about 30 minutes. Remove the chicken to a warmed platter. Degrease the pan juices and stir in the sour cream. Place over low heat just to warm the sour cream, but do not boil. Pour the sour cream mushroom sauce over the chicken and serve.

MAKES 6 SERVINGS

Another classic soup-based recipe served at many a dinner party, but a family favorite, too, was green bean casserole. The standard version incorporated canned French fried onions into the casserole and as a crunchy topping. The following was more of a dinner party dish, using as it did that sure-fire sign of Sixties elegance: blanched almonds.

## ELEGANT STRING BEAN CASSEROLE

"6 servings of company-good green beans!" said a 1961 Campbell's soup ad. This gussied up version of string beans amandine is another one of those Sixties dishes that tastes good—and at the same time absolutely awful.

2 (14$^1/_2$-ounce) cans French cut string beans, drained
1 can condensed cream of mushroom soup
$^1/_2$ cup milk
2 tablespoons dry sherry
1 tablespoon instant minced onion (fresh may be substituted)
$^1/_2$ cup blanched slivered almonds

Preheat the oven to 350°F. Mix all the ingredients together in a greased 1$^1/_2$-quart casserole, saving a few almonds for garnish. Bake for 25 minutes. Sprinkle the reserved almonds over the top and bake another 5 minutes.

MAKES 6 SERVINGS

# Nippy Nibbles, Dips,
# Dunks, and Spreads

The cocktail party was still big in the Sixties, as were the cocktail nibbles that had become standard fare at stand-up parties. But even at a relatively formal dinner, the first course was likely to be tidbits casually served in the living room.

With the advent of quick 'n' easy cooking using mixes and canned or frozen ingredients, these nibbles were liable to have peppy names to jazz them up. After all, it was safer to call that cracker spread you were about to serve your guests "aloha spread," than to tell them it was made with cream cheese, Roquefort, crushed pineapple, ginger, and chopped pecans. Aloha spread they might eat.

## PORKERS

This very simple recipe appeared in a number of cookbooks of the period, but only Jinx Kragen and Judy Perry's 1962 cookbook called it by this terminally cute name. But then the title of their cookbook was *The How to Keep Him (After You've Caught Him) Cookbook: An Irreverent and Affectionate Guide to the Well-Stuffed Spouse.* Some of their other recipes were "odious onion sandwiches," "no worry curry," "pompous paella," "baba (au rhum) black sheep," "well-bread pudding," and "gam of lamb."

1 dozen saltine crackers
1 dozen thin strips lean bacon

Preheat the broiler. Wrap each cracker with a bacon strip and broil, turning once, until the bacon is crisp.

MAKES 4 SERVINGS

Two other items, not necessarily with silly names, were fashionable for parties in the Sixties. Cocktail franks in sauce and stuffed Edam cheese made an appearance at many a sophisticated soiree then. Both have pretty much disappeared.

## FRANK 'N' SAUCE

*New York Times* writer Marian Burros confessed to having made "ruby red franks" in a sauce of cherry pie filling and red wine for the perfect cocktail tidbit in the Sixties. Here, ultrafashionable sour cream makes a less sweet, but not necessarily more appetizing, sauce.

3 tablespoons butter

1 pound cocktail franks (or substitute 1 pound hot dogs, sliced into bite-size
    pieces)

1 tablespoon flour

1 cup beef bouillon

3 tablespoons prepared chili sauce

1 tablespoon prepared mustard

2 teaspoons sugar

2 cups sour cream

Melt the butter in heavy skillet. Brown the franks in the butter on all sides and remove them from the pan. Add the flour to the pan and cook over low heat, stirring constantly, for a few minutes. Remove from the heat and slowly stir in the beef bouillon. Return to medium heat and cook, stirring constantly, until the mixture is hot and has thickened, about 5 minutes. Stir in the chili sauce, mustard, and sugar. Reduce the heat to low and stir in the sour cream. Stir in the browned franks. Heat, but do not allow to boil or the sour cream will curdle. Transfer the mixture to a chafing dish and keep warm over low heat. Serve with cocktail toothpicks.

MAKES 10 TO 12 SERVINGS

## STUFFED EDAM CHEESE

Edam cheese from Holland in its bright red wax shell was a favorite of internationally minded gourmets. One reason was its unthreatening mildness, which also made it easy to gussy up. By the end of the decade, stuffed Edam was superseding the cheese ball as the party cheese spread of choice.

1 (2-pound) Edam cheese, at room temperature

1 to 2 tablespoons half-and-half or light cream

$1/4$ cup ($1/2$ stick) butter

$1/4$ cup Madeira or sherry

1 tablespoon finely minced onion

1 teaspoon prepared mustard

Dash of cayenne pepper

Slice off the top of the cheese and carefully scoop out the center. (You may make a jagged design on the edge of the cheese shell if you like.) Mash the scooped out cheese with the half-and-half and butter until of spreadable consistency (you may use a mixer or food processor for this). Blend the Madeira, onion, and mustard together in a blender or food processor until smooth. Beat the Madeira mixture into the cheese. Add the cayenne and taste for seasoning. Put the cheese mixture back into the shell. May be refrigerated at this point for up to 5 days, but be sure to bring the cheese to room temperature before serving. Decorate with sprigs of parsley and serve with crackers and party rye bread.

MAKES 20 TO 24 SERVINGS

Dips, too, were still considered ideal cocktail party or starter fare. Indeed, dips were so popular that many could be picked up premade at the supermarket refrigerator case, and chip and snack cracker makers were busy dreaming up all kinds of variations on the standard dunkers. Corrugated potato chips ("R-R-R-Ruffles have R-R-R-Ridges") and corn chips in cornucopia shapes (Bugles) were especially designed to withstand being dragged through thick dips without breaking, while scooping up the maximum amount of flavored glop.

Not everyone was enamored of dips. Here is M. F. K. Fisher on the subject, after she was asked by a neighbor to provide the dip for a charitable function:

I scanned recipes for Bean-Bacon Chip-Dip and Saucy Crab-Clam Dip and Blue Cheese Chili Fluff and Pink Devil Dip-n-Dunk. I also read conscientiously the formulas for many other somewhat less outlandish mixtures to be paddled in by drinkers armed with everything from raw green beans to reinforced potato chips.... I closed the books and went to two large markets and stared for some time at the pretty plastic containers of dips in the cold-bins. I bought one, made of sour cream with a great deal of monosodium glutamate and not many minced clams in it, and ate some of it for lunch. I then faced the fact that I still refused, as a matter of integrity, to concoct even a reasonable facsimile of such a thing. (*With Bold Knife and Fork,* 1968)

California dip, made from sour cream and dried onion soup mix, was the Lipton company's lasting contribution to American cuisine, and one of the most popular dips of all time, right up there with clam dip. But not all onion soup mix-based dips were so pristine and elegant.

Here is one of those dips—with a difference—again from that wonderful cookbook *Conversation-Piece Recipes.* And I guarantee that if you serve this dip at your next party, there will be plenty of talk.

## COCKTAIL DUNK WITH UMPH

"The men go for this one first—and always—so make plenty of it! Surprise ingredient...is the chopped salami which gives it real umph."

$^1/_2$ pound liverwurst

I cup sour cream

$^1/_2$ cup chopped salami

I envelope onion soup mix

I teaspoon Pick-a-Peppa sauce (or healthy dash of Tabasco)

$^1/_4$ cup cashew nuts, chopped

Mash the liverwurst and sour cream together until well mixed. Stir in the rest of the ingredients. Chill at least 1 hour.

MAKES 2 CUPS

# Gooey Desserts— A Sixties Specialty

America's sweet tooth was prodigious. And while American men claimed to prefer pie and/or ice cream as their dessert of choice, American women weren't about to put up with anything so simple. When a hostess placed the final course on the table, she wanted the other ladies present to sit up and take notice…and ask for the recipe. Under most circumstances, apple pie and vanilla ice cream would not do.

While high-brow gourmets were painstakingly mixing up chocolate mousses and dessert soufflés, cooks of a less hautey persuasion were off on another tack completely. Classical French desserts were not for them. What they wanted was *American* food, and they wanted it sweet, they wanted it gooey, and they wanted it fast. Most of these homey recipes did not appear in high-brow magazines or gourmet cookbooks. Instead they were copied out and passed from cook to cook, or included in ring-bound community cookbooks.

Cheesecake was an American specialty, by way of Europe, and mighty popular it was, too, in the Fifties and Sixties. Few home cooks attempted the classic New York Cheesecake, made famous at Lindy's, with its golden crust and cheese-egg filling. Instead they made this gooey gelatinized version, in a graham cracker crust.

## CREAMY AMERICAN CHEESECAKE

One cookbook called this "mock cheesecake." Cherry or blueberry pie fillings were popular toppings for this dessert. Here crushed pineapple is used instead. If you like, you may omit the fruit topping entirely and garnish the cheesecake with additional graham cracker crumbs—a gritty but authentic variation.

**For the Crust**
I cup graham cracker crumbs
3 tablespoons sugar
3 tablespoons butter or margarine, melted

**For the Filling**
I envelope unflavored gelatin
$1/4$ cup cold water
2 (8-ounce) packages cream cheese, softened
$1/2$ cup sugar
$1/8$ teaspoon salt
$1/2$ cup milk
Pineapple Glaze (below)
I cup heavy cream, whipped until firm peaks form

Preheat the oven to 350°F. To make the crust, combine the crumbs, sugar, and butter. Press into the bottom of a 9-inch springform pan or pie pan. Bake 10 minutes. Cool.

To make the filling, soften the gelatin in the cold water in a small saucepan. Stir over low heat until dissolved. Combine the cream cheese, sugar, and salt and beat or mix in a mixer until well blended. Gradually add the dissolved gelatin and the milk, stirring constantly. Chill the mixture until slightly thickened but not set. Fold in the whipped cream. Pour into the crust and chill until firm. Remove the sides of the springform pan, if using, and top with Pineapple Glaze.

## PINEAPPLE GLAZE

I tablespoon sugar
2 teaspoons cornstarch
I (8-ounce) can crushed pineapple, undrained
I tablespoon lemon juice

Combine the sugar and cornstarch in a small saucepan. Stir in the pineapple with its juices and the lemon juice. Bring to a boil, stirring, over medium heat. Boil 1 minute. The mixture should be thickened and translucent. Let cool. Spoon over the top of the cheesecake.

MAKES I 9-INCH CAKE; 8 SERVINGS

# FRUIT COCKTAIL CAKE

This is very rich and sweet, almost more a pudding than a cake. It first appeared in the Fifties, but was still popular a decade later. My husband, who is not usually a dessert eater, said that it is *extremely* good!"

    I cup all-purpose flour
    I cup sugar
    I teaspoon baking powder
    1/4 teaspoon salt
    I large egg, beaten until light
    2 cups fruit cocktail with juice
    I teaspoon vanilla extract
    I cup firmly packed brown sugar
    1/4 cup (1/2 stick) butter
    1/2 cup walnuts or pecans, chopped

Preheat the oven to 350°F. Sift the first four ingredients into a large bowl. Add the egg, fruit cocktail, and vanilla and mix well. Pour into an 8 × 12-inch buttered and floured cake pan. Mix the brown sugar, butter, and walnuts together, then sprinkle over the top of the cake batter. Bake until the cake starts to pull away from the sides of the pan and a toothpick inserted in the center of the cake comes out clean, about 45 minutes. Cool. Serve from the pan.

MAKES 1 CAKE

Jane and Michael Stern published a version of Jell-O cake, which they called "poke cake," in *Square Meals* (1984). But their recipe called for a cake mix including pudding, and they poured the Jell-O over the baked cake instead of incorporating it into the batter. The recipe given below is, I think, an earlier version; it's from my mother's files. She made it for nearly every informal party I can remember in the early Sixties.

# JELL-O CAKE

The Jell-O gives the cake a light and spongy texture and the topping gives it gooey succulence. Be sure to sift the powdered sugar and mix it well with the fruit juice for the topping, or you'll end up with a very unappetizing lumpy glaze.

1 package vanilla or lemon cake mix
1 (3-ounce) package lemon-flavored Jell-O
$^3/_4$ cup water
4 eggs
$^3/_4$ cup mild vegetable oil
2 cups confectioners' sugar, sifted
$^1/_3$ cup fruit juice (unsweetened lemon, orange, or pineapple recommended)

Preheat the oven to 350°F. Butter and flour a 9 × 15-inch cake pan. Mix the first five ingredients together and beat until well blended. Pour into the cake pan. Bake until a cake tester inserted into the center of the cake comes out clean, about 40 minutes. Cool the cake 10 minutes in the pan. Poke holes all over the top of the cake with a fork. Mix the confectioners' sugar and fruit juice together and pour over the cake. Cool. Serve from the pan.

MAKES 1 CAKE

Pies, plain old fruit pies anyway, were not In during the Sixties: too simple, too old-fashioned, too uncreative. But there was a class of pie that a modern gal could serve and still be considered a go-go gourmet. These acceptably chic pies almost always had a crushed graham cracker or cookie crust and were filled with ice cream, or pudding, or gelatin mixed with something sweet and creamy. And they were often flavored with liqueurs.

Black-bottom pie (a gingersnap crust with a chocolate pudding layer topped with rum-flavored pudding and whipped cream) was one of these fashionable pies, as was French silk (butter, sugar, chocolate, and eggs beaten together and chilled in a crust, with whipped cream). Pies flavored like drinks were also very chic: daiquiri pie, Kahlua pie, Irish coffee pie, and especially grasshopper pie. In 1991, grasshopper pie was one of *Gourmet* magazine's choices for their favorite recipes from the last fifty years. They originally published their version in 1962.

## GRASSHOPPER PIE

The name of this mint-chocolate pie comes from the after-dinner drink, which is made by shaking $^1/_2$ ounce cream, $^1/_2$ ounce white crème de cacao, and 1 ounce crème de menthe together with ice cubes, then straining. This pie may have had its start in the Fifties when crème de menthe had considerable cachet, and by the Sixties it had quite a following. Some recipes called for gelatin and eggs—some, like one Betty Crocker version, used frosting mix—but this one uses marshmallows instead.

1½ cups chocolate cookie crumbs
¼ cup (½ stick) butter, melted
32 marshmallows
⅔ cup half-and-half or light cream
¼ cup crème de menthe
¼ cup white crème de cacao
1½ cups heavy cream, whipped until soft peaks form
Semisweet chocolate curls or additional cookie crumbs for garnish

Preheat the oven to 375°F. Mix the cookie crumbs with the butter and press into a 9-inch pie pan. Bake 8 minutes. Cool.

Place the marshmallows and half-and-half in a large saucepan and melt the marshmallows, stirring occasionally, over low heat. Cool. Stir the liqueurs into the marshmallow mixture, then fold in the whipped cream. Pour into the pie shell and freeze. Garnish with chocolate curls or sprinkle cookie crumbs over the top when serving.

MAKES ONE 9-INCH PIE; 8 SERVINGS

There was one other liquor-accented sweet recipe that swept the country in the Sixties and that was bourbon or rum balls. Because they involved no cooking and were based on ultrafashionable graham cracker or cookie crumbs, nuts, and alcohol, bourbon balls were the perfect sweet morsel for the era. They were, and are, addicting.

## BOURBON OR RUM BALLS

These little cookie confections are usually reserved for the Christmas season.

2 cups vanilla wafer crumbs (or substitute graham crackers)
1 cup confectioners' sugar, sifted
2 tablespoons unsweetened cocoa powder
1 cup finely chopped walnuts
1½ tablespoons light corn syrup or honey
¼ cup bourbon or rum
Additional confectioners' sugar, sifted, for dusting

Mix the dry ingredients together until well blended. Stir in the liquids, blending with your hands, until the mixture is of moldable consistency and not too sticky. Add additional liquid if too dry, additional sugar or crumbs if too wet. Form the mixture into balls about ¾ inch in diameter. Roll the balls in confectioners' sugar. These may be eaten right away, but are much better if stored in a tightly covered tin and aged at least 2 days.

MAKES ABOUT 40 BALLS

## THE HEALTH FOOD PHENOMENON—A REACTION TO TECHNOLOGY AND TECHNO-FOOD

Not so long ago the Federal Radiation Council reported there were no immediate health risks to the public from fallout, although radioactive contamination of food supplies has increased substantially from nuclear tests.

—*Good Housekeeping* (September 1963)

In a conversation with Clementine Paddleford at the end of the Fifties, Narcissa Chamberlain, wife of and co-author with Samuel Chamberlain (a.k.a. Phineas Beck), said that there were three types of American cooking: the regional (Boston baked beans), the foreign (paella), and the new (Jell-O cake). But by the end of the Sixties a fourth category could be added, and that was health food cooking.

America's fascination with "health food" goes back a long way. In 1830 the Reverend Sylvester Graham started promoting his unsifted whole wheat flour and set up "Graham hotels," which served bland food that "did not enflame the blood." The Kellogg brothers, William R. and Dr. John Harvey, set up their Battle Creek, Michigan, sanitarium, serving vegetarian food and Kellogg's Corn Flakes in the late 1800s. Charles W. Post borrowed the Kellogg's health ideas, bought land in Battle Creek and sold Postum, a cereal-based coffee substitute, and Grape-Nuts. With the publication of Upton Sinclair's *The Jungle* in 1906 (which exposed the horrors of America's meat-packing plants), and the scientific discoveries in nutrition in the 1920s, including the existence and importance of vitamins, health foodism and vegetarianism grew in respectability if not in size. Indeed many cookbooks of the Twenties, otherwise rife with recipes for roast beef and tamale pie, were also full of nut cutlets and cheese roasts.

Still, Americans were mostly content to go on eating as we had done, although we now preferred our food to be "vitaminized." But as more and more of our food was processed, filled with additives, or in some cases completely fake, a backlash grew. One direction this took was in the rise of gourmet cooking, with Julia Child, who thought much of American food "simply awful," leading the way.

The other reaction, with the coming of age of the Baby Boomers, was the countercultural, anti-Establishment health food movement. While the Flower Children and the hippies rejected their parents' political and social mores, they just as vehemently rejected their parents' food.

Concerned about the poisoning of their bodies and the earth by chemical fertilizers and pesticides (not to mention nuclear fallout) and armed with Rachel Carson's *Silent Spring* and Adelle Davis's *Let's Eat Right to Keep Fit*, these rebellious young adults set out to do battle with the food establishment. Out went the cans of condensed soups, with their labels full of monosodium glutamate and other suspiciously polysyllabic ingredients. Out went the squishy, soft bread made from bleached white flour. Out went the white sugar. Out went the instant white rice. Out went margarine and processed cheese. Out went canned vegetables. In came organic vegetables, raw milk products, freshly milled whole wheat flour, brown rice, yogurt, wheat germ, brewer's yeast, sunflower seeds, sprouts, honey, and blackstrap molasses.

The food establishment did not take this challenge to their authority lying down. General Foods and *McCall's* warned of famine if organic gardening practices were widely adopted. The U.S. Food and Drug Administration (FDA), supported by the American Medical Association (AMA), called claims that organic foods were more nutritious than nonorganic foods "nonsense." In 1967 the U.S. Department of Agriculture insisted that "an ample supply of nutrients is available from food purchased in regular markets at ordinary current prices." And

---

## More Food for a Nuclear Winter

Orange-flavored Tang was "the astronauts' drink" and being such a modern, and presumably scientific, concoction, it was very popular in the Sixties. Children especially loved to mix it extra-strong and then crunch the sweet crystals remaining at the bottom of the glass. Moms didn't mind—after all, Tang did supply vitamin C.

"Whipped toppings" were also popular in the Sixties, ironically as much for health reasons as for their synthetic, hence modern, appeal. Growing concern about the intake of cholesterol and saturated animal fat prompted many people to switch from real whipped cream to these fluffy, greasy toppings. Cool Whip was not marketed until 1970, but boxed whipped toppings that needed only water and stirring to bring them to life were readily available.

This confection, which combines both Cool Whip and Tang, comes from Texas.

### TANG PIE

1 (9-inch) graham cracker crust, baked
1 (14-ounce) can sweetened condensed milk
1 (8-ounce) carton sour cream
¼ cup plus 2 tablespoons Tang powder
1 (8-ounce) tub Cool Whip

Mix the milk, sour cream, and Tang together. Fold in half of the Cool Whip. Spoon into the pie shell. Top with the rest of the Cool Whip. Chill.

MAKES ONE 9-INCH PIE; 8 SERVINGS

*Good Housekeeping* (September 1967) called health foods "nutritional quackery." But the food establishment's vehemence only served to increase the hippies' conviction that modern American food was bad food.

Unfortunately, most of the people involved in the health food movement had never learned to cook. So when they went "back to the land" they also went back to zero culinarily. And, young and healthy and ignorant of good cooking as they were, as long as the food they were eating was prepared with "natural" ingredients and was full of nutrients, what it tasted like didn't really matter.

One of the most popular health foods during that period was any variation on Adelle Davis's cure-all milkshake, "Pep-Up." Made with such appetizing ingredients as magnesium oxide, granular kelp, and brewer's yeast, along with milk, yogurt, eggs, bananas, and orange juice, Pep-Up was the blueprint for nutritious health drinks and the Age of Aquarius's answer to instant breakfast.

---

## Tryabita Celery Cereal

Health food faddists have not always had the most appetizing—or successful—ideas. At the turn of the century one Dr. V. C. Price decided to combine Battle Creek, Michigan's designation as "Cereal City" and Kalamazoo, Michigan's reknown as "Celery City." He came up with celery-flavored hot cereal, which he dubbed "Tryabita."

*Mother Hubbard's Modern Cupboard* (1903) published a recipe for Tryabita bread using this unusual product, which it claimed "may truly be called the 'Staff of Life' as it contains all the nourishing qualities to make bone and muscle and feed the nerves." Despite this endorsement, the entrepreneurial Dr. Price's celery cereal failed dismally and Tryabita disappeared from the grocery shelves.

---

## HEALTH SHAKE

Many recipes for health shakes, Adelle Davis's included, called for raw, unpasteurized milk. This freaked out the medical establishment, many of whom were old enough to remember the rampant disease associated with the use of raw milk before pasteurization became virtually universal. Raw eggs were also a common component—but that was before the salmonella problems that beset us now.

1 cup milk
$\frac{1}{2}$ cup plain yogurt
$\frac{1}{2}$ cup cracked ice
1 ripe banana, peeled
$\frac{1}{4}$ cup soy flour
2 tablespoons brewer's yeast
$\frac{1}{4}$ teaspoon powdered kelp
1 teaspoon honey
1 teaspoon blackstrap molasses
$\frac{1}{2}$ teaspoon vanilla extract

Place all the ingredients in a blender. Blend at high speed until well mixed and liquefied.

MAKES 2 SERVINGS

## BUNNY BURGERS

Brown rice and carrots were two health food sacred cows. Here they are combined to make a noncow "burger." These surprisingly tasty patties are very fragile, but firm up nicely as they brown.

3 cups cooked short grain brown rice
1 cup grated carrots
2 eggs, lightly beaten
1 teaspoon vegetable seasoning salt substitute
Untoasted wheat germ and sesame seeds for dredging
Soy oil

Combine the rice, carrots, eggs, and seasoning and mix well. Form into patties. Mix the wheat germ and sesame seeds in a flat dish. Dip the patties in the wheat germ and sesame seeds. Put 1 tablespoon oil in a heavy skillet over medium heat. Cook 4 to 5 patties until nicely browned on one side, about 5 minutes, then turn and brown on the other side. Remove to a warm plate. Add more oil to the skillet and cook the remaining patties until done.

MAKES 10 PATTIES

No self-respecting young "earth mother" who had gone back to the land would consider buying supermarket bread. Instead she made her own, and she frequently filled her basic loaves with natural additives like wheat berries (whole wheat kernels), brewer's yeast, wheat germ, and soy flour. The most "far-out" earth moms had wood-burning stoves in their communal farm kitchens to bake their whole-grain breads. But even without a wood-burning stove, the simple, age-old act of transmuting yeast and grain into a nourishing loaf conferred a magical, mystical aura on the maker.

## EARTH MOTHER BREAD

Jane Fonda was an early proponent of health foods. This recipe is adapted from one that Jane herself adapted from Adelle Davis's *Let's Cook It Right*. Said *Life* magazine of Jane in 1962, "She...manages to give wholesome comestibles a gourmet glow." The recipe makes a sweet, hearty bread. Doughs high in whole grains should not be kneaded very long, as the bran cuts the developing gluten strands, interfering with the rising, and making a dense, heavy finished product.

2 packages active dry yeast
1 tablespoon honey
1 1/4 cups warm water (85°F)
5–7 cups whole wheat bread flour
1/4 cup soy flour
2 teaspoons salt
1 cup warm milk (85°F)
2 tablespoons cold-pressed soy oil
1/3 cup blackstrap molasses

In a small bowl, combine the yeast, honey, and 1/4 cup of the warm water. Allow to "proof" until the mixture is foamy and light, about 20 minutes. Place 4 cups of the whole wheat flour, the soy flour, and the salt in a large mixing bowl. Stir in the proofed yeast mixture, then stir in the rest of the water and the milk. Work in enough of the remaining flour, using your hands, if necessary, until the dough beomes soft enough to work easily without being sticky. Turn out onto a floured board and knead for 2 to 3 minutes. Place the dough in a large buttered bowl, cover with a damp cloth (or plastic wrap), and allow to rise in a warm place until doubled in bulk, about 45 minutes. Punch down. Shape the dough into two loaves and place in two greased 9 × 5-inch loaf pans. Cover and let rise until almost but not quite doubled, 30 minutes to 1 hour. Bake in a preheated 375°F oven until the bread has pulled away from the sides of the pan and is golden brown, 45 to 50 minutes. (If in doubt, take the bread out of the pan and listen to the bottom of the loaf—it needs additional baking if you hear little sizzling noises.) Immediately take the bread out of the pans and cool on a wire rack.

MAKES 2 LOAVES

# Soul Food—Another Countercultural Response

Soul food is why it is chic to have a soul sister in the kitchen.

—*Esquire* (April 1968)

New York's soul-food restaurants—and they are increasing—are discussed with enthusiasm at sophisticated cocktail gatherings.

—Craig Claiborne, "Cooking with Soul," *New York Times* (November 3, 1968)

Along with the anti-Establishment Flower Power movement came the Black Power movement. Black pride was Right On. Soul brothers and sisters stopped straightening their hair so as not to look like "The Man" (the white man, that is) and proudly wore the new Afro look. Western clothing was discarded for colorful dashikis and other African-inspired garb. And soul food, the food of slavery and poverty, became the In cooking of the late Sixties.

Many Americans had, of course, been eating soul food long before it was dubbed soul food. Ham hocks, collard greens, cornbread, and other lowly, but sustaining, foods had nourished generations of poor southerners, both black and white. But chic gourmet cooks, who had tired of French, Spanish, and Oriental cooking, were delighted to discover what was to them a new, exotic, and excitingly anti-Establishment cuisine right in their own backyard. And what could be more sophisticated for white Americans at one of Craig Claiborne's "sophisticated cocktail gatherings" than detailing a trip to a hole-in-the-wall rib joint in thrillingly dangerous Harlem or Watts? White hippies, too, found soul food to be Right On. Though few health foodies cooked soul food—too many processed, low-nutrient ingredients, too many cooked-to-death vegetables—soul food was the food of the poor and oppressed and was, therefore, axiomatically good.

Try as they might, however, most middle-class or rich Americans had a hard time downing some soul foods. "Chittlin's," or chitterlings (the small intestines of pigs), were a particular sticking point. Many soul food restaurants catering to whites, and there were quite a few, dropped chittlin's from their menus. Pigs' feet, pigs' tails, and possum were other foods that didn't go over big with people who hadn't been raised eating soulfully.

## ROAST POSSUM WITH SWEET POTATOES

This is one of those recipes that scared the daylights out of white middle-class city folk. Mrs. Johnnie Haynes won an honorable mention with it at the First

Annual Soul Food Recipe Contest sponsored by KYAC radio and the Washington Natural Gas Company on April 27, 1969. It has not been tested.

I possum
I cup salt, plus salt to taste
6 red pepper pods
I large onion, peeled and quartered
2 cloves garlic, peeled
6 sweet potatoes, peeled, left whole

First catch possum. To dress possum, scald possum with two gallons of boiling water. Skin off hide at once. Scrape well. Cut off feet and tail, and remove entrails. Cleanse thoroughly with hot water. Soak in cold water, adding 1 cup salt. Let stand for 12 hours. Remove from salted water and wash. Put possum in enough water to boil and add salt to taste. Add red pepper pods, onion, and garlic. Cook until tender. Remove possum and reserve broth. Lay possum out flat in roasting pan. Put potatoes all around possum, with sufficient amount of broth skimmed from boiling. Bake in 400°F oven until nice and brown.

MAKES 6 SERVINGS

Urban whites could still eat soulfully without having to skin a possum. Here is a safe and sanitized menu for a "Little Bit of Soul" party from a 1969 *Seventeen* magazine.

◆◆◆

## *Seventeen* Serves Up Some Soul

*Fried Chicken* ◆ *Barbecued Ribs*
*Southern Green Beans* ◆ *Potato Salad*
*Black-Eyed Peas and Rice* ◆ *Coleslaw*
*Cornbread Sticks and Butter*
*Orange Sweet Potato Pie* ◆ *Pecan Pie* ◆ *Coffee*

# SWEET POTATO PIE

Sweet potato pie is delicious, similar in taste to pumpkin pie but with a drier, more appealing texture. *Seventeen*'s original recipe called for orange juice and grated orange rind as flavorings; here bourbon and spices have been substituted. Like any custard pie, this one will continue cooking after it is removed from the oven, so it should be considered done even though it is not quite set in the middle.

2 tablespoons butter, softened
1/2 cup sugar
1 cup mashed cooked sweet potatoes
3 large eggs, beaten
1 cup light cream or half-and-half
1/2 teaspoon salt
1/4 teaspoon ground ginger
1/2 teaspoon ground allspice
1/4 teaspoon ground cloves
1 teaspoon ground cinnamon
1/8 teaspoon ground nutmeg
2 tablespoons bourbon
1 (9-inch) pie shell, unbaked

Preheat the oven to 400°F. Cream the butter and sugar together until light. Beat in the sweet potatoes and eggs and mix well. Add the cream, salt, spices, and bourbon and stir until well blended. Pour into the unbaked pie crust. Bake until the pie and crust are browned and the pie is set but not dry in the middle, about 40 minutes.

MAKES 1 (9-INCH) PIE; 6 TO 8 SERVINGS

With the difficulties involved in procuring many of the items necessary for soul food cookery—suburban supermarket meat counters not usually running to possum or pigs' feet—and the fact that much of it was a very acquired taste, the fad among the chic for soul food didn't last long. Said one African-American stockbroker in 1969: "Let white folks eat hocks and collards. I'll take a rare steak and French fries any time."

As the Sixties came to a close, American cooking was as divided as American politics. About the only thing that united the country culinarily was the lack of heritage and continuity. Cooks no longer prepared the foods their grandmothers, or even their mothers, had served. Most regional dishes had been lost—or at least relegated to the once-a-year holiday feast.

In their place was mass-market cooking. The food eaten at a "Gourmet Gang Fest" in Minnesota was likely to be identical to that served in Florida. Dinner at a gathering of health food freaks in New York would be the same as that made and eaten by a similar group in Arizona. And the hurry-up casserole crowd in Montana would feel perfectly at home sitting down to dinner in Alabama. What they all shared was their lack of culinary experience...and the naive and very enthusiastic conviction that symbolic gestures could take the place of experience. Want to be a real gourmet? Well then, whisk up a foreign specialty. It's easy! Want to make health foods? Sprinkle grated carrots and sprouts on everything and anything. Want to glamorize that casserole? Just add sour cream or cream of mushroom soup or almonds.

But if American cooks had not learned the delicate art of thoughtfully balancing a menu, or indeed of even understanding the essence of the food they cooked and ate, still the wholesale plunge into the kitchen in the Sixties was a big step. We might have been wrong in assuming that by simply making a paella we would make ourselves into gourmets. But we ate the paella and tasted something new...and learned a little in the process. And if we weren't expert bakers just because we had made our own stone-ground whole wheat loaf, still we had, perhaps for the first time, tasted bread that was honest and fresh. It was a beginning.

## Steak of the Evening, Beautiful Steak

As much as was going on culinarily in America in the Sixties, going out to dinner very often still meant going out for meat and potatoes. And it seemed that America's favorite meat was steak and its favorite potato was baked. Except for the sour cream and chives garnishing the baked potato, the only other food likely to be on the table was a small salad of iceberg lettuce, with a wedge of tomato or two, a cucumber slice, and a blob of Roquefort dressing on top.

Restaurants like The Cattleman's in New York (done up in famous New York Wild-West style), the Black Angus chain in the West, and countless "Stockyard,"s "Chuck Wagon,"s and just plain "Steak House,"s sold us grilled or broiled Porterhouse steaks, T-bone steaks, sirloin steaks, and filet mignon. But if we were really going to go all out fancy, we might gussy up the steak and have this:

# TENDERLOIN TIPS, THE CATTLEMAN'S OF NEW YORK

Tenderloin tips are not on many menus these days, but in the Sixties they were the height of genteel middle-class elegance. The tips are cut from the narrow end of the fillet, the same area from which tournedos come.

Flour for dredging
2 $\frac{1}{2}$ teaspoons salt
$\frac{1}{8}$ teaspoon pepper
3 pounds tenderloin tips, sliced on the diagonal in 1-inch pieces
$\frac{1}{4}$ cup ($\frac{1}{2}$ stick) butter
$\frac{1}{2}$ cup chopped onion
2 cloves garlic, crushed and peeled
1 pound mushrooms, sliced
$\frac{1}{4}$ cup tomato purée
$\frac{1}{4}$ cup Burgundy wine
$\frac{1}{2}$ cup beef broth
1 cup heavy cream
Dash of Tabasco sauce
1 tablespoon Worcestershire sauce
1 cup sour cream

Preheat the oven to 375°F. Mix the flour with $\frac{1}{2}$ teaspoon of the salt and the pepper, then dredge the meat in the flour. Melt 2 tablespoons of the butter in a skillet and quickly brown the meat. Transfer the beef to a 3-quart casserole. Melt the remainder of the butter in a large skillet and sauté the onions until tender. Add the garlic, 1 teaspoon of the salt, and the mushrooms and cook 5 minutes. Stir in the tomato purée, wine, and beef broth. Cook for a few minutes, scraping up all the brown bits. Pour over the steak. Bake, covered, for 30 minutes. In a small saucepan, heat the cream, Tabasco sauce, Worcestershire sauce, and the remaining salt until simmering but not boiling. Fold in the sour cream and pour over the hot steak. Stir to blend. Return the casserole to the oven until heated through, about 5 minutes.

MAKES 6 TO 8 SERVINGS

# 7

# An Exotic Interlude, II

## Other Oriental Foods in America

Real curries, as made in the Orient, never fail to delight my family. Part of the secret of the tempting flavor is the use of STEERO bouillon cubes.
—Miss Edith A. Hemingway of New Hampshire in an ad for STEERO bouillon cubes (American Kitchen Products Co.), *Woman's Home Companion* (March 1929)

Although Chinese food—meaning primarily chop suey and chow mein—was the most readily available of the "exotics," anything that hinted at the Oriental was in vogue in the America of the Twenties. Spiritualism, "ectoplasm," yogis, and Ouija boards were all the rage—and twenty-five dollars was the going rate for a course in "Indian spiritualism" in New York.

What was generally labeled "Indian" food was very popular, even if it was doubtful that any native of the subcontinent would recognize it as Indian. A *Good Housekeeping* cookbook from 1927 contained a recipe for turkey Bombay, whose peculiar ingredients included chopped apple, green pepper, turkey chunks, and tomato juice all baked under a Parmesan and egg yolk custard. Oddly enough, in 1929 Ida C. Bailey Allen gave an authentic-sounding recipe for East Indian lentils (dahl), which instructed the cook to flavor the lentils with garlic, "mixed spices" (cloves, cinnamon, and ginger perhaps?), and crushed cardamom seeds. The lentils were to be served on a platter bordered with plain boiled rice and garnished with lemon slices. The recipe, printed over sixty years ago, could go into the pages of one of the glossy cooking magazines, without being considered quaint or old-fashioned.

Yet perhaps the archetypal "exotic" food of the early twentieth century was Hindoo eggs, sometimes called eggs Delhi. This was really just good old-fashioned creamed eggs on toast (or rice). But with a dash of curry powder stirred into the cream sauce a simple nursery dish became something glamorous. That small bit of spice brought the thrill of the East, with its fabled white slave trade and opium dens, to clean-living, pure-minded Americans who had voted themselves into Prohibition.

M. F. K. Fisher wrote of concocting Hindoo eggs when she was small for her sister. In her ignorance and because she loved the taste of curry, she added more and more of the exciting brown powder to the dish: The resulting incendiary sauce blistered her little sister's tongue.

## HINDOO EGGS (CURRIED HARD-BOILED EGGS)

This mildest and most maidenly of curry sauces will not blister anyone's tongue. It is extremely old-fashioned and should not be gussied up with any real curry fixin's like coconut milk, fresh gingerroot, or cardamom seeds. Chicken, shrimp, lamb, or any leftover meats may be substituted for the eggs, however.

> 2 tablespoons butter
> 1 tablespoon finely minced onion
> 1 teaspoon curry powder (or to taste)
> 1/2 teaspoon salt
> 1 tablespoon all-purpose flour
> 1/2 cup warm beef or chicken broth
> 1 cup warm milk (half-and-half is best)
> 6 hard-boiled eggs
> Squeeze of fresh lemon juice
> Hot rice or toast

Melt the butter in a medium nonreactive skillet, add the onion and sauté over low heat until the onion is clear. Stir in the curry powder, salt, and flour and cook for 1 to 2 minutes. Off the heat, gradually stir in the broth and milk, stirring until smooth. Return to the heat and bring to a boil, lower heat to a simmer and cook about 10 minutes. The sauce should be slightly thickened and smooth. Taste for seasoning and adjust. Cut the eggs into quarters and add to the sauce. Cook just until the eggs are hot, but do not boil. Just before serving stir in a drop or two of fresh lemon juice. Serve over hot rice or toast points.

MAKES 4 SERVINGS

Curries along the lines of Hindoo eggs were about as far as most cooks were willing to go in their quest for exotic Indian food. Sometimes the curries might have a bit of chopped apple or ketchup, or even piccalilli, added to the sauce for piquancy. And occasionally a cook who had traveled might serve the curry with small dishes of chopped bacon, chutney, grated coconut, peanuts, and onions.

One such garnished curry was served at a Ladies' Luncheon given by the wife of a West Point officer in 1927. The curry itself, however, based on curry powder, flour, onion, and hot water, was strictly Occidental in flavor.

◆◆◆

# East Meets West Point Luncheon, circa 1927

*Oriental Chicken Curry in a Rice Ring with Curry*
*Garnishes*
*Fried Bananas*
*Finger Rolls*
*Canton Lemon-Ginger Sherbet*
*Coconut Macaroons*
*Ceylon Tea*

## CANTON LEMON-GINGER SHERBET

The cornstarch in this recipe substitutes for the gelatin or egg white usually used to "smooth" the texture of a sherbet. Without the cornstarch, this makes a very modern sorbet.

1 1/2 cups sugar
3 tablespoons cornstarch
2 teaspoons grated lemon rind
4 cups water
3/4 cup lemon juice (about 5–6 lemons)
1 tablespoon preserved ginger, drained and finely chopped

Mix the sugar and cornstarch in a heavy saucepan. Add the lemon rind and stir in the water. Bring to a boil and let boil 3 minutes. Remove from the heat and stir in the lemon juice and ginger. Chill and freeze in an ice cream freezer. (You may also freeze this in covered metal trays, stirring the mixture frequently once it becomes slushy. It will resemble an ice more than a sherbet with this method.)

MAKES ABOUT 9 SERVINGS

# Exotic Egypt and Pre-Trader Vic Hawaiian Delights

When King Tutankhamen's tomb was found and opened in 1922 by Howard Carter and "Porchy" Carnarvon (the earl of Carnarvon, who carried the finest port and brandy with him to Egypt), it caused a sensation. The exquisite artifacts meant to accompany the king on his trip to the afterworld inspired clothing and furniture designers, milliners, and the Hollywood dream makers to new heights of exotic Oriental design.

In exotic Dayton, Ohio, the Hotel Miami decorated its luncheon menu with motifs from King Tutankhamen's tomb. The menu itself, according to

Harvey Levenstein's *Revolution at the Table* (1988), featured exotic fare like ham and cheese sandwiches. A "King Tut Hallowe'en Party" was suggested by the October 1923 *Woman's Home Companion.* The magazine pictured a "truly Egyptian frieze cut from terra-cotta kindergarten paper" for decoration, and offered a written program for party games titled "Schedule of Tortures for the Damned." That portion of the program called "Heaven" was to be the food, which consisted of angel food cake and "Houris' Delight"—a marshmallow and pineapple concoction otherwise known as pineapple fluff (p. 20).

Pineapple was very popular in the Twenties, as were, to a lesser extent, bananas and coconut. These tropical fruits obviously suggested exotic, tropical locales, and nowhere more so than exotic, tropical Hawaii.

In those days faraway Hawaii *was* exotic. Hula dancing had long been a specialty of the exotic dancers that were so popular in the late 1910s and early 1920s. In the June 19, 1926, issue of the *New Yorker*, columnist Lois Long (a.k.a. Lipstick) described a visit to New York's "torrid, tropical" Congo Room restaurant where "two Hawaiian damsels, in grass skirts, silk stockings and high-heeled satin slippers, may be observed strumming ukuleles and guitars"—although *Vanity Fair* had commented the year before that hula dancing was becoming passé. What Hawaiian dancers were doing in the Congo Room no one seemed to worry about.

But it was just that attitude of lumping together everything that was "exotic" that was so typical of the period. It was thus not surprising that anything containing either pineapple or banana was dubbed "Hawaiian" and could, therefore, be considered exotic, even if it was just a dish of baked ham and sweet potatoes served with sautéed pineapple slices. A popular and very typical salad of the period was Honolulu salad, which consisted of a lettuce leaf topped with a slice of canned pineapple, crowned with a ball of pimiento cheese. The name was the only exciting thing about this pedestrian dish.

The odd thing about the fashion for throwing tropical fruit in a dish and labeling it Hawaiian is that real (relatively) Hawaiian food was well documented in this country before the turn of the century. Sarah Tyson Rorer's *New Cook Book* (1898) contained eleven pages of Hawaiian recipes with such ingredients as sago, taro root, green ginger, breadfruit, guava, and tamarind. Even Mrs. Rorer's chicken curry used garlic, fresh spices, and homemade coconut milk—a far cry from the cream sauce with a dab of store-bought curry powder that went into Hindoo eggs.

A surprisingly authentic menu for a Hawaiian luncheon appeared in *Ladies' Home Journal* in November 1928, complete with instructions for creating the proper tropical ambiance with fern leaves, orange crepe-paper streamers, and Hawaiian records. The magazine was quick to assure its feminine readers that the exotic food in the menu was "delicate and quickly digested."

## A Delicate Hawaiian Luncheon, circa 1928

*Salmon Lomi*
*Braised Chicken Luau with Coconut Milk and*
*Spinach*
*Baked Banana and Coconut Pudding with Cream*
*Avocado, Cucumber, and Tomato Salad*
*Grape-Grapefruit Punch*
*Pineapple Sherbet*
*Coconut Layer Cake*

## SALMON LOMI

This is traditionally called lomi-lomi salmon—*lomi-lomi* means "to rub" or "to knead," which is what you do to the salmon! It is different and quite good—a sort of salmon gazpacho. The 1928 recipe served the Lomi in tomato cups.

1 pound salted salmon
Water to cover
1 medium onion, diced (Maui or other sweet onions are best)
6 green onions, finely chopped
5 tomatoes, peeled, seeded and diced
$^1/_2$ cup crushed ice

Cover the salmon with cold water and allow to sit, covered, in the refrigerator overnight. Drain the salmon, remove the skin and bones, if any, and shred the salmon flesh. Work the onions and green onions into the salmon shreds with your hands, then add the tomatoes. Chill well, then mix in the ice and serve.

MAKES 6 SERVINGS

## BRAISED CHICKEN LUAU WITH COCONUT MILK AND SPINACH

This is another authentic Hawaiian dish, although traditionally it would be made with taro leaves (luau) rather than spinach. If you can find fresh or frozen taro leaves, by all means use them.

1 chicken (4–5 pounds), cut into serving pieces
1 teaspoon salt
Flour for dredging
2 tablespoons peanut oil or lard
$^3/_4$ cup water
2 cups Coconut Milk (below)
1 pound spinach leaves, well washed, tough stems removed, blanched for 5
    minutes in boiling water, and chopped (or 1 10-ounce package frozen
    spinach, thawed and drained)

Mix together the salt and dredging flour in a shallow bowl. Heat the oil in a large skillet over medium-high heat. Dredge the chicken pieces in the flour and sauté in hot fat until nicely browned. Add the water, cover, and cook over low heat about 20 minutes. Remove each piece of chicken as it is done to a warm platter. Pour off all but 1 tablespoon of the fat in the pan. Gradually stir in the Coconut Milk, return to the heat, and bring to a simmer. Add the spinach. When the sauce has thickened somewhat, reduce the heat to low and add the chicken pieces. Taste for seasoning and correct. Cook over low heat about 10 minutes, just to warm everything through. Serve with rice, or more traditionally, mashed potatoes!

MAKES 6 SERVINGS

## COCONUT MILK

Coconut milk and cream are both highly perishable and should be kept covered in the refrigerator where they will last up to 5 days. If you're not up to making them, they may be purchased in cans from Oriental groceries—just be sure to get the unsweetened kind.

1 1/2 cups grated coconut (fresh or dried)
1 1/2 cups boiling water
Coconut water from the shell, if available

Pour the boiling water over the coconut, add the coconut water if you have it, and let stand 30 minutes. Strain through a sieve lined with cheesecloth. Once the liquid has stopped dripping, gather the cheesecloth around the grated coconut and squeeze to extract as much milk as possible. The milk is now ready to use. If you want to get coconut cream, let the milk stand in a cool place for a few hours, then skim off the cream that has risen to the top.

MAKES ABOUT 1 1/2 CUPS COCONUT MILK OR ABOUT 1/2 CUP COCONUT CREAM

# In the Mood—Tropical Food

I didn't want to run another steak joint—that was no fun.

—Trader Vic

You are never quite the same again—once you've tasted the cosmopolitan and international cuisine that flourishes in Hawaii.

—Alice Spalding Bowen, "Give a Different Kind of Dinner Party,"
*House Beautiful* (July 1950)

In the Thirties, one of the first of the tropically themed restaurants that also served tropical food was Don the Beachcomber's in Hollywood, run by Don Beaumont-Gantt. In *House & Garden* (May 1940) June Platt said, "As a grand finale to your visit in Hollywood, go to the Beachcomber—with someone you like very much—and order one (if you are wise) of their innocent-tasting rum drinks, served in a green coconut...[and] the fried shrimps, and the chicken-almond-green-pea-pod combination, and the pineapple covered with tufts of frost." One of the most famous of Don's "innocent-tasting rum drinks" was the zombie.

## ZOMBIE

The Beachcomber's original formulation is lost in time…but everyone seems to agree that the drink consists of various fruit flavors and a knock-out quantity of rum. Trader Vic's Forties version of the drink included a dash of licorice-tasting Pernod or Herbsaint, an unusual touch. Many contemporary versions include apricot liqueur. This has neither.

Juice of 1 lime
1 ounce orange juice
$^1/_4$ ounce grenadine
1 ounce light Puerto Rican rum
1 ounce dark Jamaican rum
$^1/_2$ ounce curaçao
1 ounce 151-proof Demerara rum
Large chunk of ice
Crushed ice

Place all ingredients, except the Demerara rum, in a large mixing glass with a large piece of ice, and stir well. Pour into a 14-ounce glass $^3/_4$ full of crushed ice. Float the Demerara on top and serve with a straw.

MAKES 1 DRINK

THE OUTRIGGER

CREATED BY TRADER VIC

*Cover of luncheon menu, 1959*

Undoubtedly the ladies who supped "delicate and easily digested" exotic foods at tea rooms and feminine luncheons in the Twenties would have been horrified at the very idea of ingesting something called a zombie. But the times were changing. Prohibition was over, and the Depression was bringing a more casual—and a decidedly more masculine—approach to dining and drinking.

In northern California, ultramasculine Victor Bergeron admired Don the Beachcomber's restaurant so much that in 1938 he threw out the snowshoes and antlers decorating his steak and booze restaurant, Hinky Dink's, and put up "a bunch of South Seas stuff." But the restaurant needed a new name. Bergeron had become famous locally for trading the artifacts festooning Hinky Dink's for a handsome price, and that gave him an idea. He reportedly told his staff, "Tomorrow morning you call me Trader Vic, and if any of you bastards don't, I'll fire you." Trader Vic's was born.

Like Don the Beachcomber, Trader Vic decided to sell plenty of strong drinks, mostly rum based, and "exotic" Oriental food...carefully tailored to the American taste. He visited Cuba to learn more about the concocting of tropical drinks and went to Hawaii shortly before World War II to steep himself in its lore and cookery. What he brought back were more South Seas artifacts, and a new perspective on island food. His Chinese dishes were relatively authentic Cantonese fare (see Chapter 3)—he had learned about Chinese food in Hawaii and most of his staff were Chinese-Americans—although he did away with anything that might be too foreign to his all-American clientele. But about the so-called Polynesian dishes on his menu he said, "You can't eat real Polynesian food. It's the most horrible junk I've ever tasted." And because he was pretty sure that most Americans wouldn't know the difference anyway, he felt free to invent his own versions of Tahitian puddings and Indonesian satés.

But the point of Trader Vic's wasn't authenticity, it was fantasy. Frowning tiki gods at the entrance, tapa cloth on the walls, flaming torches to match the flaming food, grass hut motifs and South Sea island names on the menu, added up to fun. For Americans fascinated by foreign and exotic foods, it also added up to sophistication.

## SHRIMP SATÉ

Saté, or satay, in the Far East is strips of meat marinated in a pungent sauce, threaded on a stick and grilled. The word itself is a Far Eastern attempt at the word *steak*. Meat saté on a stick was popular at Trader Vic's, but his recipe for shrimp saté included neither meat, sticks, nor grills. Essentially it was shrimp in cream sauce—but exotic cream sauce to be sure. The original recipe included Trader Vic's proprietary saté seasoning. This is a spicy approximation.

2 tablespoons butter
I small onion, finely chopped
2 cloves garlic, minced
$^{1}/_{4}$ teaspoon cayenne
$^{1}/_{2}$ teaspoon ground ginger
$^{1}/_{2}$ teaspoon ground turmeric
$^{1}/_{2}$ teaspoon brown sugar
2 tablespoons soy sauce
I tablespoon smooth natural peanut butter
$^{3}/_{4}$ cup water
I pound large shrimps, peeled and deveined
I teaspoon cornstarch
I tablespoon water
$^{1}/_{4}$ cup unsweetened Coconut Milk (p. 274)
$^{1}/_{4}$ cup milk
2 tablespoons fresh lime juice

Melt the butter in a large skillet, then sauté the onion and garlic with the cayenne, ginger, and turmeric over medium heat until the onion is soft. Dissolve the brown sugar in the soy sauce and add to the onion mixture along with the peanut butter. Stir in the $^{3}/_{4}$ cup water and bring to a boil. Lower heat to a simmer, add the shrimp and cook, covered, about 10 minutes. Dissolve the cornstarch in the 1 tablespoon water and add to the pan with the Coconut Milk and milk. Cook a few minutes until thickened. Stir in lime juice and serve at once with boiled rice.

MAKES 4 SERVINGS

In 1958 Trader Vic opened a branch of his restaurant at New York's Savoy-Plaza Hotel and New Yorkers with South Seas fever no longer had to make the long trek west to sample his exotic concoctions. But by that time, all of America had the fever. Thor Heyerdahl's *Kon Tiki* had been a best-seller in 1951, *South Pacific* was everyone's favorite movie in 1958, James Michener's best-selling *Hawaii* also appeared in the late Fifties—as did America's biggest fad, the hula hoop. Americans were also visiting Hawaii in record numbers, and they wanted to recapture the island experience back home.

# Tiki Tacky

Gourmet cooking usually brings to mind fabulous dishes like Polynesian chicken.
—Mettja C. Roate, *The New Hotdog Cookbook* (n.d.)

Some of the worst food in American history—in world history perhaps—followed joyfully in the wake of Trader Vic's inspiration. It was easy (and fun!) to throw in a little pineapple or soy sauce to make a dish Poly/Waiian. If things tasted a little peculiar (and they frequently did) no one seemed to mind. After all, it was Foreign Food, from somewhere Over There, and most people didn't know what it was supposed to taste like anyway.

There were pineapple-marinated cocktail weenies roasted over the flame of Sterno embedded in a cabbage ("A new way to cook hot dogs!" gushed Betty Crocker), there were hamburgers basted with Hawaiian Punch barbecue sauce ("Turns a cookout into a luau!"), there were hot dogs baked in pineapple sweet-and-sour sauce, there were "taters rumaki" (bacon-wrapped canned potatoes), and there was even Trader Vic's lime Jell-O–chutney mold. (In the Forties Trader Vic had said that he hated gelatin salads, but by the Sixties he had changed his tune and his tastes.)

But it was exuberant food. If people didn't know what they were doing and if the tastes were often hideous and the combinations egregious, still there was a feeling of far horizons and adventure, a feeling of sophistication and daring, and above all, of fun. And it was undeniably, enthusiastically, American.

## SOUTH SEAS SKILLET MEAL

This recipe comes from a 1960s utility company pamphlet.

2 cups cubed cooked ham or pork
1 tablespoon cornstarch
1 cup water
1 (13-ounce) can pineapple tidbits and syrup
2 tablespoons soy sauce
1 tablespoon vinegar
1/2 teaspoon Worcestershire sauce
1/4 teaspoon prepared mustard
1/2 green pepper, cut into thin strips
1/2 cup chopped celery
3 cups hot chow mein noodles

Brown meat cubes in skillet. Add the cornstarch dissolved in the water, the pineapple syrup, and seasonings to meat and cook over low heat until sauce is thick and clear. Add pineapple tidbits and vegetables and cook over medium heat about 5 minutes. Serve with chow mein noodles.

MAKES 4 TO 6 SERVINGS

Polynesian restaurants—which usually meant restaurants that served the same sort of food and drink as Trader Vic's—opened by the score around the country. Washington, D.C., had the Genghis Khan, which featured flaming Mauna Loa chicken ("looks like Vesuvius"), and the Dobbs House Luau in Memphis had a flaming pool and a twenty-five-foot Easter Island idol to high-light the Polynesian mood. In Ft. Lauderdale, the Mai-Kai was considered by some to be "the best exponent of the exotic lure of the islands in the U.S.," because it featured not only exotic decor, pretty saronged waitresses, and tropical food and drink but also an "authentic" show with entertainers from Hawaii and Tahiti. Manhattan had, in addition to Trader Vic's, the Luau 400, the Hawaiian Room at the Lexington Hotel, and the Gauguin Room on the ninth floor of the Museum of Modern Art.

But wasn't the food awful? It depends. A great deal of it was Cantonese Chinese or Japanese and if prepared well, was at least good. In the 1969 *New York Times Guide to Dining Out in New York*, Craig Claiborne gave the Gauguin Room three stars (right up there with Lutèce and the Four Seasons), saying it was "one of the pleasantest dining rooms in New York" and the Polynesian food was "delicious." And if enough zombies, mai tais or fog cutters went down the hatch first, anything could taste good.

The fad for exotic Oriental and Polynesian food served up amid frowning tiki gods and flaming torches lasted well into the Sixties. Luaus became popular themes for backyard entertaining, church suppers, and high school hops. By the early Seventies there were seventeen Trader Vic's around the world, and by the time Victor Bergeron died in 1984 the corporation he headed operated twenty-one restaurants.

But by then the chic wouldn't be caught dead in a Trader Vic's. Even glitz-king Donald Trump deemed Trader Vic's tacky and wanted to evict the restaurant from Manhattan's Plaza Hotel in 1989. The Donald relented for a while when customers rushed to the doomed Vic's for just one more pu-pu platter and mai tai, but the writing was on the wall. Although some of the restaurants continued to operate in the rest of the country, Trader Vic's at the Plaza finally closed in 1993.

## A South Seas Luau

Everything is baked at a luau except the customers, who are ordinarily fried.

—"The Lowdown on a Luau, or Belly H'ai," *Saturday Review* (July 3, 1954)

Almost anything comfortable is the thing at a Hawaiian party—muumuus, of course, and aloha shirts, but sport shirts and slacks or pedal pushers are fine, too. Or you might want to make it a beachcomber party, with everyone in tattered clothes; and some of the ladies might wear sarongs.

—"How to Stage a Hawaiian Party," *Sunset* (June 1959)

Our tastes have changed. What we thought tasted exciting…and delicious…then is only strange now. But as with anything, Polynesian food if prepared well, with good ingredients, can be good. And wouldn't it be fun to have a luau party?

First you need as many flowers as you can afford, tropical if possible, but other flowers or even paper flowers will do as well. The table should be low (unless your guests are old or infirm) with low cushions to sit on. In the South Pacific the table would be covered with ti leaves, but on the mainland you could use fern fronds or other large leaves, a flowered cloth, a fish net, or brown paper with "exotic" designs drawn on. Tropical fruits in a wooden or wicker bowl, garnished with vines or flowers, makes the proper centerpiece. Or float some gardenias in low bowls. For serving dishes, as much wood and wicker as you can find—especially if you have any monkeypod bowls or platters. Coconut shells make great drink servers, but large tumblers or brandy snifters will do. Hurricane lamps, fat low candles in pottery or wooden holders, Japanese lanterns, or tiki torches outside, would add atmosphere in the lighting department. And, of course, if you happen to have any tiki god statues, old fishing floats, grass skirts, or other exotica lying around, now is the time to get them out.

For the finishing touches: Hawaiian music on the stereo (or alternatively, Yma Sumac or Martin Denny for those with a yen for the darker side of exotic).

Flower or paper leis to adorn your guests when they arrive. And by all means find out if anyone knows how to play the ukulele or dance the hula.

If you are serving outside, use hibachis to cook the rumaki and let the guests help. A real luau would feature a whole pig roasted in an underground pit, but we'll skip that. Poi, a gray slightly sour paste made from taro root, is traditional, too. If you can find poi at an import shop it will add conversation to the party...because most of your guests will hate it.

The menu below for six to eight people is only suggestive, as they used to say. If you decide to serve the entire menu, a great deal of preparation may be done ahead. The punch can be made early in the day (except for adding the ginger ale and ice), the rumaki can be ready to pop into the broiler, the shrimp for tempura may be prepared ahead and kept cold, salmon lomi may be made a few hours ahead and kept chilled, the chicken luau may be made ahead and reheated, the baked bananas can be ready to go in the oven, and the custard may be made at least a day ahead.

♦♦♦

## A Luau Menu

*Hawaiian Punch*
*Pu-Pu Platter (Rumaki and Shrimp Tempura*
*Pu-Pus)*

*Salmon Lomi (p. 272)*
*Braised Chicken Luau with Coconut Milk*
*and Spinach (p. 273)*
*Boiled Rice*
*Poi (optional)*
*Baked Bananas*
*Sliced Avocado with Lime Juice and Toasted Sesame*
*Seeds*

*Haupia (Coconut Custard)*
*Kona Coffee*

# HAWAIIAN PUNCH

Scorpions, zombies, mai tais, and so on may also be served as punches, but they are so strong the party may get more hilarious than you had planned. This punch has punch, but not too much. It is similar to a planter's punch.

I pound pineapple chunks
4 ounces dark Jamaican rum
I fifth light rum
8 ounces pineapple juice
8 ounces orange juice
4 ounces fresh lemon juice
4 ounces fresh lime juice
I quart ginger ale, chilled
Gardenias for garnish (optional)

Marinate pineapple in dark rum, chilled, overnight. On the day of the party combine the pineapple, rum, and fruit juices in a large bowl and chill at least 1 hour. Just before serving, stir in the ginger ale and add a large block of ice. Float gardenias on top of the punch if you like.

MAKES ABOUT 16 (5-OUNCE) DRINKS

# RUMAKI

Rumaki are the pu-pu everyone loved in the Fifties and Sixties, and loved to despise thereafter. Why? They are simply the South Seas version of the esteemed English savory angels on horseback, and if not too gussied up, are very good. And they are essential to any self-respecting pu-pu platter.

½ cup soy sauce
I teaspoon grated fresh ginger
½ teaspoon curry powder
I pound fresh chicken livers, cut in bite-size pieces
16 water chestnuts, halved
16 pieces bacon, cut in half

Mix together the soy sauce, ginger, and curry and let the chicken livers marinate in the mixture, refrigerated, for 1 hour, then drain. Wrap each piece of liver and water chestnut in a bacon strip and secure with a toothpick. Broil about 5 minutes, turning frequently, until bacon is done. Rumaki may also be cooked over the hibachi, in which case use long toothpicks or skewers; or they may be fried in hot oil.

MAKES 32 RUMAKI

## SHRIMP TEMPURA PU-PUS

To make a Japanese-style tempura, omit the pineapple juice and increase the amount of iced water correspondingly. The Japanese also fry vegetables in tempura batter. Try individual string beans, thin slices of sweet potato, broccoli florets, thin zucchini or eggplant rounds, mushrooms, lotus root slices, thin asparagus spears, slices of green pepper—anything that will cook through quickly.

24 large shrimp
Peanut oil for frying, or a mixture of untoasted sesame oil and peanut oil
$^1/_2$ cup all-purpose flour
$^1/_2$ cup cornstarch
$^1/_2$ teaspoon salt
I large egg, separated
$^1/_4$ cup iced water
$^1/_4$ cup chilled pineapple juice (syrup drained from canned pineapple is good)

Peel and devein the shrimps, leaving the tails on. Slit the shrimps down the backs, cutting almost all the way through, and press them open into the traditional butterfly shape. Sift flour, cornstarch, and salt together into a medium bowl. Mix the egg yolk, water, and pineapple juice and stir into the flour mixture. Beat the egg white until stiff but not dry and fold into the batter. Holding them by the tail, dip the shrimp into the batter. Fry in 375°F oil until the shrimp are a rich golden brown—either in a deep-fat fryer or in 2 inches of oil in a heavy skillet—turning once. Drain on paper towels and serve at once.

MAKES 24; SERVES 6 TO 8

## BAKED BANANAS

Bananas or sweet potatoes are traditionally baked in the luau pit with the pig. Here the bananas are baked in the oven.

$^1/_4$ cup butter
8 slightly underripe bananas, peeled
$^1/_4$ cup sugar
$^1/_4$ cup dark rum
Juice of I lime

Preheat oven to 350°F. Melt the butter in a shallow baking dish. Roll the bananas in the butter and sprinkle with sugar. Mix the rum with the lime juice and drizzle over the top. Bake 20 to 30 minutes until tender, turning the bananas halfway through the cooking time.

MAKES 8 SERVINGS

# HAUPIA

One disgruntled attendee at a luau given by Don the Beachcomber in Hawaii in the early Fifties described haupia as "a square of vulcanized pudding that tastes like white sidewalls flavored with coconut." But if you like cornstarch-coconut puddings, this is very simple and refreshing. You could replace this dessert with vanilla ice cream rolled in shredded coconut, topped with a sauce made from pineapple and apricot preserves mixed with rum—variously known as a Waikiki sundae, or Kona or Tahitian ice cream.

$\frac{1}{2}$ cup sugar
$\frac{1}{4}$ teaspoon salt
$\frac{1}{2}$ cup cornstarch
4 cups coconut milk (p. 274) or 2 cups coconut milk and 2 cups cow's milk

Stir the dry ingredients together in a large saucepan. Gradually add $\frac{1}{2}$ cup coconut milk and blend to a smooth paste. Stir in the rest of the coconut milk and cook over low heat, stirring constantly, until smooth and thickened. Pour into a 9-inch square pan and let cool, then chill. Cut into 12 squares and serve.

MAKES 12 SERVINGS

## Nouvelle Hawaiian

*Food & Wine* magazine predicted in 1992 that Hawaiian food would comprise the next "big wave" of food trends. But they weren't talking about pineapple chicken and rumaki.

Like the rest of the country, Hawaii has been seized with the nouvelle spirit. New Hawaiian dishes like seared tuna salad with cilantro-soy dressing, Kona crab cakes with warm citrus vinaigrette, sweet rice waffles with coconut chutney, and grilled spicy chicken with pineapple salsa are more in line with *Food & Wine*'s "big wave." Roy Yamaguchi of Roy's Restaurant is one of the prime exponents of the New Hawaiian cooking. In the islands, Yamaguchi has been as lionized and as emulated as Paul Prudhomme has been on the mainland.

But if it's hard to imagine a luau with a main course of seared tuna salad don't be without hope. The Kona Village Resort on the Big Island of Hawaii still offers a four-hour Polynesian feast, featuring roast pig, poi, and all the fixin's—cooked and served by descendants of the original Hawaiian settlers. They supply the leis and hula dancers, too.

# Japanese Food in America—The Ascetic Aesthetic

In Japan we have learned to eat with chop sticks very well, and it is not a bad way…. The nice little way of doing your own cooking [over a hibachi] is something to introduce for cuteness in New York.

—Alice Chipman Dewey, *Letters From China & Japan* (1920)

While the Chinese were toiling by the thousands in the American West in the late 1800s, only a few hundred Japanese had arrived on our shores. And while the Chinese opened restaurant after restaurant and introduced Americans to the thrills of Oriental cookery, very few Japanese did the same. Unlike many of the early Chinese immigrants, the Japanese assimilated rapidly into the American culture. Which is not to say they didn't suffer discrimination and humiliation in their new country, as Japanese-American internment camps during World War II so vividly illustrated.

Because the Japanese in America had lived so quietly, Japanese cooking was virtually unknown outside the West Coast before World War II. The oldest Japanese restaurant in New York, Miyako, which opened before World War I, nearly closed during World War II because of anti-Japanese sentiment. Once Miyako's owner put a picture of his son—in a U.S. Army uniform—in the window, the harassment stopped and the restaurant survived. The Japanese had added their own flavor notes and techniques to the Hawaiian melting pot, which also included Indian, Chinese, Korean, Portuguese, Filipino, and native Polynesian foods. But mainland interest in the cooking of Hawaii didn't really take hold until after the war either.

But after 1945 American interest in foreign foods sky-rocketed. Soldiers who had been stationed in Hawaii during the war, and afterward in Japan and Korea, helped spread an interest in Japanese cooking. Americans in record numbers went abroad, first in ships and then in planes, and brought back a taste for alien cuisines. Not many visited Japan, but Hawaii was a popular destination, and Americans en masse discovered sukiyaki, tempura, and teriyaki.

In 1959 there were seven Japanese restaurants in New York—but by 1969 there were thirty-six. Americans loved the atmosphere surrounding a Japanese meal almost as much as the food itself. The exotic and exquisite charm of dining in a serene tatami room (many of the better Japanese restaurants were built with materials and workmen imported from Japan), attended by a graceful kimono-clad waitress who cooked beautifully prepared foods at the low table, was second

only to the hilarity of trying to fold long Western legs clad in tight Western clothes under that table. Eating with chopsticks could also be hilarious, as could trying to pick up one of the scaldingly hot, handleless, but beautiful pottery tea cups. And finally, there was cup after thimble-size cup of delicately warmed sake.

## Sukiyaki

At a Sukiyaki party the hostess starts the festivities by cooking at the table while the guests sample the Chawan-Mushi (Japanese Custard soup). The dessert is simple to prepare and serve—chilled [canned] peaches and fortune cookies.

—*Better Homes and Gardens Guide to Entertaining* (1969)

Although it is probably the best known of all Japanese dishes, sukiyaki was not originally Japanese at all. It was introduced in Japan sometime in the sixteenth century by either the Dutch or the Portuguese and remained a foreign dish for over a hundred years. It eventually became a popular winter dish in Japan.

Sukiyaki was about the only Japanese dish known in America before World War II. In 1932, the Yoshino-Ya restaurant in New York offered a special beef sukiyaki dinner—the sukiyaki accompanied by olives, celery, and cake—for $1.25. (Chicken sukiyaki was also available for $1.50, chicken being more expensive in those days.) During the Fifties it became a popular dish for sophisticated but casual home entertaining. Craig Claiborne reported that it was one of the most requested recipes from his *New York Times* column in 1959.

# BEEF SUKIYAKI

The new electric skillet was perfect for preparing delicious sukiyaki at the table in the America of the Fifties. If you have an electric skillet or chafing dish and want to make a show, prepare the meat, vegetables, and sauce in advance and arrange them prettily, then cook them in front of your family or guests. Chicken may be substituted for the beef; the tofu and shiritaki may be omitted; celery, Chinese cabbage, or watercress may take the place of the spinach or pea pods; and bamboo shoots and soaked dried mushrooms and their liquid may be added.

2 pieces beef fat or 3 tablespoons vegetable oil
1 1/2 pounds lean tender beef, sliced very thin across the grain
2 onions, cut in thin slices
5 ounces firm tofu, cut in bite-size cubes
2 cups sliced mushrooms
1 pound spinach, stems removed, leaves cut in strips
1 1/2 cups snow peas
6 to 8 green onions, cut in 2 1/2-inch pieces
4 ounces shirataki noodles, cooked according to package instructions (see note)

**Sauce**
1/2 cup soy sauce
1/2 cup beef or chicken broth
1/4 cup sake (or sherry)
1 teaspoon sugar (or to taste)

Melt the beef fat in a heavy skillet over medium heat and remove the tried-out pieces (or use oil). Add the meat to the hot fat and brown slightly. Remove the meat to a plate (or you may leave it in the pan and push it to one side if you like it well cooked as many Japanese do) and add the onions to the pan. Cook for a few minutes, then add the tofu and mushrooms, tossing lightly. Mix the sauce ingredients and add half the sauce to the pan. Add the spinach and the rest of the sauce and cook a few more minutes. Taste for seasoning and correct. Then add the pea pods, green onions, and noodles and cook 2 minutes more. Serve at once with boiled rice. (The Japanese serve the sukiyaki with a dipping sauce of beaten raw egg, but that is not advisable in these days of salmonella.)

**Note:** Shirataki noodles may be purchased at Oriental and gourmet groceries.

MAKES 4 SERVINGS

## TEMPURA AND TERIYAKI

The delicate batter-fried Japanese specialty tempura (p. 283) was also introduced to Japan by the Portuguese in the sixteenth century. Although it remained a foreign dish for over a hundred years, by the eighteenth century the Japanese had adopted tempura as one of their own favorite foods. Tempura did not become the home-cooking rage here that sukiyaki did, perhaps because Americans were shy of deep frying, but we ordered it by the pound in Japanese restaurants. The first tempura bar opened in New York City in 1957.

Tempura is usually served with a slightly sweet soy-based dipping sauce. But, said the *New York Times* (April 24, 1955), "The...sauce...is one most Americans would not trouble to make."

## TEMPURA DIPPING SAUCE

The traditional sauce is often made with dashi, a stock flavored with dried bonito tuna and seaweed, presumably why the *Times* deemed it unsuitable for Americans. But a perfectly acceptable sauce may be made without dashi, which is widely available in Asian markets and health food stores.

> 1/4 cup Japanese soy sauce
> 1/4 cup dry sherry or sake
> 1/4 cup chicken stock
> 1/4 teaspoon grated fresh ginger
> 1 teaspoon sugar
> Prepared wasabi (Japanese horseradish condiment), optional

Mix all ingredients except wasabi, and place in individual dipping bowls. Serve with the tempura, with a dab of wasabi on the side for those who wish to heat up the dipping sauce.

MAKES 4 SERVINGS

Teriyaki was another slightly sweet Japanese dish that Americans quickly learned to love. Originally, the Japanese cooked fish with teriyaki sauce, but beef became the most popular on our shores. The meat could be marinated in the sauce, basted with it while grilling (like a barbecue sauce), or the sauce could be poured on after cooking, as Trader Vic was wont to do.

◆◆◆

## BEEF TERIYAKI

Chicken, shrimp, pork, or fish may be substituted for the beef. The beef may also be left whole, marinated for a few hours, grilled, and then sliced after cooking. This method, sans the sugar, was a very popular way with steak in the Fifties and Sixties and is still good. To give this a Japanese-Hawaiian touch, alternate the beef strips with pineapple chunks—and serve with a tropical flower impaled on the end of the skewer. (The flower should not be eaten.)

1½ pounds sirloin or tenderloin steak
½ cup soy sauce
½ cup sake or dry sherry
2 tablespoons sugar
1 clove garlic, crushed
½ teaspoon grated fresh gingerroot

Cut the meat into long, very thin slices across the grain, as for sukiyaki or beef stroganoff. Mix the rest of the ingredients and marinate the meat strips in the sauce in the refrigerator at least 1 hour, stirring occasionally. (Be sure to use a nonreactive pan for marinating.) Thread the meat strips on skewers. Pour the remaining marinade into a small pan and boil for 1 or 2 minutes. Broil or grill the meat strips slowly, basting often with the marinade, until the meat is browned. Serve at once.

MAKES 4 SERVINGS AS A MAIN DISH, OR 8 AS AN APPETIZER

## The Japanese Steak House

Anyone who has never dined in one of the several Japanese steak houses in Manhattan is missing an exceptional opportunity to sample excellent international cookery.

—Craig Claiborne, *The New York Times Guide to Dining Out in New York* (1969)

In the Sixties, Americans liked to eat steak when they went out to dinner, and they liked the exotic allure of Japanese restaurants. Enter the Japanese steak house.

There were several different "brands" of steak house, both here and in Japan, but the best known of them all was Benihana. In 1964, the first Benihana of Tokyo restaurant in the United States opened in New York. Owned and managed by twenty-four-year-old Rocky Aoki, whose father ran the chain in Japan, Benihana was a favorite both for its food and for its sense of theater.

While eight customers sat on three sides of a huge rectangular mahogany table, a chef, wearing a tall red or green hat, cooked food to order on the other side. From a wheeled cart next to the table, the chef would select the beautifully prepared meat, chicken, shrimp, and vegetables as well as the soy sauce, sesame seeds, and aji-no-moto (monosodium glutamate)…and then the show would begin. With dexterous speed and great flashing of cleavers, the chef would cut, chop, fry, and season the food on the huge flat grill on the table, right in front of the delighted customers. The food was simple and good, and the atmosphere was electric with shouts from the chefs and the ringing of the cleavers.

The interiors of the Benihana restaurants in America were carefully designed to resemble an old Japanese inn. There were folk art pottery plates, huge beams put together by Japanese craftsmen in traditional tongue-and-groove construction—and in the two New York Benihanas, the wood for the beams came from old farmhouses in Japan. Americans considered these exotic steak houses purely Japanese, but Japanese who patronized them at home considered them purely American. (In Japan, the Benihana restaurants are known as Benihana of New York.)

Although they are not the huge fad that they once were, the Benihana steak houses continue to serve and excite customers in many cities across the United States.

## Faux Fish

If the crab you find in restaurant California roll sushi is a lurid pink it probably isn't crab at all. The Japanese have a centuries-old tradition of using surimi—ground fish, shaped, colored, and flavored, to look like any number of fish and shellfish. Americans use surimi, too, although our tradition is only a few years old. In 1987 we ate almost 112 million pounds of surimi…in the form of Sea Legs.

Sea Legs, a crab "analogue," was the invention of David Berelson, who got the idea in the Seventies when he first tasted surimi. He thought the Japanese product was too rubbery and worked out his own version that was closer in taste and texture to crab. He and his wife, Riva, began marketing the imitation crab just as the salad bar fad was taking off, and Sea Legs became a megaseller. "It was a really romantic idea making a luxury product affordable," said Riva. The Berelsons also came up with shrimp and lobster analogues, which had some success.

If Sea Legs are not as socially acceptable as they once were, they are still to be found at sushi bars and surviving salad bars. But the Berelsons have been at it again. Their latest project is Mox Lox, which David hopes will make salmon affordable to everyone. For some lucky folks, says he, "Mox Lox will be their very first salmon experience."

# Sushi

In September 1934, a Japanese "bridge luncheon" was suggested by *American Home* magazine. Invitations to the luncheon were to be issued on rice paper, and "favors" of small paper fans and chopsticks tied with a ribbon were to be given to each bridge player. The menu featured sushi, but sushi made from rice boiled with candied ginger, then formed into balls and topped with smoked salmon. This nearly unrecognizable sushi was to be accompanied by tea in small porcelain cups, along with a dish of candied chestnuts mixed with mashed sweet potatoes.

That was one of the first and only mentions of sushi—at least outside of exotic manuscripts—until the great rise in popularity of Japanese food in America in the Sixties. As more and more Japanese restaurants opened here, many of them catering to visiting Japanese, Americans began to venture beyond the sukiyaki-tempura-teriyaki triad. One of the things we tried was sushi…and we liked it enough to make it one of the great food fads of the late Seventies and early Eighties.

Like the Japanese steak houses, part of the sushi bar's great appeal lay in showmanship. Garbed in traditional dress, the highly trained sushi chefs dipped, rolled, and sliced the exotic ingredients with skilled speed, a flashing of knives, and staccato shouts.

Our first hesitant taste was usually of the vinegared rice (which is what sushi means) filled perhaps with cucumber and sesame and rolled in toasted sheets of seaweed. After we were braver and more experienced, perhaps we asked for sushi topped with a slice of raw fish (sashimi)—usually red, beefy tuna. But once we had passed that Rubicon, nothing was too strange to try. Soon we were ordering sushi topped with orange sea urchin, or chewy slabs of giant clam, or slices of octopus complete with suckers. The more outré the ingredients, the more status for the Occidental consumer. On the West Coast, one of the highest status sushis featured a tiny, raw quail egg broken into a "nest" formed by a raised edge of seaweed. In New York, ordering unusual sushi by the "box" to be delivered to the office for a working lunch was the pinnacle of fashion. On both coasts, ordering a "hand roll" (which meant a roll of sushi formed by hand in a cone of seaweed rather than sushi rolled with the help of the traditional sudare mat) showed the customer to be both knowledgeable and sophisticated.

Sushi was almost never made at home, even at the height of its popularity. Many of the ingredients and techniques were too exotic or difficult to attain, even for the most ardent gourmet. But more important, the best part of eating sushi was sitting at the sushi bar, pointing to the strange and wondrous edibles lined up behind the glass (or on the laminated pictures of various sushis thoughtfully provided), and bantering with the chef as he skillfully prepared your dinner.

# CALIFORNIA ROLL SUSHI

Some say sushi was invented, much like the Occidental sandwich, by Japanese gamblers too busy to tear themselves away from the gaming tables to eat. Others say that vinegared rice was used to separate layers of salted fish, and when a hungry worker tasted the rice, sushi was born. Whichever story is true, sushi is completely Japanese, unlike sukiyaki and tempura. Still, Japanese cooks have sometimes borrowed from the West even in sushi making, as is evidenced by this crab and avocado version.

2 cups Japanese short-grain rice
2 1/2 cups water
1/4 cup rice vinegar
1/4 cup sugar
1 teaspoon salt
Paper fan or magazine
4 sheets toasted nori seaweed, cut in eight 7 × 4-inch pieces (see Note)
Sudare mat or clean dish towel
Wasabi paste (Japanese horseradish)
1 ripe avocado, peeled, cut into thin sticks
8 nice-size crab legs or pieces, cooked
1 tablespoon toasted sesame seeds
Soy sauce, wasabi paste, and pickled ginger for serving

Wash the rice under cold water until the water runs clear. Place in a sieve and let drain 1 hour. Place rice and 2 1/2 cups water in a heavy medium saucepan, cover tightly, bring to a boil, then turn heat to very low and cook 20 minutes. Remove from heat and let the pot sit undisturbed 15 more minutes. Empty the rice into a wide, shallow bowl, preferably made of wood. Mix the vinegar, sugar, and salt and pour the mixture onto the rice. Toss the rice and vinegar with a rice paddle or a wooden spoon with one hand, while you fan the rice gently with the paper fan or magazine to help dry and cool the mixture. Be sure not to mash any of the kernels. When the rice has absorbed all the vinegar and is lukewarm and glossy (about 10 minutes), the rice may be covered and set aside for up to 1 1/2 hours, but don't refrigerate.

When you are ready to make the sushi, place a piece of toasted nori on the sudare mat or a clean dishtowel. Wet your hand with water (or water and vinegar, traditionally) and dip out about 1/2 cup rice. Spread the rice on the nori, leaving about a 1/2-inch edge clear on all sides. Make a trench in the middle of the rice. Spread a little wasabi paste in the trench, top with a stick or two of avocado, a piece of crab, and sprinkle these with some of the toasted sesame seeds. Roll the mat or the dish towel away from you, enclosing the rice and fillings in the nori. Remove the mat or towel and slice the roll with a very sharp knife (it helps to wet the knife slightly) into six pieces. Serve the sushi with soy sauce, wasabi paste, and pickled ginger.

**Note:** Toasted nori may sometimes be found in Japanese markets, but it is easy to toast your own. Pass the nori sheet (chopsticks or wooden tongs work well as holders) over a gas flame several times until crisp and the color lightens somewhat. Cut in half and use.

MAKES 6 TO 8 SERVINGS

# New Cuisines from Southeast Asia

When you compare a list of Oriental restaurants in New York in Craig Claiborne's 1969 guide to those listed in the *1992 Zagat's* guide, a dramatic shift in American tastes can be seen:

| **Oriental Restaurants, 1969** | **Oriental Restaurants, 1992** |
| --- | --- |
| Chinese, 89 | Chinese, 59 |
| Japanese, 19 | Japanese, 42 |
| Polynesian, 3 | Polynesian, 0 |
| Korean, 2 | Korean, 3 |
| Burmese, 0 | Burmese, 2 |
| Indonesian, 0 | Indonesian, 2 |
| Vietnamese, 0 | Vietnamese, 6 |
| Thai, 0 | Thai, 18 |

Although Chinese restaurants were still the most numerous, our tastes and our horizons had changed. Japanese restaurants had become common and, therefore, no longer the exotic oddities that they had once seemed. Now, when we went looking for something exotic we sought out restaurants that served foods from Southeast Asia, especially Vietnam and Thailand.

Before our involvement in the "police action" in Vietnam, few Americans had ever heard of Southeast Asia, and fewer still had ever eaten Southeast Asian food. When the Vietnam War ended, many of our allies in Vietnam fled their homeland and came here. As had so many immigrants before them, the Vietnamese opened restaurants in America.

Because Vietnam had been occupied by the Chinese for centuries there are similarities in the two cuisines. But the food of Vietnam relies heavily on the ubiquitous fish sauce of Southeast Asia, called nuoc mam in Vietnam, along with hot chilies, lime, lemongrass, mint, or Vietnamese coriander, and raw fruits and vegetables, which the Chinese generally do not eat.

## Guide to Some Southeast Asian Ingredients

- *Chilies*. The Vietnamese and Thais use small, hot "bird" chilies, which are not always obtainable here. Serrano chilies or jalapeños may be substituted. To ripen green chilies, put them in a sunny window for a few days, until they start to turn red.
- *Coriander*. An herb whose fresh leaves are called cilantro or Chinese parsley. It is related to parsley with a pronounced taste and aroma. People either like it or loathe it (negative descriptions of its taste range from soap to bedbugs). Also much used in Southwestern American and Mexican cooking. No substitute.
- *Fish Sauce*. Nam pla in Thailand, nuoc mam in Vietnam, these sauces are made from salted, fermented fish. Although they do have a fishy taste, the fermentation gives the sauces a depth of flavor akin to a soy or Worcestershire sauce. Generally only the Thai variety is easily obtainable in the United States. Keeps well in the refrigerator. No substitute.
- *Fragrant Rice*. Also called Thai Jasmine rice. A perfumed long-grain rice. Basmati rice may be substituted.
- *Galanga*. Also called galangal, laos, Siamese ginger, and young ginger. A hot, sweet rhizome related to ginger. This spice was once common in European cookery, where it was known as galingale, but it disappeared there after the Middle Ages. Gingerroot may be substituted, but reduce quantities by one-third.
- *Lemongrass*. A citrusy herb that looks something like an anemic scallion. Traditionally, only the inner portions of the white bulb end are used, although some cooks use the tougher green portions when the herb will be taken out of the dish before serving. Dried lemongrass is sometimes available, but must be soaked in water to soften before using. Fresh lemongrass may be frozen. Substitute two teaspoons lime or lemon juice for each stalk of lemongrass called for.

Americans who were getting bored with Chinese food were intrigued by the new flavors of Vietnamese cooking, and raved about the contrasting sweet-sour-salty-fresh tastes. One *New York Times Magazine* article said, "The flavors…were like lightning bolts to our jaded palates." The chic rushed to try it, and Vietnamese restaurants became a fad for a while in the early Eighties. But the fad did not spread across socioeconomic boundaries, as had the Chinese food fad earlier, and as the Thai food fad would a few years later.

Still, the number of Vietnamese restaurants is slowly growing. A recent *New York Times* article praised Vietnamese food (and featured Southeast Asian–inspired clothing by fashion bigwigs like Ralph Lauren, Isaac Mizrahi, and Armani, shot on location in Vietnam). And with all the new enthusiasm for Thai cooking, cooks are turning to other parts of Southeast Asia to expand their repertoire of exotic foods. Particularly on the West Coast and in Hawaii where Pacific Rim cooking, which melds foods and techniques from all over Asia, is becoming very popular, there is again a new interest in the cooking of Vietnam.

## VIETNAMESE SPRING ROLLS WITH HOT DIPPING SAUCE

These crispy rolls appear in many guises throughout China and Southeast Asia. Cooked minced shrimp may be substituted for the crab.

        6 dried Chinese mushrooms
        2 tablespoons peanut or vegetable oil
        3 garlic cloves, chopped
        ¹/₂ teaspoon grated fresh ginger
        I pound lean ground pork
        I tablespoon fish sauce (nuoc mam or nam pla)
        I2 ounces cooked crabmeat, picked over and broken into small bits
        ¹/₂ teaspoon freshly ground black pepper
        ¹/₂ teaspoon salt
        I teaspoon sugar
        6 mint leaves, finely chopped
        6 cilantro leaves, finely chopped
        I large egg, slightly beaten
        I pound egg roll wrappers
        I¹/₂ teaspoons cornstarch
        2 tablespoons water
        Peanut oil for deep frying
        Hot Dipping Sauce (Nuoc Cham) (below)

Soak the mushrooms about 30 minutes in water to cover until they are soft. Drain them, cut off and discard any hard parts, and slice the caps into thin slivers. Set mushrooms aside. Heat the 2 tablespoons oil in a wok or heavy skillet over medium heat. Add the garlic and ginger and stir-fry until the garlic begins to color. Add the pork and cook, mashing it with a fork to break up any lumps, about 2 minutes, or until all traces of pink are gone. Drain off most of the fat from the pork, then add the fish sauce to the pan and cook for 1 minute more. Turn the pork mixture into a large bowl, add the mushrooms, crab, pepper, salt, sugar, mint, cilantro, and egg. Stir gently until well mixed. Set aside to cool slightly.

Separate the egg roll wrappers and dissolve the cornstarch in the water. Lay out each wrapper with a point toward you. Baste the edges of the wrapper with the cornstarch mixture. Take a spoonful of the stuffing, shape it into a cylinder, and place it on the wrapper point closest to you, making sure there is clearance on all sides. Fold the closest point of the wrapper over the filling, away from you. Now fold the two side edges of the wrapper over the filling, like an envelope. Roll the enclosed filling toward the open point, sealing the last point to the roll with more cornstarch mixture, if necessary. Repeat with each wrapper. Keep the filled rolls covered with plastic wrap until ready to fry, so they won't dry out.

Preheat the oven to 200°F. Heat 3 to 4 inches of oil in a wok, deep fryer, or heavy, deep skillet to 360°F. Deep-fry the rolls, 4 or 5 at a time, about 4 or 5 minutes, turning them once. They should be crisp and golden. Remove them from the oil with a slotted spoon and drain on paper towels. Keep the fried rolls warm in the oven while you fry the remainder. Serve hot with Hot Dipping Sauce.

MAKES ABOUT 16 ROLLS

## HOT DIPPING SAUCE (*NUOC CHAM*)

This sauce is infinitely variable, depending on your taste. Add more or less garlic, chili, lime juice, or sugar as you like.

    3 cloves garlic, finely chopped
    1 serrano chili, with seeds, finely chopped
    3 tablespoons sugar
    6 tablespoons fish sauce (nuoc mam or nam pla)
    3 tablespoons fresh lime juice
    1 tablespoon white vinegar
    6 tablespoons water

Pound the garlic, chili, and sugar in a mortar until smooth. Stir in the liquids, taste for seasoning, and serve. You may also make the sauce in a food processor or blender. The sauce may be covered and stored for up to 3 days in the refrigerator.

MAKES ¾ CUP

Until the mid-Seventies, about the only things most Americans knew about Thailand came from the musical *The King and I.* But after the Vietnam War, thousands of Thais flooded into America along with the Vietnamese refugees. By 1992 Los Angeles had over 350 Thai restaurants, more than any other city in the world except Bangkok.

Although Los Angeles was the center of Thai activity in America, other cities from Atlanta to Miami to Hoboken boasted at least one, if not more, Thai restaurants. And even non-Thai restaurants were serving Thai food. Wolfgang Puck's Spago served Thai spring rolls as a pre-pizza appetizer; in New York, the chef at the TriBeCa Grill served fried oysters with vegetables and nam pla and offered a Thai beef salad as an alternative to arugula with roasted red peppers.

Why Thai food has had so great an impact on the American culinary scene, while Vietnamese food has remained an exotic outsider, is difficult to pinpoint. The cuisines are similar, at least to the Western taste. The answer may simply lie in the fact that so many Thais settled in the Los Angeles area and opened restaurants there—and California has been busy exporting food fads to the rest of the country for two decades now. The Thai taste may be just another of its successful exports.

Thai food is full of bright, clear flavors—lemongrass, cilantro, lime, hot chilies, green onions, basil, mint, and galanga (a relative of ginger)—grounded by the darker tastes of garlic, tamarind, soy, and nam pla. These flavors are often brought together with the smoothing tastes of rice, noodles, sugar, or coconut milk.

Incidentally, the Thais eat either with a fork or with their fingers—never with chopsticks.

## CHICKEN AND COCONUT MILK SOUP

This popular, simple soup is well on its way to becoming Americanized. One recipe for it that appeared in a recent cooking magazine recommended half-and-half mixed with coconut extract as a substitute for the coconut milk. The classic soup calls for a whole chicken, chopped with the bones, to be poached in the coconut milk. The American version here uses chicken breasts.

1 whole chicken breast

2 cups chicken broth

3 stalks lemongrass, tender bottom portions only, cut into 1-inch pieces
   (or substitute 2 tablespoons lime juice)

1 thin slice fresh ginger, or galanga

4 cups Coconut Milk (p. 274)

3 green onions, chopped

1/4 cup coriander (cilantro) leaves, chopped

4 serrano or jalapeño chilies, seeded and chopped

2 tablespoons (or more) fresh lime juice

2 tablespoons fish sauce (nam pla), optional

Finely chopped fresh cilantro for garnish

Bone the chicken breasts and discard the skin and fat, but save the bones. Cut the chicken into bite-size pieces. Bring the chicken broth to a boil in a large saucepan. Add the chicken bones, lemongrass, and ginger. Reduce heat and simmer uncovered about 20 minutes. Remove the bones and ginger from the soup. Add the chicken meat and coconut milk and cook over low heat about 10 minutes. Add the green onions, cilantro, and chilies and bring the soup back to a boil. Remove from heat and stir in the lime juice and fish sauce. Taste for seasoning and correct. Sprinkle with cilantro leaves and serve.

MAKES 6 TO 8 SERVINGS

## CHICKEN WITH BASIL OR MINT

Thai "holy basil" is the classic seasoning in this dish but, since it is hard to find in America, any other basil or even mint may be used instead. Shrimp, squid, or beef may be substituted for the chicken. This is a spicy dish and an easy one. It is deservedly popular at Thai restaurants.

2 tablespoons peanut or vegetable oil

8 cloves garlic, coarsely chopped

3 green or red serrano or Thai hot chilies, seeded and cut into thin strips

1 pound chicken breast, boned, skinned, and cut into bite-size pieces

1 cup basil leaves, thinly sliced

1/4 cup fish sauce (nam pla)

2 tablespoons chicken stock

2 teaspoons firmly packed brown sugar

Heat oil in a wok or heavy skillet until very hot. Add garlic and stir-fry a few seconds, or until it begins to brown. Add the chilies and stir-fry a few seconds more, then add the chicken and stir-fry until nearly cooked (about 3 minutes). Add half the basil, the fish sauce, chicken stock, and sugar and cook until the sauce has thickened slightly and the basil is wilted. Stir in the rest of the basil, cooking just until it wilts. Serve immediately with boiled rice.

MAKES 4 SERVINGS

## THAI ICED COFFEE

Although modern Thais may drink cola with their meals, a light beer or the popular sweetened Thai coffee are more to American tastes. The milk and sugar in the coffee help cut down on the "burn" in many Thai dishes. Iced tea may be prepared in the same way.

Cracked ice
$^3/_4$ cup strong, cold coffee
$^1/_4$ cup sweetened condensed milk (or substitute evaporated milk and sugar to taste)

Put the ice in a tall glass and pour the coffee over it. Stir in the milk and serve.

MAKES 1 SERVING

Although Thai food and foods with a Pacific Rim accent have become very popular, indeed trendy, it is unlikely that any "exotic" cooking will again have the impact on Americans that Chinese food once did. Many of us will frequent Thai or Vietnamese restaurants, a few of us will try to duplicate some of the dishes at home. But will hostesses issue rice paper invitations to Vietnamese spring roll parties, or dress like princesses of Siam when they serve their guests Thai chicken with basil? Unlikely. Our culture, with its thousands of choices, has become too fragmented for fads to cut across all the socioeconomic lines as they used to. And, unfortunately for romantics, we have become too sophisticated and world weary for anything to be really and truly exotic anymore.

# 8

# The Seventies

## Eating Our Way to Nirvana

You've just refilled his glass with that exquisite Montrachet, and together you lie in bed, nibbling a pâté.... Doesn't a sensuous mood steal over you both, suggesting the soft, enveloping, passionate love-union to follow? And after sexual energy is spent, perhaps you prolong your mutual pleasure by sharing a delicious meal!

—Helen Gurley Brown in *Cosmo Cookery* (1971)

**A**h, the hedonistic Seventies, the Me Decade. A decade of mood rings, singles' bars, astrology, and EST. A decade of getting high...on drugs, on sex (without the fear of herpes or AIDS), on religion, on Transcendental Meditation. A decade of hot tubs and group encounters. But as hedonistic and self-absorbed as the Seventies were, they were also a decade of goofiness. How else can you describe Pet Rocks, polyester leisure suits, Earth Shoes, sky-high platform clodhoppers, patchwork pants, and the lines "Have a nice day" and "What's your sign?"? Hedonism was combined with goofiness nowhere as well as it was in food.

Simple food, like a broiled steak or a grilled chicken, was not very popular in the Seventies. Instead, everything was gussied up or had a silly name. And it was gooshy, there being no better word to describe the peculiarly unctuous, goofy texture of many of the things we ate then. Sour cream, cream cheese, mayonnaise, hollandaise, and Mornay sauce (not to mention cream of mushroom soup and cream sauce) were stirred into or poured on nearly every savory dish to give it a baroque richness. Desserts were concoctions of whipped cream (or Cool Whip or Dream Whip), or sour cream, or cream cheese, or ice cream, with sticky cornstarch glazes, or ultrasweet butterscotch or chocolate sauces on top. Cakes were baked with pudding mixes to give them that gooshy quality; broccoli and asparagus and other innocent vegetables were smothered in creamy, and often peculiar, sauces and then baked to the properly unctuous texture. Even coffee was gooshed up and gussied up with spices, chocolate, whipped cream, and liqueurs.

This trend had been evident in the Sixties, to be sure, particularly among the suburban recipe-swapping crowd who seemed to think that stirring sour cream into virtually any canned or frozen food—sweet or savory—made it fit for "company." But with the coming of age of the Baby Boomers in the late Sixties and early Seventies, young adults—and young adult tastes—began to dominate American culture. For the most part these young adults—children still, really, no matter how much they protested otherwise—liked childishly sweet and/or creamy foods. And because these young adults had come of age at the end of America's great post-World War II optimism and the beginning of its post-Vietnam gloom, they subverted their natural earnestness and abandoned themselves to hedonism and silliness, in food as in everything else. This silliness would be a strong theme in American cooking (and American culture in general) until the end of the Seventies when the Baby Boomers would finally start to mature.

Quick, which of the following are edible?

    A. Elmer Fudpuckers
    B. Screaming Yellow Zonkers
    C. Fluffernutters
    D. Harvey Wallbangers
    E. None of the above

If you answered "None of the above" your memory or your taste buds have advanced beyond the Seventies.

Elmer Fudpuckers and Harvey Wallbangers (p. 302) were both sticky, icky drinks, popular with the disco crowd. Screaming Yellow Zonkers was the brand name of a sweet snack food aimed squarely at amused hipsters suffering an attack of "marijuana munchies." Fluffernutters were, and are, peanut butter–Marshmallow Fluff sandwiches. Although the sandwich apparently originated in Massachusetts where Marshmallow Fluff is made, the silly name was dreamed up by an advertising copy writer. In a modern take on the Nero-fiddling-while-Rome-burns theme, "Doonsbury" cartoonist Garry Trudeau in 1988 depicted George Bush in the kitchen making a Fluffernutter while the Iran-Contra affair was going on.

# Brunch

Brunch didn't start in the Seventies (the word itself seems to have been coined in 1895), but it surely fit the relaxed and hedonistic style of that decade to a tee. Whether it was getting together in the late morning at a fern bar restaurant (a favorite brunch spot in Seattle sported the name Boondock Sundecker & Greenthumb) or brunching at home, brunch was a great way to socialize after a tough weekend of partying.

Drinks were an important part of brunching, with Bloody Marys and champagne and orange juice mimosas leading the pack. But other drinks that contained at least some fruit juice were popular, including two suggestively named Seventies drinks, Elmer Fudpuckers and Harvey Wallbangers. Of course, if something a little lighter but still festive was wanted, there was always sparkling rosé or sparkling burgundy.

## HARVEY WALLBANGER

The name of this drink supposedly came from a surfer named Harvey who, after consuming too much of the Galliano/vodka-based treat, walked into a wall.

Ice cubes
1 ounce vodka
4 ounces orange juice
1/2 ounce Liquore Galliano

Fill tall glass with ice cubes. Add vodka and orange juice and stir. Float Liquore Galliano on top.

MAKES 1 SERVING

Another typically Seventies drink didn't have a silly name, but did have a garish color scheme.

## TEQUILA SUNRISE

Earlier versions of this drink contained crème de cassis and club soda.

2 ounces tequila
1 ounce grenadine
3 ounces orange juice
1/2 ounce lime juice
Crushed ice
Lime slice

Shake the tequila, grenadine, and juices together with crushed ice. Strain into a glass and garnish with the lime.

MAKES 1 SERVING

If guests were nondrinkers, there was always heavenly Tang tea (although this probably wouldn't have gone over big with the health food crowd).

## HEAVENLY TANG TEA

2 cups Tang powder
$1^3/_4$ cups sugar
$^1/_2$ cup instant tea powder
1 package lemon-lime Kool Aid
$1^1/_2$ teaspoons ground cloves
$1^1/_2$ teaspoons ground cinnamon

Mix all the ingredients together and store in a covered jar. To serve, stir 2 teaspoons (or to taste) into a mug filled with hot water.

MAKES $4^1/_4$ CUPS TEA MIX

Coffee too was an important brunch drink, but plain old American coffee was no longer for the hip and young. No, indeed. We were beginning to discover freshly roasted coffee, serious coffee, and we ground it ourselves. Nor did we then brew it in an old-fashioned percolator (which had seemed so modern in the Thirties). We tried Chemex and Melitta drip coffee makers, or sturdy little stovetop espresso makers. In the Seventies, we also discovered flavored coffees, the beginnings of General Foods International Coffees. Vanilla, hazelnut, chocolate, mint, or combinations thereof were all popular—and sophisticated—coffee flavors then.

## SPICED ORANGE COFFEE

4 cups freshly brewed hot coffee
2 tablespoons firmly packed brown sugar
4 cinnamon sticks
$^1/_2$ teaspoon allspice berries
3 cloves
Rind of 2 oranges (be sure no white part is included)

In a large, nonaluminum or non–cast-iron saucepan combine all the ingredients over low heat and stir until the sugar is dissolved. Strain the liquid through a sieve into a heatproof container. Pour into coffee mugs and serve.

MAKES 4 SERVINGS

For the brunch main dish we could have served bacon and eggs or pancakes or waffles, but mostly we didn't. Instead we tried eggs Benedict ("conceivably the most sophisticated dish ever created in America," Craig Claiborne said in the September 24, 1967, *New York Times*), or French toast—but not the way our mothers had made it, with squishy white bread, and not with maple syrup.

## FRENCH TOAST, SEVENTIES STYLE

Soaking the bread overnight in the egg-milk mixture results in a puffy, very tender toast. This technique was also popular in savory concoctions (see p. 344). For health food enthusiasts, homemade whole wheat bread could take the place of the French bread, but don't soak this bread in the egg-milk mixture more than 1 hour.

> 8 slices stale French bread
> 4 eggs
> I cup milk
> 2 tablespoons Grand Marnier or cognac
> 2 tablespoons sugar
> $\frac{1}{2}$ teaspoon vanilla
> $\frac{1}{4}$ teaspoon salt
> 2 tablespoons butter
> Confectioners' sugar, strawberries, and orange slices for garnish

Place the slices of bread in a large baking pan. Mix the rest of the ingredients except the butter and garnishes together and pour over the bread. Cover and refrigerate overnight.

Melt the butter in a heavy skillet. Fry the bread in the hot butter on both sides until crisp and brown. Serve hot, sprinkled with confectioners' sugar. Garnish each serving with hulled whole strawberries or orange slices.

MAKES 4 SERVINGS

Another popular brunch item was the Dutch baby, a delicious sweet cross between a pancake and an omelet. Dutch babies are also known as puffy pancakes, German pancakes, and Norwegian pancakes and are close cousins to the French clafoutis.

## DUTCH BABY

Although babies can be served with preserves, fresh fruit, or even maple syrup, they are classically and best adorned simply with powdered sugar and lemon.

$^3/_4$ cup all-purpose flour
$^3/_4$ cup milk
$^1/_4$ teaspoon salt
I tablespoon granulated sugar
4 eggs, beaten just until foamy
3 tablespoons unsalted butter
Confectioners' sugar and lemon slices for garnish

Preheat the oven to 400°F. Place a 9-inch ovenproof skillet in the oven to heat. Mix the flour, milk, salt, and granulated sugar in a bowl. Whisk in the eggs. Place the butter in the hot skillet, swirling it around to coat all the surfaces. Pour the batter into the skillet. Put the skillet in the oven and bake until the baby is puffed, browned, and is pulling away from the sides of the pan, about 25 minutes. Cut into wedges and serve immediately (the baby will deflate as it cools). Give each diner a little bowl of confectioners' sugar to sprinkle over the pancake and some lemon slices to squeeze on top.

MAKES 4 SERVINGS

In keeping with the continuing popularity of foreign cooking, the Italian omelet, or frittata, was a big brunch dish. It was also good to serve health food enthusiasts because it incorporated vegetables into the eggs. Zucchini was a particular favorite, which was logical considering both zucchini and the omelet are Italian. Frittatas were known in the Sixties, but didn't come into their own until the Brunch Decade.

## FRITTATA WITH ZUCCHINI

Nearly any well-drained cooked vegetable may be substituted for the zucchini, but spinach, potatoes, and artichoke hearts are particularly good. A well-seasoned 10-inch frying pan that can go into the oven is best for making a frittata.

¼ cup olive oil
1 pound zucchini, thinly sliced
2 cloves garlic, minced
1 tablespoon chopped fresh oregano or Italian (flat-leaf) parsley
8 eggs
2 tablespoons water or milk
¼ teaspoon salt
Few grinds of pepper
2 tablespoons grated Parmesan cheese

Heat 2 tablespoons of the oil in a large skillet over medium-high heat. Add the zucchini and garlic, cooking and tossing them in the oil until the zucchini is soft, about 15 minutes. Stir in the oregano. Beat together the eggs, water, salt, pepper, and cheese. Stir another tablespoon of the oil into the zucchini and when the oil is heated, pour the egg mixture over the vegetables.

Cook over medium-low heat without stirring until the egg starts to set around the edges. Lift some of the egg mixture from the sides of the pan with a wide spatula, tipping the pan to let the uncooked egg flow to the bottom of the pan. Continue cooking until the egg mixture is almost set. Put a large platter over the top of the pan and invert the frittata onto the platter. Add the last tablespoon of oil to the pan, swirling it around to coat the bottom and sides. Slide the frittata back into the pan, uncooked side down, and cook about 2 minutes more. (If you are nervous about sliding the frittata in and out of the pan, or if the frittata seems to be stuck, you may place it under the broiler for 1 to 2 minutes to cook the top. Watch closely so it does not brown.) Invert the frittata onto a warm serving platter, cut into wedges, and serve.

MAKES 6 TO 8 SERVINGS

An American variation on the frittata was the Joe's special (also called Broadway Joe's special). This combination of eggs, hamburger, onions, spinach, and sometimes mushrooms made a hearty brunch with a glass of sparkling rosé wine, some French bread, and a steaming cup of café au lait.

## JOE'S SPECIAL

A long-time staple of San Francisco restaurants, Joe's special is variously reported to have been created there by (1) hungry dance-band musicians in the 1920s, (2) hungry gold miners, and (3) a famous restaurant chef who was trying out variations on a frittata. No one knows who Joe was.

2 tablespoons olive oil

1 pound ground beef, crumbled

2 medium onions, finely chopped

2 cloves garlic, minced

1/2 pound mushrooms, sliced

1 teaspoon salt

1/4 teaspoon dried oregano

Few grinds of pepper

Ground nutmeg

1 (10-ounce) package frozen chopped spinach, thawed and drained (or
substitute 1/2 pound fresh spinach, well washed, tough stems removed,
leaves chopped, and drained)

6 eggs

Heat the oil in a large, heavy skillet over medium-high heat. Brown the ground beef in the oil, stirring to break up any large chunks. Drain off all but 2 tablespoons of the fat. Reduce heat to medium and add the onions, garlic, and mushrooms. Cook until the onions are soft and the mushrooms have reabsorbed their liquid. Stir in the seasonings and spinach and cook until the spinach is nicely hot and cooked through, another 5 minutes.

In a separate bowl, stir the eggs together with a fork until just blended. Pour the eggs over the meat mixture, stirring and cooking over low heat until the eggs are set but still soft.

MAKES 4 TO 6 SERVINGS

Planning a brunch could be tough, but cookbooks came to the rescue in the Seventies with menu ideas and table setting hints. Even the staid *New York Times* put out the *Guide to Better Brunches* pamphlet in 1971, which suggested making your brunch more exciting by "adding some conversational morsels from tomorrow's *New York Times*."

My favorite brunch cookbook, however, hands down, is Ruth Macpherson's *Discover Brunch* (1977). Reading it is to travel back in time to the halcyon days of Seventies cooking when menus full of cheese, sour cream, milk, and butter were perfectly acceptable, and no one worried about fat grams.

◆◆◆

# Ruth Macpherson's Derby Day Buffet Brunch

*Mint Juleps*
*Cheese Fondue Appetizer*
*Easy Chicken Crêpes (made with cream of chicken*
*soup and sour cream)*
*French-style Green Beans (heated frozen beans with*
*butter)*
*Bing Cherry Salad Mold (made with sour cream)*
*Zucchini Bread*
*Whiskey Bundt Cake (made with vanilla pudding)*
*Coffee*

Variations on the whiskey Bundt cake, a spirited cake mix with pudding, were enormously popular in the Seventies. They were usually made with sherry—and known as sherry cake, wine cake, or just The Cake—and topped with powdered sugar, but Ruth Macpherson's version contained whiskey and added whiskey topping. Bacardi popularized a rum cake identical to the whiskey cake—except that it contained rum instead of whiskey, of course. To make sherry cake, omit the milk, whiskey, and nuts and substitute 1 cup sherry. Without either whiskey, rum, or sherry, this was Jell-O's famous pudding cake.

## WHISKEY OR RUM BUNDT CAKE

"Has to be tasted to be believed—you will find the men asking you to give the recipe to their wives," said Ruth MacPherson. The cake can be made in a tube pan, but Bundt pans were all the rage when this recipe made the rounds.

**For the Cake**

    1 (18.25) ounce package yellow cake mix

    1 (4-ounce) package instant vanilla pudding

    4 eggs

    1/2 cup vegetable oil

    1 cup milk

    1/4 cup rye whiskey or dark rum

    1 cup chopped pecans or walnuts, dusted with flour

**For the Glaze**

    1/3 cup butter

    1/4 cup water

    3/4 cup sugar

    1/4 cup rye whiskey or dark rum

Preheat the oven to 350°F. Grease and flour a 12-cup Bundt pan. Combine all the cake ingredients except the nuts and beat with a mixer on medium speed for 5 minutes. Stir in the nuts. Pour the batter into the prepared pan. Bake until the cake pulls away slightly from the edges of the pan and a toothpick inserted in the center of the cake comes out clean, about 50 minutes.

While the cake is baking, make the glaze. In a small saucepan over low heat, melt the butter, then stir in the sugar, water, and whiskey or rum. Boil 5 minutes, stirring constantly. Remove from the heat and keep warm. Remove the cake from the oven and immediately pour half the glaze over the cake. Leave the cake in the pan for 25 minutes. Remove from the pan and pour over the rest of the glaze.

MAKES 1 CAKE

One other variation on whiskey or sherry cake must be mentioned and that is the Elmer Fudpucker cake. To make a Fudpucker cake, substitute $^{1}/_{4}$ cup vodka, $^{1}/_{4}$ cup apricot nectar, and $^{1}/_{4}$ cup apricot brandy for the milk and whiskey or rum. Glaze the warm cake with 1 cup confectioners' sugar mixed with 2 tablespoons apricot nectar, 2 tablespoons vodka, and 2 tablespoons apricot brandy.

## ZUCCHINI BREAD

This quick bread was full of zucchini, brown sugar, and vegetable oil, all of which were considered good for you in the 1970s. For anyone who has not tried this bread, the zucchini adds almost no flavor but contributes moistness to the crumbs.

 3 large eggs
 2 cups firmly packed brown sugar
 I cup vegetable oil
 2 teaspoons vanilla extract
 3 cups sifted flour
 I teaspoon salt
 I teaspoon baking powder
 I teaspoon baking soda
 I teaspoon ground cinnamon
 2 cups loosely packed grated zucchini
 I cup chopped walnuts

Preheat the oven to 325°F. In a large bowl beat the eggs, sugar, oil, and vanilla together until thick and creamy. Sift together the dry ingredients and stir them into the eggs, blending well. Stir in the zucchini and nuts. Pour the batter into two greased and floured 9 × 5-inch loaf pans. Bake until a toothpick inserted in the center comes out clean, about 70 minutes. Remove from the pans and cool on a wire rack.

MAKES TWO (9 × 5-INCH) LOAVES

Another "healthy" quick bread that was all the rage then was pumpkin bread. Both pumpkin bread and zucchini bread freeze very well, if you're wondering what to do with all those loaves.

## PUMPKIN BREAD

2 large eggs

3 1/2 cups sugar

1 cup vegetable oil

1 (29-ounce) can solid pack pumpkin

5 cups all-purpose flour

4 teaspoons baking soda

1 teaspoon salt

1 teaspoon ground cinnamon

1 teaspoon ground nutmeg

2 cups raisins

2 cups chopped nuts

Preheat the oven to 350°F. In a large bowl, beat together the eggs, sugar, and oil until thick and creamy. Beat in the pumpkin. Sift together the dry ingredients in another large bowl and stir into the pumpkin mixture in several additions. Stir in the raisins and nuts. Pour the batter into 4 greased and floured 9 × 5-inch loaf pans. Bake until a toothpick inserted into the center comes out clean, 60 to 70 minutes. Remove from the pans and cool on wire racks.

MAKES 4 (9 × 5-INCH) LOAVES

# Crêpes

Which came first?—The brunch or the crêpe?

—Dean Hewitt, *The New York Times Guide to Better Brunches* (1971)

If you plan to have a strawberry crêpe and sparkling Burgundy brunch for five hundred people, it might be wise to buy more than one crêpe pan.

—Irena Kirshman, *Crêpes & Flaming Desserts* (1969)

What beef Wellington was to the Sixties, crêpes were to the Seventies. And more so. Crêpes were far easier to make than beef Wellington, and they were infinitely more versatile. They could be served as an appetizer, a main course, or a dessert, and they could be served at breakfast, lunch, supper, and dinner...and certainly at brunch. And best of all, nearly every one of the myriad possible fillings would include the rich, creamy sauces so typical of the Seventies. Crêpes were so popular that Aunt Jemima came out with crêpe mix and frozen crêpe batter in 1977.

Crêpes were not new to America in the 1970s. Crêpes suzette had been the dessert of sophisticates for forty years. But as French-accented "gourmet" cooking took hold in the 1960s, the possibilities inherent in crêpes became apparent. One of the strongest popularizing forces was Hungarian expatriate Leslie Fono who, with his wife, Paulette, opened one of the first crêperies in San Francisco, the Magic Pan, in 1965. The restaurant, with its eponymous patented crêpe-making machine, specialized in crêpes stuffed with every imaginable filling. The Magic Pan was extremely successful and soon opened branches in other major cities. Other crêperies opened around the country, but only the Magic Pan seemed to have the staying power to survive the Seventies. (And indeed longer—one of the last Magic Pans closed in Paramus, New Jersey, in 1989.) One of the Magic Pan's specialties was brunch—and they even found a way to serve popular Eggs Benedict in a crêpe.

## BASIC CRÊPES

1 cup all-purpose flour
Pinch of salt
3 large eggs
1 1/2 cups milk
1 tablespoon melted butter
Oil or clarified butter for cooking

Sift the flour and salt into a mixing bowl. In a separate bowl beat the eggs lightly, then stir in the milk and 1 tablespoon melted butter. Beat the liquid gradually into the dry ingredients, beating just until the batter is smooth. It should be the consistency of heavy cream. The crêpes will be most tender if the batter is left to sit, covered, in the refrigerator at least 1 hour before cooking. If the batter thickens on standing, thin it with a little water.

To cook the crêpes, brush a 6- to 7-inch well-seasoned crêpe or nonstick pan with a thin film of oil or clarified butter. Heat the pan until hot but not smoking. Pour about 2 tablespoons of the batter into the pan and immediately tip the pan in all directions to spread the batter in a thin circle. Pour out any excess. Cook over medium heat until the top of the crêpe is dry and the bottom is lightly browned. Turn the crêpe and cook on the other side about 20 seconds. Remove the crêpe to a plate, wipe out the pan, if necessary, and grease it again. Continue cooking the rest of the crêpes. The finished crêpes may be kept warm in a low oven covered with a kitchen towel or stacked between pieces of foil, waxed paper, or plastic wrap and stored tightly covered in the refrigerator for later use. They may also be frozen for up to one month.

MAKES 12 TO 14 CRÊPES

# CHICKEN AND MUSHROOM CRÊPES

These crêpes, with their cream sauce, cheese, and sour cream, are rich and gooey—and certainly have no place in a low-fat diet. But who was worried about that in the early Seventies?

7 tablespoons butter
$^1/_2$ pound mushrooms, sliced
5 tablespoons flour
I cup milk
I cup chicken broth
$^1/_2$ cup heavy cream
Salt and pepper
$^1/_8$ teaspoon cayenne pepper
$^1/_4$ teaspoon ground nutmeg
I cup shredded Gruyère cheese
$1^1/_2$ to 2 cups bite-size pieces cooked chicken
$^1/_2$ cup sour cream
12 cooked Basic Crêpes (p. 312)
$^1/_2$ cup grated Parmesan cheese

Preheat the oven to 350°F. Melt 2 tablespoons of the butter in a skillet over medium heat, then stir in the mushrooms and cook until the mushrooms are soft and all their liquid has been reabsorbed. Remove from the heat and set aside. Melt the remaining butter in a heavy saucepan over low heat. Stir in the flour, cooking for a few minutes. Remove the pan from the heat and gradually whisk in the milk and broth. Return the pan to medium heat and when the mixture is thick and smooth, stir in the cream, salt, pepper, cayenne, and nutmeg. Remove from the heat and set aside half the sauce. Into the remaining sauce stir the Gruyère, chicken, mushrooms, and sour cream.

Spoon a thin layer of the reserved cream sauce over the bottom of a greased oven-to-table baking dish. Spoon a little of the chicken mixture onto each crêpe and roll the crêpes. Arrange the rolled crêpes close together in the baking dish. Spoon the remaining cream sauce over the rolled crêpes. Sprinkle with the Parmesan and bake until browned and bubbly, 20 to 30 minutes.

MAKES 6 SERVINGS

# ICE-CREAM SUNDAE BUTTER PECAN CRÊPES

Real kids' stuff, this, yet sophisticated enough for "gourmets." And pretty yummy, if you're in the mood for baroque desserts. This recipe was developed from the description of the butter pecan crêpes served at the Clos Normand Restaurant in the April 1971 issue of *Gourmet*. Toasted salted pecans have been substituted for Clos Normand's toasted almonds.

**For the Caramel Sauce**
> 1 1/4 cups sugar
> 1/3 cup warm heavy cream
> Pinch of salt
> 1/2 teaspoon vanilla extract

**For the Toasted Salted Pecans**
> 1 cup pecan halves
> 1 teaspoon butter, melted
> Salt

**To Assemble the Dessert**
> 6 hot cooked Basic Crêpes (p. 312), or use the sweeter crêpes from Crêpes
>    Suzette (p. 159)
> Butter pecan ice cream

In a heavy skillet (cast iron works well) melt the sugar over low heat, stirring constantly. When the sugar has melted and reached a light golden color, remove from the heat. Very carefully and slowly stir in the cream and salt. (Be *very* careful, because the hot sugar syrup can burn mightily if it splashes.) Return the pan to the heat and stir the sugar and cream together until smooth. Remove from the heat, cool slightly, then stir in the vanilla. Pour the warm sauce into a bowl or pan and keep it warm over hot water.

Toss the pecans with the butter, place them on a baking sheet, and toast them in a preheated 400°F oven, or in a heavy skillet on top of the stove until they smell toasted and are golden brown. Remove from the heat and sprinkle with a little salt. Set aside.

Place each warm crêpe on a warm dessert plate. Put a scoop or two of ice cream on each crêpe and drizzle a little warm caramel sauce over the ice cream. Fold the crêpe over the filling. Spoon more warm caramel sauce over each crêpe and scatter the pecans over the top.

MAKES 6 CRÊPES

♦♦♦

# A Glorious Holiday Brunch, Circa 1975

*Harvey Wallbanger Wassail Cup*
*Quiche Lorraine*
*Mixed Grill of Lamb Chops, Sausages, Tomatoes,*
*and Peppers*
*Moselle Wine*
*Pancake Puff (Dutch Baby) with Strawberries and*
*Whipped Cream*
*Brandied Mocha Chocolate with Whipped Cream*

Along with beef Wellington, the other pastry-based dish that became popular in the Sixties—and on and on into the Seventies—was quiche. Cut small as an appetizer (or baked in tiny tartlet tins for even more panache) or served in large slices as the perfect centerpiece for an elegant brunch or festive late night supper, quiche was sophisticated, easy to make, and delicious. At least, it started out that way.

According to *Larousse Gastronomique,* quiche originated in the Lorraine area of France, which has often come under the domination of Germany. The word *quiche* (Old French: *kiche*) is probably a corruption of the German word *kuchen,* which means "cake." The dish can be traced back to the sixteenth century, when it was made with a bread dough base rather than the flaky pastry now used.

There is nothing so simple, so full of the good flavors of rich cream, eggs, and smoky bacon as a basic quiche Lorraine. However, to be really good it must be made with the best ingredients. Try it with organic eggs from range-fed chickens, absolutely fresh cream (not ultrapasteurized), and thick-cut, farmer-style bacon. Why bother to ingest all those fat grams unless what you're eating is superb?

## QUICHE LORRAINE

A true quiche Lorraine contains no cheese, although very few cookbooks will tell you that.

**For the Pastry**

1 1/2 cups all-purpose flour
1/4 teaspoon salt
1/2 cup (1 stick) chilled unsalted butter, cut into 1/4-inch bits
1 tablespoon fresh lemon juice
2 to 4 tablespoons ice water
Egg wash made with 1 egg white beaten with 1 tablespoon water

**For the Filling**

4 to 5 thick slices lean bacon
3 tablespoons unsalted butter
4 eggs
1 1/2 cups heavy cream
1/4 teaspoon salt
Freshly ground pepper and nutmeg

For the pastry, sift the flour and salt together into a large mixing bowl. Add the butter bits and work them into the flour with a pastry blender or two knives (or your fingers, if you have a cool hand with pastry) until the mixture resembles coarse meal. Pour in the lemon juice and 2 tablespoons of the ice water. Mix lightly until the dough starts to gather into a ball. If the dough is still crumbly, add additional water, drop by drop. Dust the pastry ball lightly with flour and refrigerate, covered tightly, for at least 1/2 hour.

Preheat the oven to 400°F. Remove the pastry from the refrigerator and roll out on a lightly floured board to make a circle 12 inches across.

Butter an 8- or 9-inch pie pan (or a false-bottomed tart pan if you wish to unmold the quiche). Gently lay the pastry over the pan and fit it into the sides and bottom without stretching it. If you are using a pan with fluted sides, roll the rolling pin over the edges of the pan to trim off the excess pastry. Otherwise, flute the pastry around the top of the pan with your fingers, trimming off excess pastry with a sharp knife. Prick the bottom of the pastry all over with a fork, without piercing it all the way through.

Bake for 10 minutes. Remove from the oven and brush the bottom of the pastry with the egg wash. Bake again until it starts to brown, about 5 minutes. Cool on a wire rack.

Lower the oven to 350°F. Make the filling. If the bacon is heavily smoked, blanch it for 5 minutes in boiling water, then pat it dry. Melt 1 tablespoon of the butter in a heavy skillet. Add the bacon and cook until it is cooked but not crisp.

Drain it well, patting off the fat with paper towels. Cut the bacon into small pieces and scatter them over the bottom of the cooked pastry shell. Beat the eggs lightly, in a medium bowl, then pour in the cream, mixing well. Season with the salt, a grinding of pepper, and a grating of nutmeg. Melt the remaining butter in a small heavy pan until it just starts to color and give off a nutty aroma. Mix the melted butter into the custard. Pour the custard into the tart shell. Bake the quiche until the custard has puffed and browned and a knife plunged into the side of the custard comes out clean, 25 to 30 minutes. Serve hot or warm.

MAKES 1 QUICHE

In a review of New York's Leopard restaurant in the February 1970 issue of *Gourmet,* Donald Aspinwall Allan praised the appetizers because "there is always a good quiche," including onion, ham, leek, or anchovy and olive. Restaurants and caterers soon learned that while quiche was both a popular and hearty appetizer, it was also sturdy, and could be held for hours. If the crust became slightly soggy, no one complained.

Quiche's enduring popularity into the Seventies had a great deal to do with the scope it allowed creative cooks. As one *Bon Appétit* reader commented, while inquiring after the recipe for the moussaka quiche (with eggplant, tomatoes, onion, and lamb) served at The Cottage Crest in Massachusetts, "There seems to be no end to culinary imagination when it comes to making quiches." Another *Bon Appétit* reader contributed a cottage cheese quiche topped with canned French-fried onion rings as a "light supper dish that is an excellent source of protein." *Gourmet* (October 1971) even published a recipe for a cranberry-carrot dessert quiche to be served with whipped cream. Plain old quiche Lorraine—with cheese, of course—was still around, but it was generally considered much too boring. And besides, what more elegant way for American homemakers to use up their leftovers than in a fashionable quiche?

By the early Eighties Americans had been served too many quiches—at bad restaurants, at every catered event, even at the corner deli—and the dish took a nose dive in popularity. Even Craig Claiborne, quiche's early promoter, declared that he wouldn't be caught dead serving it.

Of late, however, quiche has been making a slight comeback. Considering how simple and elegant a dish it is—when well made—it's not surprising. And don't forget quiche's seemingly infinite capacity to absorb the creative cook's fillips.

## Who Really Put the Quiche on the American Table?

One of the first U.S. recipes for quiche appeared in *American Home* magazine in April 1941 as "tart Normandy." It was an accurate gastronomic rendition of quiche Lorraine, if geographically quite a few kilometers off. A few years later Herman Smith wrote about his cook Stina's quiche d'Alsace (in *Stina*, 1945), but the recipe turned out to be an egg-thickened cream sauce poured over cubed chicken, ham, and hard-boiled eggs, served in a pastry shell. James Beard's catering company, Hors d'Oeuvres, Inc., served quiche to many an upscale Manhattan crowd in the Forties, and Dione Lucas published a quiche Lorraine recipe in her *Cordon Bleu Cook Book* (1947), adding just a smidgen of grated Parmesan (and a shake of cayenne pepper) to her custard. In January 1951 *House and Garden* suggested "that wonderful cheese and onion pie, quiche Lorraine" as the perfect hearty dish for hungry skiers. Also calling it a "cheese and onion pie," Craig Claiborne reported on January 4, 1959, that quiche Lorraine was one of the *New York Times* food department's four most requested recipes of 1958. (The other three were paella, sukiyaki, and chocolate cake.)

Both Claiborne and Beard claimed to have introduced quiche to America. Given the evidence, this is unlikely, although undoubtedly both men did much to popularize the dish. But it wasn't until Julia Child's eighty-seventh television show for *The French Chef* in the mid-Sixties that quiche became America's favorite pie. Mrs. Child encouraged her audience to flavor the basic custard with everything from the classic bacon (or cheese) to chopped spinach, asparagus, mushrooms, chicken livers, or shellfish. The "Era of the Quiche," as Betty Fussell called it in *Masters of American Cookery* (1983), had begun, and there was no holding anyone back.

## LATTER-DAY SPINACH-FETA QUICHE

In September 1992, *Parenting* magazine asked readers, "Remember quiche? That old-fashioned one-dish dinner is slated for a comeback. It's a breeze to prepare, and kids love its creamy texture." Using a small number of eggs and reduced-fat dairy products, the magazine gave readers several (relatively) low-fat alternatives to that rich dish of old, including broccoli-tomato-cheddar quiche and zucchini-pepper-ricotta quiche. This is a Greek-accented version.

2 large eggs

I cup I percent milk

$^2/_3$ cup crumbled feta cheese, rinsed to remove excess salt

$^1/_3$ cup grated Parmesan cheese

$^1/_2$ teaspoon ground nutmeg

I teaspoon dillweed

3 tablespoons chopped fresh Italian (flat-leaf) parsley

I (10-ounce) box frozen chopped spinach, cooked according to package instructions and drained

3 tablespoons minced onions, sautéed in a little butter until soft

I (9-inch) pie crust, unbaked

Preheat the oven to 350°F. Place the eggs, milk, feta, and Parmesan in a bowl and stir until blended. Stir in the seasonings, spinach, and onions. Pour everything into the crust and bake for 45 to 60 minutes. or until puffed and brown.

MAKES I QUICHE

# The International Gourmet Heads South

International cooking still set gourmets apart from nongourmets, and French cooking was still king. Coq au vin, bouillabaisse, and any sort of duckling with fruit sauce were popular "posh" dishes, whether at home or at a restaurant. But the fashion in international food was moving south toward the Mediterranean. German and Scandinavian foods, which had been popular in the Fifties and Sixties, had definitely lost much of their cachet, and even French food seemed excessively classical. The most fashionable foods now had an Italian or Greek accent.

There was one category of French dish, though, that was a favorite with nearly everyone, young and old, high-brow gourmet and low, and that was pâté. Strong, dark flavors were In and nothing was more darkly sensuous and hedonistic than a well-seasoned mixture of meats and fats. A few brave souls made their own at home from mile-long recipes, but most pâtés were purchased either in cans or from the charcuteries springing up in the major cities that also sold cheese, French-style breads, and fancy condiments.

For the cook who did want to make a pâté but wasn't about to attempt a classic version, there were, of course, recipes that started with "take ¹/₂ pound liverwurst." But there were also the more honest, if less deluxe, recipes based on chicken livers.

## CHICKEN LIVER–MUSHROOM PÂTÉ

"A handsomely garnished pâté is an important element to assure successful entertaining," according to *Your Secret Servant,* a small 1970s cookbook. This one is delicious.

³/₄ cup (1 ¹/₂ sticks) butter
¹/₂ pound mushrooms, chopped
1 clove garlic, minced
¹/₃ cup minced onion
1 bay leaf
1 pound chicken livers
1 teaspoon salt
2 tablespoons brandy
2 drops Tabasco sauce
¹/₂ teaspoon freshly ground black pepper
Additional butter for sealing crocks, if desired

Melt ¹/₄ cup of butter in a large heavy skillet. Add the mushrooms, garlic, onion, and bay leaf and sauté over low heat until the onions are soft. Clean and remove the membranes from the chicken livers, cutting away any black or green spots. Cut the chicken livers in pieces, then add them to the vegetable mixture with the salt and cook until the livers are cooked, but still a little pink inside. Cool slightly. Remove the bay leaf and put the chicken liver mixture in a blender or food processor along with the brandy, Tabasco sauce, pepper, and ¹/₂ cup of butter. Blend until smooth. Taste for seasoning and correct, adding more salt, Tabasco sauce, pepper, or brandy as needed. Turn into serving crocks and chill, tightly covered, overnight. The pâté may be held, chilled, for up to 1 week if melted butter is poured over the top.

MAKES 3 CUPS

The vogue for food with a Mediterranean accent meant that Spanish paella was still going strong as a dinner party dish. The Italian-American fish stew cioppino, a cousin of paella and bouillabaisse, was another popular item.

## CIOPPINO

This fish stew originated with the Italian fishermen working in the San Francisco area and is still featured at many restaurants there. It can be served with rice but, in keeping with its place of birth, is best with a crusty loaf of sourdough bread.

1/3 cup olive oil
3 medium onions, chopped
1 medium green bell pepper, seeded and chopped
8 cloves garlic, minced
2 cups peeled, seeded, and chopped tomatoes
1/4 cup tomato paste
2 cups dry white wine
1/4 cup coarsely chopped Italian (flat-leaf) parsley
1 bay leaf
1/2 teaspoon dried oregano
1/2 teaspoon dried thyme
1/2 teaspoon dried or 1/4 cup chopped fresh basil
1 teaspoon salt
1 large Dungeness crab, cut into serving pieces (other crabs or lobster may be substituted)
1 pound firm-fleshed sea fish fillet such as snapper, skinned and cut into chunks
1 pound medium shrimp, shelled and deveined
2 dozen small clams, scrubbed
2 dozen small mussels, scrubbed and debearded
1/4 cup chopped Italian (flat-leaf) parsley for garnish

In a large kettle heat the olive oil, then sauté the onions, green pepper, and garlic over medium heat until soft. Add the tomatoes, tomato paste, 1 cup of the wine, the herbs, and salt and bring to a boil. Lower the heat and simmer 10 to 15 minutes. Add the crab and chunks of fish to the pot, pushing them down into the sauce, and cook over low heat, covered, about 10 minutes. Add the shrimp, cover again, and cook until the shrimp are pink.

In a separate pot, steam the clams and mussels in the remaining 1 cup wine (add a little water, if necessary) until they open. Discard any that do not open. Add the clams and mussels to the kettle. Strain the clam cooking liquid through fine cheesecloth and add it to the kettle.

Cover and cook another 3 to 5 minutes over low heat. (If the stew is too liquidy, remove the fish and shellfish and boil down the liquid. Then return the fish and shellfish to the pot.) Taste for seasoning and serve sprinkled with parsley.

MAKES 6 TO 8 SERVINGS

Other dishes with that Mediterranean touch were fashionable, too. Italian osso bucco (braised veal shanks) was considered very sophisticated, as was the Sicilian appetizer caponata (an eggplant-based relish or salad). Both of these can still be found at Italian restaurants (and caponata is available canned). One Italian dish that was all the rage then but is almost never seen now is lobster fra diavolo. It is very similar to the cioppino recipe given earlier except that $1^{1}/_{2}$ pounds of lobster are substituted for the crabs, fish, and shellfish. The lobster is usually removed and served separately, and the sauce is served with linguine.

As popular as Italian food was, tomato-based pasta sauces—except for the fra diavolo—were definitely Out. Spaghetti and meatballs were entirely too pedestrian and too redolent of family potluck suppers and the neighborhood Neapolitan restaurant. Spaghetti was In, but only with the white sauces more typical of northern Italian cooking. These sauces tended to be very rich and creamy—it was the gooshy Seventies, after all.

## SPAGHETTI CARBONARA

Rich, creamy, and delicious. Believe it or not, the fat in this recipe has been substantially reduced from the original.

I pound spaghetti
$^{1}/_{2}$ pound bacon
$^{1}/_{2}$ cup (I stick) butter, softened
I cup grated Parmesan cheese
6 eggs
I cup light cream or half-and-half
Freshly ground pepper

Cook the pasta in boiling salted water until al dente. Drain and keep warm. While the pasta is cooking, fry the bacon until almost crisp, drain on paper towels, then cut into bite-size pieces. Cream the butter until light, then mix in the Parmesan. Beat the eggs into the butter mixture one at a time, then beat in the cream. Place the butter mixture in a large, heavy skillet (nonstick is best) and heat, but do not allow it to boil. Add the warm pasta and most of the bacon to the butter mixture and toss together over low heat until the pasta is coated with the sauce. Turn into a warm serving dish and garnish with the rest of the bacon and freshly ground black pepper.

MAKES 6 SERVINGS

## FETTUCINE ALFREDO

Another drop-dead rich and creamy pasta dish. According to the *Dictionary of American Food and Drink,* it was created in Rome in 1920 by restaurateur Alfredo di Lellio and was popularized in America by di Lellio's clients Douglas Fairbanks and Mary Pickford. The Alfredo sauce is usually made in this country with butter, cheese, and cream and sometimes even eggs, but it is best with just butter and cheese.

$^3/_4$ cup (1 $^1/_2$ sticks) butter, softened
1 cup freshly grated Parmesan
1 pound fettucine (fresh is best, but use dried if fresh isn't available)
Extra Parmesan for serving

Cream the butter until very light and fluffy. Mix in the Parmesan. Put half the butter mixture in a hot serving bowl. Cook the pasta until al dente and drain. Pour the hot pasta into the serving bowl and top with the remaining butter mixture. Toss the pasta and butter mixture together until the pasta is well coated. Serve immediately on warm plates. Pass around additional cheese.

MAKES 6 SERVINGS

Another creamy pasta dish that was all the rage in the Seventies was pasta primavera. Craig Claiborne called it "by far the most talked-about dish in Manhattan" in 1977. And while this dish was wholly American, it was Italian in feel, and it was rich and creamy.

There is no question that pasta primavera was invented in New York at Le Cirque restaurant. But whether it was first made by Le Cirque owner, Sirio Maccioni, when he decided to add vegetables to his Alfredo sauce, or by Le Cirque cofounder Jean Vergnes in conjunction with Le Cirque chef Jean-Louis Todeschini after Vergnes tasted a pasta with vegetables made by friend and cookbook writer Ed Giobbi, is still a matter of debate.

# PASTA PRIMAVERA

This pasta dish held on to its popularity through the Eighties, when Ed Giobbi called it "the most popular pasta recipe in America." Le Cirque still makes pasta primavera, but the dish is not, and never has been, on their menu.

    I cup snow peas
    ¹/₂ cup asparagus tips
    I cup broccoli florets
    I cup tiny peas
    ¹/₄ cup plus I teaspoon butter
    I cup sliced mushrooms
    I cup sliced zucchini
    I cup peeled and seeded tomato chunks
    Salt
    ³/₄ cup heavy cream, warmed
    ¹/₃ cup pine nuts
    I pound spaghetti or fettucine, cooked al dente
    ¹/₃ cup basil leaves, torn into small pieces
    ¹/₂ cup grated Parmesan cheese

Steam the snow peas, asparagus, broccoli, and peas until crisp-tender. Set aside and chill until ready to assemble the dish. Melt 3 tablespoons of the butter in a large skillet and sauté the mushrooms and zucchini over medium heat until tender. Set aside.

Melt 1 tablespoon of the butter in a small skillet and sauté the tomatoes over medium heat until their liquid is almost evaporated Stir ¹/₄ cup of the cream into the tomatoes and set aside.

Melt the remaining butter in a small saucepan and sauté the pine nuts over low heat until they are aromatic but not brown. Set aside.

Add the steamed vegetables to the pan containing the mushrooms and zucchini and cook briefly until warmed through. Salt to taste. Add the rest of the cream to the vegetables and heat until the cream is hot but not boiling. Add the pasta to the vegetables, then the basil and Parmesan and toss all together over low heat until the pasta is coated with the cream sauce. Taste for seasoning and add more salt, cream, or Parmesan as needed. Gently stir in the tomatoes and cream mixture and sprinkle the pine nuts over the top. Serve immediately on warm plates and pass around additional Parmesan at the table.

MAKES 6 SERVINGS

Greek cooking was not very well known in the United States, but there was one Greek dish that caught on in the Seventies. Moussaka—with its dark Mediterranean flavors of eggplant, lamb, and tomato, and nicely gooshy bechamel and egg topping—was a logical Seventies favorite. One creative Massachusetts restaurant combined two trends and came up with a moussaka quiche (p. 317).

## MOUSSAKA

Eggplant is usually used in most American moussakas, but zucchini or combinations of zucchini, eggplant, tomatoes, and potatoes are also good and authentic. An equally authentic Greek dish, but one that is less rich, can be made by omitting the creamy topping and spreading a simple tomato sauce over the top eggplant slices before baking.

**For the Filling**
   2 medium eggplants
   Salt
   6 tablespoons olive oil
   2 small onions, chopped
   1 clove garlic, minced
   1 1/2 pounds ground lamb or beef
   1/2 cup dry red wine
   1 1/2 cups peeled, seeded, and chopped tomatoes (canned are fine)
   1/4 cup chopped fresh parsley
   1/2 teaspoon dried oregano

**For the Topping and Assembly**
   1/4 cup (1/2 stick) butter
   1/4 cup all-purpose flour
   3 cups warm milk
   3 large egg yolks
   1/4 teaspoons ground nutmeg
   1 cup grated Parmesan cheese (Greek mizithra or kefalotíri cheese is more
      authentic, but hard to come by)
   Salt and pepper

For the filling, peel the eggplants, slice them into rounds, salt them heavily, and let them drain in a colander for 1/2 hour. Rinse them well and pat dry with paper towels. Heat half the olive oil in a large skillet over medium-high heat. Add the eggplants and cook until they are soft. Remove from the pan and drain on paper towels. Heat the rest of the olive oil and sauté the onions over medium heat until they are soft, then add the garlic and lamb. Cook, stirring, until the lamb is no longer pink, about 5 minutes. Pour off any excess fat and stir in the wine, tomatoes, parsley, and oregano. Bring to a boil, then lower the heat and simmer, uncovered, about 30 minutes. Taste for seasoning and correct.

Preheat the oven to 350°F. For the topping, melt the butter in a large saucepan over low heat, stir in the flour, and cook, stirring contantly, without browning for about 3 minutes. Remove from the heat and gradually stir in the warm milk. Return to the heat and cook, stirring, until the sauce is hot, thick, and smooth. Beat the egg yolks in a separate bowl and stir some of the white sauce into the eggs to warm them. Pour the warmed egg mixture back into the white sauce and cook over low heat, stirring constantly, until thick. Do not boil or the eggs will curdle. Remove from the heat and stir in the nutmeg and half the grated cheese. Taste for seasoning and add salt and pepper as necessary.

Grease a 9 × 12-inch oven-to-table baking dish and arrange half the eggplant slices on the bottom. Spread all of the meat mixture over the eggplant, then cover the meat mixture with the rest of the eggplant. Spread the topping over the top of the dish, sprinkle with the rest of the grated cheese, and bake until the top is crusty and golden brown, about 40 minutes. Remove the pan to a rack and let the casserole cool about 15 minutes. Cut the moussaka into squares and serve.

MAKES 8 TO 10 SERVINGS

## Salads

Salads also had undergone a sea change in America. For gourmets, of course, gelatin-based salads were definitely Out, as were salads made with the dreaded iceberg lettuce. What was In were two main-dish salads, salad niçoise and Caesar salad, both with a nicely Mediterranean zip to them. But for a salad as a side dish, nothing was more popular than one made with spinach—particularly if it was served with a goopy, cheesy dressing.

## SPINACH SALAD WITH CHEDDAR CHEESE DRESSING

The Cheddar Cheese Dressing was adapted from one served in the Seventies at the Proud Popover in Boston. Crumbled bleu cheese may be substituted for the Cheddar—or you could skip the goopy dressing entirely and serve the salad with a simple tart vinaigrette. After the first bite of this salad, one taster said, "Ah! Maxwell's Plum, 1978!"

**For the Dressing**

  ¹/₂ cup mayonnaise

  ¹/₂ teaspoon Worcestershire sauce

  ¹/₂ teaspoon prepared horseradish

  ¹/₂ cup vegetable oil (corn or safflower oil would be most typical of the period)

  1 teaspoon white wine vinegar

  1 teaspoon lemon juice

  Salt and pepper

  ¹/₃ cup grated Cheddar cheese

  1 green onion, finely chopped

**For the Salad**

  1 pound tender fresh spinach, well washed, dried, and tough stems removed

  6 pieces bacon, fried until crisp, patted dry, and crumbled

  10 white mushrooms, sliced

  1 small red onion, thinly sliced and separated into rings

For the dressing, combine the mayonnaise, Worcestershire sauce, and horse-radish in a blender or food processor and blend at high speed. With the blender or processor running, very slowly add the oil and then add the vinegar and lemon juice. The mixture should have the consistency of a thin mayonnaise. Taste for seasoning, adding lemon juice, vinegar, and salt and pepper as necessary. Pour the dressing into a bowl and stir in the cheese and green onion. The dressing may be refrigerated at this point.

For the salad, put the spinach, crumbled bacon, mushrooms, and onion rings in a serving bowl and toss together. Serve at once with the dressing.

MAKES 6 SERVINGS

# Desserts

Desserts with a Mediterranean twist were more problematic. Middle Eastern or Greek baklava was popular, but it was very pesky to make at home and few attempted it. The rich Sicilian cake/confection cassata was also popular, but again pesky to make, and it was a little too rich after all those heavy, creamy entrées, even for the Seventies. (On the other hand, many were just as likely to finish up with a heart-stoppingly rich dessert like Ice Cream Sundae Butter Pecan Crêpes [p. 314] or a fudge nut pie.)

Fruit was a logical ending to a heavy meal and it fit the Mediterranean theme, but few Americans were content to end a meal with just plain fruit. There were two gussied-up fruit desserts that were popular and easy—and gooshy, of course.

## FRUIT WITH SOUR CREAM AND BROWN SUGAR

There are two methods for this dessert. One is to mix the sour cream and brown sugar with the fruit, as in this recipe. The other is to pass bowls of sour cream and brown sugar and allow the guests to dip the fruit (unhulled strawberries, or chunks of other fruit on toothpicks) first into the sour cream and then into the sugar.

$^1/_2$ cup sour cream
$^1/_3$ cup firmly packed brown sugar
$2^1/_2$ cups fruit (blueberries, fresh pineapple chunks, strawberry halves, etc.)

Mix the sour cream and brown sugar together, reserving 1 tablespoon of the brown sugar. Toss the sour cream mixture with the fruits and chill. Just before serving, sprinkle with the reserved brown sugar. For a real period touch, serve in balloon-style wineglasses.

MAKES 4 SERVINGS

## GLAZED STRAWBERRY PIE

This pie, with its fruits glistening like jewels under a glaze, was all the rage in the Seventies. For some of us, then and now, it was terribly disappointing to find out it was only raw fruit and pie crust. Other fresh fruits in season may be substituted for the strawberries in the pie and in the glaze.

1 cup crushed strawberries
2 teaspoons cornstarch
$^1/_4$ cup granulated sugar
2 cups beautiful whole strawberries, hulled
1 (9-inch) pie shell, baked (or use baked tartlet shells)
1 cup heavy cream, whipped until soft peaks form

Put the crushed berries in a small saucepan. Mix the cornstarch and sugar and add them to the pan. Cook over low heat, stirring constantly, until the sugar is dissolved and the sauce has thickened and cleared. Cool. Arrange the whole berries in a pleasing pattern in the pie shell—pointy end up in concentric circles was very common in the Seventies. Spoon the crushed fruit glaze over the fruit, using just enough to cover smoothly. Cover and chill until ready to serve. Cut the pie and top each slice with whipped cream.

# Dining Out in the Seventies

Throughout the restaurant there is a fascinating miscellany of antiques, old photographs, and unclassifiable odds and ends, such as a portrait of the restaurant's "founder," which was selected as much for its crossed eyes as its last-century frame.

—Review of the Chronicle (Pasadena), *Gourmet* (September 1974)

There were, of course, the old standby French and Continental restaurants, but by the early 1970s, their menus had become pretty staid, too. Nearly every "good" restaurant with serious pretensions offered the following dishes on the menu:

---

### Appetizers
*Oeufs en Gelée (Eggs in Aspic)*
*Quiche*
*Pâté Maison*

### Entrées
*Duckling à l'Orange*
*Beef Wellington*
*Chicken Kiev*
*Seafood with Mornay Sauce*
*Lobster with Pernod*
*Chicken Véronique*
*Cassoulet*
*Frogs' Legs*
*Steak au Poivre*

### Desserts
*Chocolate Mousse*
*Grand Marnier Soufflé*
*Ice Cream Coupe with Liqueurs*
*Tarte Tatin*
*Dessert Crêpes*

---

Even if the food was good, it was boring after a while. How many Oeufs en Gelée can one person eat? The young crowd was tired of the same old food, served in the gracious, quiet dining rooms. And mostly they couldn't afford such places anyway. Enter the zany, goofy restaurants, catering to the young and the hip. These new restaurants might sport silly names, or amusing decor (often with a theme), or they might just be decorated with ferns (indoor plants were de rigueur in the Seventies) and Tiffany lamps. Many of these "fun" restaurants also doubled as singles' bars, that important cultural phenomenon of the hormone-rich Seventies. The food was nearly always international (as opposed to Continental), eclectic, casual, and often of the sticky, sweet, or gooshy variety. But the food was less important than the experience.

There was Spats, a Restaurant Associates creation in New York (Restaurant Associates was also responsible for the goofy "gourmet" Forum of the Twelve Caesars in the late 1950s and early 1960s). Spats, which prided itself on its chilled pumpkin bisque, was done up in 1930s-style with black and beige decor. The waiters wore spats, and even the phone number fit the 1930s theme: It was BR9-1934. The Blue Boar, filled with humorous antiques, served beef Wellington with fruit sauce and salads dressed with cheese and mayonnaise. There was La Bibliotheque, whose menu, done up to look like the French paper *Le Monde*, listed such entrées as veal scaloppini Voltaire and filet mignon Camus. There were also the Frog & Nightgown in Raleigh, North Carolina; Tumbledown Dick's in Cos Cob, Connecticut; and Boondock Sundecker & Greenthumb in Seattle. And there was the Chowderhead in Golden Beach, Oregon, famous for its "Merry Old Sole."

## MERRY OLD SOLE (SOLE STUFFED WITH CRAB AND CHEESE)

Otherwise inoffensive filets of sole (one hoped they were not too old) were frequently stuffed with crab—to the benefit of neither fish—in the Seventies. But the Chowderhead's version, rich with cheese and sauce, took the idea over the top. The original recipe included scallops but they are omitted here.

I cup cooked crabmeat, picked over for cartilage
~~I cup cooked tiny shrimp~~
I cup shredded Monterey Jack cheese
4 large fillets of sole
I cup dry white wine
I cup warm Hollandaise Sauce (p. 194)
Paprika and minced fresh parsley for garnish

Preheat the oven to 400°F. Mix the crab, shrimp, and cheese together. Place one-quarter of the filling on top of each fillet and roll the fillet around it. Secure with a toothpick. Place the stuffed fillets in a buttered casserole, seam side down, pour the wine around the fish, and bake until the fish flakes, 10 to 15 minutes. Preheat the broiler. Remove the fillets to a heatproof serving platter. Spoon the Hollandaise Sauce over the top of each fillet and place under the broiler until the sauce bubbles and browns slightly, 2 to 3 minutes. Remove the toothpicks. Sprinkle the fillets with paprika and parsley and serve.

MAKES 4 SERVINGS

## PUMPKIN-ORANGE BISQUE

Unusual fruit or vegetable cream soups were very popular in the Seventies at the more trendy and ambitious restaurants.

3 tablespoons butter
$^3/_4$ cup finely chopped onions
1 teaspoon sugar
$^3/_4$ teaspoon dried thyme
4 cups chicken broth
$^1/_3$ cup orange juice
2 cups fresh or canned pumpkin purée
Salt
$^1/_2$ cup heavy cream
Ground nutmeg
Freshly ground black pepper

In a large kettle, melt the butter over low heat. Add the onions and sauté until soft. Stir in the sugar and thyme and continue cooking for a few minutes, until the thyme is aromatic. Add the broth and orange juice and simmer, uncovered, about 15 minutes. Strain out the onions, purée them with a little of the liquid in a blender or food processor, and return them to the pot. Stir in the pumpkin purée and bring to a simmer. Taste for salt and correct the seasoning. Simmer another 10 minutes. Stir in the cream and heat but do not allow to boil. Just before serving, stir in a little freshly ground nutmeg and black pepper. Serve the soup in a tureen or in a large pumpkin shell that has been hollowed out. The soup may also be served cold—just be sure to check the seasonings again after the soup is chilled.

MAKES 6 TO 8 SERVINGS

## Maxwell's Plum—Restaurant as "Happening"

*I don't really remember the food. There was too much else going on.*

—A Maxwell's Plum regular.

One of the most popular, and certainly the most outrageous, of the new restaurants wasn't a new restaurant at all. Maxwell's Plum (the name, like many of that era, was silly for silliness's sake and meant nothing) was opened in Manhattan in 1966 by Warner LeRoy, son of Hollywood's legendary producer-director Mervyn LeRoy. The restaurant was often described as a three-ring circus, not only because of everything going on there, which was plenty, but because, under one glittering roof, it contained a casual café, a formal dining room, and a brass-bound bar that was the model for singles' bars for years. The food was generally considered pretty good and ran from foot-long hot dogs served in the café to ultrarich saumon en croûte in the main dining room, under the direction of Chef Jean Vergnes. The wine cellars contained more than eighty thousand bottles (one reviewer called the wine list "preposterous"), ranging from $175 bottles of cheval-blanc 1947 to $5.75 bottles of red Bordeaux.

But food and wine were not the point of Maxwell's Plum: theater was. The restaurant was an enormous stage setting for the antics of its hip, mostly young clientele. And what a stage setting. The ceiling of the main dining room was, according to LeRoy, "the largest single sheet of stained glass in the world." Windows and mirrors glittered with cut glass, the copper ceiling in the café was studded with floral motifs in high relief, art deco and art nouveau figures and objects abounded, and plants and huge Tiffany-glass chandeliers hung from the ceiling. "It was a magical, happy place," said one restaurant goer. "It just made you feel good to be there."

Maxwell's Plum was such a big hit that reservations were no guarantee of a table (fourteen hundred meals were served on weekends at the height of its popularity) and the bar resembled "an anchovy tin turned inside out," according to Jay Jacobs in *Gourmet* (May 1973). The restaurant continued to be a happening place for more than a decade, and even in its decline was able to attract promising young chefs.

Maxwell's Plum finally closed in 1989. The stained glass chandeliers and other extraordinary fixtures were auctioned off, along with some of Warner LeRoy's 1970s velvet suits. Said LeRoy at the auction, "I think it's great. I ran a wonderful show, and now the show's over."

## Salad Bars, "Freshly Baked" Bread, and Surf & Turf

No one knows exactly who opened the first salad bar, but one of the first and certainly the largest was at one of those restaurants with a funny name, R.J. Grunts, in Chicago. (You didn't think it was going to be Le Cirque, did you?)

R.J. Grunts opened in 1971, and its salad bar featured forty different items. The cofounder of the restaurant, Rich Melman, was "into" macrobiotic foods and R.J. Grunts's salad bar reflected his countercultural health food ideals.

But as the salad bar idea swept the country, its healthfulness dwindled. In fact, the most popular places for salad bars were likely to be restaurants featuring steaks or "surf and turf," not exactly palaces of macrobiotic cooking. The salad bars usually had a big bowl of iceberg lettuce (often brown around the edges), perhaps a bowl of spinach leaves, and cherry tomatoes, sliced pickled beets, sliced cucumbers, sliced onions, sliced radishes, shredded carrots, garbanzo beans, various sprouts, sunflower seeds, artificial bacon bits, and shredded cheese. And there were, of course, plenty of gloppy mayonnaise-based salad dressings.

It was almost a given that a salad bar restaurant would be "themed." Victoriana was particularly popular, and countless restaurants strove for that olde-tyme atmosphere—while serving completely modern food, of course. The Wall Street in Indianapolis featured surf and turf with a salad bar and "turn-of-the-century stock market decor." The Victoria Station restaurants patterned themselves after railroad cars, going so far as to use a separate car for each of the many dining rooms. But anything that looked old would do. Many restaurants turned to darkened walls, quasi-baronial brass fixtures, and for tables, those well-known antique artifacts…polyurethaned wooden hatch covers.

It was also a given that if a restaurant had hatch-cover tables and a salad bar, it would have "freshly baked" little loaves of bread, served on cute little cutting boards, with a small bowl of whipped nonbutter alongside. The bread was indeed freshly baked at the restaurant, but it was baked from preshaped frozen dough. One company supplied the restaurants not only with the dough but with the knives and cutting boards for serving as well.

The food at these restaurants was usually of the most basic variety, and frequently consisted of mass-market frozen entrées. Steaks there would be, perhaps a shrimp or chicken kebab, and for the big spenders, steak and rock lobster tails…surf and turf. (One Spanish restaurant advertised "mar y tierra"—land and sea.) There would be a choice of baked or fried potatoes or rice pilaf. There would be the salad bar and the little loaves of bread. And then there would be dessert.

The patrons of these restaurants were usually young and the desserts reflected their still childish tastes. Not for them cheese and fruit, or even the complications of French pastry. They wanted and got sweet, rich, gooey desserts: ice cream pies with chocolate sauce and nuts, carrot cake with cream cheese frosting (p. 338), and cheesecake flavored with Kahlua or chocolate. Or they ordered after-dinner dessert coffee.

These dessert coffees, which had become popular in the late Sixties, were the last gasp for hard liquor. Hippies-turned-Baby Boomers did not drink the martinis or Scotch on the rocks that their parents had considered essential to a sophisticated good time. If they drank at all, it was likely to be "white spirits" like vodka, tequila, or light rum in something sweet like a Harvey Wallbanger, tequila sunrise, strawberry daiquiri, or piña colada. Even these childishly sweet drinks were giving way to "lite" wine spritzers, or kir (white wine and cassis)— and for the bubblegum set, ultrasweet apple- or peach-flavored "wines."

Dessert coffees were usually based on sweet liqueurs like Kahlua or Amaretto mixed with coffee and sweetened whipped cream. (Amaretto was increasingly popular and was even used in a sauce for prawns in one rich and icky Seventies recipe.) These drinks were modeled after Irish coffee, which had been introduced at San Francisco's famed Buena Vista bar in 1952.

## IRISH COFFEE AMARETTO

I sugar cube
I jigger Irish whiskey
I jigger Amaretto
5 ounces hot, strong coffee
Whipped cream

Crush the sugar cube in the bottom of a tall, warm coffee mug. Add the whiskey and Amaretto. Fill the mug with coffee and float whipped cream on top.

MAKES I SERVING

## KRAZY KAHLUA KOFFEE

Better Home and Gardens *Holiday Cooking & Entertaining Ideas* (1975) suggested Cool Whip, rather than whipped cream, as the topper here.

2/3 cup Kahlua
1/3 cup crème de cacao
1/3 cup brandy
6 cups hot, strong coffee
Whipped cream

In a decanter mix the liqueurs. For each serving pour a jigger of the mixture into a warm, tall mug and fill the mug with the coffee. Top with whipped cream.

MAKES 8 SERVINGS

Kahlua was very popular, both as a drink and as a flavoring, during the Me Decade. For some reason, it became the vogue to make it at home in the Seventies. Why this was so is unclear, because the end result bore only a vague resemblance to the real thing, and it was a lot more trouble and not much cheaper than buying real Kahlua. But making it seemed to please people.

## HOMEMADE "KAHLUA"

The real McCoy is made from coffee beans, cocoa beans, vanilla, and brandy. The homemade potion skips the cocoa and is often based on vodka.

    4 cups freshly made strong coffee
    4 cups sugar
    1 vanilla bean, cut into 4 pieces
    1 gallon jug with screw-on cap
    1 fifth vodka or brandy

Heat the coffee and sugar in a large saucepan, stirring until the sugar is dissolved. Remove from the heat and add the vanilla bean pieces. When lukewarm, pour the mixture into a sterilized gallon jug. Add the vodka or brandy. Put a small plastic bag over the top and screw on the cap. Keep in a cool, dark place, shaking the mixture twice a week. Age three weeks. Strain through a coffee filter and decant the strained "kahlua" into smaller jars.

MAKES 2 FIFTHS

# Health Foods in the Seventies—Pardon Me, Waiter, But There's Some Granola in My Fondue

Health food, which had so alarmed the food and nutrition establishments in the Sixties, started appearing outside hippie enclaves and communes in the Seventies. Mainstream cookbooks like Virginia Pasley's *In Celebration of Food* (1974) offered menus for "your vegetarian young people home from college."

Many magazines, including *Bon Appétit,* started up "natural foods" columns. Even *Gourmet,* while it didn't feature health foods, occasionally gave recipes for such things as soybeans with feta and peppers or bean sprout–mushroom salad. The food processing giants realized that "natural" products sold and scrambled to turn out "home-style" breads, yogurts with no additives, and especially granola.

Of all the health foods, granola was the one that seemed to have the broadest appeal. Nearly every big company had its own version: General Mills put out Nature Valley, Kellogg's had Country Valley, Pet made Heartland, and Colgate-Palmolive came up with Alpen (which, unfortunately, sounded a little too much like the popular dog food Alpo). Quaker Oats had Quaker 100% Natural Cereal, which in 1974 was one of the top five selling brands of cereal, quite a feat considering that no other new brand had made the top five in almost thirty years.

It was hard not to like granola: It was laved with honey and oil and loaded with calories. But the calories were "natural" calories, at least in the granola that was bought in bulk at health food stores or made at home. Many of the supermarket store brands were packed with sugar, brown sugar, corn syrup, and highly processed saturated palm and coconut oils. (In the Nineties, some manufacturers saw the "lite" and started making low-fat, fruit juice–sweetened granolas.)

## OLD-FASHIONED GRANOLA

All sorts of variations are possible. Maple syrup may replace part of the honey, various nuts and grains may be substituted, and dried fruits can be added. If you do add dried fruits, it is better to stir them into the granola after it comes out of the oven so they don't get hard. And if you've forgotten what homemade granola tastes like, this one is very good.

> 1 cup raw honey
> 1/2 cup cold-pressed safflower, corn, or canola oil
> 1 tablespoon vanilla extract or 2 teaspoons ground cinnamon
> 1/2 teaspoon sea salt
> 7 cups rolled (old-fashioned) oats
> 1 cup toasted wheat germ
> 1/2 cup unblanched sliced almonds
> 1/2 cup sesame seeds
> 1/2 cup sunflower seeds
> 1 cup unsweetened shredded coconut

Preheat the oven to 350°F. In a small saucepan stir together the honey and oil and heat slightly until thin. Remove from the heat and stir in the vanilla. In a large bowl combine the rest of the ingredients, then pour the honey mixture over the top. Stir the mixture, then rub it between your hands, making sure everything is coated with the honey. Spread the mixture over the bottom of a large baking pan. Bake, stirring every 5 minutes, until the mixture is golden brown and crisp, 20 to 25 minutes. Cool and store in covered jars.

MAKES ABOUT 12 CUPS

Granola was the perfect breakfast food with fruit and milk or yogurt and was often carried in plastic sandwich bags for snacks. It was also sometimes used in desserts as the topping for fruit crisps or sprinkled over ice cream or fruits. Few felt the urge to incorporate it into savory dishes as did *The Granola Cookbook* (1973), which gave recipes for granola eggs Benedict, granola quiche Lorraine, granola eggplant Parmesan...and granola fondue.

## GRANOLA FONDUE

This recipe has not been tested.

$\frac{1}{2}$ cup (1 stick) butter
3 tablespoons whole wheat flour
$\frac{1}{2}$ teaspoon sea salt
$\frac{1}{2}$ teaspoon pepper
2 garlic cloves, minced
$2\frac{1}{4}$ cups warm milk
5 egg yolks, lightly beaten
$\frac{1}{4}$ cup granola
$\frac{3}{4}$ cup grated Parmesan
Dippers: whole wheat bread chunks, raw vegetables, apples

Melt the butter in a large saucepan and stir in the flour, salt, pepper, and garlic. Cook over low heat for a few minutes. Off the heat gradually stir in the milk, then return to the heat and cook until the mixture is smooth and has thickened slightly. Add some of the milk to the egg yolks to warm them, then stir the eggs into the milk. Cook over low heat, stirring constantly, until the mixture thickens. Stir in the granola and cheese and serve with dippers.

MAKES ABOUT 6 SERVINGS

Like granola, carrot cake was a high-fat, high-calorie food that was still considered healthy. After all, it had vegetables in it, didn't it? Although its origins are unclear, carrot cake may have been a descendant of German carrot bread, according to Evan Jones in *American Food* (1981). The American version first became popular in the Sixties, but its combination of gooshiness and healthfulness made carrot cake a sure-fire Seventies hit. It became a standard at every health food restaurant—and you could be sure of finding it on the dessert menu at any restaurant that sported polyurethaned hatch-cover tables.

## CARROT CAKE WITH CREAM CHEESE FROSTING

There are as many versions of carrot cake as there are cooks. Many of them are high in oil—so much so that it oozes out with every fatty bite. The oil has been reduced in this recipe, but if you want that Seventies feel, go ahead and increase the oil to one full cup.

4 eggs
2 cups sugar
$2/3$ cup mild vegetable oil (canola oil is a good, but modern, choice)
2 cups all-purpose flour
$1/2$ teaspoon salt
2 teaspoons baking soda
2 teaspoons cinnamon
1 cup chopped walnuts
3 cups finely grated carrots
Honey-Sweetened Cream Cheese Frosting (below)

Preheat the oven to 350°F. In a large bowl beat the eggs until light and lemon colored. Beat in the sugar and oil. Sift together the flour salt, baking soda, and cinnamon. Add the flour mixture to the egg mixture in four parts, stirring well after each addition. Gently stir in the walnuts and carrots. Pour the batter into a lightly greased 9-inch tube pan and bake 55 to 60 minutes, or until a toothpick inserted in the thickest part of the cake comes out clean. (Cake may also be baked in a 13 × 9-inch pan at 300°F for 60 to 70 minutes.) Cool on a wire rack for 10 minutes, then run a knife around the edge of the pan to loosen and turn the cake out onto the rack to cool. Frost with Honey-Sweetened Cream Cheese Frosting, or with Philly-Vanilly Frosting (p. 77).

MAKES 1 (9-INCH) TUBE CAKE

### HONEY-SWEETENED CREAM CHEESE FROSTING

The earliest carrot cakes were glazed with a fruit purée, but fluffy, rich, cream cheese frosting soon became the favorite. Here, a honey-sweetened cream cheese frosting is used, in keeping with the "healthfulness" of this dessert. This recipe comes from a 1978 cookbook called *Snackers*.

2 (8-ounce) packages cream cheese, softened
6 tablespoons honey, or to taste
I teaspoon vanilla extract

In a mixing bowl, mash the cream cheese with the honey and vanilla. Beat until the honey is incorporated and the mixture light and fluffy. Taste and add additional honey if you like a sweeter frosting.

MAKES ABOUT 2 CUPS FROSTING

While health food drinks based on brewer's yeast and nutritional powders remained acceptable fare in the die-hard health food camp, other blended drinks like smoothees became more widely popular.

## STRAWBERRY-BANANA SMOOTHEE

The addition of a scoop of ice cream to a smoothee made it a cooler.

I cup cold milk
$^3/_4$ cup sliced strawberries
$^1/_2$ large banana, peeled
I tablespoon honey
I teaspoon lemon juice
I cup crushed ice

Place all the ingredients in a blender and blend at high speed until smooth and frothy.

MAKES 2 SERVINGS

Home-baked breads also moved out of the commune kitchen and into the mainstream. Magazines from *Woman's Day* to *Gourmet* ran features on the joys of bread making. James Beard published "the definitive bread book" in 1973, *Beard on Bread,* but books on bread abounded, from the *Tassajara Bread Book* (from the vegetarian Zen Mountain Center) to Mariana Honig's *Breads of the World,* which included a recipe for the newly popular pita bread. Bread even became a fashion-ably earthy accessory to accent Harvest Gold or Burnished Copper kitchen appli-ances and was molded into baskets or braided into intricate shapes and then lacquered.

To go along with all the homemade bread everyone was up to their armpits in, homemade soup became very fashionable. Such peasant fare seemed simple, honest, and nourishing—not to mention righteous—compared with the baroque and/or ersatz food so many Americans were eating. Restaurants offering nothing more than bread and soup opened across the country, including Manhattan's La Potagerie, whose chef was Jacques Pépin.

## New American Health Food

Much of the health food cooking in the country had progressed beyond the Food as Fuel stage ("Lamb Brains with Wheat Germ will supply B vitamins, lecithin, hefty amounts of protein, and vitamin E"). With its emphasis on fresh, unprocessed, and organic foods, the health food movement encouraged a closer connection between the food people ate and its source. In fact, one could argue that the New American Cooking owed as much as to the health food movement as it did to French nouvelle cuisine.

Edward Espe Brown (who would collaborate with Deborah Madison on the *Greens Cookbook* in the Eighties) had worked at the Tassajara Zen Mountain Center in northern California and put out the *Tassajara Bread Book,* with its wonderful, nourishing recipes. Mollie Katzen's *Moosewood Cookbook,* with recipes from the Moosewood cooperative restaurant in Ithaca, New York, highlighted innovative vegetarian cooking, although some of her food was a little heavy on cheese, butter, and eggs for Nineties tastes. (A new edition of the cookbook is now out with many lightened recipes.) Anna Thomas came out with *The Vegetarian Epicure* in 1972, which featured such interesting and unusual dishes as chestnut soufflé and cheese ramekins with artichoke purée. (The latest version of Thomas's book is due out in 1995.)

But even less serious health food cooking was beginning to show some sophistication. Here is a recipe from a compilation cookbook (which also included such things as curried goat, Portuguese fish stew, and Greek rice salad). It is a sort of crustless quiche, packed with vegetables, that is good, simple, and wins the award for the best title for a Seventies recipe.

## VEGETABLE CURRY CHEESE PIE OF THE YEAR WITHOUT THE DAMN CRUST

1/4 cup vegetable oil or butter, plus additional as needed
4 cups peeled and diced potatoes
2 onions, chopped
3 garlic cloves, minced
1/2 pound mushrooms, sliced
1 cup thinly sliced carrots, blanched in boiling water 4 minutes
1 cup broccoli florets, blanched in boiling water 4 minutes
1 cup grated Monterey Jack cheese
1 cup cottage cheese or ricotta
2 large eggs, beaten slightly
1/2 teaspoon salt
Freshly ground black pepper
3 teaspoons curry powder or to taste
1/2 cup freshly grated Parmesan cheese

Preheat the oven to 400°F. Heat the oil in a large, heavy skillet. Sauté the potatoes in the hot oil until tender. Put the potatoes in a large bowl. Sauté the onions, garlic, and mushrooms in the skillet until soft, adding additional oil as needed. Add the mushroom mixture, the carrots, and broccoli to the potatoes. Mix the Monterey Jack and ricotta cheeses, eggs, and seasonings together, then add this mixture to the vegetables and mix thoroughly but gently. Pour the mixture into a greased 9 × 13-inch baking dish, sprinkle the top with the grated Parmesan, and bake until lightly browned, about 30 minutes. Serve with a garden salad and whole wheat rolls.

MAKES 8 SERVINGS

# Suburban Gourmets

While their children were disporting themselves in singles' bars or health food restaurants, Seventies suburbanites were cooking up some pretty strange food. Like the younger set's food, what the older crowd was making tended to be gooey, gloppy, and gooshy.

But unlike their children, many older people had embraced processed or even synthetic foods wholeheartedly. Particularly in desserts was the trend apparent, with cake mixes, pudding mixes, Cool Whip, Dream Whip, and soda pop being common ingredients. Even in savory foods processed shortcuts were not only respectable, they were downright chic.

## TOMATO SPINACH SOUFFLÉ CUPS ÉLÉGANTE

"Serve…as a first course, as a luncheon dish, or as a distinguished vegetable," said the contributor.

**Note:** I have tried this recipe every-which-way. I've used thawed, frozen, and partially frozen soufflé. I have lowered and raised the oven temperature and baked the cups for longer and shorter times than indicated, until my supermarket ran out of frozen spinach soufflé. No matter what I tried, the soufflé would not puff as promised. But this is still a fine and (theoretically) elegant idea.

> 5 large tomatoes, hollowed out and drained
> 3 slices bacon, fried crisp, patted dry and crumbled
> 1 12-ounce package frozen Stouffer's spinach soufflé
> ½ cup grated Parmesan cheese

Preheat the oven to 350°F. Place the tomato cups in a buttered casserole, just large enough so that they fit snugly. Sprinkle the crumbled bacon into the cups. Fill the cups with the soufflé and dust the tops with the cheese. Bake until the soufflés have puffed and browned (see Note above), 20 to 25 minutes. Serve immediately.

MAKES 5 SERVINGS

Savory mousses were also "élégante" and made the perfect chic appetizer. These cool, creamy concoctions weren't classic egg white mousses, rather, they were molded salads with the main ingredients pulverized in the blender or, more and more, the food processor. Avocado was a popular mousse base, as was canned liver pâté, but seafood mousses were probably the favorite.

# LOBSTER-ASPARAGUS MOUSSE

Said Ruth Macpherson, "Guests are always trying to guess at the ingredients in this marvelous appetizer." It is surprisingly good. Use only a glass, pottery, or stainless mold for this mousse as the ingredients may react to an aluminum or copper mold.

1 teaspoon butter
$^1\!/_2$ cup finely chopped onion
$1^1\!/_2$ cups canned asparagus, drained and $^1\!/_4$ cup of the liquid reserved
2 envelopes unflavored gelatin
11–12 ounces lobster chunks (frozen or canned is fine)
1 can condensed cream of asparagus soup
3 (8-ounce) packages cream cheese
1 cup mayonnaise
$^1\!/_2$ teaspoon salt
Fresh parsley sprigs, thin cucumber slices, and halved Spanish olives for garnish
Crisp crackers and thinly sliced brown bread for serving

Melt the butter in a small skillet and sauté the onion over low heat until soft. Place the sautéed onion, canned asparagus, $^1\!/_4$ cup of the asparagus liquid, the gelatin, and lobster in a blender or food processor and purée. In a large pot heat the soup and cream cheese together over low heat, stirring until smooth. Add the puréed ingredients, mayonnaise, and salt to the soup mixture and cook over low heat until heated through but not hot. Pour into an oiled 2-quart mold and chill until set. Unmold onto a chilled platter, garnish with parsley sprigs, cucumber, and olives, and serve with crackers and brown bread.

MAKES ENOUGH FOR 10 TO 12 GUESTS

Dips were still acceptable as a suburban appetizer—but for real elegance the dip had to be hot. And hot crab dip was hot in the Seventies.

# HOT CRAB DIP

This recipe was also popular baked, with slivered almonds on top.

1 (8-ounce) package cream cheese
1 (6-ounce) can crabmeat, drained and flaked
2 tablespoons grated onion
1 tablespoon mayonnaise
1 teaspoon Worcestershire sauce
$^1\!/_2$ teaspoon prepared horseradish
$^1\!/_4$ teaspoon salt
Milk

In the top of a double boiler over simmering water melt the cream cheese, stirring until smooth. Add the rest of the ingredients, except the milk, and cook over low heat until hot. Thin to dipping consistency with milk if necessary. Serve immediately in a heated bowl, with crackers or other dippers.

MAKES ABOUT 2½ CUPS

Spinach and broccoli were very popular with suburban gourmets—probably because these two vegetables were so easily gussied up. In a casserole or in a soufflé, a package of frozen broccoli or spinach mixed with some combination of sour cream, mayonnaise, cream cheese, or canned soup made a dandy vegetable side dish.

## BROCCOLI CASSEROLE

Spinach could be substituted for the broccoli—probably no one would notice.

    I teaspoon butter
    I small onion, minced
    I (10-ounce) package frozen chopped broccoli, thawed and drained
    I can condensed cream of mushroom soup
    ¼ cup mayonnaise
    ½ cup sour cream
    I large egg, lightly beaten
    ¾ cup crushed Ritz crackers
    Butter

Preheat the oven to 350°F. Melt the butter in a small skillet and sauté the onion over low heat until soft. Combine the onion, broccoli, soup, mayonnaise, sour cream, and egg in a medium bowl and blend well. Turn into a buttered 1-quart casserole. Sprinkle with the cracker crumbs and dot with butter. Bake until brown and bubbly, 30 to 35 minutes.

MAKES 4 SERVINGS

Casseroles in general were big items, but the puffy sandwich casserole took suburbia by storm in the Seventies. Known variously as baked sandwiches, cheese cloud, Danish soufflé, sandwich soufflé, and cheese strata (like the similar Italian dish), this casserole used the same technique as French Toast, Seventies Style (p. 304): soaking bread in milk and eggs overnight.

# Crockery Cookery

New appliances were cluttering up America's kitchens like mad in the Seventies. The blender was still popular, but many of its jobs were being taken over by the sexy food processor, particularly in serious gourmet kitchens. The microwave was becoming more popular and less frightening, although it wasn't yet revolutionizing American cooking as many had predicted. But the Crock-Pot (which is a trademark of the Rival Manufacturing Co., but has became the generic name for any electric crockery appliance) was the electronic appliance of the Seventies.

The homely little Crock-Pot was perfect for the working wife who wanted to come home to lemon chicken made with frozen lemonade concentrate or good 'n' easy stew made with onion soup mix and condensed cream of mushroom soup.

While today most electric crockery cookers are gathering dust on the back of kitchen shelves, they can still be useful gadgets for anything that needs long, slow, untended cooking. Bean dishes and stews can be wonderful and wonderfully easy made in these cookers. But as with any other appliance, the resulting dish is only as good as the ingredients that go into it.

## CROCKERY CHICKEN STEW WITH WINE AND TARRAGON

The wine and herbs make this easy dish a "gourmet treat."

4 medium waxy potatoes, peeled and cut into large chunks
3 pounds chicken thighs and legs
2 tablespoons butter
Salt and pepper
2 medium onions, cut into large chunks
1/2 cup dry white wine
1 teaspoon dried tarragon, crumbled

Put the potatoes in the bottom of the cooker. Rinse the chicken and pat dry. In a heavy skillet melt the butter and brown the chicken parts on all sides. Salt and pepper them and place them in the cooker. Pour off all but 1 tablespoon of fat from the skillet. Sauté the onions for a few minutes in the skillet and add them to the pot. Add the wine to the skillet and cook for 1 minute, scraping up all the brown bits. Sprinkle the tarragon over the contents of the cooker and pour the wine over the top. Cover and cook on low setting 6 to 8 hours. Skim off the fat and serve.

MAKES 4 TO 6 SERVINGS

## SANDWICH CASSEROLE

This can be a simple dish of bread, cheese, milk, and eggs or a more rococo affair incorporating sausage, ham, seafood, and vegetables. It makes a fine brunch or supper dish.

8 slices firm white bread, crusts removed
4 slices sharp cheddar cheese
4 slices ham
4 eggs
2 cups milk
$\frac{1}{2}$ teaspoon salt
$\frac{1}{2}$ teaspoon dry mustard
Dash of Tabasco sauce
$\frac{1}{4}$ cup ($\frac{1}{2}$ stick) butter, melted
$\frac{1}{3}$ cup grated Parmesan cheese

Make four sandwiches with the bread, ham, and cheese. Put sandwiches side by side in a buttered 8-inch-square glass or ceramic casserole. Beat the eggs, then add the milk, salt, mustard, and Tabasco sauce. Pour over the sandwiches. Cover the casserole and refrigerate overnight (or at least 8 hours).

Preheat the oven to 350°F. Pour the melted butter over the top of the sandwiches, sprinkle with the grated cheese and bake until puffed and golden brown, 50 to 60 minutes. Serve immediately.

MAKES 4 SERVINGS

# Suburban Gourmet Desserts

And now we come to the real raison d'être of suburban cookbooks, if not suburban cooking: dessert. One of the most popular desserts was Whiskey or Rum Bundt Cake, or The Cake (p. 309), which could be flavored with various liqueurs. Cakes flavored with Coke, Fresca, and 7UP also made the rounds, and carrot cake, "healthy" but yummy, was as common in suburbia as it was in health food enclaves. But there was one other cake that, although it never appeared in the pages of *Gourmet,* did appear in nearly every compilation cookbook in the Seventies.

## WACKY CAKE OR CRAZY CAKE

This easy, chocolatey, and moist cake was "wacky" because of the unusual mixing method. It's still a great cake for young children to help with.

1 1/2 cups all-purpose flour

1 cup sugar

3 tablespoons unsweetened cocoa powder

1 teaspoon baking soda

1 teaspoon baking powder

1/2 teaspoon salt

1 teaspoon vanilla extract

1 tablespoon mild vinegar

6 tablespoons mild vegetable oil

1 cup water

Preheat the oven to 350°F. Grease a 9-inch-square baking dish. Sift the dry ingredients directly into the pan. Make three holes in the mixture. In one put the vanilla, in one put the vinegar, and in the last put the oil. Pour the water over all. Mix well with a fork but don't beat. Bake until a cake tester inserted in the center of the cake comes out clean, about 30 minutes.

MAKES 1 (9-INCH) CAKE

Apple cakes of various types were extremely popular in the Seventies, both with Suburban Gourmets and their more urban brethren.

## APPLE CAKE

This recipe was copied at many a club meeting across the country in the Seventies—but unlike other such formulas, it still tastes good. And it doesn't have a particularly strange texture, although it is very moist. I believe the original recipe first appeared in *Sunset* magazine in the early 1950s, although that version called for melted chocolate rather than cocoa. I have reduced the sugar here by 1/2 cup.

4 cups cored, peeled, and chopped apples

1 1/2 cups sugar

1/2 cup mild vegetable oil or melted butter

1 cup walnuts, chopped

2 large eggs, beaten

2 teaspoons vanilla extract

2 cups all-purpose flour

2 teaspoons baking soda

2 teaspoons ground cinnamon

2 tablespoons cocoa powder

1 teaspoon salt

Preheat the oven to 350°F. Mix the apples and sugar together in a large bowl. In a separate bowl, mix the oil, nuts, eggs, and vanilla together. Add the egg mixture to the apples and mix well. Sift the dry ingredients together and fold into the apple mixture. Pour the batter into a greased 9 × 13-inch pan and bake until a cake tester inserted in the center of the cake comes out clean, 45 to 50 minutes.

MAKES 1 (9 × 13-INCH) CAKE

Impossible pie was another one of those "weird" dessert recipes that seemed to catch people's fancies in the Seventies. The same recipe, omitting the sweet stuff and substituting cheese, hamburger, onion, etc., made impossible quiche.

## IMPOSSIBLE PIE

The "impossible" part was that the Bisquick settled to the bottom of the pan and made its own crust.

    4 eggs
    2 cups milk
    $1/4$ cup ($1/2$ stick) butter, melted
    $1/2$ teaspoon vanilla extract
    $1/2$ cup sugar
    $1/2$ cup Bisquick
    1 cup unsweetened shredded coconut

Preheat the oven to 350°F. Put all the ingredients except the coconut in a blender and mix well on low speed. Stir in the coconut. Pour into a buttered 10-inch pie pan and bake until a knife inserted at the edge of the pie comes out clean, 40 to 45 minutes. Cool and serve.

MAKES 1 (10-INCH) PIE

## STRAWBERRY SQUARES

In 1975, this dessert was one of *Better Homes and Gardens* choices for their fifteen "all-time favorite" recipes from their test kitchens. The original recipe used 2 uncooked egg whites and $2/3$ cup sugar, beaten with the strawberries until light. To get around the raw egg white problem you could substitute an Italian meringue, but in keeping with the philosophy of the recipe, I have used marshmallows instead.

**For the Base and Topping**

 1 cup all-purpose flour
 1/4 cup firmly packed brown sugar
 1/2 cup walnuts, chopped
 1/4 cup (1/2 stick) butter or margarine, melted
 Pinch of salt

**For the Filling**

 1 tablespoon gelatin
 2 tablespoons lemon juice
 1/2 cup boiling water
 24 marshmallows
 1/2 cup sugar
 1 (10-ounce) package frozen strawberries, thawed
 1 cup heavy cream, whipped until firm peaks form, or 1 (4 1/2 ounce) container
  Cool Whip

Preheat the oven to 350°F. Mix all the base and topping ingredients together and spread in a shallow pan. Bake for 20 minutes, stirring occasionally. Cool and set aside.

For the filling, put gelatin, lemon juice, and boiling water in a blender container and blend on high 1 minute. Add marshmallows and sugar and blend on high until smooth. Drop a few strawberries into blender and blend for a few seconds. Continue adding strawberies and blending until all the strawberries are used. Pour into a large bowl, cover, and chill until the mixture is thick and almost set, about 30 minutes. Beat the strawberry mixture with a mixer or egg beater until frothy, about 1 minute. Fold in the whipped cream.

Sprinkle half the base and topping mixture over the bottom of a greased 9 × 13-inch pan. Cover with the filling and sprinkle the remaining base and topping mixture on top. Cover tightly and freeze 8 hours or overnight. Cut into squares and serve.

MAKES 12 TO 15 SERVINGS

## LEMON BARS

Everyone had a recipe for lemon bars in the Seventies after they appeared in *Betty Crocker's Cooky Book* (1963). They are still popular...and still good. Betty now sells a lemon bar mix.

**For the Pastry**

    2 cups all-purpose flour
    ½ cup confectioners' sugar
    I cup (2 sticks) butter

**For the Topping**

    4 eggs
    I ½ cups sugar
    6 tablespoons lemon juice
    I teaspoon grated lemon rind
    ¼ cup all-purpose flour
    ½ teaspoon baking powder
    Sifted confectioners' sugar

Preheat the oven to 350°F. Sift the flour and sugar together. Cut in the butter using a pastry blender or two knives until the mixture resembles cornmeal. Pat the dough into an ungreased 9 × 13-inch pan. Bake until set and just beginning to color, 12 to 15 minutes. Set on a wire rack to cool.

Beat the eggs for the topping until light and lemon colored. Beat in the sugar, lemon juice, and lemon rind. Sift the flour and baking powder together and stir into the egg mixture.

Pour the egg mixture over the baked pastry and bake until the topping is set and golden brown, 20 to 25 minutes. Remove to a wire rack and sift confectioners' sugar over the top. Cut into squares when cool.

MAKES ABOUT 24 (2-INCH-SQUARE) BARS

# The Times They Are a-Changin'—American Nouvelle

The market is the beginning. We want only what is seasonal. We don't even think about tomatoes between October and July.

    —Alice Waters, Chez Panisse restaurant (Berkeley, California)

Anyone who knows the fragrance of tomatoes ripening in the sun, the sweetness of berries so ripe they practically fall into the hand, or the flavor of asparagus and corn when picked and cooked right away knows food at its pleasurable best. This quality is what we wanted to be able to offer in our restaurant.

—Deborah Madison, Greens restaurant (Fort Mason, California)

In the Seventies there were the Old Guard restaurants still churning out beef Wellington and chicken Véronique; there were the Fun restaurants with their "Merry Old Sole" and "Krazy Kahlua Koffee"; there were the Suburban Gourmets cranking out broccoli-mayonnaise casserole and wacky cake. And there were the health food freaks who found virtue, if not pleasure, in soybeans with feta or granola fondue. As divergent as these cooking styles were, they all shared something crucial: Food was not the point. Adherence to the rules, or "goofing" on the rules, or quick 'n' easy cooking, or counting protein grams might have been the point. But food, as the direct and daily connection between Human and Earth, was not.

Yet something was stirring. In France in the late Sixties young chefs rebelled against the stultifying codification of classical French cooking. Paul Bocuse, Pierre Troisgros and Jean Troisgros, and Roger Vergé were some of the leaders of the rebellion, which sought a lighter hand, more innovation, a return to regional cooking, and the use of fresh seasonal ingredients. In 1973 this new style gained a name when *Gault-Millau* magazine dubbed it "la nouvelle cuisine."

## SCALLOP-VEGETABLE TERRINE WITH TOMATO COULIS

Delicate terrines made from seafood and/or vegetables became very fashionable in the early days of nouvelle cuisine—although such terrines weren't nouvelle at all, but standards of classic French cookery. Tomato coulis (nouvelle tomato sauce) was a popular accompaniment to many dishes. Crème fraîche replaced American sour cream (and French heavy cream) in the new cooking.

1 pound scallops
2 egg whites
1 teaspoon salt
1/4 teaspoon freshly ground black pepper
Few grains cayenne pepper
2 cups crème fraîche (p. 368)
1/4 pound young green beans, blanched in boiling water for 3 minutes, and cooled
1/4 pound young carrots, cut into strips, blanched in boiling water for 3 minutes, and cooled
1 1/2 cups Tomato Coulis (below)

In a food processor or blender, purée the scallops with the egg whites, salt, pepper, and cayenne. Force the mixture through a fine sieve. Chill the mixture, covered, in a metal bowl for 2 hours.

Preheat the oven to 375°F. Set the bowl of scallop purée in a larger bowl filled with cracked ice and cold water. Using a wooden paddle or a large wooden spoon, stir in 1½ cups of the crème fraîche, ¼ cup at a time, and continue stirring until the mixture is firm and light. Spoon one-third of the scallop mixture into a buttered 1½ quart rectangular terrine. Arrange half the vegetables, end-to-end lengthwise, over the mixture. Cover with one-third of the scallop mixture and arrange the rest of the vegetables over that. Finish with the rest of the scallop mixture.

Cover the terrine with a buttered piece of waxed paper cut to fit the terrine, place the lid on top, and place the terrine in a large baking dish, adding enough hot water to come two-thirds of the way up the sides of the terrine. Bake for 25 to 30 minutes, or until the mixture is just firm. Place the terrine on a rack, remove the lid and waxed paper, and let rest about 10 minutes. Turn the terrine out onto a platter, and slice into 8 slices.

Mix the Tomato Coulis with the remaining crème fraîche. Spoon some of this sauce on 8 serving plates and place a slice of the terrine on top. Serve at once with a bowl of the remaining sauce.

MAKES 8 SERVINGS

## TOMATO COULIS

 1 tablespoon butter
 1 shallot, minced
 2 garlic cloves, minced
 2 pounds ripe tomatoes, peeled, seeded, and chopped
 ½ teaspoon dried thyme
 1 teaspoon freshly ground black pepper
 1 bay leaf

Melt the butter in a heavy nonaluminum or non–cast iron skillet and sauté the shallot and garlic over low heat until soft. Add the rest of the ingredients, cover, and cook about 5 minutes. Remove the cover and cook over low heat, stirring occasionally, until the sauce is thick, about 30 minutes. Remove the bay leaf and purée the mixture in a food processor or blender.

MAKES ABOUT 1½ CUPS

In America too something was stirring. Partly in response to what was happening in France, partly as a result of the burgeoning health food movement, partly in reaction to the sameness, awfulness, or deadness of much of our cooking, American cooks began to look at food in a new way.

Alice Waters's Chez Panisse, which opened in Berkeley in 1971, was the most famous of the new restaurants, and it certainly had the most far-reaching impact. Although Chez Panisse started out serving primarily French dishes, these were not from the codified haute cuisine of Escoffier and Carême. Instead the restaurant relied on recipes from Richard Olney and Elizabeth David that were no less authentic but were lighter and more Provençal in feel. As time went on, Waters and then chef and co-owner Jeremiah Tower would begin to create dishes that reflected the northern California lifestyle. Throughout its evolution, Chez Panisse emphasized simple food (the recipes were not necessarily simple, how-ever) made from fresh, seasonal ingredients of the highest quality.

In Seattle, Robert Rosellini, whose family had for years run two old-line Italian restaurants, opened Rosellini's Other Place in 1974. While the Other Place did not have the countrywide impact that Chez Panisse did, Rosellini, like Alice Waters, highlighted regional foods cooked simply. He described his menus, which changed with the seasons, as a "moving image of the Pacific Northwest," and said, "I think my cuisine keeps getting simpler and cleaner and purer." All of the foods served in the restaurant were grown or produced in the Northwest, many on farms developed by Rosellini.

◆◆◆

## Rosellini's Other Place, Menu from January 1975

*Cream Soup of Wild Chantarelle and Morel*
*Mushrooms*
*Butter Roasted Pheasant with Pan Juices*
*Roasted New Potatoes*
*Salad of Bitter Greens*
*Wines from the St. Michelle Winery*
*Oregon Hazelnut Torte*

For success such a simple, but carefully balanced, menu depended on the best ingredients, perfectly cooked. That was the point, and it was what Rosellini and his more famous compatriots were trying do. It was revolutionary, but it was also obvious.

Many young chefs responded with enthusiasm to the new cooking, particularly on the West Coast. In southern California, chefs and restaurateurs like Wolfgang Puck of Ma Maison, Jean Bertranou of La Chaumière and then L'Ermitage, and Michael McCarty of Michael's brought nouvelle-inspired dishes to their chic and wealthy clientele. Whether they were serving an American nouvelle mesquite-grilled Sonoma County lamb or a French nouvelle salad of warm lobster medallions with baby green beans, or vegetarian nouvelle green ravioli with ricotta and fresh herbs, they, along with Alice Waters and her chefs, laid the groundwork for what would come to be known as California Cuisine. In northern California, the exciting vegetarian restaurant Greens opened in 1979, with Deborah Madison as chef.

Indeed, California's influence on the changing culinary scene was profound. In the northern part of the state, the wineries were beginning to produce wines that Hugh Johnson in the October 1970 issue of *Gourmet* reported with surprise were "at the peaks not quite so good [as French wines], but on the average maybe better." *Gourmet* itself finally recognized that the culinary center of America had shifted away from still staid New York when it started reviewing California restaurants in its January 1974 issue.

## CALIFORNIA BAKED GOAT CHEESE
## WITH GARDEN SALAD

Goat cheese, especially if locally produced, was all the rage with the new chefs. Served warm on a salad, it was incredible, in the lingo of the times. Jeremiah Tower says he started this salad fad in 1973 when he couldn't get Chez Panisse guests to eat goat cheese plain. He plopped a round of the cheese in the middle of a mixed green salad and the rest is history.

8 ounces fresh goat cheese, cut into 1/2-inch-thick rounds
1/2 cup extra virgin olive oil
3 to 4 sprigs fresh thyme
3 to 4 sprigs fresh basil
I garlic clove, mashed with a knife and peeled
2 to 3 tablespoons red wine vinegar
Salt and freshly ground black pepper to taste
1/2 pound arugula, washed and dried
I small head radicchio, washed and dried
I small head butter lettuce, washed and dried

Marinate the goat cheese in the olive oil with the fresh herbs and garlic overnight. Just before serving, preheat the oven to 400°F. Remove the cheese from the marinade and strain the marinade, reserving the oil. Bake the cheese on a lightly oiled baking sheet until bubbling, about 6 minutes. Whisk the vinegar, salt, and pepper in a small bowl, whisk in the reserved oil, then taste for balance. Toss the greens with the vinaigrette and arrange on salad plates. Place the baked cheese on top of the greens and serve at once.

MAKES 4 SERVINGS

Things were happening in the rest of the country as well. In New York Lawrence Forgione studied the French nouvelle style under Michel Guérard in the kitchens of the très trendy disco Regine's before moving on to become the chef at the River Café in Brooklyn. Forgione's style became more and more American and, like Alice Waters and Robert Rosellini, he developed relationships with local growers to provide fresh, seasonal foods. In New Orleans the rotund Paul Prudhomme and his wife opened K-Paul's Louisiana Kitchen, serving Cajun-style food made from the freshest local ingredients...not in a traditional flocked-velvet dining room, but in a down-home, lunchroom atmosphere. Forgione and Prudhomme would become two of the prime movers of the New American Cuisine in the 1980s.

Many cooks, in restaurants and at home, missed the point of the new cooking entirely and seized on the gimmicks—and the excesses of the nouvelle style, both American and French, were legion. Diners frequently were faced with tiny, exquisitely arranged—and exquisitely expensive—portions served on large plates, barely cooked fish or chicken, outlandish combinations (lobster with vanilla sauce was infamous), and clouds of mesquite-wood smoke that billowed out from countless grills.

But a few heeded the lessons of Bocuse, of the Troisgros brothers, and of Waters and Tower and sought to bring the best local and seasonal ingredients, perfectly cooked, to the table. It was an exciting time in American culinary history.

# 9

# The Eighties

## For Richer, for Poorer: Status Food and Comfort Food

The keynote was greed: the underlying philosophy was image over reality.
—Charles Panati on the 1980s

Many of those young chefs pay more attention to the way food is arranged than the way it tastes.
—M. F. K. Fisher, interview with Mimi Sheraton, *Time* (January 26, 1987)

With the arrival of the Eighties, America plunged into a new orgy of spending: on luxurious housing; on fancy cars; and on fancy, fashionable food. Gone were the sad, bad old days of a disgraced President Nixon, of Gerald Ford and his antiinflation WINS buttons, of Jimmy Carter's plain living, and of the Iran hostage debacle. The rich Reagans were in power now, the hostage crisis was over, the stock market was booming, and American confidence was returning. The new first lady, in contrast to the three unassuming women who had occupied the White House before her, epitomized the sharp-edged glamour of the new decade with her Reagan Red designer suits and glittering designer gowns (the designers were, of course, American). One of Nancy Reagan's first moves was to restore veal, which the Carters had considered too "elitist," to White House menus.

The Baby Boomers who had goofed on life in the Seventies had grown up to be Yuppies. Consumed with the serious task of disposing of the inordinately high cash flow that a two-income family generated, they bought BMWs, condos, and high-priced take-out from fashionable charcuteries—expensive frozen "gourmet" meals to pop in the microwave...or they went out to eat. For with all the glitz and ready cash of the so-called Greed Decade, no one seemed to have any time.

Eating, which Americans had always had ambivalent feelings about anyway, took time. So the new breed made eating count. They power-breakfasted and power-lunched, combining business with doubtful pleasure. When they went out to dinner, it wasn't to a quiet corner bistro where they could relax over a favorite and familiar dish. It was to an expensive, flashy, trendy place, where the fame of the chef, or the hipness of the food, might help guarantee their place in the demanding, unending struggle for status.

Yuppies certainly didn't have time to cook, at least not the old-fashioned time-consuming day-in-day-out cooking that Grandma had done. If they cooked, it had damned well better be worth their while. So cooking was reserved for parties, and the recipes were likely to be complicated restaurant-style creations from the pages of glossy cookbooks written by famous chefs.

The Decade of Greed was also the Decade of the Foodie, and Foodies were nothing if not greedy for new taste sensations, exotic new foods, expensive and high-status new ingredients. Note that this was not the age of the "eatie," if such a word were to exist. It wasn't eating that was important—not enough time for that—it was the individual foods that grabbed everyone's attention. Whether it was raspberry vinegar, green peppercorns, onion marmalade, walnut oil, or sun-dried tomatoes, it was the trendy ingredients or the newest way of combining seared tuna with lime-ginger chutney that took center stage.

The age of the Foodie brought with it the age of the star chef and the star chef's cookbook. In describing the new cooking, one of these star chefs said, with typical Eighties hubris, "I have gone on…to develop a style of cooking which, in its influence and scope, drawing on bar and grill, bistro, brasserie, and classical restaurant food, has become a new American classic." Significantly, nowhere in that impressive listing did he mention home cooking.

# Toto, I Don't Think We're in Kansas Anymore: New American Cooking

Using a technique picked up from a Hunanese chef, [Mark] Stech-Novak caramelized the skin of a Petaluma smoked duck with maple syrup and green peppercorn purée and served it forth with a piquant raspberry sauce studded with fresh whole berries.

—Caroline Bates, review of Le St. Tropez (San Francisco), *Gourmet* (November 1982)

You can't get a nice Coq au Vin anywhere anymore. When you go to a restaurant now, you never know what they're going to serve.

—An older restaurant goer (late 1980s)

Calvin Trillin said in the Seventies that four of the five best restaurants in the world were in Kansas City. Whether you agreed with him or not (there is some doubt whether he agreed with himself), by the Eighties American cooking was In in America. But what was meant by American cooking had little to do with the recipes in Irma Rombauer's *Joy of Cooking.*

## California Cuisine

It's great to take a piece of tuna and throw it on coals and serve it with a seasoned butter, but I don't think that's a big advance over what my father did in the backyard. In fact, no offense to the California cooks, they didn't invent coriander butter, either.

—Paula Wolfert, *Cook's* (January/February 1986)

California Cuisine, characterized by light sauces, fresh, and often Mediterranean- or Mexican-style combinations and ingredients, beautiful presentation, and a breezy informality, continued to fascinate. Alice Waters and Chez Panisse were still setting trends in northern California (one reviewer called the 1982 *Chez Panisse Menu Cookbook* "one of the few unquestionably brilliant books to appear in several years"), while Jeremiah Tower had moved on to an even trendier level with his San Francisco–area restaurants Balboa Café, Santa Fe Bar & Grill, and Stars.

Like his earlier partner, Alice Waters, and unlike many who tried their hand at the new cooking, Jeremiah Tower had strong, clear ideas of what he wanted food to taste like. His cooking, cutting edge and trendy as it was, had a purity and simplicity that indeed made it classic, although much of it was a little too "haute" for the home cook to whip up after a day at the office.

### Food and Fantasy

Remember, you don't always have to serve a dish in the correct piece of china—just the appropriate piece. These red and white grapefruit sections look quite right in a very shallow soup plate (it's the Twintons pattern by Poole of England).

—Martha Stewart, *Quick Cook Menus* (1988)

> If your setup includes a little guest house…treat its weekend occupants to the luxury of having breakfast in private at whatever time suits their mood. Equip the house with a small refrigerator, a coffee maker, and an extra cabinet filled with simple breakfast fixings.
>
> —Lee Bailey, *Lee Bailey's Country Weekends* (1983)

Yuppies who dressed for success, power-lunched, and aerobicized (in Nikes or Reeboks) also longed for a break from their high-pressure lives. But their fantasies were as status seeking as their realities: Instead of a deserted tropical beach, what Yups pictured was an English country house with graceful, beautiful people in summer whites playing croquet on beautiful lawns.

To satisfy this landed aristocracy fantasy in clothing and home furnishings the Yuppie Baby Boomers could turn to Ralph Lauren. For fantasy in food, they had Lee Bailey and Martha Stewart.

Lee Bailey's first book, *Lee Bailey's Country Weekends,* was based on the charming assumption that we all had not only country houses to repair to after the workweek, but that these houses were large enough to accommodate several guests. The book was organized not by types of food, but by where the food would be eaten. In "Under the Arbor" ("an idyllic place to have an evening meal") Mr. Bailey suggested beef brisket with new potatoes. In "On the Boat Dock" he advised chicken wings in hot pepper-butter sauce with bulgur salad. In "By the Pool" it was black forest ham and sweet red pepper and eggplant condiment. On what to do if you had neither an arbor, a boat dock, nor a pool—let alone a country house—he was silent.

Martha Stewart wasn't as concerned about where you and your guests ate your meal as she was about what you ate it on. In a typical description of a winter Sunday dinner meal that centered around roast pork with onions and prunes she said, "For this meal…I chose plates from my collection of old silver luster, made in England by Johnson Bros., pearl-handled flatware by Joseph Rogers & Sons, and a bouquet of peony tulips tucked into a silver biscuit container." But Stewart was no silver-and-damask snob. She was perfectly happy to advise you to serve a vegetarian pasta dinner on Fiestaware (she could serve twenty on the Fiestaware handed down from her maternal grandmother, augmented by pieces picked up at yard sales, and was glad to tell you so), or to use pink-lace pattern Depression glass to offset your grilled swordfish with chervil butter.

With neither Bailey nor Stewart was food the point. Image was all, and the image they both projected—and presumably their readers aspired to—was one of the leisured, moneyed class. It might not have been England, but it was as close to the upper-class ideal as most Americans would ever get.

*Alice Waters*

Like many of the what seemed like thousands of new cookbooks that came out in the Eighties, Tower's first cookbook was large and glossy, filled with gorgeous full-color pictures. This made for a lovely coffee table book. But did anyone really want to take such a beauty into the kitchen where it might get splattered with grease and drops of fig-mint relish? Fame, more than user-friendliness, seemed to be the point. (In fairness to Tower, quite a few of the recipes in his book are accessible to the experienced home cook, like the two below. But I still wouldn't bring his cookbook into the kitchen.)

## Tea

Upscale wannabes who had been watching too much *Masterpiece Theater* decided in the early Eighties that English afternoon tea was the ticket to social success. Not wanting to miss an opportunity to rake in even more dollars from their status-hungry patrons, fashionable hotels and trendy restaurants began serving fashionable, trendy, and often hideously expensive tea.

To the amusement of British onlookers, many of these precious afternoon rituals were called "high tea." Although this sounded very upper crust to Americans, high tea in England was a supper of hearty dishes usually partaken of by the lower classes. One snooty Englishman found fault with the Lucullan displays of the dainty sandwiches, fancy small cakes, and trifles that Americans liked for tea. "At the best homes," he sniffed, "only small bread-and-butter sandwiches are served."

Americans were not from the "best homes" (meaning upper-class English homes, of course), and we liked to get our money's worth from afternoon tea. Although some establishments served such things as golden caviar and vegetable pâtés, the most successful stuck to what Americans perceived as typically English tea fare. Trumps, an upscale Los Angeles restaurant whose starkly trendy decor included free-form concrete tables, served this sumptuous, yet proper, tea:

◆◆◆

# Tea at Trumps,
# circa 1983

*Sherry, White Wine, or Perrier*
*English Breakfast or Darjeeling Tea*
*Assortment of Finger Sandwiches filled with Curried Chicken,*
*Smoked Salmon, and Cucumber*
*Scones with Devonshire Cream and*
*Strawberry Jam*
*Fingerprint Cookies and Pecan Sandies*
*Fresh Fruit Tartlets and Lemon Curd Tartlets*
*Petit Fours*

For most of us, however, afternoon tea was too expensive in both money and time. Nor did tea fit either the American lifestyle or the American psyche. The fad, which had never reached beyond rich Baby Boomers anyway, faded quickly.

Reading about cream of corn soup in a century-old cookbook in the mid-1970s is what Jeremiah Tower says awoke him to the idea of American food. The original recipe called for crayfish butter, Tower's adaptation changed that to crayfish cream. In the recipe given here, two 1980s essentials are added to the soup: Roasted red peppers replace Tower's crayfish cream, and whole corn kernels are added to his smooth purée.

Variations on cream of corn soup were extremely popular: Recipes for it appeared everywhere, including one of Martha Stewart's glossy tomes and the first cookbook from Texas's Mansion on Turtle Creek restaurant. Michael McCarty, of Michael's in Santa Monica, said *his* corn soup, with jalapeño, lime, and coriander accents, was the definitive version.

## CREAM OF CORN SOUP WITH ROASTED RED PEPPER CREAM AND CORN KERNELS

If you really want to be super trendy, early Eighties-style, make an equal quantity of puréed black bean soup, then pour the bean soup and the corn soup into bowls simultaneously so that they do not mix, then pipe red pepper purée over the top in squiggles. Soup as modern art.

2 tablespoons unsalted butter
3 or 4 fresh oregano leaves
$1/3$ cup finely chopped Maui or Walla Walla sweet onion
2 cups very hot fresh chicken stock
7 ears fresh, very young, sweet corn
$1/2$ teaspoon salt
$1/2$ cup heavy cream
1 Roasted Red Pepper (p. 363)
1 teaspoon canned chipotle chili
1 cup light cream
Salt and freshly ground black pepper

Melt the butter in a large, heavy soup pot and add the oregano, the onion, and $1/4$ cup of the stock. Cover and cook over low heat about 5 minutes. Slice the kernels off the cobs, making sure you are not getting any of the tough cob with the kernels. Run the back of your knife downward over the cob to extract any last little bits of corn juice. Reserve the cobs. Add the rest of the stock to the pot, along with the corn, its juice, the salt, and as many corn cobs as will fit in the pot, and bring to a boil. Remove from the heat and let cool to lukewarm. Remove the corn cobs, strain out about $1/2$ cup of corn kernels, then purée the rest of the soup in a blender or food processor. Strain the purée through a fine sieve.

Whip the heavy cream to soft peaks. Purée the roasted red pepper with the chipotle chili and fold it into the whipped cream. At serving time, reheat the corn purée with the light cream and the corn kernels. Check for seasoning and spoon into soup plates. Add a spoonful of the red pepper cream mixture to each serving.

MAKES 8 SERVINGS

## ROASTED RED PEPPERS

Roasting peppers (and fresh hot chilies) was practically a national sport in the Eighties. To roast them, you can grill them on the barbecue, broil them, char them over a gas flame, or simply bake them at high temperature until blackened. The broiler is suggested here. If you have a highly sensitive smoke alarm, open the windows wide and turn on a fan. This recipe sets my alarm off every time.

4 large meaty red peppers

Preheat broiler. Place peppers on broiling pan and broil as close to the heat as possible until the skins blacken. Immediately wrap peppers in damp paper towels, place in a plastic bag and let sit for 20 minutes. Take them out of the bag, slip skins off peppers, and remove stems and seeds. Some people resort to washing the pepper under running water to get off the last little black bits but try not to do this, because the nice roasted flavors washes off too.

The peppers may now be puréed for the corn soup recipe given above. They may also be cut in strips, salted, and tossed with chopped garlic and olive oil for a wonderful appetizer.

MAKES 4 ROASTED PEPPERS

What grilling was to the late Seventies, roasting was to the Eighties. Everything was roasted, which really meant "baked," especially vegetables. And especially garlic.

Both Jeremiah Tower and Alice Waters take credit for introducing roasted whole garlic at Chez Panisse. Tower said that he learned of the idea from Richard Olney, American expatriate, superb cook, and author of (among others) *The French Menu Cookbook* and *Simple French Food*. (A recipe for garlic purée based on whole baked heads of garlic appeared in the latter book in 1974.)

# ROASTED GARLIC WITH WHITE CHEESE, OLIVES, AND GRILLED TOASTS

No one served toast in the Eighties, only "toasts."

4 heads new, unsprouted garlic
6 to 7 sprigs fresh thyme, broken into small pieces
$1/3$ cup unsalted butter, melted
$1/3$ cup extra virgin olive oil
Salt and freshly ground black pepper
$1/2$ cup fresh goat cheese
$1/4$ cup heavy cream
Italian bread, cut into thin slices
Olive oil for grilling the bread
2 or 3 kinds of green and black olives (but *not* the pitted California type)

Preheat the oven to 275°F. Cut each head of garlic in half horizontally, brush the cut sides with olive oil, and put the heads back together. Arrange them in a shallow baking dish, place half the thyme around them, pour the melted butter and half the olive oil over them, and salt and pepper them. Cover and bake until the garlic is very soft but not at all browned, about $1^1/_2$ hours, basting the heads occasionally with the oil and butter in the pan.

Put the garlic heads on a serving plate. Mash the cheese with the cream to a spreadable consistency and scoop the cheese onto a serving plate. Pour the remaining olive oil over the cheese and sprinkle with the remaining thyme sprigs. Brush the bread slices lightly with olive oil and grill them on both sides until crisp and golden. Serve the bread with the baked garlic, cheese, olives, and plenty of napkins. Each guest squeezes some of the garlic onto a toast, and tops the garlic with some of the cheese.

MAKES 4 SERVINGS

In northern California, too, the Greens restaurant and its founding chef, Deborah Madison, continued to offer sometimes celestial and always creative and satisfying vegetarian food. The first Greens cookbook, by Madison with Edward Espe Brown, came out in 1987. Unlike many of the other books that carried the name of a famous restaurant, this one contained recipes that the home cook could easily make, with (mostly) readily available ingredients.

# New American Cooking, Not-So-Haute-Style

Although the star chefs were publishing cookbooks by the pound, most Americans who still cooked regularly were not ready for a steady diet of poached duck with duck sausage and horseradish sauce. On the low end of the culinary scale, there were still plenty of cookbooks offering hurry-up tuna crunch and such. But for those of us with higher aspirations, our well-thumbed copies of *Joy of Cooking* and Julia Child's early works did not reflect the new food tastes we were becoming accustomed to.

Of the many good cookbooks published in the Eighties, one we turned to constantly, because it not only reflected the new styles but was also generally reliable, was *The Silver Palate Cookbook*. Written by Sheila Lukins and Julee Rosso, who also ran the Silver Palate shop in Manhattan, the book told us how to make "American" classics like beef stroganoff and gazpacho, as well as newer dishes like carrots in raspberry vinegar and spinach pasta with salmon and cream. Although it had its faults (too much fruit with meat, some "inauthentic" recipes), this book was probably the new American classic, no matter what certain star chefs thought. The book was a best-seller and was recently issued in a tenth-anniversary edition.

The other books we turned to were anything by Jeff Smith, the Frugal Gourmet. This Methodist-minister-turned cook was the Eighties answer to Julia Child. On his popular PBS series he gamboled across the kitchen, laughed at himself, made messes, stuck his fingers in the sauce, and admonished us to enjoy our food. He was obviously enjoying himself, and like Mrs. Child's, his appeal was that he not only could cook but was also "one of us." Unlike Mrs. Child's, his recipes tended to be simple home cooking, often American, although he frequently ventured into foreign cuisines.

Jeff Smith was so popular that by the end of the Eighties there was a "Frug" backlash. It became fashionable to say that many of his foreign recipes were bastardizations (some were: he put milk in Greek avgolemono soup, which is heresy), that he had no technique, no training, etc., etc. But no matter what your opinion of him was, Smith contributed two important things to American cooking in the Eighties: He made cooking seem unintimidating, and he made us feel that the sharing of home-cooked food with friends and family was one of life's happier necessities.

## LINGUINE WITH CARAMELIZED ONIONS AND WALNUTS

In *The Greens Cookbook,* Deborah Madison made this dish with fresh pasta seasoned with rosemary. While it is very good that way, the sauce is too delicious to wait for only those times when the cook is ambitious enough to make fresh noodles. The original recipe also called for grated Gruyère to be stirred into the pasta before serving: I like it better without. Madison used white wine, but I like the color and flavor red gives the dish. One taster said this strongly flavored dish was the best thing she had ever eaten.

3 tablespoons butter
3 tablespoons extra virgin olive oil
2 bay leaves
1/2 teaspoon finely chopped fresh rosemary
1/2 teaspoon dried thyme or 6 sprigs fresh
5 large onions (red are best but yellow will do), very thinly sliced
1 teaspoon salt
1 cup walnuts, coarsely chopped (be sure they are not rancid—
 many supermarket nuts are)
2 tablespoons walnut oil or olive oil
1 pound linguine (or make your own pasta adding 1 tablespoon finely chopped
 fresh rosemary to the dough)
2 cloves garlic, minced
1 cup dry red wine
1 cup water
Freshly ground black pepper
Freshly grated Parmesan cheese

Melt the butter with the olive oil over low heat in a large, heavy skillet and sauté the herbs in the mixture until they are fragrant. Add the onions and salt to the herbs. Cook over low heat, stirring occasionally, until the onions have taken on a rich, golden color, about 20 minutes. While the onions are cooking, toast the chopped walnuts in a small pan over low heat in the walnut oil until they are fragrant, about 5 minutes, being careful not to let them burn.

Cook the pasta in boiling salted water until al dente, drain it, and keep it warm while you finish the sauce. Add the garlic and wine to the onions, raise the heat to medium-high, and cook, stirring, until the wine has reduced by about half. Add the water and allow the sauce to cook down about one-third. Stir in half the walnuts and cook for 1 minute more. Taste for seasoning, adding salt if necessary and a few grinds of fresh pepper. Add the pasta to the sauce, along with the rest of the walnuts. Toss well to mix everything together. Serve with Parmesan on the table.

MAKES 4 SERVINGS

Asian cooking techniques and ingredients had long been an accepated part of West Coast cookery and, not surprisingly, were incorporated into California Cuisine too. In San Francisco in the Eighties, Ken Hom was startling many with his unusual blend of Chinese, French, and American ingredients and techniques. He confidently sauced mussels with Chinese black beans mixed with tomato coulis and basil; marinated chicken in rice wine, soy sauce, and ancho chili paste; and made savory cornmeal waffles with sesame oil, scallions, and ginger. He also made a variation of the popular corn soup (p. 362) flavored with Chinese chili bean paste, ginger, and lemongrass.)

Whether Ken Hom started the trend for Franco-American-Asian food, or whether he was just one of the medium's best practitioners, others soon got into the game. Wolfgang Puck (see p. 370 for more on him) opened a very popular Chinese-French restaurant, Chinoise-on-Main, in southern California, which also boasted the super-trendy French-Japanese La Petite Chaya. You could be just about assured in the mid-Eighties that the trendiest, highest-priced, and smallest-portioned restaurants would be serving Asian-inspired food.

## BAKED APPLES WITH GINGER, LEMONGRASS, AND CRÈME FRAÎCHE

Baked apples are not French haute cuisine, but they are part of old-fashioned American cooking…and the new chefs loved nothing better than "updating" old favorites. Ken Hom sliced the apples and cooked them with lemongrass and vanilla beans in little foil packets. Here the apples are baked and candied ginger replaces the vanilla beans. If fresh lemongrass is not available, fresh lemon zest may be substituted.

> 4 firm baking apples (Rome Beauty or McIntosh are good)
> 2 tablespoons firmly packed brown sugar
> 2 teaspoons minced candied ginger
> 2 tablespoons minced fresh lemongrass (or 2 teaspoons minced lemon zest)
> 1 tablespoon unsalted butter
> Crème Fraîche (below) or sour cream, whipped cream, or ice cream

Preheat the oven to 350°F. Core the apples and pare off the upper third of their skins. Mix the sugar, ginger, lemongrass, and butter together and stuff the mixture into each apple core. Put the apples in a baking dish just big enough to hold them, cover, and bake until the apples are soft all the way through (test with a toothpick), about 40 minutes. Let them cool slightly, then serve with the Crème Fraîche.

MAKES 4 SERVINGS

## CRÈME FRAÎCHE

Real crème fraîche, the French answer to American sour cream, is impossible to make in this country with generally available dairy products. But you can come up with a close approximation if you can get heavy cream that has not been ultrapasteurized. This luscious, tangy cream was very much in vogue in the Eighties. Unlike sour cream or yogurt, crème fraîche will not curdle when it is heated.

> I cup heavy cream, not ultrapasteurized
> I tablespoon buttermilk

In a clean bowl or jar mix together the cream and buttermilk. Cover tightly and let sit in a warm, dark place 24 hours. By then the cream should have thickened to the consistency of a thin yogurt. If not, let it sit up to another 12 hours. Refrigerate, covered, for up to 1 week.

It was in glitzy Los Angeles that the glitziest and trendiest new restaurants operated. Michael McCarty perhaps did the most to set the style for California restaurants with Michael's, which opened in 1979 in Santa Monica. With its garden patio, its pale peach walls hung with original and expensive modern art, and waiters in chinos and pink Oxford shirts, Michael's was the epitome of the casual, yet very chic, California restaurant. It was also very expensive. One struggling writer who treated herself and three friends to a visit to Michael's in the Eighties was stunned when the check arrived. "It was literally more than my rent," she said.

The food at Michael's was casual yet chic, too, tending to simple grilled items sauced with variously flavored vinaigrettes, cream sauces, or beurre blanc. The top half of every entrée plate was decorated with a vegetable mosaic—an artful array of baby vegetables that had been blanched and then tossed with appropriate flavorings and oils. Was McCarty's way with vegetables the inspiration behind those huge stalks of lukewarm, crunchy broccoli that appear on the entrée plates at so many American restaurants now?

## GRILLED SCALLOPS WITH WATERCRESS-LIME BEURRE BLANC

Raspberries were pretty much passé by the mid-1980s, but Michael McCarty garnished this dish with three berries per plate anyway, calling it "a funny old holdover from the days of nouvelle cuisine." He said he liked the color and taste contrast between the fruit and the white shellfish and sauce. McCarty was also a proponent of slightly underdone poultry, fish, and shellfish. Although that idea was a popular one in the 1980s with young chefs, it is not recommended in the salmonella-prone 1990s.

2 cups Beurre Blanc (below)
2 bunches fresh watercress, leaves finely chopped and stems discarded
Juice of 3 limes, strained
30 large scallops
6 tablespoons clarified butter
Salt and freshly ground pepper (the original specified white pepper)
18 fresh raspberries for garnish

Preheat the grill or broiler. Prepare the Beurre Blanc and stir in the chopped watercress and lime juice. Keep the sauce warm in the top of a double boiler over simmering water. Brush the scallops with the clarified butter and season with salt and pepper. Grill or broil them about 2 minutes per side. To give them that restaurant look of cross-hatched grill marks, rotate the scallops on the grill 90° after the first minute of cooking. For each serving, spoon the Beurre Blanc on the plate, place 5 scallops on top of the sauce, and garnish with 3 raspberries.

MAKES 6 SERVINGS

## BEURRE BLANC

Beurre blanc, a sort of béarnaise without egg yolks, was the haute sauce of the 1980s. It is a classic French sauce with fish and is delicious and useful to know, if you can stand the calories.

2 shallots, finely chopped
1/2 cup white wine vinegar
1 cup dry white wine or fish stock
1 cup (2 sticks) salted butter, chilled and cut into small pieces
1 tablespoon heavy cream (optional)

In the top of a nonaluminum double boiler, combine the shallots, vinegar, and wine. Bring to a boil and cook over high heat until the liquid is reduced by about 1/3 cup. Place the pan over simmering water and whisk in the butter a few pieces at a time. Keep the sauce warm in the double boiler. The cream may be added to help stabilize the sauce—in which case the sauce becomes known as beurre nantais.

MAKES ABOUT 2 CUPS

And then there was Wolfgang Puck, probably the most famous of the star chefs of the Eighties. Austrian born, French trained, and irrepressibly exuberant, Puck refused to take haute cuisine seriously (although he took his cooking very seriously indeed). Instead of the usual chef's white toque, Puck sported a baseball cap (which became a fad among other young chefs) and delighted in shocking the Old Guard with untraditional restaurant fare like pizza with smoked salmon and golden caviar or American chocolate chip cookies. Of those who criticized his straying from the tenets of the classic cuisine, he said, "Maybe they don't change the water in their bathtubs for years at a time either!"

In the Seventies, Puck had taken over the kitchens at Patrick Terrail's Ma Maison in L.A., which quickly became the hottest restaurant in town, complete with an unlisted phone number. In 1982, he went out on a limb to open Spago, originally conceived as a pizzeria. But what a pizzeria! Instead of the standard tomato, mozzarella, pepperoni fare, Puck offered pizza with duck sausage, or goat cheese and Black Forest ham, or artichokes and fresh wild mushrooms. The restaurant was an overnight sensation. Reservations were taken months in advance (at least for plebs—Hollywood's highest and mightiest could usually get a table), and Puck quickly expanded Spago's menu to include things like squid ink pasta with smoked scallops or quail on garlic corn cakes with zinfandel-thyme sauce.

Spago's success encouraged Puck to open an even less traditional restaurant, Chinoise on Main, in Santa Monica, in 1983. With outrageous "Felliniesque" decor designed by his wife, Barbara, he served up Sino-French concoctions like lobster with rice wine and ginger cream sauce or rack of lamb with cilantro and miso (an interesting choice, because Puck said that he hated cilantro because "it tastes like soap"). Chinoise didn't take off at first as Spago had done. People weren't quite ready for a "Chinese" restaurant that didn't serve Chinese food, but it was an immediate hit with the Hollywood gang (Victoria Principal hosted one of her New Year's Eve parties there). Still, Chinoise eventually became a success, if not quite the household name Spago had been, and it certainly did much to add to Puck's image as the "wild and crazy" chef.

## PIZZA WITH EGGPLANT, GOAT CHEESE, AND BASIL

Jeremiah Tower again gets credit for the first stylish, individual pizzas in America, which he made at Chez Panisse in 1974. But it was Wolfgang Puck who made pizza the inescapable appetizer at trendy restaurants. Pizza may be topped with everything from cheese and tomatoes to duck sausage (hard to find these days and too much trouble for most people to make), or roasted peppers, or tuna fish and capers or—after baking—smoked salmon, crème fraîche, and caviar.

Extra-virgin olive oil

1 pound baby eggplants, cut into $^1/_4$-inch rounds

Salt and freshly ground black pepper

1 recipe Pizza Dough (below)

$1^1/_2$ cups unpuréed Tomato Coulis (p. 352)

4 large garlic cloves, blanched in boiling water for 10 minutes,
  then peeled and finely chopped

$^1/_4$ cup finely chopped fresh basil

6 ounces fresh goat cheese, cubed

Fresh basil sprigs for garnish

Preheat the oven, preferably equipped with a baking stone, to 500°F for 20 to 30 minutes. Heat 2 to 3 tablespoons of olive oil in a large skillet over medium heat, then add the eggplant and sauté until soft and slightly browned. Season with salt and pepper and set aside. Divide the pizza dough into four segments and roll or stretch each one out to a 7- to 8-inch circle. Brush each circle with olive oil. Spread the Tomato Coulis on each pizza round and scatter the garlic and chopped basil over the top of the coulis. Arrange the eggplant slices on the sauce and top with the goat cheese.

Slide the pizza onto the hot stone, or place on a baking sheet, and bake until the crust is golden and the cheese has melted, 10 to 12 minutes. Garnish with basil sprigs and serve.

MAKES 4 (7- TO 8-INCH) PIZZAS

## PIZZA DOUGH

Many home cooks are intimidated by yeasted doughs. Pizza is a good beginner course, because the dough is quickly and easily put together, and it can be ready for the oven in about one hour. Whole wheat flour is used here to give the dough extra flavor, but all white may be used.

1 package active dry yeast

2–3 cups all-purpose unbleached flour (or bread flour, if you can get it)

$1^1/_4$ cups lukewarm water

2 tablespoons olive oil

1 cup whole wheat flour

1 teaspoon salt

In a large bowl stir the yeast and 1 tablespoon of the white flour into $^1/_2$ cup of the water until dissolved and let it "proof"—bubbles should show all over the surface in about 5 minutes. (If the yeast doesn't start to bubble, it is no good and you must start over.) Stir in the rest of the water, the oil, then the flours and salt, holding out about 1 cup of the white flour. The dough should be soft and workable but not sticky. Add additional flour as necessary to get the right texture.

Turn the dough onto a lightly floured surface and knead until very smooth and elastic, about 10 minutes. Put the dough in a clean, oiled bowl and turn it over to coat all sides with the oil. Cover and let rise in a warm spot until doubled in bulk, 35 to 40 minutes. Punch down the dough, divide it into four sections, and continue as directed in the main recipe.

## Other Regional Cuisines

The development and success of California Cuisine spawned a rush to "regional" cooking all over the country. But, as John Mariani pointed out, regional cooking often meant that the goat cheese pizza would be topped with fiddlehead ferns in New England and with andouille sausage in Louisiana.

### Cajun Food

Perhaps the greatest craze, following the California Cuisine fad, was for Louisiana Cajun food. Of course, Cajun food was not a new development in Louisiana. It had been simmering along quite nicely ever since the French Acadians were booted out of Nova Scotia in the 1700s and found shelter in the bayous of south Louisiana. Cajun food differed from Creole food (Creoles are the descendants of the French and Spanish who settled the region) in being somewhat simpler and usually hotter than its complex, rich cousin. Both Creoles and Cajuns use French techniques, and indigenous produce, along with foodstuffs and techniques brought by African slaves, to produce a fully developed, wonderful cuisine. And they both take their cuisines very seriously. New Orleans residents have been known to quit speaking to each other over an argument about whether gumbo should be thickened with okra or filé powder (never both).

So New American Cooking didn't have a great effect on Louisiana, but Louisiana certainly had an effect on New American Cooking. And mostly because of another one of those star chefs, Paul Prudhomme, owner and chef of K-Paul's Louisiana Kitchen.

Prudhomme is a Cajun and he mostly cooks Cajun, although he is just as adept at Creole cooking, which he practiced for years at the Brennan sisters' famous restaurant, Commander's Palace. As much as his cooking, good as it is, it is Prudhomme's outsized personality, along with his physique, that made him—and Cajun food—famous. And perhaps his most famous dish (aside from gumbo made without roux, a shocking departure for many Louisianians) was blackened redfish, which he created in March 1980. This method of cooking fish in a white-hot skillet became so popular so quickly that as early as 1982 one San Francisco restaurant was serving blackened tuna (raw in the middle, of course)...with ginger chutney. The immense popularity of blackened redfish also led to the redfish being placed on the endangered species list.

## Grazing and Tapas

Americans seemed to like snacking better than sitting down to a square meal. Although gourmets had previously derided this preference, in the Eighties snacking became chic. But because it needed an up-market label to be truly chic, snacking was now called grazing.

Grazing meant that restaurant goers (and chefs) no longer had to make an effort to think out a cohesive, balanced menu. Now all you had to do was order as many different appetizers as you thought you could eat. Individual pizzas, each with a different topping, were perhaps the most popular grazing items, but fajitas, tuna or salmon tartare, grilled goat cheese, and blinis with sour cream and caviar were also trendy.

In the mid-Eighties a subset of the grazing craze took hold. Tapas, which are Spanish bar snacks, became a sensation in New York after Felipe Rojas-Lombardi started serving them at the Ballroom restaurant in 1983. Trendy restaurants and pubs quickly picked up on the tapas fad and tapas bars opened in many of the big cities. But the tapas fad did not last long. As much as Americans liked snacking, the food at tapas bars was just a little too unfamiliar and perhaps a little too *brown* for our liking. And it wasn't the sort of food we were ready to make at home. One of Rojas-Lombardi's tapas menus from the Eighties is listed here:

---

*Rabbit Escabeche*
*Pickled Artichokes*
*Eggs with Romesco Sauce*
*Spareribs with Black Mustard Seeds*
*Eggplant and Mushroom Ragu*
*Snails with Red Kidney Beans*
*Country Ham*
*Savory Duck Stew with Olives and Potatoes*
*Butternut Squash and Tomato Stew*
*Shrimp à la Gallega*
*Cod Fritters*
*Spiced Shredded Beef with Potatoes*
*Curried Lamb Empanadas*
*Potatoes with Chili and Cheese Sauce*

---

## PAUL PRUDHOMME'S BLACKENED REDFISH

The original recipe (in *Chef Paul Prudhomme's Louisiana Kitchen*, 1984) called for a whole grocery list of herbs and spices. Chef Paul became upset about the liberties many cooks took with that list and now prefers this recipe, which calls for his proprietary seasoning blend. (In addition to being a good cook, Chef Paul is quite a businessman.)

It's a good idea to have a fire extinguisher handy when making this recipe.

1½ cups (3 sticks) unsalted butter, melted and kept warm
6 (8- to 10-ounce) redfish fillets, ½ inch thick, or substitute other firm-fleshed
    fish such as pompano, red snapper, salmon, or tuna
3 tablespoons Chef Paul Prudhomme's Blackened Redfish Magic™

Make the hottest fire you can manage on a charcoal or gas grill. Heat a large cast-iron skillet over very high heat on the stove until it is beyond the smoking stage and you see white ash in the skillet bottom, at least 10 minutes. Using thick potholders, carefully transfer the hot skillet to the grill.

Put half the melted butter in a flat dish big enough to hold a fillet. Dip each fillet in the butter, coating both sides well. Sprinkle the Blackened Redfish Magic generously and evenly on both sides of the fillets. Place 2 fillets in the skillet and cook uncovered until the underside becomes deep brown, almost black (but not burned), about 2 minutes. Turn the fish over and pour 1 teaspoon butter on top of each fillet. ***Be careful here***, because the butter may flame up. Cook until dark brown on the second side, about 2 minutes more. Remove the cooked fillets to heated serving plates. Cook the remaining fillets in the same way. Serve the fillets with ramekins filled with the remaining melted butter.

MAKES 6 SERVINGS

By the mid-Eighties nearly every major American city had a Cajun restaurant, or if it didn't, its trendy restaurants were sure to serve at least some variety of Cajun food. For a while, it seemed you couldn't turn around without meeting some sort of blackened fish, or gumbo (the trendiest were made with duck sausage), or jambalaya. But overexposure, and the fact that most so-called Cajun food was just bad food with a lot of spices, put an end to this fad. Even the man who started the craze, Paul Prudhomme, said he "did a little jig" when ersatz Louisiana cooking passed from the scene. By the late 1980s, Cajun food was Out...except in Louisiana, where they know a delicious thing when they eat it.

*Paul Prudhomme*

## BREAD PUDDING WITH PECAN BOURBON SAUCE

Bread pudding was another one of those old-fashioned all-American dishes that were de rigueur for trendy chefs. Although bread puddings were made around the country with every sort of "regional" accent, one of the most popular was one with a Southern, especially southern Louisiana, twang. The flavors in this pudding may be varied by substituting rum for the bourbon, candied orange and lemon peel for the raisins, cinnamon for the nutmeg, etc.

    2 cups milk
    4 cups stale Italian or French bread cubes, with crusts on
    1/4 cup (1/2 stick) unsalted butter, melted
    1/4 cup Bourbon whiskey
    2 large eggs, lightly beaten
    3/4 cup sugar
    1/4 teaspoon salt
    1 teaspoon vanilla extract
    1/2 teaspoon freshly ground nutmeg
    1/2 cup raisins
    1/2 cup toasted pecans
    Bourbon-Pecan Sauce (below)
    Heavy or whipped cream (optional)

Preheat the oven to 350°F. Scald the milk by heating it in a saucepan to the point where tiny bubbles start to form around the edges. Put the bread cubes in a large bowl and pour the milk over them. Let them sit until the milk has cooled, pushing the bread cubes down into the milk occasionally.

Meanwhile, mix the eggs, sugar, salt, vanilla, and nutmeg together. When the bread mixture has cooled, add the egg mixture, stirring to blend well. Then add the raisins and pecans. Pour into a buttered 2-quart casserole and bake until a knife inserted in the center comes out clean, 40 to 45 minutes. Let the pudding cool slightly, then serve it warm with the Bourbon-Pecan Sauce and, if you like, some heavy or whipped cream.

MAKES 8 SERVINGS

### BOURBON-PECAN SAUCE

This is nothing more than old-fashioned lemon or vanilla cornstarch sauce made to taste like a spirited pecan pie.

½ cup sugar

2 tablespoons cornstarch

1 ½ cups boiling water

½ cup dark corn syrup

¼ cup (½ stick) unsalted butter

1 teaspoon vanilla extract

¼ cup Bourbon whiskey

½ cup toasted pecans

In a deep saucepan, mix the sugar and cornstarch together. Stir the boiling water gradually into the sugar mixture, then stir in the corn syrup. Bring to a boil and boil 1 minute, stirring constantly. Turn down the heat to the lowest setting and stir in the butter, vanilla, Bourbon, and pecans. Remove from the heat and keep warm until serving time.

MAKES ABOUT 2 CUPS

## The South, Midwest, Northwest, and Northeast

Interestingly, as popular as Louisiana-style cooking was for a while, traditional Southern cooking, which was also highly developed, did not become a fad, at least not per se. When old-fashioned American cooking became popular (updated, of course) much of it was Southern cooking—fried chicken, biscuits, spoon bread, pecan pie, etc. But Southern food had no trendy proponents and was thus spared.

In New England, in the Midwest, and in the Pacific Northwest, young chefs were as excited as everyone else about the New Cooking and started using fresh, local ingredients in trendy ways. Robert Rosellini continued to turn out astoundingly good food at the Other Place in Seattle, but he was not trendy enough or flashy enough to gain national prominence. Steven Raichlen and Lydia Shire were well known in New England, but although they might have been recognized by Foodie cognoscenti, they were not household names. And the pink singing scallops of Washington State or the fiddlehead ferns of Maine were too localized a taste to become a craze.

Midwestern cooking gained something of a foothold with the return of old-fashioned Americana in the late Eighties. Meat loaf, corned beef hash, coleslaw, and oatmeal cookies were what many Americans had cut their teeth on, and they welcomed the return of these simple, if often updated, dishes. However, Midwestern cooking again had no well-known fashionable proponents. But Midwestern ingredients did. In the early Eighties, Larry Forgione of Brooklyn's

River Café (and later of An American Place in Manhattan), along with Justin Rashid and Kate Marshall of Michigan, started American Spoon Foods, which sold the best of Michigan's foodstuffs by mail. Especially popular were Spoon Foods's dried cherries and Michigan morel mushrooms, but the company also sold wild fruit jellies, native hickory nuts, and Michigan maple cream, among many other trendy, high-quality items.

## The American Southwest

If I hear any more about chic Tex-Mex or blue cornmeal, I'll throw up.
—M. F. K. Fisher, interview with Mimi Sheraton, *Time* (January 26, 1987)

California Cuisine might have been the beginning of the New American cooking in the late Seventies, but in the Eighties the trendiest cooking was that of the American Southwest. Whether it was Cal-Mex, Tex-Mex, or Santa Fe inspired, this style had more food fads under one generalized umbrella than any other "cuisine." What with grilling, corn, blue corn, beans, chilies, cilantro, salsa, quail, trout, jicama, limes, mangoes, and squash blossoms, how could it fail to become a long-lived hit?

The California chefs had done a great deal to start the fad for all things Southwest, cooking as they did in a state that had once been part of Mexico. They used beans, corn, fresh and dried chilies, and cilantro freely, often in unconventional ways, and they grilled food over mesquite (a shrub from the Southwest). Jeremiah Tower liked to make Russian blinis (to be served with sturgeon and caviar) with cornmeal instead of buckwheat. At the Santa Fe Bar & Grill in San Francisco he served Eggs in Hell, Texas style (hard-boiled eggs with red pepper purée, barbecue sauce, and cilantro) and chiles rellenos (stuffed chilies) with a sauce of black beans. Michael Roberts of L.A.'s très trendy Trumps featured plantains and American caviar with refried beans. Not surprisingly, New York was way behind this Southwestern trend, and it wasn't until 1982 that the first Manhattan restaurant began grilling with mesquite imported from Texas.

Who really put Southwestern cooking on the map outside of California is difficult to pinpoint. It just seemed to spread like the wildfire inherent in its characteristic hot chilies. But one of the first to bring this initially simple cooking to national attention was Huntley Dent, with his *Feast of Santa Fe* (1985).

To read Dent's book is to be transported to a sun-baked land where the bones of the earth show clearly and food—corn, beans, chilies, and squash—is hard won and treated simply, with great respect. Said Dent, "At first it barely seems credible that a stew could be satisfying if it consisted only of meat, onion and red chili, so cookbook writers rush in to clothe the naked and begin to amplify." If you are looking for an "amplified" recipe for blue corn pancakes with sturgeon and caviar, you won't find it in Dent's book. But you will find recipes for blue cornmeal mush (blue cornmeal, salt, water, and lard) and pinto beans (dried beans, water, salt pork, onion, garlic, cumin, oregano, salt, and pepper). And, of course, plenty of recipes for various salsas, fresh and cooked, and other deliciously simple things. Which is not to say that the recipes in *Feast of Santa Fe* are unsophisticated: it's just that their sophistication lies in their purity.

## SIMPLE CHICKEN SOUP WITH SALSA

This soup was served at a party given by a Mexican-American family. They didn't have much money, but their hospitality was boundless and the simple soup, accompanied by corn tortillas and pinto beans, delicious.

> 3 cups hot cooked rice
> I cup or more shredded cooked chicken, if you have it
> Salsa Cruda (below)
> 8 cups hot chicken broth seasoned to taste with salt and pepper

Place $^1/_2$ cup of the rice in each soup bowl, top with a little chicken if you are using it, and then add a large spoonful of the salsa. Ladle in the hot broth and serve the soup with the rest of the salsa on the table for each guest to add as desired. If accompanied by beans and tortillas, this makes a filling and economical meal.

MAKES 6 SERVINGS

### SALSA CRUDA (FRESH SALSA, A.K.A. PICO DE GALLO)

Everyone has their own pet way of making fresh salsa, but this is one of the simplest. Cooks with sensitive hands often wear gloves when working with chilies. In any case, be sure to wash your hands, the knife, and the cutting board thoroughly after cleaning and chopping the chilies. The slightest bit of chili oil finding its way into an eye or other tender portion of the anatomy will burn like the blazes.

> 3 medium tomatoes (peeled if you like)
> I to 3 jalapeño peppers, seeds and veins removed
> 3 green onions
> $^1/_2$ cup cilantro (fresh coriander or Chinese parsley) leaves
> I tablespoon fresh lime juice
> Salt and freshly ground black pepper

Chop all the vegetables fine (a food processor works, but don't keep it on more than a few seconds). Mix together well. (If you like, you may now chop them together to form a finer, more cohesive mass.) Season with the lime juice and salt and pepper.

MAKES ABOUT 2 CUPS

As simple as the food of the Southwest was in its native incarnations, the "greatyoungchefs," as Paula Wolfert called them, soon changed that. Mark Miller, who had cooked with Alice Waters at Chez Panisse, opened the Coyote Café in New Mexico in 1986 with offerings like smoked chili pasta with duck. In Dallas, Dean Fearing, chef at the high-toned Mansion on Turtle Creek, decided he could emulate the California chefs with Texas ingredients and techniques. The result was warm lobster taco with yellow tomato salsa and jicama salad (the Mansion's signature appetizer) and pan-seared veal chops with a sauce of tangerines, smoked peppers, and wild rice, accompanied by a marigold mint and jicama compote. In an effort to bring his food to home cooks, Fearing put out *The Mansion on Turtle Creek Cookbook* in 1987. But many of the recipes called for such ingredients as quail demi-glace, cold-smoked pheasant, and smoked corn—not the sort of things to whip up of an afternoon with items from your average supermarket. Fearing's friendly rival in Dallas was Stephan Pyles, a native Texan who had worked at his family's Truck Stop Café before opening the ultratrendy Routh Street Café in 1983 with partner John Dayton. Pyles's cooking was similar in ingredients and philosophy to that of Fearing (one of Routh Street's earliest offerings was a lobster enchilada with red pepper crème fraîche and caviar). Both Pyles and Fearing did much to popularize southwestern foods, particularly when Pyles opened two Texas-style restaurants in the Midwest.

## BLUE CORN PANCAKES WITH CILANTRO CREAM AND BLACK BEAN CAVIAR

Funny-colored foods were In in the Eighties, as were Southwest foods. So what could possibly be more In than blue corn? Much more finicky to grow than standard corn, blue corn is rare (although it is available at some specialty markets outside the Southwest) and expensive. Its flavor is slightly smokier than that of standard corn, but if you are unable to find blue cornmeal, substitute yellow or white measure for measure. This recipe is an amusing Southwest visual take on blinis with sour cream and caviar, which were so trendy in the Eighties. However, its flavor is more akin to haute cuisine nachos, which were also popular on a lower culinary scale.

 1 recipe Blue Corn Pancakes (below)
 1 recipe Black Bean Caviar (below)
 1 recipe Cilantro Cream (below)
 Cilantro (or Chinese parsley) sprigs for garnish

Put the warm pancakes on warmed plates. Put some of the warm Black Bean Caviar in the center of each pancake, then spoon some of the Cilantro Cream on top. Garnish each pancake with sprigs of cilantro.

MAKES ABOUT 20 SMALL PANCAKES

## BLUE CORN PANCAKES

 1 $\frac{1}{3}$ cups blue cornmeal
 1 $\frac{1}{4}$ teaspoons salt
 $\frac{1}{2}$ teaspoon baking soda
 $\frac{1}{4}$ cup sifted all-purpose unbleached flour
 $\frac{1}{4}$ cup ($\frac{1}{2}$ stick) chilled unsalted butter, cut into pieces
 2 cups buttermilk
 Mild vegetable oil or clarified butter for frying

While you are making the batter, heat a heavy skillet or griddle to the point at which a drop of water skitters across its surface. Preheat the oven to 200°F. Mix the dry ingredients together in a bowl. Cut the butter into the dry ingredients with a pastry blender or two knives until the mixture has the consistency of coarse meal. Stir the buttermilk into the cornmeal mixture with a few quick strokes.

Brush the hot skillet or griddle with a little oil and drop the batter into the pan by spoonfuls (the cakes should be about 2 to 2$\frac{1}{2}$ inches wide for best results with this tender batter). Cook until bubbles appear and the top surface starts to look dry, then turn the cakes over and cook 1 or 2 minutes more on the second side. Remove the finished cakes to a rack in the warm oven and continue making the rest of the pancakes. You may need to stir the batter slightly between bakings because the cornmeal tends to settle to the bottom of the bowl.

MAKES ABOUT 20 (2-INCH) PANCAKES

## BLACK BEAN CAVIAR

$^3/_4$ cup dried black beans, picked over, rinsed, and soaked overnight in cool
    water to cover
4 cups water
I small smoked pork hock
I tablespoon olive oil or bacon grease
I tablespoon chopped onion
I garlic clove, minced
2 serrano or jalapeño chilies, seeds and veins removed and minced
I teaspoon dried oregano, crumbled
Salt and freshly ground black pepper
2 tablespoons fresh lime juice
2 tablespoons finely chopped green onion
2 tablespoons finely chopped fresh tomato
2 tablespoons seeded and diced red bell pepper
2 tablespoon seeded and diced yellow bell pepper

Drain the soaked beans. Place them in a large kettle, cover them with the fresh water, add the pork hock, bring to a boil, then lower the heat so the liquid just simmers. In a small skillet heat the olive oil, then sauté the onion, garlic, half of the minced serrano chilies, and oregano until the vegetables are soft. Add this mixture to the beans. Cook the beans, removing the scum that rises to the top initially, until the beans are tender but not mushy, 45 to 60 minutes. (If the beans were very dry, it may take up to 2 hours to reach this point.) Taste for seasoning, adding salt and pepper if necessary.

Drain the beans, reserving the liquid, and set aside. Place $^1/_2$ cup of the beans in a blender or food processor and purée them, adding some of the cooking liquid as necessary to keep the mass moving. Mix the puréed beans with the reserved whole beans and keep warm. Just before serving, fold in the lime juice, green onions, tomato, bell peppers, and remaining chili. Taste for seasoning and correct.

MAKES ABOUT 2 CUPS

## CILANTRO CREAM

I $^1/_2$ cups fresh cilantro (or Chinese parsley) leaves
3 tablespoons milk
I cup sour cream or crème fraîche (p. 368)

Purée the cilantro with the milk in a blender or food processor. Push the purée through a fine sieve into a bowl and mix it with the sour cream. Cover and set aside in a cool place.

MAKES 1 CUP

Although natives of Georgia or Alabama would argue with the notion, Texans consider themselves part of the South. Southern crab cakes, often with a Caribbean or Tex-Mex slant, were popular items at trendy Texan restaurants. And one of the most popular southern-style Texas dishes was pecan pie, especially if it was made with chocolate.

## PECAN PIE WITH CHOCOLATE CHIPS

Some cooks made a black bottom pecan pie by covering the bottom of the pie shell with melted chocolate before adding the filling. This version is easier and just as deadly.

1 deep (9-inch) pie shell, unbaked
1 large egg white, lightly beaten
1/4 cup (1/2 stick) unsalted butter
1 cup firmly packed dark brown sugar
4 eggs
1 cup dark corn syrup
1 cup coarsely chopped pecans
1 teaspoon vanilla extract
1/2 cup semisweet chocolate chips
1/2 cup pecan halves
Unsweetened whipped cream for garnish

Preheat the oven to 350°F. Brush the bottom of the pie shell with the egg white and set aside. Cream the butter until light, then mix in the brown sugar. Beat in the eggs one at a time. Stir in the corn syrup, chopped pecans, and vanilla. Spread the chocolate chips over the bottom of the pie shell. Pour the egg mixture over the chips, then arrange the pecan halves over the top. Bake until a knife inserted halfway between the center and the edge comes out clean, 40 to 50 minutes. Remove to a cooling rack and let cool at least 30 minutes before cutting. Serve with the whipped cream.

MAKES 1 (9-INCH) PIE

Southwestern cooking is still very popular in this country, even if it is not as trendy as it once was. With our seemingly endless delight in chilies and salsas, it seems likely that many elements of Southwest style will become firmly integrated into American cookery.

# Cooking from the New American Pantry

## Fruited and Anything but Plain: Kiwis, Raspberries, and Other Fashionable Fruits

Unless you've been cruising about in a submarine for the last several years without surfacing, you will undoubtedly have met up with the kiwifruit.
—Elizabeth Schneider, *Uncommon Fruits & Vegetables* (1986)

[Kiwifruit is] An insipid, expensive fruit with a phony, cutesy name—I say it's a Chinese gooseberry and I say to hell with it.
—John Thorne, *Simple Cooking* (1987)

Fruit in general, and exotic fruits in particular, were very popular in the Eighties. The hautest chefs might not have been using raspberries and kiwis very much anymore (although the rest of us still were), but a dish hardly seemed complete without its accompaniment of fresh mango chutney, or pineapple-corn kernel salsa, or blood orange beurre blanc, or carambola (starfruit) sorbet.

This craze for exotic fruits (and vegetables, too) got part of its impetus from their use in both nouvelle and New American cuisine. But American's concern for lighter diets, lower fat, and higher fiber and carbohydrates also played a large role. New immigrants from the Caribbean and Asia brought a taste and a market for many of the new exotics, while new methods of shipping and handling—not to mention the efforts of Frieda Caplan of Frieda's Finest Specialty Produce in California who nearly single-handedly made kiwifruit a national staple—added to American's fad-fruit-of-the-month mania.

Kiwis were without doubt the most popular of the exotic fruits in the late Seventies and early Eighties. Besides making a beautiful garnish for meats, fish, and poultry with their bright green flesh and black seeds, they were used heavily in salads and in tarts, fruit terrines, compotes, and sorbets. Unfortunately, their overuse and abuse at the hands of trendy but not always good restaurant cooks caused a kiwi backlash. Kiwis were as Out in the mid-Eighties as they had been In earlier.

Now that they are being successfully grown in the United States as well as in New Zealand, kiwis have become an inexpensive and welcome addition to the winter fruit bowl. And when handled properly and not overripe, they are tartly sweet and delicious.

## KIWI, CARAMBOLA, AND RASPBERRY TART

Fruit tarts—simple pastry shells filled with pastry cream, topped with glazed fresh fruits—were extremely popular in the early Eighties. The selection of fruits for this recipe showcases particularly trendy fruits of that era, but any ripe and pleasing fruits may be used.

> 1 (9-inch) Tart Shell, baked and cooled (below)
> Apricot Glaze (below)
> 1 1/2 cups Pastry Cream (below)
> 4 kiwis, peeled and thinly sliced
> 4 carambolas (starfruits), thinly sliced
> 1 pint fresh raspberries, picked over, but not washed

Brush the Tart Shell with a little of the Apricot Glaze. Spread the Pastry Cream in the tart shell. Arrange the fruits in as artistic a fashion as you can over the pastry cream. Brush the fruit with the glaze. The tart may be held up to 2 hours in a cool place, but is best served right away.

MAKES 1 (9-INCH) TART

### TART SHELL

> 1 1/2 cups all-purpose unbleached flour
> 1 tablespoon sugar
> 1/4 teaspoon salt
> 1 large egg yolk
> 1/2 teaspoon vanilla extract
> 1 tablespoon lemon juice
> 1/2 cup (1 stick) unsalted butter, chilled and cut into bits

Sift the flour, sugar, and salt together into a mixing bowl, making a well in the middle. Place the egg yolk, vanilla, and lemon juice in the well and work them into the flour mixture with your fingers. Cut the butter into the flour mixture with a pastry blender, two knives, or your fingers until the mixture forms a ball. Cover and refrigerate the dough at least 30 minutes.

Preheat the oven to 400°F. Roll out the dough on a floured surface to a round big enough to fit your pan (the dough should be about ⅛ inch thick). Butter a 9-inch tart pan (with a false bottom if you plan to unmold the tart) and line the pan with the dough. Fit the dough into the sides of the pan without stretching, then trim and crimp the edges. Line the dough with aluminum foil and weight by filling with rice or beans. Bake about 6 minutes. Remove the foil and rice or beans and discard, prick the bottom of the tart in several places with a fork, then bake until the pastry is a light golden color, another 4 to 5 minutes. Cool on a wire rack in the pan or unmold the shell and cool on a wire rack.

MAKES 1 (9-INCH) TART SHELL

## APRICOT GLAZE

1 cup apricot preserves, pushed through a sieve
1 tablespoon sugar
1 tablespoon light corn syrup
1 tablespoon lemon juice
1 tablespoon Cointreau

Cook the preserves with the sugar and corn syrup in a heavy saucepan until the sugar is dissolved. Turn off the heat, let cool slightly, and stir in lemon juice and the Cointreau. Keep warm over hot water until ready to use. This will keep indefinitely in the refrigerator if tightly covered. Rewarm in a double boiler before using.

MAKES 1 CUP GLAZE

## PASTRY CREAM

2 cups milk
½ cup sugar
2 tablespoons all-purpose unbleached flour
3 egg yolks
1 tablespoon butter
1 teaspoon vanilla extract
1 tablespoon Cointreau

Scald the milk in a heavy, nonaluminum saucepan over medium-low heat until fine bubbles just start forming around the edges of the pan. Remove from the heat. While the milk is heating, stir the sugar and flour together in the top of a double boiler. Over simmering water, whisk the hot milk mixture into the sugar and flour. Cook, stirring constantly, until the mixture has thickened and will coat the spoon, about 10 minutes.

In a separate bowl, beat the egg yolks lightly with a whisk, then whisk in a little of the hot milk mixture to temper them. Slowly stir the warmed yolks into the rest of the hot milk and cook, whisking constantly, another 10 minutes. The mixture should have thickened considerably and should heavily coat a spoon at this point. Remove from the heat and stir in the butter, vanilla, and Cointreau. Cover the top of the pastry cream with a light film of butter or milk (or plastic wrap pressed down onto the surface of the cream) to prevent a skin from forming and chill. This will keep 2 to 3 days in the refrigerator.

MAKES ABOUT 2½ CUPS

Fruit sorbets—made with exotic fruits, of course—were also popular desserts (see sidebar p. 391). The favorite flavors were kiwi, passion fruit, raspberry, blood orange, red grapefruit, and black currant.

## PASSION FRUIT SORBET

You may substitute any other sieved fruit purée or fruit juice for the passion fruit.

²/₃ cup sugar
2 cups water
2 cups passion fruit pulp, sieved

Combine the sugar and water in a heavy saucepan and bring to a boil. Remove from the heat and let cool. Stir half the syrup into the fruit purée and taste for sweetness, adding more syrup until the taste is right. Place the mixture in an ice cream freezer and freeze, following the manufacturer's instructions. (The mixture may also be frozen in a refrigerator tray; take it out to beat it as the ice crystals form. This makes more of a grainy ice than a smooth sorbet.)

MAKES ABOUT 1½ QUARTS

Fruits were not just confined to the dessert course in the Eighties. Fruits combined with meats was a hallmark of the New Cooking and was very popular, at least with trendy types. When *The Silver Palate Cookbook* appeared in 1982, one otherwise complimentary reviewer, who was very fond of foods from The Silver Palate shop in New York, complained that meat/fruit combinations were getting out of hand. Said he, "Meat and poultry dishes include everything from prunes, raspberries, and orange juice, to marmalades, and black currant jam." Some writers tried to find a link between these new combinations and the historical American usage of sweet and sour relishes with meat. But it is unlikely that many of the Foodies flinging mangoes into the sauce for a pork roast had ever tasted these relishes, with the exception of the traditional cranberry sauce with Thanksgiving turkey.

Raspberries were one of the first fruits to be combined with meats, especially in the form of raspberry vinegar. While raspberries are not exotic, they are expensive, fragile, and rare.

---

## The Eighties Pantry

Keeping track of what was In and what was Out in foodland during the Eighties was not easy, but these were some of the essentials.

### Staples

- Beans, dried (particularly black beans and French lentils)
- Cherries, dried
- Chocolate, white
- Cornmeal, blue
- Oil, walnut
- Olive oil, extra virgin
- Pasta, especially fresh (better if tinted with spinach, herbs, tomatoes, or squid ink)
- Polenta
- Tomatoes, sun-dried
- Vinegar, balsamic
- Vinegar, raspberry (and blueberry)

### Dairy Products

- Brie
- Crème fraîche
- Goat cheese
- Mascarpone

### Herbs and Seasonings

- Basil, fresh
- Chilies, fresh and dried
- Coriander, fresh
- Garlic, generally roasted
- Gingerroot, fresh
- Lemongrass
- Mint, fresh
- Peppercorns, green (and pink)
- Saffron
- Sage leaves, fresh
- Vanilla, Tahitian

## Produce

- Arugula (rocket or roquette)
- Bell peppers (all colors but green), generally roasted
- Corn kernels
- Fiddlehead ferns
- Figs
- Flowers, edible
- Kiwifruit
- Limes
- Mâche (lamb's quarters)
- Mangoes
- Mesclun (mixed baby greens for salads)
- Mushrooms, wild (chanterelles, morels, cepes, shiitake, enokidaki)
- Okra
- Oranges, blood
- Radicchio
- Squash blossoms
- Vegetables, baby
- Vegetables, funny-colored (purple cauliflower, blue potatoes, brown bell peppers, yellow tomatoes, etc.)

## Poultry, Game, Meat, and Fish

- Bay scallops
- Buffalo
- Chicken, free-range
- Crayfish
- Duck
- Proscuitto and pancetta
- Spot prawns
- Swordfish
- Venison
- Yellowfin tuna

## Miscellaneous

- Aioli
- Butters, flavored (cilantro-lime-ginger, etc.)
- Caviar, fresh American
- Chutneys, relishes, and salsas
- Croissants, brioche, muffins, foccacio, and walnut yeast bread
- Onion marmalade or confit
- Pesto
- Zabaglione sauce (both sweet and savory)

## Potables

- Amaretto (low brow)
- Armagnac (high brow)
- Boutique beers
- Calvados (high brow)
- Cassis (mixed with champagne, mostly)
- Red wines, California (especially zinfandel)
- Sambucca (middle brow)
- Water, mineral (especially Perrier)

# RASPBERRY CHICKEN

This recipe is a good one, even if you usually hate fruit/meat combinations.

1 (4–5 pound) chicken, cut into serving pieces
2 tablespoons unsalted butter
Salt and freshly ground pepper
¼ cup raspberry vinegar (see note)
½ cup chicken broth
2 tablespoons mashed raspberries
1 tablespoon light brown sugar
2 garlic cloves, mashed
½ cup Crème Fraîche (p. 368)
½ cup fresh raspberries for garnish

Remove as much fat as possible from the chicken pieces. Melt the butter over medium heat in a large, heavy skillet. Salt and pepper the chicken. Sauté the chicken on both sides, until golden brown. Remove the chicken to a platter. Pour off all but 1 tablespoon of the fat from the pan. Add the vinegar and broth to the pan and bring to a boil, scraping up any browned bits. In a small bowl mix the mashed raspberries, the brown sugar, and the garlic, then stir this mixture into the pan. Return the chicken pieces to the pan, lower the heat to a simmer, cover the pan, and cook about 10 minutes. Turn the chicken pieces over, cover, and continue simmering 10–20 minutes more, removing the individual pieces from the pan as they are done. (The breast meat and smaller wing pieces will usually finish cooking before the leg and thigh pieces.) Cover the chicken pieces with foil and keep them warm on a large serving platter while you make the sauce. Skim off as much fat from the pan juices as you can. Turn the heat to high and boil the pan juices until reduced by about half. Stir in the crème fraîche and boil 1 minute more. Taste for seasoning and correct. Pour the sauce over the chicken, scatter the whole raspberries over the top, and serve.

**Note:** Raspberry vinegar is available at specialty food shops, but can just as easily be made at home by combining 1 quart white wine vinegar with 1 pint fresh or frozen (unsweetened) raspberries and letting it stand at least 2 days before straining into bottles. Commercial raspberry vinegar can range tremendously in acidity, so taste your brand before using it.

Makes 4 to 6 servings

# The Big Chill

> I love sorbet. You're serving fresh fruit, but with art…. And it's fun. Like the night I folded shredded prosciutto into a melon sorbet mixture as a prosciutto and melon first course.
> —Harley Baldwin (New York developer), *Cuisine* (March 1983)

In the Eighties, Americans couldn't seem to get enough of cold, sweet stuff. Whether it was sorbets, ices, granitas, gelati, or good old American ice creams, we consumed them all by the gallon. And we bought ice-cream makers by the cartload to make these frozen sweets at home.

Premium high-fat ice creams were the decade-long favorite. At the beginning of the Eighties ice-cream manufacturers with Scandinavian-sounding names like Häagen-Dazs and Frusen Glädjé were popular, but ice cream's down-home feel soon brought the all-American Ben & Jerry's and Steve's to prominence.

Softer but just as rich, Italian gelati were a huge fad in the early Eighties. Gelaterias (usually decorated in high-tech Italian style) serving gelato flavors like espresso, amaretto, and tangerine opened in big cities across the country. The gelati fad soon peaked and faded, however, perhaps because many stores started selling gelati made from inferior quality mixes.

Trendy restaurants seemed to feel compelled in the Eighties to offer sorbets between courses as palate refreshers, although many of the sorbets were far too sweet to do any such thing. For dessert, sorbets often appeared in combinations of three exotic fruit flavors (chosen for both color and flavor compatibility). The three little spoon-shaped scoops of sorbet were often artfully arranged on a puddle of fruit coulis or sabayon sauce.

About the only frozen dessert that dropped in popularity in those years was sherbet…the kind that came in lemon, pineapple, orange, and rainbow flavors in plastic tubs at the supermarket. (Sherbet is sorbet with egg white or gelatin added to increase the mix's volume and give a smoother texture.) Sorbet was chic, but sherbet was strictly for nerds.

# Green Peppercorns

The fresh green berries of *Piper nigrum* (pepper) had been used by the natives of the Malagasy Republic for years, but until some bright Malaysian figured out how to can and freeze green peppercorns in the 1960s, they were unknown in the West. In France, where the processed green peppercorns arrived first, they caused a sensation. By the mid-Seventies they appeared on the menus of such bastions of the haute cuisine as Le Grand Véfour, La Tour d'Argent, and Taillevent. In London respected food writer Elizabeth David was one of the first to set forth their merits, creating unusual recipes to demonstrate green peppercorns' versatility. One of the first American mentions of green peppercorns was in 1969 in Donald Aspinwall Allan's review in *Gourmet* magazine of La Seine restaurant in New York. Allan liked the restaurant's duck with green peppercorn sauce but felt compelled to explain to the uninitiated that the peppercorns "are soft, like capers, with delightful pungency."

Although by the Eighties green peppercorns had become something of a cliché with the "greatyoungchefs," who moved on to other seasonings-of-the-moment, more humble cooks both in restaurants and at home used them extensively. Green peppercorn vinegar, pâté with green peppercorns, steak au poivre vert, duck with green peppercorn sauce, and even green peppercorn dip were encountered with frequency. By the mid-Eighties the green peppercorn fad had peaked, but the deliciously pungent little berries continued (and continue) to be used.

> Many of the trendiest chefs left behind green peppercorns for the newer and even trendier pink peppercorns in the early Eighties. Unfortunately, when it was discovered that pink peppercorns, which are not members of the Piperaceae family at all but come from the weed *Schinus terebinthifolius*, caused acute allergic reactions in some eaters, they were hastily abandoned.

## DUCK BREAST AU POIVRE VERT

Duck was In in a big way in the Eighties, and duck breast particularly so (one of its more frequent incarnations was as warm duck breast salad). Here the duck breast is treated much like a steak cooked au poivre, and indeed, steak, rabbit, chicken breasts, or veal paillards may be substituted for the duck in this recipe. If you cut and bone the duck breasts yourself, you may prepare duck stock from the carcass. Otherwise chicken stock may be substituted. Frozen green peppercorns or those packed in water may be used as is. If they are packed in brine, they should be drained and rinsed in cool water before using.

2 whole duck breasts, split, boned, and skinned
1 clove garlic, cut in half
2 tablespoons green peppercorns, chopped
Salt
2 tablespoons unsalted butter
1 tablespoon olive oil
$\frac{1}{3}$ cup dry white wine
2 tablespoons Cognac
1 tablespoon green peppercorns, left whole
$\frac{1}{3}$ cup duck or chicken stock
$\frac{1}{2}$ cup heavy cream

Rub the duck breasts with the cut garlic clove, then press the chopped peppercorns into both sides of the breasts. Sprinkle lightly with a little salt (if you use brined peppercorns, the salt may be unnecessary). In a large, heavy skillet melt the butter with the olive oil over high heat until the butter foams but does not smoke. Sear the breasts on both sides in the hot fat, then lower the heat slightly and cook them about 3 to 4 minutes on each side. Remove the breasts to a warm platter and keep warm while you make the sauce.

Add the wine and Cognac to the skillet, heat on high, and cook, scraping up all the browned bits, until reduced by half. Add the whole peppercorns and stock and cook, still over high heat, until reduced slightly. Stir in the heavy cream and cook, stirring constantly, until the sauce has thickened. Taste for seasonings and adjust. Pour the sauce over the breasts and serve.

MAKES 4 SERVINGS

## Chocolate, Dark and Otherwise

If food in general has not replaced sex in the puritanical canon, chocolate in particular has.

—Betty Fussell, *Masters of American Cookery* (1983)

The only thing more trendy than trendy fruit desserts in the Eighties was chocolate. We consumed the finest imported chocolate candies, dense and swooningly rich chocolate decadence cakes, chocolate tortes filled and frosted with chocolate ganaches and buttercreams, exquisite fruits enrobed in chocolate, chocolate truffles flavored with nuts and liqueurs, chocolate pecan pies, double-fudge chocolate brownies, and chocolate chocolate-chip cookies. There was even a magazine devoted to chocolate. Americans might have been eating more fruits, vegetables, fish, and poultry, but we more than made up for any "lite" main courses with thousand-calorie chocolate desserts.

In addition to the palatal delights afforded by chocolate, chocolate was prized for its visual appeal, although many of the chocolate fantasies constructed in the Eighties were more suited to the abilities of accomplished pastry chefs than to the home cook. Magazines like *Bon Appétit* and *Gourmet* seemed to love recipes that featured delicate chocolate butterflies alighting on a frozen mousse, meringue swans swimming in a chocolate pool, and chocolate leaves that had apparently just fluttered down onto an autumnal pie. Cakes were wrapped in chocolate like fantastic presents and tied with chocolate ribbons. I remember one birthday party in the early Eighties where the cake, made by a home cook, was decorated to look like a woven chocolate basket filled with chocolate-dipped strawberries. Very beautiful, but difficult to cut.

And then there was white chocolate. After chef Michel Fitoussi created a white chocolate mousse in New York City in 1977, we couldn't get enough. Mousse was perhaps the most popular of the white chocolate desserts, but white chocolate was soon finding its way into truffles, brownies ("whities" might have been more appropriate), dessert sauces, cakes, pavés, tortes, tarts, cheesecakes, ice cream, and white chocolate chip cookies. Pastry chefs appreciated white chocolate's malleability and, as they had done with dark chocolate, were soon molding it into fantastic flowers, ribbons, butterflies, and leaves to decorate cakes that had already been wrapped in sheets of the stuff.

Truffles were one of the most ubiquitous of the chocolate goodies we seemed to be consuming with abandon, although they were rare in the United States before 1980. But once we got a taste for them we were doomed. Truffles appeared with the espresso (after the pears poached in zinfandel) at the most high-tech chic restaurants and were made at home and given as glamorous little gifts in suburbia.

Although truffles are not as In as they once were, there has been no truffle backlash. These succulent little morsels will disappear at the end of a dinner party just as quickly now as they did in the Eighties.

## DARK CHOCOLATE TRUFFLES

Finely chopped nuts, candied citrus peels, crystallized ginger, and so on may be worked into the truffle mixture before molding. You may also enclose a whole nut or raspberry or other luscious tidbit as a surprise in the middle of the truffle. Many professionals enrobe the truffle mixture in a shell of dipping chocolate, but here the truffles are simply rolled in cocoa powder—which does, after all, make them look more like their fungal namesakes. Use only the best cream (not ultrapasteurized), butter, chocolate, and flavorings for these. Or why else make them?

¼ cup heavy cream

8 ounces semisweet chocolate, broken into pieces

2 tablespoons unsalted butter, softened

½ teaspoon vanilla extract or 1 tablespoon Grand Marnier, rum, Cognac, cold
    espresso coffee, framboise, or other flavoring

½ cup sifted unsweetened cocoa powder

Boil the cream in a small, heavy saucepan until reduced by half. Remove from the heat, stir in the chocolate, and return to low heat, stirring until the chocolate melts. Remove from the heat and add the softened butter and flavoring, whisking until smooth. Freeze until firm enough to shape, about 20 minutes. Scoop up the mixture by large teaspoonfuls and form into 1-inch balls. Roll the balls in the cocoa powder. Chill, covered. (Truffles may be frozen for up to 1 month.) Allow truffles to come to room temperature (assuming the room is relatively cool!) before serving.

Makes about 12

White chocolate is not technically chocolate at all, because it contains no cocoa powder (which gives dark chocolate its characteristic color, taste, and aroma), but is simply cocoa butter flavored with milk and vanilla. Many people love the creamy unctuousness of white chocolate, while others find it cloyingly sweet and rich.

## WHITE CHOCOLATE AND RASPBERRY MOUSSE WITH RASPBERRY SAUCE

White chocolate was often combined with berries to offset some of its unadulterated richness. This delicious and very pretty mouse should be made the day before it is served.

8 ounces fresh raspberries, or frozen unsweetened berries, thawed

⅓ cup granulated sugar

1 teaspoon gelatin soaked in 1 tablespoon cold water

1 tablespoon framboise (cassis, kirsch, or Cognac may be substituted)

1 teaspoon raspberry vinegar or lemon juice

6 ounces white chocolate, chopped

2½ cups heavy cream

½ cup confectioners' sugar

2 teaspoons vanilla extract

Raspberry Sauce (below)

Fresh whole raspberries for garnish

Line a 9 × 5-inch loaf pan with plastic wrap. Purée the berries in a blender or food processor and strain through a fine sieve to remove the seeds. Place the strained purée in a small, heavy saucepan with the granulated sugar and cook over medium heat until the mixture boils and the sugar is dissolved. Stir in the soaked gelatin. Let cool slightly, then stir in the framboise and vinegar. Cover and chill until the mixture is almost set.

In a small, heavy saucepan over medium heat, melt the chocolate with $^1\!/_2$ cup of the cream. Remove from the heat and let cool to room temperature.

In a large bowl, whip the remaining cream with the confectioners' sugar and vanilla until stiff peaks form, then gently fold in the chocolate mixture.

Place $1^1\!/_3$ cups of the chocolate mixture in a medium bowl and gently fold in the strained berry purée. Fill the loaf pan with half of the remaining chocolate mixture. Top with the raspberry mixture and cover with the rest of the chocolate mixture. Cover with plastic wrap and freeze overnight. To serve, unmold the frozen mousse, peeling off the plastic wrap. Slice into $^1\!/_2$-inch slices, spoon some of the Raspberry Sauce over each slice, and garnish with whole berries.

MAKES 8 SERVINGS

## RASPBERRY SAUCE

I cup raspberries
I teaspoon sugar
I teaspoon framboise (or the same liqueur used in the mousse)

Purée the raspberries with the sugar in a blender or food processor. Strain the purée through a fine sieve to remove the seeds and stir in the liqueur.

## WHITE CHOCOLATE BROWNIES

My sister's comment, when she gave me this recipe, that she hated white chocolate but loved these brownies says it all. Very similar brownies were made in the Eighties at Stephan Pyle's Routh Street Café in Texas and at the Honey Bear Bakery in Seattle.

$^1\!/_2$ cup (I stick) unsalted butter
8 ounces white chocolate chips
2 large eggs
$^1\!/_2$ cup sugar
$^1\!/_2$ teaspoon vanilla extract
I cup all-purpose unbleached flour
$^1\!/_2$ teaspoon salt
8 ounces semisweet chocolate chips

Preheat the oven to 350°F. Melt the butter in a small saucepan. Remove from the heat and add half the white chocolate, stirring until melted. In a large mixing bowl, beat the eggs until frothy, then gradually add the sugar, beating until thick and pale lemon colored, about 3 minutes. Stir the melted chocolate mixture and vanilla into the eggs. Sift the flour with the salt and mix into the egg mixture until just combined. Stir in the semisweet chocolate and remaining white chocolate chips. Pour the batter into a buttered and floured 8-inch-square pan and bake until a toothpick inserted in the center comes out almost clean, 25 to 30 minutes. Cool in the pan on a wire rack.

MAKES 16 SQUARES

# New Italian Cooking

## Whatever Happened to Spaghetti and Meatballs?

Grandma would never recognize what the 1980s have done to her dear old macaroni salad.

—Marian Burros, *Cuisine* (July/August 1981)

The fad for Mediterranean foods that had started in the Seventies continued into the Eighties, although it focused more and more on the cooking of Italy. The most obviously Italian of foods was pasta, the eating of which fit neatly into the new health dicta of upping carbohydrates and lowering protein and fat intake—at least if the accompanying sauces were not too heavy in cream, cheese, eggs, and other gorgeously fatty items.

Of course, in the culinarily correct Eighties, pasta was pasta, not spaghetti, and it wasn't served with meatballs anymore, except by the untrendy. Nor was it macaroni and cheese...although it might be pasta with three cheeses. (In the decade in which practically every ingredient in a dish was part of the dish's title, people seemed to get a real charge out of numbering things, hence "pasta with three cheeses," "pasta with smoked salmon and three onions," "blinis with sour cream and three caviars," etc. Three was the most popular number.)

In the first place, fresh pasta was In. If you didn't make it at home in your own pasta machine, you could buy it at stores like Auntie Pasta's in San Francisco or Pasta, Inc., in Washington, D.C., or maybe even at the good old supermarket. In the second place, the pasta was often flavored—and colored—with tomato or spinach, or if you were feeling adventuresome, beets, saffron, chilies, or herbs. Even black pasta, made with squid ink, was very In for a short while.

Pasta salad was one of the biggest of the pasta fads, taking hold in the early Eighties. In *Masters of American Cookery* (1983), Betty Fussell credits Craig Claiborne with starting the craze when he gave his sister's recipe for cold spaghetti in a mustard-flavored mayonnaise. By the middle of the decade, salad bars and take-out delis featured every sort of pasta salad imaginable, from Hawaiian salad (pasta shells, pineapple, ham, and macadamia nuts) to Greek salad (orzo, lamb, cucumbers, garbanzos, and yogurt). Pasta salads did not survive the decade, and with rare exceptions, they are not only Out, they are gone.

## PASTA SALAD WITH OLIVES, YELLOW TOMATOES, AND THREE PEPPERS

The trick to making salads with cold starches, whether it be pasta, rice, or what have you, is to keep the starches from developing a hard, dry, unappealing texture. Refrigeration will definitely bring out the worst in these cold starches. As soon as the pasta (or rice) is cooked, drained, and cooled slightly, toss it with the dressing and the rest of the ingredients and serve as soon as possible. This is a pleasant salad, the bright flavors and colors of the vegetables contrasting nicely with the earthiness of the olives. Although Eighties-trendy yellow tomatoes are called for, red tomatoes work just as well.

1/2 pound fusilli, rotelle, or small shells
3 tablespoons extra virgin olive oil
1 medium green bell pepper, seeded and coarsely chopped
1 medium red bell pepper, seeded and coarsely chopped
1 medium yellow bell pepper, seeded and coarsely chopped
3 green onions, finely chopped
15 to 20 Greek olives (kalamata or other soft black olives), pitted and coarsely chopped
2 tablespoons white wine vinegar
Salt and pepper
1/2 teaspoon dried Greek oregano, crumbled
1/2 teaspoon dried thyme, crumbled
Romaine leaves for garnish
Small yellow tomatoes, cut in half, for garnish

Cook the pasta in boiling salted water until al dente. Drain the pasta, rinse in cold water, then drain again. Mix the cooled pasta with 1 tablespoon of the olive oil. Gently toss the pasta with the chopped vegetables and olives, using two forks to avoid mashing the pasta. In a small bowl, mix the vinegar with a little salt and pepper and the herbs, then stir in the remaining olive oil. Pour the vinaigrette over the salad and toss gently but thoroughly so that everything is coated evenly. Taste for seasoning and correct. Set aside, covered, in a cool place (not the refrigerator) for 30 minutes to let the flavors marry. Line a serving platter or large flat bowl with the romaine leaves and arrange the salad on top of the leaves. Garnish with the tomatoes.

MAKES 4 TO 6 SERVINGS

Freshly cooked hot pastas with sauces were popular, too, but in general, the rich and creamy sauces popular in the Seventies were abandoned for lustily flavored olive oil sauces. Genoese pesto was a particular favorite, showing up not only on pasta, but as a flavorful garnish for baked potatoes, ripe tomatoes, pizza, and anything else cooks could think of to use this delicious sauce on as well. Pesto was so popular that Stouffers came out with a frozen linguini with pesto entrée in 1987. Really trendy chefs with Southwest leanings made pesto with cilantro, but fortunately that fad didn't last long.

## ANGEL HAIR PASTA WITH PESTO

Delicate angel hair pasta was very In in the Eighties, but any thin stranded pasta may be used. Every pesto I have ever seen has been made with olive oil, except Marcella Hazan's, which is made with butter instead. She's Italian and I'm not, but olive oil is used here. Traditionally, pesto is made with a mortar and pestle (from which it derives its name), but the food processor works tolerably well. A blender will also work, but you'll have to make the pesto in batches.

    1 pound angel hair pasta
    2 tablespoons unsalted butter
    1 cup fresh basil leaves (about 1 large bunch)
    2 medium garlic cloves, sliced
    Pinch of salt
    1/2 cup extra virgin olive oil
    1/3 cup pine nuts or walnuts
    1/3 cup freshly grated Parmesan or Romano cheese
    Additional grated cheese for serving

Cook the pasta in boiling salted water just until al dente, then drain and toss with the butter. Keep warm. While the pasta is cooking, place the basil leaves, garlic, a little salt, half the olive oil, the nuts, and the cheese into a food processor and chop finely. Add more of the olive oil as needed to keep the mass moving. When it is finely chopped, taste for seasoning, adding more salt, cheese, or more oil to taste. Process 1 minute more until the pesto is a fine, cohesive paste, but before it becomes a smooth purée.

To serve you may either toss the pasta with the pesto or put the pesto in a serving bowl, place the pasta on warm plates, and allow everyone to spoon and toss the pesto themselves. Pass grated cheese. (Pesto will darken on contact with the air, so if you aren't serving it immediately, film the top with olive oil or press plastic wrap onto the surface and keep it cool.)

MAKES 1 CUP PESTO; **6** TO **8** SERVINGS WITH PASTA

Drawing by Leo Cullum; © 1988 The New Yorker Magazine, Inc.

Pasta with vodka-enhanced sauce was another trendy food in the mid-Eighties. Although cooks later devised such dishes as pasta with vodka, sour cream, and two caviars, the first and probably the best was a simple dish of penne (a thick, tubular pasta), vodka, tomatoes, and cream. According to Barbara Kafka in *Food for Friends* (1984), it was fashionable in Italy before Joanna's Restaurant in New York put it on the menu and made it a fad in the United States.

## PENNE WITH VODKA SAUCE

Barbara Kafka substituted a spicy Hungarian paprika for the Italian recipe's red pepper flakes. This version returns to the original spice. Summer-ripe fresh tomatoes are essential.

    1 pound penne
    3 tablespoon unsalted butter
    2 tablespoons extra virgin olive oil
    2 garlic cloves, minced
    1/2 teaspoon dried red pepper flakes
    6 tablespoons vodka
    2 cups peeled, seeded, and chopped fresh tomatoes
    2 cups heavy cream
    1/2 teaspoon salt
    Freshly ground black pepper
    3 tablespoons finely chopped Italian (flat-leaf) parsley
    Freshly grated Parmesan cheese and a peppermill for the table

Cook the pasta in boiling, salted water until just al dente. Drain, toss with 1 tablespoon of the butter, and keep warm. While the pasta is cooking, melt the rest of the butter with the olive oil in a heavy skillet. Cook the garlic and red pepper flakes in the hot oil mixture over low heat until fragrant. Add 3 tablespoons of the vodka to the skillet and cook down over high heat until syrupy. Add the chopped tomatoes and continue cooking over high heat until the tomatoes have rendered up their juices and start to look dry. Remove from the heat, stir in the cream and the rest of the vodka, and cook over medium heat until thickened and reduced by about one-third. Taste for seasoning and add salt and freshly ground black pepper. Cook 1 minute more to let the salt cook into the sauce. Put the hot pasta in a warm serving bowl and add the sauce and parsley. Toss to coat well and serve immediately. Grated Parmesan and a peppermill should be passed at the table.

MAKES 8 SERVINGS

## Risotto and Polenta

It remains only to be borne in mind that the simpler the risotto the better.

—Elizabeth David, *Italian Food* (1954)

Various things called risottos had been made in America for years, but these rice-based dishes were usually more like a dry pilaf than the creamy northern Italian classic. With our new interest in the foods of Italy, more authentic risotto and polenta, that other northern Italian grain dish, became fashionable alternatives to the seemingly ubiquitous pasta.

Risotto seems to be unique in rice cookery in that the object is to release as much of the grain's starch into the cooking liquid as possible. This is what forms risotto's characteristic creaminess coupled with the slight al dente core in each grain of rice. To make it work correctly, you must use the very short-grained and starchy Italian Arborio rice.

## RISOTTO WITH ASPARAGUS AND PINE NUTS

Risotto is almost infinitely variable, so long as you take Elizabeth David's injunction to keep it simple to heart. The pine nuts and asparagus may be omitted and the risotto served plain with a little saffron and beef marrow stirred in (which makes risotto alla Milanese, the classic accompaniment to osso bucco). Truffles, if you have them, mushrooms, artichoke hearts, peas, chicken, game, shellfish, etc. all make good additions to a basic risotto.

1/4 cup (1/2 stick) unsalted butter
1 medium onion, finely chopped
1 1/2 cups Arborio rice
1 cup dry white wine
1/4 teaspoon salt
4 cups chicken stock, kept at a simmer in a pan
1/2 cup pine nuts, toasted lightly
1 pound fresh asparagus, tough stems pared, cut into bite-size pieces, and
    cooked in boiling salted water until crisp-tender
1/4 cup (1/2 stick) unsalted butter, melted
1/2 cup freshly grated Parmesan cheese
Freshly ground black pepper
Additional grated Parmesan for the table

Melt the unsalted butter in a heavy, medium saucepan and sauté the onion over medium-low heat until soft and golden, but not browned. Add the rice and stir until it is coated with the butter, but do not let the rice color. Pour in the wine and cook over medium heat, stirring occasionally, until the wine has almost evaporated. Stir in the salt now and enough hot stock to just cover the rice and cook, stirring occasionally until the stock is almost absorbed. Repeat this procedure, covering the rice with the stock each time, and stirring and cooking until the rice is tender, but still firm in the middle, and the mixture is thick and creamy, 20 to 25 minutes. Near the end of the cooking, watch the risotto carefully so it does not stick to the pan, adding a little hot water if necessary to finish the cooking.

Stir in the pine nuts, asparagus, melted butter, and cheese. Taste for salt and add, if necessary, with a little freshly ground pepper. Serve immediately and pass grated cheese at the table. The Italians also pass additional melted butter, but Americans usually omit this extra richness.

MAKES 6 APPETIZER SERVINGS

Chez Panisse was one of the first non-Italian restaurants to serve polenta, perhaps because of the influence of Elizabeth David's *Italian Food.* It soon became a common starch at trendy restaurants, usually served cut into shapes, brushed with olive oil, and grilled. Nothing went better with dark, autumnal, and fashionable dishes like grilled little birds or wild mushroom ragout than a bed of crisp yet creamy (and trendy) polenta.

Polenta is cornmeal mush, either eaten as its stodgy self, enriched with cheese, or served with mushroom or tomato sauce. It also can be chilled, cut into slices, and then grilled, fried, or broiled. Italian polenta is usually a coarser grain than American cornmeal, but if you can't get the former the latter works fine.

Most recipes for polenta whisk the uncooked grain into boiling water. For me this method brings only lumps. Instead I follow *Joy of Cooking*'s technique of mixing the polenta with cold water, then adding hot liquid. Works every time.

## POLENTA WITH TWO CHEESES WITH WILD MUSHROOMS AND SAUSAGE

The original recipe called for a lot more butter and cheese, cream and bacon. This version, while hardly low fat, has been lightened considerably.

**For the Polenta**
    2 cups yellow cornmeal or polenta, preferably water-ground
    2 cups cold water
    1 teaspoon salt
    5 cups boiling water
    1 cup warm milk
    $1/4$ cup freshly grated Parmesan cheese
    1 cup grated mozzarella or Monterey Jack cheese
    Tiny dash of Tabasco sauce

### For the Wild Mushrooms and Sausage

1 1/2 ounces dried porcini mushrooms, soaked in boiling water to cover
    for 30 minutes

1 1/2 pounds sweet Italian sausage (other mild sausage in casings may be
    substituted)

1/2 cup boiling water

1 tablespoon butter or extra virgin olive oil, if needed

1 pound cultivated mushrooms, sliced

1/4 cup dry full-bodied red wine

2 tablespoons finely chopped fresh Italian (flat-leaf) parsley

1 garlic clove, minced

1/2 teaspoon lemon zest, minced

Preheat the oven to 350°F. In a large saucepan combine the polenta with
the cold water and salt, stirring vigorously to discourage lumps. Over low heat
slowly stir the 5 cups boiling water into the polenta, then raise the heat to medium and cook, stirring frequently, until very thick, about 15 minutes. Stir in the
milk and when it has been absorbed, stir in half the Parmesan and mozzarella
cheeses and the Tabasco sauce. Remove from the heat, taste for seasoning, and
correct. Pour the polenta into a well-buttered shallow 2-quart oven-to-table baking dish. Sprinkle the rest of the cheeses over the top and bake until the cheese is
bubbly and beginning to brown, about 20 minutes. Remove from the oven and
let stand about 10 minutes before serving with the mushrooms and sausage.

While the polenta is cooking, drain the mushrooms, reserving the soaking
liquid. Slice the softened mushrooms, strain the liquid through a double thickness of paper towels, and set both aside.

Prick the sausages in a few places and put them in a large heavy skillet
with the 1/2 cup boiling water. Cover the pan and simmer about 8 minutes. Pour
off the liquid and cook the sausages over low heat, shaking the pan, until the
sausages are browned. Remove from the pan and keep warm. There should be
about 1 tablespoon of fat in the pan. Pour off any excess, or add up to 1 tablespoon butter or olive oil as needed. Increase the heat to high, add the wild and
cultivated mushrooms, and cook, stirring constantly, until the mushrooms start
to brown and the cooking liquid has been reabsorbed. Stir in the wine and a few
tablespoons of the strained mushroom soaking liquid and cook for a few minutes
over high heat until the liquid is reduced to about 1 tablespoon. Chop the
parsley, garlic, and lemon zest together until thoroughly mixed and very
fine. (This is the Italian seasoning gremolata, which is delicious in many savory

preparations.) Slice the sausages into ¹/₃-inch slices and add them to the mushrooms, sautéing over high heat until heated through. Then stir in the gremolata and cook, stirring constantly, until aromatic, about 3 minutes. Taste for seasoning and correct. Turn the mixture into a warm serving dish and serve with the polenta.

MAKES 8 SERVINGS

# "Healthful" Food and
# Fear of Food

Concern over additives fed a resurgence of concern over nutrition and health, particularly as the "baby boomers" matured into a generation of extraordinarily self-absorbed people with pronounced narcissistic tendencies.

—Harvey A. Levenstein, *Revolution at the Table* (1988)

By the Eighties the health food movement had evolved away from nutritional quacks pushing blackstrap molasses, yogurt, and wheat germ. Health food had become healthful food. The star chefs of the New American cooking routinely used organic produce and free-range poultry. Americans claimed to be eating far more fruits and vegetables than they had in years (whether they actually did is the subject of some debate). Whole grain breads and cereals were common supermarket fare, even if most of those sold were highly sweetened and prepared with hydrogenated fats. Red meat consumption was down, chicken consumption was way up, and we ate more dried beans and fish when we went out to restaurants. So why were we so fat and unhealthy? And why were we so afraid of food?

In the Sixties Baby Boomers had vowed never to trust anyone over the age of thirty. When the last of the Boomers passed that Rubicon in the Eighties they found that they were not immune to wrinkles, sagging flesh, and expanding waistlines—not to mention the other joys of aging like arthritis, cancer, and heart disease. To stave off the ravages of time, many tried diets similar to that popularized by former engineer Nathan Pritikin who, after finding out that his cholesterol level was abnormally high, devised a strenuous no-added-fat regimen. Unfortunately, Pritikin's recipes for vichyssoise made with skim milk and cornstarch and his egg white "omelets" tasted awful. But eating "lite" became important because it was good for our bodies, if not necessarily our palates.

# Lite-Styles of the Rich and Famous

In the good old days, rich Americans (as well as rich Europeans) ate vast quantities of rich and exotic foods. In the new age, rich Americans ate tiny quantities of low-fat and exotic foods. To make this dieting sound chi-chi, it was called "spa cuisine."

According to John Mariani, the term *spa cuisine* was coined in 1983 by Four Seasons chef Seppi Renggli for the hotel chain's diet menu. Diet entrée selections included sautéed sea scallops with angel hair pasta, asparagus, and curry jus ($16.00); sautéed cod fillet with steamed spaghetti squash and red pepper coulis ($14.50); and roasted Cornish hen with potato purée, peas, and thyme jus ($15.00). Other expensive big city restaurants soon picked up on this trend. New York's renovated Rainbow Room featured its "Evergreen Fitness Menu" from which, for under five hundred calories and over $30, patrons could select game consommé with quail breast, paillard of veal with broccoli purée, and blueberries and oranges with yogurt crème.

And of course, spas like Florida's Bonaventure and southern California's Golden Door, in exchange for a small fortune, offered patrons relaxation, exercise, massage, and herbal, mud, and mineral wraps, along with some of the most fashionably trendy spa cuisine in the Western world. The following menu was served at the Golden Door in 1985:

*Leek Timbales*
*Tiger Prawns with Tomato Concassée and*
*Radicchio Leaves*
*Brown and Wild Rice Pilaf with Wheat*
*Berries, Pine Nuts, and Cilantro*
*Orange, Kiwi, Banana, and Date Sorbet*

---

At the other end of the diet scale, for those of us who couldn't afford spa cuisine, was Jane Brody. Ms. Brody had been writing on science and health for the *New York Times* since 1965 and had also written a number of books with a health and nutrition slant. In 1985, she came out with *Jane Brody's Good Food Book* ("Living the High-Carbohydrate Way"), which was filled with nutritional information as well as recipes that were as low fat and high carbohydrate as she could make them without being ridiculous. The information was sound, and the recipes were not only edible but often quite good. Still, things like chicken and barley bake, terrific turkey loaf, and lentil-and-bulgur patty sandwiches were a far cry from game consommé with quail breast or tiger prawns with tomato concassée and radicchio leaves.

We discovered fiber, which was supposed not only to make us regular but also to discourage colon and rectal cancers. So we tried to eat higher fiber foods, to the extent of fortifying bread with wood fiber (fortunately, a short-lived phenomenon). Then we discovered oat bran, which contained soluble fiber and was supposed to help clean up our clogged arteries. Demand for oat bran became so high that suppliers could charge anything they wanted for it and many stores periodically ran out.

We discovered omega-3 fatty acids, found in the fats of cold-water fish like salmon, that lowered harmful low-density lipoprotein (LDL) serum cholesterol, and we tried to eat more fish or we took nasty-tasting fish-oil supplements. We discovered that many fruits and vegetables contained potent anticancer compounds, so we tried to eat more broccoli, carrots, and cantaloupe. We discovered that the monounsaturated fats present in olive and canola oils lowered cholesterol in general and bad LDL-type cholesterol in particular, and we started cooking with them, to the extent of creating a market for tasteless "lite" olive oil. We were told that wine, particularly red wine, was an antiviral agent, a bactericide, and protected against heart disease, so we tried to drink a little every day. We were told that the cuisines of the countries surrounding the Mediterranean promoted longevity, so we tried to "eat Mediterranean."

While we were discovering certain foods as the magic bullets that could cure our ills, we also discovered that what we ate could kill us. Egg yolks and butter had been considered bad for decades, but new information showed that hydrogenated and polyunsaturated vegetable oil, which raised bad LDL-type serum cholesterol levels, could be worse. Pesticide residues in fruits and vegetables could cause cancer, particularly in our children. Antibiotic residues in milk and meat could make our own bodies less able to fight infection. Artificial dyes, additives, and preservatives could cause cancers, allergies, and asthma. Broiling or grilling poultry, fish, and meats could cause cancer-promoting compounds to form. Nitrates in bacon, ham, and other cured meats could cause stomach cancer, as could eating too many pickled foods. And on, and on, and on.

Fear of red meat was rampant in the Eighties. A grilled, fatty steak—that most American of foods—was considered to be a nutritional time bomb with a short fuse. But for those who wanted to slip an occasional steak past the food censors, the noted life-extension researcher Dr. Roy Walford supplied an (almost) guilt-free recipe.

## 170–DEGREE STEAK

1 pound beef sirloin steak, $^3/_4$ to 1 inch thick, trimmed of all fat
1 oven cooking bag and twist tie

Put water in the top and bottom pots of a double boiler. Bring the water in the upper part of the double boiler to the 160°-to-180°F range. Wrap the steak in an oven cooking bag, pressing the bag tightly against the steak and expressing all air bubbles. Seal the bag securely with a twist tie. Place the wrapped steak in the top of the double boiler and keep the water temperature at 160° to 180°F. Cook for 10 to 12 minutes for a medium-rare steak, turning the steak in the water halfway through the cooking. Remove from the cooking bag and serve at once.

MAKES 2 LARGE SERVINGS

At the same time that we were dosing ourselves with oat bran and fish oils and worrying about the pesticide content in apples, we were also gorging ourselves on chocolate truffles, chocolate decadence cake, and Heath Bar Crunch premium high-butterfat ice cream. In a recent issue of their *Simple Cooking* newsletter, John and Matt Lewis Thorne said that Americans were going through "an obsessive seesawing between conspicuous consumption and fear of its consequences…leading us all into a cul-de-sac, epitomized by an ever more pervasive fear of food."

In the early Nineties more nutritional information continued to beset us: Rice bran and wheat bran were found to be as effective as oat bran in lowering serum LDL-type cholesterol levels, and the natural pesticides in fruits and vegetables were discovered to be possibly more toxic than synthetic pesticides. But all this confusing and sometimes frightening information seems to have numbed us, and a counterreaction to our fear of food is setting in. Just recently Americans have upped their intake of meat and fats again. And that most feared of all oral gratifications—cigarette smoking—is once again becoming popular, at least occasionally, with Baby Boomers tired of worrying about health.

## Breads of the Eighties: Croissants and Muffins

In the late Seventies and early Eighties Americans went wild for flaky, buttery croissants. At first these treats were reserved for Sunday morning, washed down with frothy home-brewed cappuccino. This *petit déjeuner,* so alien to the American style of breakfasting, seemed *très* French and *très* chic and no one seemed worried about the calories or fats. Croissant shops, decorated in French red, white, and blue, sprang up across the country. But croissants quickly moved out of their strictly breakfast status and were soon being filled with ham and cheese, spinach, mushrooms, broccoli, and ratatouille for quick lunchtime bites. By the time one fast-food chain started to sell Croissantwiches and the supermarket freezer case was stocked with frozen croissant pizzas, the croissant craze was pretty much over.

When croissants passed from favor, supposedly healthier and all-American muffins took their place. As these quick breads grew in popularity in the Eighties, they also grew in size, and gigantic "Texas muffins" became the norm (although cute little mini-muffins were also available). Ironically, these giant muffins—which were often full of fruit, zucchini, carrots, oat bran, and nuts—were perceived as healthful, even though they were also full of giant-size helpings of fat and sugar. One nutritional analysis showed some muffins to contain as many as 824 calories (half an average woman's daily allowance) and 29 grams of fat (the same as three small bags of potato chips). Muffins were so popular for a while that a recipe for "refrigerator muffins" made the rounds. People could dip into the refrigerated mix and whip up a fresh batch of muffins whenever the mood hit.

## OAT BRAN RAISIN MUFFINS

Standard size or giant muffin tins may be used. The large tins may require a few more minutes' baking time. A higher proportion of oat bran to wheat bran may be used, if you like a strong taste of oats.

1 cup all-purpose flour
1 cup whole wheat flour
2 tablespoons sugar
1/2 teaspoon salt
1 1/2 teaspoons baking soda
1 1/2 cups oat bran
1 cup wheat bran
2 cups plain yogurt
1 large egg, beaten
1/2 cup dark molasses
1/4 cup (1/2 stick) butter, melted, or mild vegetable oil
3/4 cup raisins

Preheat the oven to 400°F. Sift the flour, sugar, salt, and baking soda together in a large mixing bowl and stir in the bran. Make a well in the center of the dry ingredients. Mix the yogurt, egg, molasses, and butter together and add this mixture to the dry ingredients along with the raisins. Combine with a few quick strokes, using a fork. Spoon the batter into generously buttered muffin tins and bake 20 to 25 minutes or until the muffins are nicely browned and pulling away from the sides of the tin.

MAKES ABOUT 24 (2-INCH) OR 12 TEXAS-SIZE MUFFINS

# A Kinder, Gentler America: The End of the Eighties

There is only one kind of grilled cheese sandwich: the kind Mommy made for lunch on cold days.

—Holly Garrison, *Comfort Food* (1988)

As the Greed Decade and the Reagan years came to an end, high-salaried, high-consumption, status-seeking, image-conscious America was rocked by the stock market collapse and the junk bond and savings & loan scandals. People were scared. Those who hadn't lost their jobs or endured pay cuts hunkered down and stopped spending. And one of the first places they stopped spending was at high-ticket restaurants.

Many of the trendiest and most expensive restaurants closed. Those that survived simplified their menus and lowered prices. "If you've got it, flaunt it" food like herb-flecked pasta with two cheeses and three caviars was replaced by chicken pot pie. Which was not to say that trendiness stopped. But the pace slowed down, and the newest trend was for Comfort Food just like Mom used to make—good old American classics, albeit often updated good old American classics. Excess was Out, nurturing was In.

Jane and Michael Stern were at the forefront of the Comfort Food trend with *Square Meals* (1984). With chapters like "Lunch Counter Cooking," "Sunday Dinner," and "Nursery Food," the Sterns made it seem not only okay but trendy to make and eat meat loaf (which became a staple at many restaurants in the late Eighties) and noodleburger casserole (which did not). It was considered terribly amusing to serve something as deliberately unhip as "cherry Coke Jell-O salad" at a dinner party for rich Yuppies. Ernest M. Mickler's *White Trash Cooking* (1986) took this trend to its campy limit with things like potato chip sandwiches. Because everything needed a label in the Eighties, so-Out-they're-In-again dishes were labeled Retro Foods. (It also became fashionable for the chic and famous to confess to a weakness for Retro and Comfort Foods. The chef of Manhattan's superexpensive, supertrendy restaurant, the Quilted Giraffe, admitted that he wolfed down Oreo cookies while he worked.)

But when economic disaster struck, campy Retro Food was transformed into soothing Comfort Food. Many of the most popular Comfort Foods were what Mommy and Grandma were making in the Twenties, Thirties, and Forties.

Postwar Meat Loaf (p. 141), American Biscuits (p. 53), Middle-American Chili con Carne (p. 60), Three-Bean Salad (p. 177), Marshmallow-Coconut Cake (p. 25), and Hot Fudge Pudding Cake (p. 147) appeared not only at home but on the menus of the bistro-style restaurants that were becoming fashionable.

But Comfort Food didn't just mean down-home American cooking. We also turned to Italian food to soothe our shattered nerves in the late Eighties. Perhaps because spaghetti and meatballs and lasagna had long been some of our favorite "American" comfort foods, not to mention the fact that we had been eating high-tech Italian foods for a decade, hearty Italian cooking seemed almost as friendly and familiar as meat loaf.

---

## When Mommy Can't Cook

Staying at home instead of going out to restaurants became an economic necessity for many at the end of the decade. To remove any embarrassment this stay-at-home behavior might cause former movers and shakers it was dubbed "cocooning" and became fashionable. Unfortunately, many of the new stay-at-homers had never learned to cook. This restaurant conversation was reported in *Newsday* in 1988:

> WOMAN #1: *"Where were you last night?"*
> WOMAN #2: *"You think I eat out every night?*
> *I cooked."*
> WOMAN #1: *"What did you make?"*
> WOMAN #2: *"Lean Cuisine."*

---

By the late Eighties microwavable foods were the most common new products in supermarkets (more than 760 were introduced in 1987 alone). And one 1988 survey found that 41 percent of American families were bringing home a complete cooked meal at least twice a month.

Many Americans were apparently so incompetent in the kitchen that they didn't even know how to reheat their purchased meals. Said one noncooking Mommy interviewed by *Newsday* as she waited in line at a take-out counter, "These days it's eat out or take out."

Tummy-filling, soul-warming beans (particularly in the style of Tuscany), pasta, and polenta were all popular Italian comfort foods. But because Americans seemed to get a great deal of comfort from sweet dishes, the simple but rich Italian semifreddo (chilled) pudding called tiramisù became very fashionable. It had indeed been a trendy dessert at the most high-tech restaurants before the Crash, but didn't catch on nationwide until after. It helped that the dessert is made with mascarpone, an Italian cream cheese that was very trendy.

## TIRAMISÙ, CAFÉ LOUIS

I have usually steered clear of recipes using raw eggs for health reasons. Unfortunately, most recipes for tiramisù, including this delicious one from Chef Louis Hernandez of Hoboken's Café Louis, use uncooked beaten egg whites to lighten the mixture. In place of the egg whites, you could substitute 1 cup heavy cream, whipped, which makes a much richer dessert. For a lighter touch, you could substitute that old-time stand-in for whipped cream, whipped evaporated milk (for directions, see 1960s Evaporated Milk Chocolate Chiffon Pie, p. 153).

> 5 large eggs, separated
> $1/2$ cup + 1 tablespoon sugar
> 16 ounces mascarpone cheese
> 6 cups brewed espresso, at room temperature
> $1/4$ cup Kahlua or Grand Marnier
> 72 small ladyfingers
> $1/2$ cup cocoa powder, sifted
> Chocolate Sauce (below)
> Whipped cream and whole strawberries for garnish

In the top of a double boiler, over but not in simmering water, beat the egg yolks and sugar together until they are hot, thick, and lemon colored. Turn the egg yolk mixture into a large bowl and whisk in the mascarpone. Whip the egg whites until stiff but not dry and fold them into the mascarpone mixture.

Pour the espresso into a bowl and stir in the liqueur. Dip 24 of the ladyfingers one at a time into the espresso mixture, and place them on the bottom of a 9 × 12-inch pan (you should have two rows of 12 ladyfingers). Spread half the mascarpone mixture over the ladyfingers. Dip the next 24 ladyfingers into the espresso mixture and place them over the mascarpone mixture in the pan. Spread the remaining mascarpone mixture over the top of the ladyfingers. Dip the last 24 ladyfingers into the espresso mixture and place them over the mascarpone mixture. (You should now have two layers of the mascarpone mixture sandwiched between three layers of ladyfingers.) Cover with plastic wrap and refrigerate 8 hours or overnight.

To serve, cut the Tiramisù into 12 pieces and put them on individual plates. Sprinkle each piece with cocoa powder, spoon some Chocolate Sauce over the top of each, and garnish with whipped cream and strawberries.

MAKES 12 SERVINGS

## CHOCOLATE SAUCE

$^2/_3$ cup heavy cream
2 tablespoons sugar
6 ounces semi-sweet chocolate, chopped
2 tablespoons butter

Put the cream and sugar into a small, heavy saucepan and bring to a boil, stirring until the sugar is dissolved. Remove from the heat and add the chocolate and butter, stirring until melted. Cool to room temperature.

MAKES 1 CUP

The Comfort Food phenomenon also fit right into the New American cooking trend. Old cookbooks and regional American cooking styles were studied for old-fashioned gems that might be suitable for new restaurant menus. Shaker lemon pie was one such recipe that appeared from coast to coast for a while. Southern fried chicken with biscuits and mashed potatoes was also very popular. Of course, the chicken was coated in an incendiary batter, the biscuits were "herb flecked," and the potatoes were mashed with their skins on...with garlic. Grandma would have been horrified.

## SOOTHING MASHED POTATOES, NEW AMERICAN COOKING–STYLE

6 medium nonwaxy potatoes
6 cups water
1 to 1$^1/_2$ teaspoons salt
4 cloves garlic, mashed and any green sprouts removed
3 tablespoons butter
$^1/_3$ cup warm milk, light cream, or half-and-half
Freshly ground black pepper

Scrub the potatoes thoroughly and cut out any blemishes, sprouts, or bad spots, but leave the skins on. Bring the water to a boil in a large saucepan with $^1/_2$ teaspoon of the salt. Add the potatoes and garlic cloves and cook them, covered, until the potatoes are just tender but not falling apart, 25 to 30 minutes. Drain the water from the potatoes, place a folded towel over the pot, and let sit 5 minutes, shaking the pot occasionally. (This will make the potatoes extra mealy and fluffy.) Mash the potatoes with their skins and the garlic cloves with a potato masher (or use an old-fashioned ricer). Taste them for salt, and beat in the butter, salt as needed, and the warm milk with a fork until they are light and airy. Taste again for seasoning and adjust, beating in the pepper. Serve at once.

MAKES 4 SERVINGS

# 10

# The Nineties

## Fin-de-Siècle Cooking in the Fusion Decade

**A**s George Bush ended his tenure in office in a blaze of mediocrity in the first years of the Nineties, Americans were still disheartened, still hunkered down. The economy was showing some signs of improvement, but not enough to start people spending again. Baby Boomers were aging, and having children, and those things, combined with the dull economy, led them to stay away from restaurants and eat at home more often. The rising Generation X was going out with a vengeance, but these young people, as young people always have done, headed to crowded bars to drink and snack…not to dine.

Restaurant going remained flat, and trendiness remained flat, too. If people did treat themselves to a night out, pork chops and mashed potatoes for $12.95 at the corner bistro seemed more appealing than free-range duckling with maple-mango chutney for $22.95 at the flashy restaurant in town. (Even New York's expensive Four Seasons restaurant switched from its $85 per-person à la carte menu to a $26.50 to $37.50 three-course prix fixe menu.)

But if the fast-paced trendiness of the greedy Eighties was gone, there were still some definite trends in the early Nineties.

Cuisina Povera—the cuisine of poverty—in the form of beans, was a big fad at the beginning of the decade. We were all feeling poor, whether we were or not, but to eat poor stylishly seemed critical to our well-being. Beans were also good for us and so politically correct if cooked without meat. Tuscan beans with olive oil (extra virgin, of course) showed up in chic trattorias and in all the glossy food magazines. American baked beans were okay, even fashionable—but only if made in the authentic old style. If they came out of a famous-maker can and were gussied up with molasses and ketchup, and even—horrors!—hot dogs, as our mothers had done, they were definitely not okay. For those of us who still craved a little animal protein with our legumes, fish and beans were the thing. Shrimp with lentils, salmon with black beans…these were adjudged much more hip than pork and beans. And because cod was a traditional food of the European poor, what could be a better Nineties match than cod and beans?

## COD WITH LENTILS AND OLIVE OIL

¼ cup plus 2 tablespoons olive oil
1 medium onion, chopped
1 celery stalk, chopped
1 garlic clove, minced
1 bay leaf
1½ cups lentils
5 cups hot chicken stock or water
Salt to taste
4 (8-ounce) cod fillets
Freshly ground black pepper to taste
½ cup dry white wine

Heat the 2 tablespoons of the olive oil in a large saucepan and add the onion and celery. Cook over low heat until soft. Add the garlic and bay leaf and continue cooking until the garlic is soft. Stir in the lentils and toss with the vegetables for 1 minute, then add the hot chicken stock and bring to a boil. Reduce heat and simmer until the lentils are almost tender, stirring occasionally (about 30 minutes). Taste for seasoning and add salt if necessary. Finish cooking the lentils and set aside, but keep them warm. Heat the ¼ cup olive oil in a large heavy skillet and cook the cod fillets over medium-high heat on one side about 6 minutes, seasoning with salt and pepper. Turn the fillets and finish cooking, about another 3–6 minutes, until the fish is opaque all the way through. Using a slotted spoon, spoon the lentils onto hot plates and top with the cod fillets. Add the wine to the skillet and cook over high heat until reduced by about half. Pour the wine over the cod fillets and serve at once.

MAKES 4 SERVINGS

Food hot with chilies was also very big, whether it was pork loin with spicy banana-tomatillo salsa, Thai coconut soup, or Jamaican jerk chicken. In 1993, there were six books in print solely about chilies, not to mention the legions of books that contained chili-fired recipes. "Mouth surfing," as one chili aficionado called the effect of eating hot chilies, became so popular that even desserts were often spiked with fiery flavors. Citrus-chili sorbet was one offering, and in 1993, at least two cookbooks gave recipes for sweet chili custard. The hottest chili, the habañero, which is purportedly 100 times more fiery than the jalapeño, became the hottest fad, although chili experts recommended that habañeros be eaten— and handled—with caution.

Hot salsa was still one of America's favorite condiments, and cooks served salsas up under various names. As long as they had heat and bite, what did it matter if theses condiments were called salsas, chutneys, sambals, or even relishes? Though the classic Southwestern fresh salsa (p. 379) based on tomatoes was still popular, it was more fashionable to make salsas with fruit, black beans, or corn.

Salsas and their relatives were quick and easy to make—a boon for restaurateur and home cook alike—and were low in fat and high in vitamins and minerals. Said John Willoughby in "Eating With Relish" (*Eating Well,* July/August 1991), "the lively preparations we know best as salsas…are more in tune with our own changing habits of eating and cooking than are the sauces of classical European haute cuisine."

## FRESH PEACH SALSA

This spicy peach salsa, which is not unlike a fresh Indonesian sambal or an uncooked chutney, is very good with grilled pork tenderloin, the fashionable meat of the early Nineties.

1 1/2 cups peeled, ripe, firm peaches, cut into 1/2-inch dice
1/4 cup minced red onion
1/2 small red pepper, seeded and cut into 1/4-inch dice
1 fresh serrano or jalapeño chili, seeded and finely chopped
1 teaspoon honey
1 tablespoon fresh lime juice
1/4 teaspoon freshly ground cardamon seeds
1/4 teaspoon freshly ground coriander seeds
Pinch salt

Mix all ingredients. Taste for seasoning and correct. Cover and let sit at room temperature for 30 minutes before serving. Refrigerate if you are going to hold the salsa any longer.

MAKES ABOUT 1 1/2 CUPS

American food was still fashionable, although many chefs and their customers were getting a little bored with it. More popular than American food was food of the rest of the New World. The fashionability of Pan-American cooking was not surprising considering the fact that so many of our new immigrants were from Central or South America and the Caribbean. Americans had also developed a taste for chilies and cilantro and were happy to find ways to expand these tastes with the admixture of tropical fruits and seasonings. Many of the Pan-American dishes, in addition to their attractive spiciness, contained beans, corn, potatoes, or pork—American favorites—or fish, which we liked for its health benefits. Mexican cooking became our preferred ethnic food (aside from the ubiquitous pizza). Brazilian cooking, which with its African base is a little like American Soul food with a tropical slant, was also fashionable. A few cooks even attempted feijoada, a colossal, complicated, and hearty Brazilian bean-based festival dish.

Food from the Caribbean, whether it was Cuban moros y cristianos (black beans and rice), Jamaican jerk chicken (chicken marinated and grilled with an incendiary habañero chili paste), Grenadian grouper with chilies and onions, or even stone crab tostadas from Key West, was all the rage in the early Nineties.

## CALYPSO PORK LOIN WITH BLACK BEANS

This Caribbean-style pork roast is also popular in Brazil, where it is served with plantains and collard greens, and in Cuba, where the meat is served hot with steamed rice. For this recipe, the pork is served at room temperature, accompanied by a cool salad of beans and avocado.

**For the Pork**
    1 teaspoon grated orange peel
    2 cloves garlic, peeled and minced
    1 slice fresh ginger, peeled and minced
    1 1/2 teaspoons salt
    3/4 teaspoon ground allspice
    1 cup orange juice
    1 teaspoon Tabasco sauce
    1 tablespoon firmly packed light or dark brown sugar
    1 teaspoon freshly ground black pepper
    1 boned and rolled pork loin, about 2–3 pounds

**For the Sauce**
    1 cup fresh orange juice
    1/4 cup cider vinegar
    1 teaspoon grated orange peel

1 slice ginger, peeled and minced

1 garlic clove, peeled and minced

1 bay leaf

Sugar to taste

### For the Black Bean and Avocado Salad

1 (16-ounce) can black beans, rinsed and drained

½ small red onion, peeled and diced

½ cup cilantro leaves, coarsely chopped

¼ cup olive oil

2 tablespoons fresh orange juice

2 tablespoons fresh lime juice

Salt and freshly ground pepper

2 avocados, peeled and pitted, cut into large dice

8 orange slices, for garnish

Combine all the pork ingredients, except the pork, in a large casserole or baking pan. Put the pork loin in the pan and turn to coat with the mixture. Marinate, covered, in the refrigerator, for at least 3 hours or overnight, turning the pork occasionally. Preheat oven to 450°F. Set the loin on a baking rack in a roasting pan and bake until a meat thermometer inserted in the center of the roast registers 155°F, about 35 minutes. Set pork aside to cool while you make the sauce.

Combine all ingredients for the sauce in a small heavy saucepan. Bring to a boil, then reduce heat so the mixture just simmers. Cook until sauce is slightly syrupy, about 15 minutes. Correct seasonings, adding sugar or more vinegar as necessary. Strain sauce and set aside to cool.

To make the salad, mix the beans with the onion and cilantro in a small bowl. Toss with the oil, 1 tablespoon of the orange juice, and the lime juice. Taste for seasoning and correct, adding salt and pepper as necessary. Toss the avocado cubes with the remaining orange juice. Just before serving gently mix the avocado into the bean mixture.

To serve, mound the bean salad in the center of a serving platter. Cut the pork loin into slices and arrange them on a platter around the bean salad. Drizzle the sauce over the pork and garnish the platter with the orange slices.

MAKES 6 TO 8 SERVINGS

Perhaps the most significant trend in the Nineties, and the one that will endure, is so-called Fusion cooking. This blending of cuisines from different countries became fashionable in the Eighties on the West Coast at Japanese-French and Chinese-Italian-French restaurants. In the Nineties this blending has lost much of its trendiness, but has gained in acceptance. American cooks feel increasingly comfortable combining ingredients and techniques from around the world, without worrying about "authenticity" anymore.

Of course Americans have always been Fusion cooks. As a nation of immigrants we have constantly adapted Old World foods to our own ways of doing things. Chili con carne, tamale pie, pizza, spaghetti and meatballs, jambalaya, and pasta primavera, among many others, can all be considered Fusion dishes. The difference now is that we are consciously melding cuisines, rather than simply adapting foreign foods to American tastes and ingredients.

A typical daily menu at a fashionable Los Angeles restaurant (whose chef is a woman of African-American and Japanese heritage) consists of Yucatan chicken-and-duck sausage, goat cheese flan with grilled Japanese eggplant, sticky rice tamale wrapped in bamboo, tempura tuna salad, and grilled acorn squash filled with vegetable ragout. And a national fern bar restaurant chain now offers Szechwan shrimp Alfredo: fettucini with Alfredo sauce, mixed with shrimp, broccoli, water chestnuts, mushrooms, garlic, ginger, sun-dried tomatoes, and Hoisin sauce. Whether this ultimate Fusion dish is good or not I will probably never know, but it clearly reflects the wave of the future.

American food has changed dramatically since the Twenties. Organically grown baby lettuces have replaced marshmallows and gelatin in our salads. Fish, pasta, beans, and poultry are frequently preferred to beef or pork. Sauces are no longer flour, cream, or egg thickened but are often simple pan juices or fruit- or vegetable-based salsas. Virtually nothing is considered exotic anymore, and certainly not Chinese and Italian food, which once seemed almost dangerously foreign. The classics of the French haute cuisine are no longer de rigueur for the finest dining, although French technique still reigns supreme. And the revolution in frozen foods coupled with the wide acceptance of the microwave in the home have brought changes in our eating habits unthought of seventy years ago.

Certainly, much of our food is better now, more varied, fresher, and lighter than it was. We can buy fresh goat cheeses made right here, and handmade breads baked in brick ovens; we can get extra virgin olive, walnut, and avocado oils from California, and good wines from many states; we can sample dried cherries from Wisconsin, fresh wild mushrooms from the forests of the Northwest, and corn, dried beans, and chilies of ancient lineage from the Southwest; and we can try exotic tropical fruits and vegetables unheard of in the Twenties—and many of these for a decent price. It can even be argued that many frozen microwavable entrées are better-tasting and more nutritious than some of the "home-cooked" dishes of the Twenties, concocted from canned ingredients.

But with all this bounteous choice, do we really care anymore about what constitutes good food than the Twenties housewife with her banana-popcorn salad? *Mademoiselle* recently ran a "health" article on low-fat potato chips and fat-free brownies titled "Eat Junk and Still Lose Weight." Another recent story in the *New York Times* was about the rich and powerful who go to the finest restaurants in town and demand scrambled eggs or mashed potatoes. Said one of these "haute brats," as they are called, "When negotiating million-dollar deals, all the food tastes like sawdust." Besides, he added, "The sign of a great restaurant is not the food, not the atmosphere: it's being known."

Many of us no longer cook at all, and many of us who do cook do so only occasionally. Yet there is a hard core of people who cook often, and well, and a growing number of people who, because of the uncertain economy and a desire to spend more time with their families, are trying to learn how to cook.

For we must all eat. In America we have the bounty and the culinary heritage to cook and eat virtually anything we wish. Whether we choose to nourish ourselves with a meal of frozen fish sticks and fat-free brownies, or with food—whether simple or sophisticated—that is chosen and prepared with love and respect, is up to us.

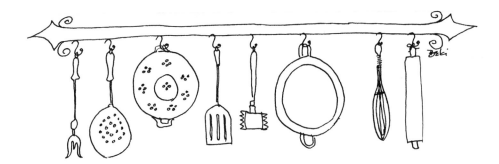

# Sources and Permissions

**A** complete bibliography is out of the question in a popular work of this kind, but I have given sources for quotations and historical information in the text wherever possible. Unless otherwise indicated, all recipes are from author's files. In addition to the recipe sources below, there are a number of books that were invaluable in my research:

Fussel, Betty. *Masters of American Cooking*. New York: Times Books, 1983.

Levenstein, Harvey. *Paradox of Plenty*. New York: Oxford University Press, 1993.

Levenstein, Harvey. *Revolution at the Table*. New York: Oxford University Press, 1988.

Mariani, John. *America Eats Out*. New York: William Morrow and Company, Inc., 1991.

Mariani, John. *The Dictionary of American Food and Drink*. New York: Ticknor & Fields, 1983.

Schremp, Gerry. *Kitchen Culture: Fifty Years of Food Fads*. New York: Pharos Books, 1991.

# Recipes

## Chapter 1: The Twenties

**Water Lily Salad**—Association of Hawaiian Pineapple Canners. *Pictorial Review* Aug. 1926.

**Alice Bradley's Kitchenette Valentine Salad**—Bradley, Alice. "Holiday Refreshments Planned for Easy Entertaining." *Woman's Home Companion* Feb. 1927.

**Three P's Salad**—Smith, Isabel Cotton. *The Blue Book of Cookery*. Hoboken, NJ: Jersey Observer, 1926.

**1920s' Ginger Ale Salad**—Adapted from Allen, Ida C. Bailey. *Mrs. Allen on Cooking, Menus, Service*. Garden City, NY: Doubleday, Doran & Company, Inc., 1929.

**Fruit & Flower Mission Frozen Cheese Salad**—Seattle Fruit & Flower Mission. *Fruit & Flower Mission Cook Book*. Seattle: 1924.

**Tomato Frappé, *Pictorial Review***—Stegner, Mabel J. "Ice-Box Cooking." *Pictorial Review* June 1929.

**Frozen Fruit Salad**—Adapted from *The Kelvinator Book of Recipes*. Detroit: Kelvinator Corporation [c. 1930].

**Caesar Salad**—Adapted from Mariani, John F. *The Dictionary of American Food and Drink*. New York: Ticknor & Fields, 1983.

**Marmalade Sandwiches for Ladies**—Adapted from King, Caroline B. "Hostess Dishes from the Tea Rooms." *The Ladies' Home Journal* Oct. 1923.

**Tea Shop Cornflake Macaroons**—Adapted from King, Caroline B. "Hostess Dishes from the Tea Rooms." *The Ladies' Home Journal* Oct. 1923.

**Heavenly Hash**—Seattle Fruit & Flower Mission. *Fruit & Flower Mission Cook Book*. Seattle: 1924.

**Flapper Pudding (Icebox Cake)**—Adapted from *Pictorial Review Standard Cook Book*. New York: The Pictorial Review Company, 1934.

**Pineapple Fluff**—Adapted from Allen, Ida C. Bailey. *Mrs. Allen on Cooking, Menus, Service*. Garden City, NY: Doubleday, Doran & Company, Inc., 1929.

**Lady Baltimore Cake**—Gay, Lettie, ed. 200 *Years of Charleston Cooking*. New York: Harrison Smith & Robert Haas, 1934. Used by permission of University of South Carolina Press.

**Mrs. Fred Mensch's 1910 Devil Cake**—*Cookery Craft*. Grants Pass, OR: Women of Bethany Presbyterian Church, 1910. Adapted from a recipe contributed by Mrs. Fred Mensch.

**Henry Fonda's Mother's Spanish (Mexican) Rice**—Adapted from Turner, Grace, ed. *The Celebrities' Cook Book*. New York: Thomas Y. Crowell Company, 1948.

**1920s' Tamale Loaf**—Seattle Fruit & Flower Mission. *Fruit & Flower Mission Cook Book*. Seattle: 1924.

**1924 Italian Spaghetti**—Seattle Fruit & Flower Mission. *Fruit & Flower Mission Cook Book*. Seattle: 1924.

# Chapter 2: The Thirties

**Sweet Potato–Marshmallow Surprises**—Massie, Larry B. and Priscilla. *Walnut Pickles and Watermelon Cake: A Century of Michigan Cooking*. Detroit: Wayne State University Press, 1990. Adapted from recipes contributed by Mrs. H. A. Flick and Mrs. H. D. Cox.

**Veal-Ham Pinwheels from the Roaster**—Beveridge, Elizabeth. "A Hot Meal in a Cool Place." *Woman's Home Companion* July 1939.

**Stuffed Peach Salad**—*Pictorial Review Standard Cook Book*. New York: The Pictorial Review Company, 1934.

**Absurd Rictim Chitti**—Adapted from Smith, Isabel Cotton. *The Blue Book of Cookery*. Funk & Wagnalls Company, 1939.

**Chipped Beef and Pineapple, Mystery Chef**—MacPherson, John. *The Mystery Chef's Own Cook Book*. Philadelphia: The Blakiston Company, 1934.

**Basic Waffles**—Adapted from *48 Delicious Recipes...Waffle-ized*. Westinghouse [c. 1930].

**Gingerbread Waffles**—Adapted from *48 Delicious Recipes... Waffle-ized*. Westinghouse [c. 1930].

**Cheese Dreams, Procter & Gamble**—Adapted from *The Art of Cooking and Serving*. Cincinnati: Procter & Gamble, 1937.

**Middle-American Chili Con Carne**—Adapted from *Betty Crocker's Picture Cook Book*. General Mills, Inc. and McGraw-Hill Book Company, Inc., 1950.

**Peanut Butter Tea Sandwiches**—Adapted from Moats, Leone B. "The Old-Fashioned Tea Party Returns." *House & Garden* April 1933.

**Rolled Sandwiches (Diplomas)**—Adapted from Galvin, Agnes Mary. "From Four to Six." *Pictorial Review* Nov. 1931.

**Date-Nut Bread for Tea Sandwiches**—From my mother, Louise M. Lovegren, [c. 1958].

**Taste-T Bridge Tea Sandwiches**—Kraft-Phenix Cheese Corp. *Kitchen Fresh Ideas*, 1933. Used by permission of Kraft General Foods, Inc.

**Sparkling Punch for Summer Tea**—Adapted from Taylor, Demetria M. "The Young People Entertain During August Holidays." *Good Housekeeping* Aug. 1931.

**Betty Co-Ed Surprise Sandwich Loaf**—Adapted from *Pictorial Review Standard Cook Book*. New York: The Pictorial Review Company, 1934.

**Checkerboard Sandwich Loaves**—Adapted from *Pictorial Review Standard Cook Book*. New York: The Pictorial Review Company, 1934.

**Nosegay Cocktail**—Adapted from "Spring Song of Foods." *Better Homes & Gardens* Apr. 1936.

**Meringue Torte**—Adapted from Huttenlocher, Fae. "All Set for Fun." *Better Homes & Gardens* Feb. 1938.

**Angel Pie**—"Cooks' Round Table of Endorsed Recipes." *Better Homes & Gardens* June 1936. Adapted from a recipe contributed by Mrs. K. M. Boettner of Rockport, MO.

**Pastry Party Loaf**—Adapted from Kirk, Dorothy. "And the Food Was Simply Marvelous." *Woman's Home Companion* Nov. 1939.

**Salad Pumpkins**—Adapted from Kirk, Dorothy. "And the Food Was Simply Marvelous." *Woman's Home Companion* Nov. 1939.

**Mystery Cake, Campbell Soup**—Marshall, Anne, Director of Home Economics, Campbell Soup Co. *Cooking with Condensed Soups*. Campbell Soup Co., n.d. Courtesy of Campbell Soup Co.

**Philly-Vanilly Frosting**—Massie, Larry B. and Priscilla. *Walnut Pickles and Watermelon Cake: A Century of Michigan Cooking*. Detroit: Wayne State University Press, 1990. Adapted from a recipe contributed by Mrs. Harry Fawley.

**Cream Mongole Soup**—Adapted from Pierce, Anne. "Food that Stops the Conversation." *Good Housekeeping* Sept. 1939.

**Boula**—Adapted from Ellsworth, Mary Grosvenor. *Much Depends on Dinner*. New York: Alfred A. Knopf, 1939.

**Clam Juice Cocktail, American Home**—Brandsness, Margaret Carson. "Dinner party plans for the three-in-one-hostess." *American Home* Mar. 1935.

**Blueberry Flip**—Nichols, Nell B. "The Talk of the Party." *Woman's Home Companion* Oct. 1934.

**Burning Bush**—Nichols, Nell B. "The Talk of the Party." *Woman's Home Companion* Oct. 1934.

# Chapter 3: An Exotic Interlude, I

**Cream Cheese and Fig Sandwiches**—Bradley, Alice. "Mah Jung Refreshments." *Woman's Home Companion* Jan. 1924.

**Mrs. Allen's Chinese Chop Suey**—Adapted from Allen, Ida C. Bailey. *Mrs. Allen on Cooking, Menus, Service*. Garden City, NY: Doubleday, Doran & Company, Inc., 1929.

**Chicken Chow Mein**—Adapted from Bergeron, Victor. *Trader Vic's Pacific Island Cookbook*. New York: Doubleday & Company, Inc., 1968.

**Chicken Chow Mein Reubenola**—Turner, Grace, ed. *The Celebrities' Cookbook*. New York: Thomas Y. Crowell Company, 1948.

**Buwei Yang Chao's Wine Smothers Meat Slices**—Chao, Buwei Yang. *How to Cook and Eat in Chinese*. © 1945, 1949, 1963, 1970 by Buwei Yang Chao. Reprinted by permission of Random House, Inc.

**Paper-Wrapped Chicken**—Adapted from Brown, Helen Evans. *Helen Brown's West Coast Cook Book*. Boston: Little, Brown and Company, 1952.

**Stir-Fried Bean Curd (Tofu) with Pork and Vegetables**—Adapted from Miller, Gloria Bley. *The Thousand Recipe Chinese Cookbook*. New York: Fireside Books, 1966. By permission of the author.

**Moo Shu Pork**—Adapted from Miller, Gloria Bley. *The Thousand Recipe Chinese Cookbook*. New York: Fireside Books, 1966. By permission of the author.

**Chinese Chicken Salad**—Picot, Leonce, ed. *Great Restaurants of the United States and their Recipes*. Ft. Lauderdale, FL: Research Unlimited, Inc., 1966. Adapted from a recipe contributed by Johnny Kan.

# Chapter 4: The Forties

**Prewar Bananas Flambés Kirsch**—The American Friends of France. *Spécialités de la Maison*. New York: 1940. Recipe contributed by Mrs. Douglas Ives.

**Patriotic Pinwheel Meat Roll**—Adapted from *Betty Crocker's Your Share*. Minneapolis: General Mills, Inc., 1943.

**White Market Lamb Neck Casserole**—Berolzheimer, Ruth, ed. *The American Woman's Cook Book* from the *Delineator Cook Book*. Chicago: Consolidated Book Publishers, 1945.

**Home Front Ring of Plenty with Cheesy Halibut Sauce**—Adapted from *Betty Crocker's Picture Cook Book*. General Mills, Inc. and McGraw-Hill Book Company, Inc., 1950.

**Sludge, or How to Keep Alive**—Fisher, M. F. K. *How to Cook a Wolf*. © 1942 by M. F. K. Fisher. Published in 1942 by Duell, Sloan and Pearce. Included in M. F. K. Fisher: *The Art of Eating*, published 1990 by Collier Books/Macmillan.

**Red, White, and Blue Carrot-Nut Ring with Lima Beans**—Safford, Virginia, ed. *Food of My Friends*. Minneapolis: University of Minnesota Press, 1944. Adapted from a recipe contributed by Mrs. Gideon Seymour.

**Boiled Tongue**—Adapted from Paine, Florence. "Don't Stop Entertaining Just Because He's Away." *House Beautiful* May 1944.

**Chocolate Drop Cookies with No-Sugar Chocolate Icing**—World War II era.

**All-American Maple-Nut Angel Food Cake with Maple-Nut Cream Filling**—Adapted from Berolzheimer, Ruth, ed. *The American Woman's Cook Book* from the *Delineator Cook Book*. Chicago: Consolidated Book Publishers, 1945.

**Postwar Meat Loaf**—Adapted from Nickerson, Jane. "Meat Loaf Theme." *New York Times Magazine* 11 Apr. 1948.

**Swiss Steak**—Adapted from the Home Institute of the *New York Herald Tribune*, comp. *Home Institute Cook Book*. New York: Charles Scribner's Sons, 1947.

**Mock Drumsticks**—Bradley, Alice. *The Alice Bradley Menu Cook Book* [c. World War II].

**Sea Captain's Special**—*Esquire's Handbook for Hosts*. New York: Grosset & Dunlap, 1949. Used by permission of Esquire, Inc. and the Hearst Corp.

**Hot Fudge Pudding Cake**—Adapted from Callahan, Genevieve. *The California Cook Book*. New York: M. Barrows & Company, Inc., 1946.

**Sheila Hibben's Orange-Lemon Pudding Cake from Florida**—Hibben, Sheila. *American Regional Cookery*. Boston: Little, Brown and Company, 1946. Used by permission of Jill Hellendale.

**Eggnog Chiffon Pie**—Dunne, Ida Lee. *The American Hostess*. Akron, OH: The Dunne Press, 1948. Recipe contributed by Mrs. Walter Huber.

**1960s Evaporated Milk Chocolate Chiffon Pie**—Atlanta Power Squadron Auxiliary. *Galley Gab*. 1963. Recipe contributed by Marcia Beutner.

**Spice Islands Coconut Chiffon Cake**—Adapted from Williams, Ruth J. *It's Easy with Wesson Oil* [c. 1950].

**French Casserole of Sausage and Corn**—Berolzheimer, Ruth, ed. *The American Woman's Cook Book* from the *Delineator Cook Book*. Chicago: Consolidated Book Publishers, 1945.

**Crème Vichyssoise, General Electric Institute**—*The New Art of Simplified Cooking*. General Electric Co., 1940. Courtesy of General Electric.

**Semiclassic Crêpes Suzette**—Adapted from the Culinary Arts Institute. *The Creole Cookbook*. Chicago: 1954.

**Zabaglione**—Dunne, Ida Lee, ed. *The American Hostess*. The Dunne Press, 1948. Adapted from a recipe contributed by Mrs. Julia Cooley Altrocchi of Berkeley, CA.

**Strawberries Romanoff à la Mode Americaine**—Adapted from Brown, Helen Evans. *The West Coast Cook Book*. Boston: Little, Brown and Company, 1952.

**Poulet Sauté au Citron (Chicken with Lemon Cream Sauce)**—Lucas, Dione. *The Cordon Bleu Cook Book*. Boston: Little, Brown and Company, 1947. Used by permission of Marion Gorman.

# Chapter 5: The Fifties

**Steaks Ranchero, Arthur Froehlich**—Dunn, Helen, comp. *Celebrity Recipes*. Helen Dunn Associates, Inc., 1958. Recipe contributed by Arthur Froehlich.

**Cowboy-type Spicy Barbecue Sauce**—*Let's Eat Outdoors* [c. 1955]. Recipe contributed by McCormick®/Schilling®. Courtesy McCormick®/Schilling®.

**Gourmet-type Barbecue Sauce**—Dunn, Helen, comp. *Celebrity Recipes*. Helen Dunn Associates, Inc., 1958. Recipe contributed by Armand Hammer.

**Barbecued Bologna for Men à la Crisco**—The Procter & Gamble Company. *Praise for the Cook*. Cincinnati: The Procter & Gamble Company, 1959. Used with permission of The Procter & Gamble Company.

**Rosin Baked Potatoes**—"America is Bit by the Barbecue Bug." *Look* 12 July 1955.

**Three-Bean Salad**—*Let's Eat Outdoors* [c. 1955]. Adapted from a recipe contributed by Stokely-Van Camp.

**Party Kebabs**—Adapted from *Better Homes & Gardens Barbecue Book*. Des Moines, IA: Meredith Publishing Company, 1956.

**Caramel Apple Kebabs**—"America's Big Cook-Out." *Look* 13 July 1954.

**Brown Rice Pilaf**—Adapted from Rieman, Margo. *Twelve Company Dinners*. New York: Simon and Schuster, 1957.

**Baby Borscht**—Linton, Adelin. "The Latest Time-Saving Staple on the Pantry Shelf." *House Beautiful* Apr. 1952. Recipe reprinted with permission of *House Beautiful*, © April 1952, by The Hearst Corporation. All rights reserved.

**Velvety Crab and Cheese Soufflé**—Adapted from Corbitt, Helen. *Helen Corbitt's Cookbook*. Boston: Houghton Mifflin Company, 1957.

**Uncanny Salmi of Duck with Wild Rice**—"20th-Century Short Cuts to Old-Fashioned Dishes." *House & Garden* Feb. 1953. Courtesy HG, © 1953, renewed 1981, by Conde Nast Publications, Inc.

**Working-gal Tomato Aspic Rounds with Hearts of Celery Salad**—Adapted from Bergeron, Victor. "A Ready-Made Start for Better Recipes." *House Beautiful* Mar. 1953.

**Finest Tomato Aspic**—Adapted from a Stokely-Van Camp ad. *American Home* Sept. 1947.

**Extra-fresh Apricot-Orange Parfait Pie**—Adapted from McCully, Helen. "Short-cut Foods Revolutionize American Cooking." *McCalls* Jan. 1955.

**Fruit Cocktail-Spam Buffet Party Loaf**—From a Del Monte ad. *Woman's Home Companion* June 1954.

**A Classic Beef Stroganoff**—Adapted from Rombauer, Irma S. *The Joy of Cooking*. New York: The Bobs-Merrill Company, 1946.

**Hamburger Stroganoff**—Adapted from *Betty Crocker's Good and Easy Cook Book*. New York: Golden Press, 1954.

**Semi-Authentic Chicken Divan**—Adapted from Harvey, Peggy. *When the Cook's Away*. Chicago: Henry Regnery Company, 1952.

**Chicken Divan Continental**—Nissly, Catherine. "Take a Can of Soup." *The American Home* Oct. 1953.

**Lobster Thermidor Classique**—Adapted from Sardi, Vincent, Jr., and Helen Bryson. *Curtain Up at Sardi's*. New York: Random House, 1957.

**Lobster Thermidor, Can-Opener Gourmet-Style**—Cannon, Poppy. *The Can-Opener Cookbook*. New York: Thomas Y. Crowell Company, 1953. © 1951, 1952, 1959 by Poppy Cannon. Reprinted by permission of HarperCollins Publishers, Inc.

**Baked Alaska**—Adapted from National Dairy Products Corp. *641 Tested Recipes from the Sealtest Kitchens*. 1954.

**Tournedos Rossini**—Adapted from Allen, Ida C. Bailey. *Gastronomique*. Doubleday & Company, Inc., 1958.

**Swedish Meatballs (Köttbuller)**—Culinary Arts Institute. *The American Peoples Cookbook*. Chicago: Spencer Press, Inc., 1956. Adapted from a recipe contributed by Mrs. Carl J. Erickson of Leonard, MN.

**Kraft Music Hall Clam Appetizer Dip**—Kraft Kitchens. *44 Wonderful Ways to Use Philadelphia Brand Cream Cheese* [c. 1950]. Courtesy of Kraft General Foods.

**Gourmet Herb Dip**—Adapted from Corbitt, Helen. *Helen Corbitt's Cookbook*. Boston: Houghton Mifflin Company, 1957.

**Nippy Cheese Ball**—Adapted from the Culinary Arts Institute. *The American Peoples Cookbook*. Chicago: Spencer Press, Inc., 1956.

**Wedgies a.k.a. Bologna Pie**—Various sources, including Knopf, Mildred O. *The Perfect Hostess Cook Book*. New York: Alfred A. Knopf, 1950.

**Urbane Cocktail Party Martinis**—Adapted from Edmunds, Lowell. *The Silver Bullet*. Westport, CT: Greenwood Press, 1981.

**TV Mix—Nuts and Bolts Style**—Culinary Arts Institute. *The American Peoples Cookbook*. Chicago: Spencer Press, Inc. 1956.

# Chapter 6: The Sixties

**Chicken Breasts with Tarragon, Instant Haute Cuisine**—Solomon, Esther Riva. *Instant Haute Cuisine*. © 1962, 1963 by The Curtis Publishing Company.

**Chocolate-Cherry Delight Cake**—Adapted from Better Homes and Gardens Books. *Better Homes and Gardens Guide to Entertaining*. Meredith Publishing, 1969.

**Baked Beans au Glow-Glow**—Adapted from Poister, John J. *The Pyromaniac's Cookbook*. Garden City, NY: Doubleday & Company, Inc. 1968.

**Lobster in Pineapple Boats Flambé**—Adapted from Neumann, Ruth Vendley. *Conversation-Piece Recipes*. Chicago: Reilly & Lee Co., 1962.

**Flaming Blue Iceberg**—Adapted from Neumann, Ruth Vendley. *Conversation-Piece Recipes*. Chicago: Reilly & Lee Co., 1962.

**Veal Orloff**—Adapted from Child, Julia. *The French Chef Cookbook*. New York: Alfred A. Knopf, 1969.

**Beef Wellington with Madeira Sauce**—Adapted from Tracy, Marian. *Parties from the Freezer*. New York: Charles Scribner's Sons: 1962.

**Ham Wellington**—From a gas company booklet [c. 1965].

**Grand Marnier Torte**—Hillman, Libby. *The Best From Libby Hillman's Kitchen: Treasured Recipes from 50 Years of Cooking and Teaching*. Woodstock, VT: The Countryman Press, 1993. Courtesy of Libby Hillman.

**Cheese Fondue Vaudoise**—Adapted from Smith, Olga C. "What's Cooking in Switzerland?" *House & Garden* Apr. 1954.

**Billi-bi**—Adapted from Bradshaw, George, and Ruth Norman. *Cook Until Done*. New York: M. Barrows and Company, 1962.

**Split-second Gourmet with a Blender Gazpacho**—Adapted from Graves, Eleanor. *Great Dinners from Life*. New York: Time-Life Books, 1969.

**Jellied Gazpacho**—Knox Gelatine, Inc. *Knox On-Camera Recipes*. Johnstown, NY: 1962. Used by permission of Nabisco Foods Group.

**Porkers**—Various sources, including Kragen, Jinx, and Judy Perry. *The How to Keep Him (After You've Caught Him) Cookbook*. New York: Doubleday & Company, Inc., 1968.

**Frank 'n' Sauce**—Adapted from Reed, Ann, and Marilyn Pfaltz. *Your Secret Servant*. New York: Charles Scribner's Sons, 1970.

**Stuffed Edam Cheese**—Adapted from Hillman, Libby. *The Menu Cookbook for Entertaining*. New York: Hearthside Press Incorporated Publishers, 1968.

**Cocktail Dunk with Umph**—Neumann, Ruth Vendley. *Conversation-Piece Recipes*. Chicago: Reilly & Lee Co., 1962.

**Pot Roast à l'Oignon—a.k.a. Sweep Steak**—Various sources including the back of Lipton Onion Soup Mix boxes; and Bracken, Peg. *The I Hate to Cook Book*. Greenwich, CT: Fawcett Publications, Inc., 1960.

**Crab and Artichoke Casserole**—Adapted from Home Service Department, Washington Natural Gas Company. *Skillet Meals & Casseroles with a Flair!* [c. 1965].

**Golden Gourmet Chicken**—Developed by Laura Marlow and the author. 1969.

**Elegant String Bean Casserole**—Adapted from Home Service Department, Washington Natural Gas Company. *Skillet Meals & Casseroles with a Flair!* [c. 1965].

**Creamy American Cheesecake**—Adapted from Kraft, Inc. *The Philadelphia Brand Cream Cheese Cookbook*. 1981.

**Fruit Cocktail Cake**—Ballard-Cochran Unit 40. *American Legion Auxiliary Cook Book*. Seattle, WA: n.d.

**Jell-O Cake**—From my mother, Louise M. Lovegren [c. 1968].

**Grasshopper Pie**—Adapted from General Mills, Inc. *Betty Crocker's Hostess Cookbook*. New York: Golden Press, 1967.

**Bourbon or Rum Balls**—Laura Marlow. 30 Nov. 1963.

**Tang Pie**—Recipe from a Texan friend who shall continue to remain nameless. 1992.

**Health Shake**—Adapted from Davis, Adelle. *Let's Eat Right to Keep Fit.* New York: Harcourt Brace Jovanovich, Inc., 1954, 1970.

**Bunny Burgers**—Adapted from Kinderlehrer, Jane. *Confessions of a Sneaky Organic Cook.* Emmaus, PA: Rodale Press, Inc., 1971.

**Earth Mother Bread**—Adapted from a recipe by Fonda, Jane. "Jane's Buckwheat Bread." *Life* 23 Nov. 1962.

**Roast Possum with Sweet Potatoes**—Radio KYAC. *Soul Food.* Seattle: [c. 1969]. Recipe contributed by Mrs. Johnnie Haynes.

**Sweet Potato Pie**—Adapted from "Serve Up Some Soul." *Seventeen* Sept. 1969.

**Tenderloin Tips, The Cattleman's of New York**—Adapted from Truax, Carol, and S. Omar Barker. *The Cattleman's Steak Book.* New York: Grosset & Dunlap, 1967.

# Chapter 7: An Exotic Interlude, II

**Canton Lemon-Ginger Sherbet**—Adapted from Jervey, Phyllis Pulliam. "The Merry Wives of West Point Entertain." *Pictorial Review* Mar. 1927.

**Salmon Lomi**—Adapted from Maddox, Marguerite. "Entertaining with a Hawaiian Luncheon." *Ladies' Home Journal* Nov. 1928.

**Braised Chicken Luau with Coconut Milk and Spinach**—Adapted from Maddox, Marguerite. "Entertaining with a Hawaiian Luncheon." *Ladies' Home Journal* Nov. 1928.

**Zombie**—Adapted from Trader Vic. *Trader Vic's Bartender's Guide, Revised.* New York: Doubleday & Company, Inc. © 1947, 1972 Victor Bergeron.

**Shrimp Saté**—Adapted from Trader Vic. *Trader Vic's Book of Food & Drink.* New York: Doubleday & Company. © 1946 Victor Bergeron.

**South Seas Skillet Meal**—A 1960s utilities company pamphlet.

**Hawaiian Punch**—Adapted from Trader Vic. *Trader Vic's Bartender's Guide, Revised.* New York: Doubleday & Company, Inc. © 1947, 1972 Victor Bergeron.

**Rumaki**—Adapted from Claiborne, Craig. "Now a Polynesian Trend in Food." *New York Times* 5 Jan. 1958.

**Shrimp Tempura Pu-Pus**—Adapted from FitzGerald, Don, ed. *Hawaii Cook Book*. Chatsworth, CA: The Pacifica House, Inc., 1965.

**Baked Bananas**—Adapted from Bowen, Alice Spalding. "Give a Different Kind of Dinner Party." *House Beautiful* July 1950.

**Haupia**—Adapted from FitzGerald, Don, ed. *Hawaii Cook Book*. Chatsworth, CA: The Pacifica House, Inc., 1965.

**Sukiyaki**—Adapted from Tarr, Yvonne Young. "The 10 Minute Gourmet Cookbook." *Ladies' Home Journal*. Jan. 1966.

**Beef Teriyaki**—Adapted from Shenton, James P., and Angelo M. Pellegrini, Dale Brown, Israel Shenker, Peter Wood, and the editors of Time-Life Books. *American Cooking: The Melting Pot*. New York: Time-Life Books, 1971.

**California Roll Sushi**—Sahatijian, Bette. "Sushi to the Rescue." *Cuisine* Oct. 1984. Adapted from Kay Shimizu.

**Vietnamese Spring Rolls with Hot Dipping Sauce (Nuoc Cham)**—Adapted from the editors of Time-Life Books. *Foods of the World Series: Pacific and Southeast Asian Cooking*. New York: Time-Life Books, 1970.

**Chicken and Coconut Milk Soup**—Smith, Scott. "Lemongrass of Thailand." *Bon Appétit* June 1992. Adapted from Sarah Tenaglia.

**Chicken with Basil or Mint**—Henderson, Janice Wald. "Thai Cooking Translated." *Bon Appétit* July 1988. Adapted from Nancie McDermott.

# Chapter 8: The Seventies

**Harvey Wallbanger**—Adapted from Liquore Galliano® pamphlet, n.d.

**Tequila Sunrise**—Adapted from Mario, Thomas. *Playboy's Bar Guide*. Chicago: Playboy Press, 1971.

**Heavenly Tang Tea**—Women of the International Neighbors Club of Copper County (Houghton, MI). *Passport to International and Copper County Cooking*. 1975.

**Spiced Orange Coffee**—Adapted from Macpherson, Ruth. *Discover Brunch*. Maplewood, NJ: Hammond, Inc., 1977.

**French Toast, Seventies Style**—Ladies Auxiliary of the Carteret (NJ) B.P.O.E. #2235. *Recipes from the Best People on Earth*. 1974.

**Dutch Baby**—Adapted from Capitol Hill Business and Professional Women's Club (Seattle). *Capitol Cooks*. 1973.

**Frittata with Zucchini**—Adapted from "Yours from Italy…Two Frittatas." *Sunset* May 1968.

**Joe's Special**—Adapted from the Firehouse restaurant. "R.S.V.P." *Bon Appétit* Feb. 1978.

**Whiskey or Rum Bundt Cake**—Various sources, including Macpherson, Ruth. *Discover Brunch*. Maplewood, NJ: Hammond, Inc., 1977; and Bacardi Imports, Inc., Bacardi rum ad, *Bon Appétit* Jan. 1976.

**Zucchini Bread**—Adapted from Jekyll Island Garden Club (Jekyll Island, Georgia). *Golden Isles Cuisine*. Waycross, GA: Dot Gibson Publications, 1978.

**Chicken and Mushroom Crêpes**—Adapted from Hewitt, Jean. *The New York Times Guide to Better Brunches*. New York: The New York Times Company, 1971.

**Ice-Cream Sundae Butter Pecan Crêpes**—Allen, Donald Aspinwall. "Along the Avenues." *Gourmet* Apr. 1971. Adapted from the description of a recipe from Clos Normand restaurant.

**Quiche Lorraine**—Adapted from Fisher, M. F. K., and the editors of Time-Life Books. *Foods of the World Series: The Cooking of Provincial France*. Time Inc., 1968.

**Latter-day Spinach-Feta Quiche**—Adapted from "What's Cooking." *Parenting* Sept. 1992.

**Chicken Liver–Mushroom Pâté**—Adapted from the Women's Board of Rush Presbyterian St. Lukes Medical Center (Chicago). *Good Taste*. 1979.

**Cioppino**—Adapted from various sources including John Clancy, in Dale Brown and the editors of Time-Life Books. *Foods of the World Series: American Cooking*. Time Inc., 1971; and Clayton, Bernard, Jr. *The Complete Book of Soups and Stews*. Fireside Books, 1984.

**Spaghetti Carbonara**—Adapted from Ladies Auxiliary of the Carteret (NJ) B.P.O.E. #2235. *Recipes from the Best People on Earth*. 1974.

**Pasta Primavera**—Adapted from Le Cirque restaurant (New York). "R.S.V.P." *Bon Appétit* Feb. 1978.

**Moussaka**—Adapted from *Betty Crocker's Dinner Parties*. New York: Golden Press, 1974.

**Spinach Salad with Cheddar Cheese Dressing**—Adapted from the Proud Popover restaurant (Boston). "R.S.V.P." *Bon Appétit* Oct. 1979.

**Fruit with Sour Cream and Brown Sugar**—Given to author by Sigrid Solheim [c. 1978].

**Glazed Strawberry Pie**—Adapted from Dyer, Ceil. *The After Work Entertaining Cookbook*. New York: David McKay Co., 1976.

**Merry Old Sole (Sole Stuffed with Crab and Cheese)**—Adapted from the Chowderhead restaurant (Gold Beach, OR). "R.S.V.P." *Bon Appétit* Oct. 1979.

**Pumpkin-Orange Bisque**—Adapted from the Women's Board of Rush Presbyterian St. Lukes Medical Center (Chicago). *Good Taste*. 1979.

**Homemade "Kahlua"**—Capitol Hill Business and Professional Women's Club (Seattle). *Capitol Cooks*. 1973. Adapted from a recipe contributed by Jim Hurja.

**Irish Coffee Amaretto**—Adapted from Trader Vic. *Trader Vic's Bartender's Guide, Revised*. New York: Doubleday & Company, Inc. © 1947, 1972 Victor Bergeron.

**Krazy Kahlua Koffee**—Adapted from *Better Homes and Gardens Holiday Cooking & Entertaining Ideas*. Special Interest Publications, Magazine Division, Meredith Corporation, 1975.

**Old-fashioned Granola**—Adapted from Ewald, Ellen Buchman. *Recipes for a Small Planet*. New York: Ballantine Books, 1973.

**Granola Fondue**—Meller, Eric, and Jane Kaplan. *The Granola Cookbook*. New York: Arco Publishing Co., Inc., 1973.

**Strawberry-Banana Smoothee**—Adapted from Brown, Bonnie. *Sunbeam Portable Electric Cookery*. Chicago: A Benjamin Company/Rutledge Book, Sunbeam Corporation, 1970.

**Carrot Cake**—Given to the author by Beki Petras [c. 1985].

**Honey-Sweetened Cream Cheese Frosting**—Adapted from Wallace, Maureen and Jim. *Snackers*. Seattle: Madrona Publishers, Inc., 1978.

**Vegetable Curry Cheese Pie of the Year Without the Damn Crust**—Adapted from parents, children, and staff of the Kingston Community School. *Vegetable Curry Cheese Pie of the Year Without the Damn Crust and Other Recipes* [c. 1970].

**Tomato Spinach Soufflé Cups Elegante**—Adapted from the Women's Board of Rush Presbyterian St. Lukes Medical Center (Chicago). *Good Taste*. 1979.

**Lobster-Asparagus Mousse**—Adapted from Macpherson, Ruth. *Discover Brunch*. Maplewood, NJ: Hammond, Inc., 1977.

**Crockery Chicken Stew with Wine and Tarragon**—Adapted from Neill, Marilyn. *Rival Crock-Pot ™ Cooking*. New York: Golden Press, 1975.

**Hot Crab Dip**—Various sources, including Jekyll Island Garden Club (Jekyll Island, GA). *Golden Isles Cuisine.* Waycross, GA: Dot Gibson Publications, 1978; and Birch Bay Village Ladies' Club (Birch Bay Village, WA). *Our Favorite Recipes.* 1983.

**Broccoli Casserole**—Adapted from a recipe contributed by Fox, Karalee. "Too Busy to Cook." *Bon Appétit* Nov. 1979.

**Sandwich Casserole**—YWCA (Oakland, CA). *Holiday Harvest Cook Book.* 1974.

**Wacky Cake or Crazy Cake**—Various sources including The Women of Covenant Presbyterian Church (Charlotte, NC). *Covenant Shares.* 1977. Recipe contributed by Mrs. W. C. McIntyre; and James Beard. *James Beard's American Cookery.* Boston: Little, Brown and Company, 1972.

**Apple Cake**—From my mother, Louise M. Lovegren [c. 1970].

**Impossible Pie**—Various sources, including the English Altar and Rosary Society of the Sacred Heart of Jesus Church (Carteret, NJ). *A Book of Our Favorite Recipes.* 1976. Recipe contributed by Mary Hodroski.

**Strawberry Squares**—Adapted from Jekyll Island Garden Club (Jekyll Island, GA). *Golden Isles Cuisine.* Waycross, GA: Dot Gibson Publications, 1978.

**Lemon Bars**—From my mother, Louise M. Lovegren [c. 1970].

**Scallop-Vegetable Terrine with Tomato Coulis**—"50 Favorite Recipes: Seafood." *Gourmet* Jan. 1991. Adapted from Jourdan, Daniel. *Hostellerie de La Fuste.* Valensole-Manosque, France, 1978.

**California Baked Goat Cheese with Garden Salad**—Adapted from Waters, Alice L. *The Chez Panisse Menu Cookbook.* New York: Random House, 1982.

# Chapter 9: The Eighties

**Cream of Corn Soup with Roasted Red Pepper Cream and Corn Kernels**—Adapted from Tower, Jeremiah. *New American Classics.* New York: Harper & Row, 1986.

**Roasted Garlic with White Cheese, Olives, and Grilled Toasts**—Adapted from Tower, Jeremiah. *New American Classics.* New York: Harper & Row, 1986; and Waters, Alice L. *The Chez Panisse Menu Cookbook.* New York: Random House, 1982.

**Linguine with Caramelized Onions and Walnuts**—Adapted from Madison, Deborah, and Edward Espe Brown. *The Greens Cookbook.* © 1987 by Edward Espe Brown and Deborah Madison. Used by permission of Bantam Books, a division of Bantam Doubleday Dell Publishing Group, Inc.

**Baked Apples with Ginger, Lemongrass, and Crème Fraîche**—Adapted from Hom, Ken. *Ken Hom's East Meets West Cuisine.* New York: Simon and Schuster, 1987.

**Grilled Scallops with Watercress-Lime Beurre Blanc**—McCarty, Michael. *Michael's Cookbook.* New York: Macmillan Publishing Co., 1989. Used by permission.

**Pizza with Eggplant, Goat Cheese, and Basil**—Adapted from Puck, Wolfgang. *The Wolfgang Puck Cookbook.* New York: Random House, 1986.

**Paul Prudhomme's Blackened Redfish**—© 1984 Paul Prudhomme. Courtesy of Paul Prudhomme.

**Bread Pudding with Pecan Bourbon Sauce**—Adapted from Brennan, Ella and Dicken. *The Commander's Palace New Orleans Cookbook.* Clarkson N. Potter, Inc., 1984.

**Simple Chicken Soup with Salsa**—Given to the author by Tony Garcia. 1983.

**Salsa Cruda (Fresh Salsa, a.k.a. Pico de Gallo)**—Adapted from Dent, Huntley. *The Feast of Santa Fe.* New York: Simon and Schuster, 1985.

**Blue Corn Pancakes with Cilantro Cream and Black Bean Caviar**—Adapted from Pyles, Stephan. *The New Texas Cuisine.* New York: Doubleday, 1993.

**Pecan Pie with Chocolate Chips**—Adapted from Fearing, Dean. *The Mansion on Turtle Creek Cookbook.* New York: Grove Weidenfeld, 1987.

**Pasta Salad with Olives, Yellow Tomatoes, and Three Peppers**—Adapted from Meyer, Susan Janine. *Pasta Salads!* Freedom, CA: The Crossing Press, 1986.

**Penne with Vodka Sauce**—Adapted from Kafka, Barbara. *Food for Friends.* New York: Harper & Row, 1984.

**Risotto with Asparagus and Pine Nuts**—Adapted from Sax, Irene. "A Culinary Command Post." *Cuisine* Mar. 1983.

**Polenta with Two Cheeses with Wild Mushrooms and Sausage**—Adapted from Simmons, Marie. "Polenta Express." *Cuisine* Oct. 1984.

**Kiwi, Carambola, and Raspberry Tart**—Adapted from Raichlen, Steven. *A Taste of the Mountains Cooking School Cookbook.* New York: Poseidon Press, 1986.

**Passion Fruit Sorbet**—McCarty, Michael. *Michael's Cookbook.* New York: Macmillan Publishing Co., 1989. Used by permission.

**Raspberry Chicken**—Behr, Edward. *The Art of Eating.* Spring 1994. Adapted from Charles Barrier; and Casas, Penelope. "Chicken with Blackberries." *Food & Wine* Aug. 1994.

**Duck Breast au Poivre Vert**—Adapted from Lucas, Jimella, and Nanci Main. *The Ark Restaurant Cookbook.* Penguin Books, 1983.

**Dark Chocolate Truffles**—Adapted from Tenaglia, Sarah. "The Elegant Temptation." *Bon Appétit* Jan. 1987.

**White Chocolate and Raspberry Mousse with Raspberry Sauce**—Adapted from Crowther, Lane S. "A Festive Champagne Brunch." *Bon Appétit* Apr. 1991.

**White Chocolate Brownies**—From my sister, Tany Maes. 1988.

**175-Degree Steak**—Walford, Roy L., M.D. *The 120-Year Diet.* New York: Simon and Schuster, 1986.

**Tiramisù, Cafe Louis**—Courtesy of Chef Louis Hernandez. Cafe Louis, Hoboken, NJ. [c. 1994].

**Soothing Mashed Potatoes, New American Cooking–Style**—Adapted from "Dinners for 79¢ or Less." *Woman's Day* 23 Feb. 1993.

# Chapter 10: The Nineties

**Cod with Lentils and Olive Oil**—"R.S.V.P." *Bon Appétit* Mar. 1992. Adapted from a recipe contributed by Le Petit Marguery (Paris).

**Fresh Peach Salsa**—Adapted from Simonds, Nina. "Feel the Burn." *Bazaar* June 1993.

**Calypso Pork Tenderloin with Black Beans**—Adapted from Kaplan, Karen, and Kristine Kidd. "Island Menus." *Bon Appétit* Aug. 1992; and from Chef Robert H. Kinkead, Twenty-One Federal restaurant (Washington, DC). "Recipe File." *Food Arts* May 1993.

# Illustrations

Ad for Magic Chef, page 45, courtesy of Magic Chef © 1935 Magic Chef. Originally appeared in *Woman's Home Companion*, June 1935.

Photograph of Buwei Yang Chow, page 96, courtesy of Rulan Chao Pian.

Ad for Certo, page 115, courtesy of Kraft General Foods, Inc. Used with permission. Originally appeared in *Woman's Home Companion*, August 1944.

Ad for Magic Chef, page 134, courtesy of Magic Chef © 1947 Magic Chef. Originally appeared *Woman's Home Companion*, March 1947.

Photograph of Sheila Hibben, page 150, courtesy of Jill Hellendale.

Photographs of kitchens, pages 169, 235 and 308, courtesy of Armstrong World Industries.

Magic Chef Model 69L, (c. 1954), page 181, courtesy of Magic Chef.

Original line drawings, pages 199, 206 and 222, Beki Petras.

Photograph of Julia Child, page 226, courtesy of Julia Child's Kitchen.

Front and back covers of Trader Vic's "The Outrigger" luncheon menu, pages 275 and 280, courtesy of Trader Vic's.

Artwork, page 340, by Julie Maas, from Thomas, Anna, *The Vegetarian Epicure*. Copyright © 1972 by Anna Thomas. Reprinted by permission of Alfred A. Knopf, Inc.

Photograph of Alice Waters, page 360, courtesy of Alice Waters, by F.L. Avery, 1994.

Photograph of Paul Prudhomme, page 375, courtesy of Paul Prudhomme.

Drawing, page 400, by Leo Cullum; © 1988, the *New Yorker* Magazine, Inc.

**On the back cover:**

The Procter & Gamble Company, *Praise for the Cook*, Cincinnati: The Procter & Gamble Company, 1959. Used with permission of The Procter & Gamble Company.

Photograph of Benihana chef courtesy of Benihana of Tokyo, Inc.

# INDEX

Page numbers in italics refer to illustrations.

almond(s):
  carrot ring with lima beans,
    red, white, and blue,
    128
  elegant string bean
    casserole, 249
  green beans amandine, 230
Amaretto Irish coffee, 334
American Spoon Foods, 378
*American Regional Cookery*
  (Hibben), 150–51
appetizers, 83–84
  burning bush, 84
  chicken liver-mushroom
    pâté, 320
  cocktail dunk with umph,
    252–53
  cocktail lilies, 211
  frank 'n' sauce, 250–51
  gourmet herb dip, 209
  hot crab dip, 343–44
  *Kraft Music Hall* clam dip,
    208
  lobster-asparagus mousse,
    343
  nippy cheese ball, 210
  paper-wrapped chicken,
    100–101
  porkers, 250
  rumaki, 282
  shrimp tempura pu-pus,
    283
  stuffed Edam cheese,
    251–52
  wedgies (bologna pie),
    210–11
apple(s):
  baked, with ginger,
    lemongrass, and
    crème fraîche, 367
  cake, 347–48
  caramel kebabs, 179

appliances, 46, 47, 345
apricot:
  glaze, 386
  orange parfait pie,
    extra-fresh, 188–89
artichoke(s), 80
  and crab casserole, 248
Asian foods, 367
  southeast, 293–99
  *see also* Oriental foods
asparagus:
  Alice Bradley's kitchenette
    valentine salad, 4–5
  lobster mousse, 343
  risotto with pine nuts and,
    402–3
aspic, 7
  tomato, 186, 230
    finest, 186–87
    rounds with hearts
    of celery salad,
    working gal, 188

baby food, 184
bacon:
  porkers, 250
  quiche Lorraine, 315–17
  rumaki, 282
  spaghetti carbonara,
    322–23
  veal-ham pinwheels from
    the roaster, 47
Bailey, Lee, 359
baked Alaska, 200, 201–2, *201*
  pie, 202
banana(s):
  baked, 283
  candlestick salad, 5
  flambés kirsch, prewar, 119
  monkey pudding, 21
  and popcorn salad, 5

salad, 2–4
  strawberry smoothee, 339
barbecue(d), 168–80
  grills, 174
  kebabs, 178–80
  pork (cha sui), 100
  sauces, 170
    cowboy-type spicy, 171
    gourmet-type, 171–72
basil:
  angel hair pasta with pesto,
    399–400
  chicken with, 298–99
  pizza with eggplant, goat
    cheese and, 370–71
bean(s), 415–16
  baked, 177, 415–16
    au glow-glow, 223
  black
    calypso pork loin with,
      418–19
    caviar, 382
    caviar, blue corn pancakes
      with cilantro cream
      and, 380–81
  cod with lentils and olive
    oil, 416
  green
    amandine, 230
    elegant casserole, 249
  lima, red, white, and blue
    carrot-nut ring with,
      128
  middle-American chili con
    carne, 60–61
  three-, salad, 176–77
bean curd (tofu), stir-fried,
  with pork and vegetables,
  104
Beard, James, 155, 158, 164,
  178, 198, 202, 244

Beaumont-Gantt, Don, *see* Don
  the Beachcomber
beef, 173
  basic fondue bourguig-
    nonne, 240–41
  boiled tongue, 132
  chipped, 51
    burning bush, 84
    creamed, 50
    and pineapple, Mystery
      Chef, 51
  ground, 121, 141
    hamburger stroganoff,
      193
    Joe's special, 306–7
    patriotic pinwheel meat
      roll, 122
    postwar meat loaf, 141
  middle-American chili con
    carne, 60–61
  moussaka, 325–26
  1920s humble tamale pie,
    35
  pot roast à l'oignon (sweep
    steak), 247–48
  steak, 173, 266, 407
    170-degree, 407–8
    planked, directions for,
      82
    ranchero, Arthur
      Froehlich, 170
  stroganoff, 191–92
    classic, 192
    hamburger, 193
  sukiyaki, 287
  Swiss steak, 141–42
  tenderloin tips, The Cattle-
    man's of New York, 267
  teriyaki, 289
  tournedos Rossini, 203
  Wellington, 231, 232–35
    with Madeira sauce,
      232–33
Benihana, 289–90
Bergeron, Victor, *see*
  Trader Vic

beurre blanc, 369
  watercress-lime, grilled
    scallops with, 368–69
beverages:
  blueberry flip, 83
  clam juice cocktail,
    American Home, 81
  Hawaiian punch, 282
  heavenly Tang tea, 303
  sparkling punch for
    summer tea, 65
  *see also* coffee
beverages, alcoholic, 29–30,
  82, 145, 211–12,
  333–34
  Harvey Wallbanger, 302
  homemade "Kahlua," 335
  Irish coffee Amaretto, 334
  krazy Kahlua koffee, 334
  martinis, 211–12
    urbane cocktail party, 212
  sea captain's special, 145
  tequila sunrise, 302–3
  zombie, 274–76
billi-bi, 243
bird's nest salad, 4
biscuits, 52
  American, 53
blueberry flip, 83
bologna:
  barbecued, for men à la
    Crisco, 172
  cocktail lilies, 211
  pie (wedgies), 210–11
borscht, baby, 184
boula, 77, 78–79
bourbon:
  balls, 257
  pecan sauce, 376–77
    bread pudding with, 376
Bracken, Peg, 247
Bradley, Alice, 4, 11, 38
bran, oat, 407, 408
  raisin muffins, 409
Brazilian food, 418

bread, 333, 339
  croissants and muffins,
    408–9
  date-nut, for tea sandwiches,
    63
  earth mother, 262
  garlic, 172–73
    foil-wrapped, 175
  oat bran raisin muffins, 409
  pudding with pecan
    bourbon sauce, 376
  pumpkin, 310, 311
  zucchini, 310
  *see also* sandwich
broccoli, 80
  casserole, 344
  chicken divan continental,
    195
  semi-authentic chicken
    divan, 194–95
Brody, Jane, 406
Brown, Edward Espe, 340, 364
Brown, Helen Evans, 98, 100,
  101
brownies, white chocolate,
  396–97
brunch, 302–19
buffet, smorgasbord, 204
*Bull Cook* and *Authentic
  Historical Recipes and
  Practices* (Herter and Herter),
  244
burgers, bunny, 261
burning bush, 84
butter, 132–34
butter pecan ice-cream sundae
  crêpes, 314

Caesar salad, 13–14
Cajun food, 372–77
cakes, 21–28
  angel food, 136–37
    all-American maple-nut,
      137–38
  apple, 347–48
  boiled icing for, 27

bomb shelter chocolate-
    cherry delight, 219
carrot, 337–38
    with cream cheese
        frosting, 338
chiffon, 146, 154
        Spice Island coconut, 154
Elmer Fudpucker, 310
fruit cocktail, 255
Grand Marnier torte,
    236–37
icebox (flapper pudding),
    18–20
Jell-O, 255–56
Lady Baltimore, 23–24
marshmallow-coconut, 25
Mrs. Fred Mensch's 1910
    devil, 26–27
mystery, Campbell's soup,
    76
Philly-vanilly frosting for,
    77
pineapple upside-down,
    27–28
pudding, 146, 147, 309
    hot fudge, 147
    Sheila Hibben's orange-
        lemon, from Florida,
        148
wacky or crazy, 346–47
whiskey or rum Bundt, 309
California cuisine, 354,
    358–72, 378
canapés, see appetizers
candlestick salad, 5
candy, 146
    dark chocolate truffles,
        394–95
    M&Ms, 135
Cannon, Poppy, 181, 183,
    193, 198
carambola, kiwi, and raspberry
    tart, 385
caramel apple kebabs, 179
Caribbean food, 418
    calypso pork loin with
        black beans, 418–19
carrot(s):
    bunny burgers, 261
    cake, 337–38

with cream cheese
        frosting, 338
    nut ring with lima beans,
        red, white, and blue, 128
    salad pumpkins, 75
casseroles, 344
    broccoli, 344
    crab and artichoke, 248
    elegant string bean, 249
    French, of sausage and corn,
        156–57
    sandwich, 344, 346
    white market lamb neck,
        123
celery:
    cereal, 260
    hearts of, salad, working-
        gal tomato aspic
        rounds with, 188
cereals:
    old-fashioned granola,
        336–37
    snack mix, 214–15
    tea shop cornflake maca
        roons, 16–17
    Tryabita celery, 260
    TV mix—nuts and bolts
        style, 215
chafing dishes, 46, 47, 48, 50,
    204, 206–7, 287
Chao, Buwei Yang, 96–97, 96,
    100
    wine smothers meat slices,
        97
cha sui (barbecued pork), 100
cheese(s):
    absurd rictim chitti, 49
    American Welsh rabbit, 48
    ball, 209–10
        nippy, 210
    California baked goat, with
        garden salad, 354–55
    Cheddar, dressing, spinach
        salad with, 326–27
    cream
        Alice Bradley's kitchen-
            ette valentine salad,
            4–5
        bird's nest salad, 4

burning bush, 84
    creamy American cheese-
        cake, 253–54
    and fig sandwiches, 88
    frosting, carrot cake with,
        338
    frosting, honey-
        sweetened, 338–39
    gourmet herb dip, 209
    hot crab dip, 343–44
    Kraft Music Hall clam
        appetizer dip, 208
    marmalade sandwiches for
        ladies, 16
    and olive sandwiches, 62
    Philly-vanilly frosting, 77
    salad, Fruit & Flower
        Mission frozen, 11–12
    tea sandwiches, date-nut
        bread for, 63
    wedgies (bologna pie),
        210–11
dreams, Procter & Gamble,
    57
fondue, 238, 239–40
    Vaudoise, 238
goat, pizza with eggplant,
    basil and, 370–71
home front ring of plenty
    with cheesy halibut
    sauce, 126–27
latter-day spinach-feta
    quiche, 318–19
sandwich, grilled (cheese
    dream), 56–58
sandwich casserole, 346
sole stuffed with crab and
    (merry old sole), 330–31
stuffed Edam, 251–52
two, polenta with, with
    wild mushrooms and
    sausage, 403–5
vegetable curry pie of the
    year without the damn
    crust, 341
Velveeta, 185
    and crab soufflé, velvety,
        185

cheese(s) (*continued*)
  Welsh rabbit (rarebit),
    46–49
  white, roasted garlic with
    olives, grilled toasts
    and, 363–64
cheesecake, creamy American,
  253–54
cherry-chocolate delight cake,
  bomb shelter, 219
Chez Panisse, 353, 354, 358,
  380, 403
chicken:
  with basil or mint, 298–99
  braised, luau with coconut
    milk and spinach, 273
  breasts with tarragon,
    *Instant Haute Cuisine*, 218
  chow mein, 91–92
  chow mein Reubenola
    (circa 1948), 94
  and coconut milk soup,
    297–98
  divan, 191, 193–95
    continental, 195
    semi-authentic, 194–95
  golden gourmet, 248–49
  with lemon cream sauce,
    166
  liver(s):
    mushroom pâté, 320
    rumaki, 282
  and mushroom crêpes, 313
  paper-wrapped, 100–101
  pastry party loaf, 74–75
  raspberry, 390
  salad, Chinese, 109–10
  soup with salsa, simple,
    379
  stew with wine and
    tarragon, crockery, 345
Child, Julia, 163, 165, 221,
  225–28, 226, 230, 235,
  244, 245, 247, 258, 365
chili con carne, 58–61
  middle-American, 60–61
chilies, 294, 416–17, 418

Chinese food, 85–113, 268,
  276
  Buwei Yang Chao's wine
    smothers meat slices, 97
  chicken salad, 109–10
  chop suey, 89–91, 93, 94,
    105
  chow mein, 91–94
  cooking at home, 103–6
  dim sum, 106–7
  evolution in fad for,
    106–11
  mah-jongg party menu,
    circa 1924, 88
  moo shu pork, 108–9
  MSG in, 105
  names of dishes in, 86
  1960s revolution in cooking
    of, 103–6
  paper-wrapped chicken,
    100–101
  popular dishes in 1940s and
    1950s, 100–101
  prophets of the new
    Chinese cooking,
    95–99
  spareribs, 100
  stir-fried bean curd (tofu)
    with pork and vegetables,
    104
  Szechwan, 107–11, 112
  Tibetan, 111, 112
  Trader Vic's dinner party
    menu, 1946, 99, 100
  after World War II, 95
Chinese restaurants, 101–2,
  103, 107–8, 293
  MSG in, 105
  top 11, in United States,
    112–13
chocolate, 135, 393–97
  cherry delight cake, bomb
    shelter, 219
  chiffon pie, 1960s evapo-
    rated milk, 153
  chip
    cookies, 146–47
    pecan pie with, 383

dark, truffles, 394–95
  drop cookies with no-sugar
    chocolate icing, 136
  fondue, 241
    hip dip, 242
  Grand Marnier sauce, 237
  grasshopper pie, 256–57
  hot fudge pudding cake,
    147
  icing, no-sugar, 136
  Mrs. Fred Mensch's 1910
    devil cake, 26–27
  sauce, 413
  wacky cake or crazy cake,
    346–47
  white, 394, 395
    brownies, 396–97
    and raspberry mousse
      with raspberry sauce,
      395–96
cholesterol, 407, 408
chop suey, 89–91, 93, 94, 105
  Mrs. Allen's Chinese,
    90–91
  chow mein, 91–94
    chicken, 91–92
    Reubenola (circa 1948),
      94
cilantro, 418
  cream, 382–83
    blue corn pancakes with
      black bean caviar and,
      380–81
cioppino, 321–22
clam(s):
  appetizer dip, *Kraft Music
    Hall*, 208
  cioppino, 321–22
  juice cocktail, *American
    Home*, 81
club luncheons, 65–73
cocktail lilies, 211
cocktail parties:
  in Thirties, 82–84
  in Forties, 144–45
  in Fifties, 207–12
  in Sixties, 250–52

cocktails, *see* beverages, alcoholic
coconut:
  chiffon cake, Spice Islands, 154
  haupia, 284
  impossible pie, 348
  marshmallow cake, 25
coconut milk, 274
  braised chicken luau with spinach and, 273
  and chicken soup, 297–98
cod with lentils and olive oil, 416
coffee, 144, 303
  dessert, 333–34
  homemade "Kahlua," 335
  Irish, Amaretto, 334
  krazy Kahlua koffee, 334
  spiced orange, 303
  Thai iced, 299
comfort food, 410–13
cookies:
  bourbon or rum balls, 257
  chocolate chip, 146–47
  chocolate drop, with no-sugar chocolate icing, 136
  tea shop cornflake macaroons, 16–17
  white chocolate brownies, 396–97
*Cooking of China*, The (Hahn and Lin), 103
Cool Whip, 259
  Tang pie, 259
*Cordon Bleu Cook Book* (Lucas), 165
coriander, 294
corn:
  cream of, soup with roasted red pepper cream and corn kernels, 362–63
  French casserole of sausage and, 156–57
cornflake macaroons, tea shop, 16–17

cornmeal:
  blue, pancakes, 381
    with cilantro cream and black bean caviar, 380–81
  1920s humble tamale pie, 35
  1920s tamale loaf, 34
  polenta, 402, 403
    with two cheeses with wild mushrooms and sausage, 403–5
crab, 290
  and artichoke casserole, 248
  and cheese soufflé, velvety, 185
  cioppino, 321–22
  dip, hot, 343–44
  sole stuffed with cheese and (merry old sole), 330–31
crackers:
  common, 52
  porkers, 250
cream, whipped:
  angel pie, 73
  heavenly hash, 18
  monkey pudding, 21
creamed chipped beef, 50
crème de menthe:
  grasshopper pie, 256–57
  lemon sherbet with, 198
crème fraîche, 368
  baked apples with ginger, lemongrass and, 367
crème vichyssoise, General Electric Institute, 157–58
crêpes, 311–14
  basic, 312–13
  chicken and mushroom, 313
  ice-cream sundae butter pecan, 314
  suzette, 158–59, *161*, 312
  semiclassic, 159–60
Crock-Pot, 345
croissants, 408–9
"Crumbs of Comfort" (W. D. Lovegren), 3

cuisina povera, 415
curry(ied), 269–70
  hard-boiled eggs (Hindoo eggs), 268–69
  vegetable cheese pie of the year without the damn crust, 341

date-nut bread for tea sandwiches, 63
Davis, Adelle, 258, 260, 262
de Groot, Roy Andries, 222, 224
de Wolfe, Elsie, 79, 80
dehydrated foods, 118
Dent, Huntly, 378-79
Depression, Great, 40, 41–42, 44, 84, 139, 167, 190, 276
dessert coffees, 333–34
dessert parties, 135–39
desserts, 17–28, 146–54, 158–64, 253–57, 327–28, 333, 346–50
  baked Alaska, 201–2
  baked apples with ginger, lemongrass, and crème fraîche, 367
  baked bananas, 283
  bourbon or rum balls, 257
  bread pudding with pecan bourbon sauce, 376
  Canton lemon-ginger sherbet, 270
  caramel apple kebabs, 179
  chocolate chip cookies, 146–47
  chocolate drop cookies with no-sugar chocolate icing, 136
  creamy American cheese cake, 253–54
  flapper pudding (icebox cake), 18–20
  frozen fruit salad, 12–13
  fruit with sour cream and brown sugar, 328
  gingerbread waffles, 55
  haupia, 284

desserts (*continued*)
    heavenly hash, 18
    hip dip chocolate fondue,
        242
    ice-cream sundae butter
        pecan crêpes, 314
    kiwi, carambola, and rasp
        berry tart, 385
    lemon bars, 349–50
    lemon sherbet with crème
        de menthe, 198
    meringue tortes, 72
    monkey pudding, 21
    passion fruit sorbet, 387
    pineapple fluff, 20
    prewar bananas flambés
        kirsch, 119
    semiclassic crêpes suzette,
        159–60
    strawberries Romanoff à la
        mode americaine, 164
    strawberry squares, 348–49
    tea shop cornflake
        macaroons, 16–17
    tiramisù, Café Louis,
        412–13
    white chocolate and rasp-
        berry mousse with
        raspberry sauce, 395–96
    white chocolate brownies,
        396–97
    zabaglione, 162
    *see also* cakes; pies, dessert
dim sum, 106–7
dips, 208, 252
    cocktail dunk with umph,
        252–53
    gourmet herb, 209
    hot crab, 343–44
    *Kraft Music Hall* clam, 208
Don the Beachcomber, 274,
        276, 284
dried foods, 118
drumsticks, mock, 143
duck:
    breast au poivre vert,
        392–93
    pressed, 100

    uncanny salmi of, with wild
        rice, 187–88
Dutch baby, 304–5

Edmunds, Lowell, 212
egg foo yung, 100
eggnog chiffon pie, 149
eggplant:
    burning bush, 84
    moussaka, 325–26
    pizza with goat cheese,
        basil and, 370–71
eggs:
    frittata with zucchini,
        305–6
    Hindoo (curried hard-
        boiled eggs), 268–69
    Joe's special, 306–7
Egli, Konrad, 240, 241
Eighties, 356–414
    end of, 410–14
    health food in, 405–8
    ingredients used in,
        384–97
    Italian cooking in,
        397–405
    New American Cooking in,
        357–84
    restaurants in, 358, 364,
        367, 368, 370, 374,
        378, 380, 410, 411
Elmer Fudpucker cake, 310
entertaining:
    in Thirties, 44–61, 73–77
    in Fifties, 207–16
    in Sixties, 230–42, 246–49
    in wartime, 129–39
    *see also* appetizers; parties

farm food, 68
Fearing, Dean, 380
fettucine Alfredo, 323
fiber, 407
Fifties, 168–216
    barbecue cookery in,
        168–80
    Chinese food in, 100–101

    entertaining in, 207–16
    foreign foods in, 198–205
    instant haute cuisine in,
        181–98
fig and cream cheese
    sandwiches, 88
fish:
    cioppino, 321–22
    cod with lentils and olive
        oil, 416
    faux, 290
    home front ring of plenty
        with cheesy halibut
        sauce, 126–27
    merry old sole (sole stuffed
        with crab and cheese),
        330–31
    Paul Prudhomme's black-
        ened redfish, 374
    salmon lomi, 272–73
    *see also* seafood
Fisher, M. F. K., 130–31, 150,
        155, 158, 161, 198, 244,
        245, 252, 269
fish sauce (nam pla; nuoc
    mam), 294
flambéed food, 220–25
flapper pudding (icebox cake),
        18–20
FNB (Food and Nutrition
    Board), 116
foil-wrapped garlic bread, 175
Fonda, Henry, 32
    Spanish (Mexican) rice, 32
fondue, 237–42
    basic, bourguignonne,
        240–41
    cheese, 238, 239–40
        Vaudoise, 238
    chocolate, 241
        hip dip, 242
    granola, 337
Fono, Leslie and Paulette, 312
Food and Nutrition Board
    (FNB), 116
food groups, 116–17
Food Pyramid, 117

football, TV, party menu, 214
foreign foods:
    in Twenties, 31–40
    in Forties, 155–67
    in Fifties, 198–205
    in Sixties, 244–46
    in Seventies, 319–27
    *see also specific types*
Forties, 114–67
    Chinese food in, 100–101
    desserts in, 146–54,
        158–64
    eating orgy in, 139–54
    gourmet cooking in,
        155–67
    see also World War II
frank 'n' sauce, 250–51
French food, 40, 155–60, 165,
    199–203, 319–20. *See also*
    nouvelle cuisine
    casserole of sausage and
        corn, 156–57
    crème vichyssoise, General
        Electric Institute,
        157–58
    Julia Child and, 225–28,
        *226*, 230
    poulet sauté au citron
        (chicken with lemon
        cream sauce), 166
    scallop-vegetable terrine
        with tomato coulis, 351-2
    semiclassic crêpes suzette,
        159–60
    three-course peasant
        supper, 199–200
French toast, Seventies style,
    304
frittata with zucchini, 305–6
frosting:
    honey-sweetened cream
        cheese, 338–39
    Philly-vanilly, 77
Frugal Gourmet, 365
fruit, 384–88
    cocktail, 189, 191
        cake, 255
        nosegay, 70–71
        Spam buffet party loaf,
            190–91

flaming blue iceberg,
    224–25
salad, frozen, 12–13
with sour cream and brown
    sugar, 328
*see also specific fruits*
Fusion cooking, 420

galanga, 294
garlic:
    bread, 172–73
        foil-wrapped, 175
    roasted, with white cheese,
        olives, and grilled
        toasts, 363–64
gazpacho, 244, 245
    jellied, 246
    split-second gourmet with
        a blender, 245
gelati, 391
gelatin, 7–8
    extra-fresh apricot-orange
        parfait pie, 188–89
    finest tomato aspic, 186–87
    fruit cocktail-Spam buffet
        party loaf, 190–91
    ginger ale salad, 8–9
    jellied gazpacho, 246
    salad pumpkins, 75
ginger:
    baked apples with
        lemongrass, crème
        fraîche and, 367
    lemon sherbet, Canton, 270
ginger, Siamese (galanga), 294
ginger ale salad, 8–9
gingerbread waffles, 55
*Gourmet* magazine, 158, 159
graham cracker pie shell, 152
Grand Marnier, 236
    chocolate sauce, 237
    torte, 236–37
granola, 336, 337
    fondue, 337
    old-fashioned, 336–37
grasshopper pie, 256–57
grazing, 373
Greek food, 325
    moussaka, 325–26

green bean(s):
    amandine, 230
    casserole, elegant, 249
Greens restaurant, 351, 364
grills, 174
    *see also* barbecue

Hahn, Emily, 103
halibut sauce, cheesy, home
    front ring of plenty
    with, 126–27
Halloween buffet supper, 74
ham:
    party kebabs, 178
    sandwich casserole, 346
    South Seas skillet meal, 278
    veal pinwheels from the
        roaster, 47
    Wellington, 236
Harvey Wallbanger, 302
haupia, 284
Hawaiian food, 271–74, 278,
    279
    braised chicken luau with
        coconut milk and
        spinach, 273
    luaus, 279–84
    nouvelle, 284
    salmon lomi, 272–73
health food:
    in Sixties, 258–62, 335
    in Seventies, 335–41, 351,
        353
    in Eighties, 405–8
health shake, 260–61
heavenly hash, 18
Herter, George Leonard and
    Berthe E., 244
hibachis, 174, 281, 285
Hibben, Sheila, 150–51, *150*
    orange-lemon pudding cake
        from Florida, 148
    thoroughly American dinner
        menu, 151
hi-fi dining, 213, 215–16
Hindoo eggs (curried hard-
    boiled eggs), 268–69
Hom, Ken, 367
honey-sweetened cream cheese
    frosting, 338–39

hot fudge pudding cake, 147
*How to Cook and Eat in Chinese* (Chao), 96
*How to Cook a Wolf* (Fisher), 130–31

icebox cake (flapper pudding), 18–20
iceboxes, 10
ice cream, 391
  baked Alaska, 201–2
    pie, 202
ice cream (*continued*)
  extra-fresh apricot-orange parfait pie, 188–89
  sundae butter pecan crêpes, 314
icing:
  boiled, for devil cake, 27
  no-sugar chocolate, 136
*I Hate to Cook Book, The* (Bracken), 247
Indian food, 268–69
  Hindoo eggs (curried hard-boiled eggs), 268–69
instant cuisine, 181–98, 217–19
international foods, *see* foreign foods
Irish coffee Amaretto, 334
Italian food, 35–39, 161–63, 320–23, 397–405, 411–12
  angel hair pasta with pesto, 399–400
  cioppino, 321–22
  dinner party menu, circa 1926, 38
  fettucine Alfredo, 323
  Mrs. Altrocchi's savory and exotic formal dinner, 163
  1924 spaghetti, 37
  pasta salad with olives, yellow tomatoes, and three peppers, 398–99
  penne with vodka sauce, 401
  polenta with two cheeses with wild mushrooms and sausage, 403–5

risotto with asparagus and pine nuts, 402–3
spaghetti carbonara, 322–23
tiramisù, Café Louis, 412–13
zabaglione, 162

Japanese food, 285–93
  sukiyaki, 286–87
  sushi, 290, 291–93
  tempura, 288
  teriyaki, 288–89
Japanese restaurants, 285–86, 293
  steak houses, 289–90, 291
Jell-O, 7–8
  cake, 255–56
jewel salad, 8
Joe's special, 306–7
*Joy of Cooking* (Rombauer), 221, 247, 358, 365

K rations, 126
"Kahlua," homemade, 335
Kahlua koffee, krazy, 334
kebabs, 178–80
  caramel apple, 179
  company dinner with pilaf, 180
  party, 178
kiwi, 384–85
  carambola, and raspberry tart, 385
köttbuller (Swedish meatballs), 205

Lady Baltimore cake, 23–24
lamb:
  moussaka, 325–26
  neck casserole, white market, 123
  patriotic pinwheel meat roll, 122
lemon:
  angel pie, 73
  bars, 349–50
  chiffon pie, *152*
  cream sauce, chicken with, 166
  curd, 73

flapper pudding (icebox cake), 18–20
ginger sherbet, Canton, 270
orange pudding cake from Florida, Sheila Hibben's, 148
sauce for gingerbread waffles, 55
sherbet with crème de menthe, 198
lemongrass, 294
  baked apples with ginger, crème fraîche and, 367
lentils, cod with olive oil and, 416
Le Pavillon, opening night menu of, 155–56
lettuce, 6
lima beans, red, white, and blue carrot-nut ring with, 128
lime-watercress beurre blanc, grilled scallops with, 368–69
Lin, Florence, 103
linguine with caramelized onions and walnuts, 366
liver(s), chicken:
  mushroom pâté, 320
  rumaki, 282
lobster:
  asparagus mousse, 343
  in pineapple boats flambé, 224
  thermidor, 191, 195–97
    can-opener gourmet-style, 197
    classique, 197
Louisiana Cajun food, 372–77
Lovegren, W. D., 3
luaus, 279–84
  menu for, 281
Lucas, Dione, 165, 198
luncheons, club, 65–73

macaroni, 35
  home front ring of plenty with cheesy halibut sauce, 126–27

macaroons, tea shop cornflake,
16–17
McCarty, Michael, 362, 368
MacPherson, John,
*see* Mystery Chef
Macpherson, Ruth, 307, 309
Derby Day buffet brunch,
308
Madeira sauce, 233–34
beef Wellington with,
232–33
Madison, Deborah, 340, 351,
354, 364
Magic Pan, the, 312
mah-jongg, 87
parties, 88
Chinese menu, circa
1924, 88
menus:
after-television intellectual
supper, 213
American dinner party, circa
1927, 39
Betty Crocker's extra-
special dinner party
starring beef Wellington,
231
carving-up-the-world postwar party, 140
Chinese mah-jongg party,
circa 1924, 88
delicate Hawaiian
luncheon, circa 1928, 272
East meets West Point
luncheon, circa 1927, 270
Fifties sophisticates' hi-fi
dinner, 216
glorious holiday brunch,
circa 1975, 315
*Good Housekeeping*'s poke
bonnet luncheon, 69
Halloween buffet supper,
74
Italian dinner party, circa
1926, 38
kebab company dinner with
pilaf, 180
luau, 281

maidless dinner, I, 80
for a modern epicure, 184
Monday in the Army,
1942, 125
Mrs. Altrocchi's savory and
exotic Italian formal
dinner, 163
no ration-point, for a
Monday, 1943, 121
opening night, Le Pavillon,
October 15, 1941,
155–56
planked dinner, 82
progressive dinner, 133
Rosellini's Other Place,
January 1975, 353
Ruth Macpherson's Derby
Day buffet brunch, 308
*Seventeen* serves up some
soul, 264
Sheila Hibben's thoroughly
American dinner, 151
smorgasbord buffet, 204
Spam quick-cook stove-top
special, 191
stop-em-dead low-point
after-church lunch, 130
Sunday night supper of
dreams, 58
tea at Trumps, circa 1983,
361
three-course French peasant
supper, 199–200
thrifty, for the winter of
1931, 44
Trader Vic's Chinese dinner
party, 1946, 99, 100
TV football party, 214
valentine pink-and-white
luncheon, 68
White House, for Chief
Justice Warren,
January 29, 1957,
195–96
meringue:
angel pie, 73
baked Alaska, 201–2
pie, 202

flapper pudding (icebox
cake), 18–20
Italian, 19
tortes, 72
Mexican food, 358, 378, 418
chili con carne, 58–61
Henry Fonda's mother's
rice, 32
Midwestern food, 377–78
soldiers and, 124–25, 144
Miller, Gloria Bley, 103–4
mint:
chicken with, 298–99
grasshopper pie, 256–57
lemon sherbet with crème
de menthe, 198
mock drumsticks, 143
Mongole soup, 77–78
cream, 78
monkey pudding, 21
monosodium glutamate
(MSG), 105
moo shu pork, 108–9
moussaka, 325–26
mousse:
savory, 342
lobster-asparagus, 343
white chocolate and
raspberry, with
raspberry sauce, 395–96
MSG (monosodium
glutamate), 105
muffins, 409
oat bran raisin, 409
mushroom(s):
and chicken crêpes, 313
chicken liver pâté, 320
wild, polenta with two
cheese with sausage
and, 403–5
mussels:
billi-bi, 243
cioppino, 321–22
mystery cake, Campbell's soup,
76
Mystery Chef (John
MacPherson), 51, 58, 78

nam pla (fish sauce), 294
Nineties, 415–21
nosegay cocktail, 70–71
nouvelle cuisine, 350–55
nuoc cham (hot dipping sauce),
    296–97
nuoc mam (fish sauce), 294
nut(s):
    see almond(s); pecan; pine;
walnut

oat bran, 407, 408
    raisin muffins, 409
olive(s):
    and cheese sandwiches, 62
    pasta salad with yellow
        tomatoes, three peppers
        and, 398–99
    roasted garlic with white
        cheese, grilled toasts
        and, 364
omelets, 165
    frittata with zucchini,
        305–6
onions:
    caramelized, linguine with
        walnuts and, 366
    crème vichyssoise, General
        Electric Institute,
        157–58
orange:
    apricot parfait pie, extra-
        fresh, 188–89
    coffee, spiced, 303
    Grand Marnier torte,
        236–37
    lemon pudding cake
        from Florida, Sheila
        Hibben's, 148
    pumpkin bisque, 331
Oriental foods, 268–99
    Indian, 268–69
    luaus, 279–84
    southeast Asian, 293–99
    tropical, 274–84
    see also Chinese food;
        Hawaiian food;
        Japanese food

paella, 244, 245
Pan-American food, 418
pancakes, blue corn, 381
    with cilantro cream and
        black bean caviar,
        380–81
paper-wrapped chicken,
    100–101
party mix (TV mix), 214–15
    nuts and bolts style, 215
passion fruit sorbet, 387
pasta, 35, 37, 397, 400
    angel hair, with pesto,
        399–400
    fettucine Alfredo, 323
    linguine with caramelized
        onions and walnuts, 366
    1924 Italian spaghetti, 37
    penne with vodka sauce,
        401
    primavera, 323–24
    salad, 398
        with olives, yellow toma-
            toes, and three peppers,
            398–99
    spaghetti carbonara,
        322–23
pastry cream, 386–87
pastry party loaf, 74–75
pâté, chicken liver-mushroom,
    320
peach:
    fresh, salsa, 417
    stuffed, salad, 48
peanut butter tea sandwiches,
    62
peanuts:
    three p's salad, 7
    TV mix—nuts and bolts
        style, 215
pear salad, 6
peas:
    snow, 105–6
    three p's salad, 7
pecan:
    bourbon sauce, 376–77
    bread pudding with, 376

butter, ice-cream sundae
    crêpes, 314
pie with chocolate chips,
    383
penne with vodka sauce, 401
pepper(s):
    chili, 416–17, 418
    roasted red, 363
        cream, cream of corn soup
            with corn kernels and,
            362–63
    three, pasta salad with
        olives, yellow tomatoes
        and, 398–99
pepper, black, 177
peppercorns:
    green, 392
        duck breast au poivre
            vert, 392–93
    pink, 392
pesto, angel hair pasta with,
    399–400
pickles, 6
    three p's salad, 7
pico de gallo (salsa cruda; fresh
    salsa), 379–80
pies, dessert:
    angel, 73
    baked Alaska, 202
    chiffon, 146, 148–49
        alternative, 153
        eggnog, 149
        lemon, 152
        1960s evaporated milk
            chocolate, 153
    extra-fresh apricot-orange
        parfait, 188–89
    glazed strawberry, 328
    graham cracker shell for,
        152
    grasshopper, 256–57
    impossible, 348
    pecan, with chocolate chips,
        383
    sweet potato, 265
    Tang, 259, 259
pies, savory:
    latter-day spinach-feta
        quiche, 318–19

pies, savory (continued)
    1920s humble tamale, 35
    quiche Lorraine, 315–17
    tamale, 33, 34
    vegetable curry cheese, of
        the year without the
        damn crust, 341
pilaf, 179–80
    brown rice, 180
    kebab company dinner
        with, 180
pineapple, 271–72
    Alice Bradley's kitchenette
        valentine salad, 4–5
    candlestick salad, 5
    chipped beef and, Mystery
        Chef, 51
    flapper pudding (icebox
        cake), 18–20
    fluff, 20
    glaze, 254
    Hawaiian punch, 282
    heavenly hash, 18
    party kebabs, 178
    pudding, 20
    salad pumpkins, 75
    South Seas skillet meal, 278
    upside-down cake, 27–28
    water lily salad, 4
pine nuts, risotto with
    asparagus and, 402–3
pizza, 35, 370, 418
    dough, 371–72
    with eggplant, goat cheese,
        and basil, 370–71
planked dinners, 81–82
planked steak, directions for,
    82
polenta, 402, 403
    with two cheeses with wild
        mushrooms and
        sausage, 403–5
Polynesian food, 276, 278,
    279, 280
    luaus, 279–84
popcorn and banana salad, 5
pork, 173
    barbecued (cha sui), 100
    Buwei Yang Chao's wine
        smothers meat slices, 97

loin with black beans,
    calypso, 418–19
moo shu, 108–9
Mrs. Allen's Chinese chop
    suey, 90–91
South Seas skillet meal, 278
stir-fried bean curd (tofu)
    with vegetables and, 104
see also ham
porkers, 250
possum, roast, with sweet
    potatoes, 263–64
postwar parties, 140
potatoes:
    crème vichyssoise, General
        Electric Institute,
        157–58
    rosin-baked, 175–76
    soothing mashed, new
        American cooking-style,
        413–14
pot roast à l'oignon (sweep
    steak), 247–48
poulet sauté au citron (chicken
    with lemon cream
    sauce), 166
poultry:
    duck breast au poivre vert,
        392–93
    uncanny salmi of duck with
        wild rice, 187–88
    see also chicken
poverty, cuisine of, 415
progressive dinner, 133
Prohibition, 29–30, 37, 40,
    46, 167, 276
    end of, 41, 82
protein, 173
Prudhomme, Paul, 372–73,
    374, 375
    blackened redfish, 374
Puck, Wolfgang, 367, 370
pudding, 17–21
    bread, with pecan bourbon
        sauce, 376
    cakes, 146, 147, 309
        hot fudge, 147
    Sheila Hibben's orange-
        lemon, from Florida,
        148

flapper (icebox cake),
    18–20
haupia, 284
heavenly hash, 18
monkey, 21
pineapple, 20
pineapple fluff, 20
pumpkin:
    bread, 310, 311
    orange bisque, 331
punch:
    Hawaiian, 282
    sparkling, for summer tea,
        65
Pyles, Stephan, 380

quiche, 317, 318
    latter-day spinach-feta,
        318–19
    Lorraine, 315–17, 318

rabbit (rarebit), Welsh, 46–49
    absurd rictim chitti, 49
    American, 48
raspberry:
    chicken, 390
    kiwi, and carambola tart,
        385
    sauce, 396
    and white chocolate mousse
        with raspberry sauce,
        395–96
rationing, 119, 120, 122, 124,
    126, 128, 129, 132, 133,
    135, 139, 144, 146, 190
    no ration-point menu for a
        Monday, 1943, 121
Recommended Daily
    Allowances (RDAs), 116
record players, hi-fi, 213,
    215–16
redfish, Paul Prudhomme's
    blackened, 374
refrigerators, 7, 9–11
restaurants:
    Chinese, 101–2, 103,
        107–8, 293
    MSG and, 105
    top 11, in United States,
        112–13

in Eighties, 358, 364, 367,
    368, 370, 374, 378,
    380, 410, 411
  Japanese, 285–86, 293
    steak houses, 289–90,
      291
  in Nineties, 415
  in Seventies, 329–34, 351
  steak in, 266
rice:
  brown
    bunny burgers, 261
    pilaf, 180
  fragrant, 294
  fried, 100
  Henry Fonda's mother's
    Spanish (Mexican), 32
  risotto, 402
    with asparagus and pine
      nuts, 402–3
  wild, 230
    uncanny salmi of duck
      with, 187–88
rictim chitti, absurd, 49
risotto, 402
  with asparagus and pine
    nuts, 402–3
roasted:
  garlic with white cheese,
    olives, and grilled
    toasts, 363–64
  red peppers, 363
roasters, electric, 47
roasting, 363
Romanoff, Mike, 163
Rombauer, Irma S., 221, 358
  Joy of Cooking, 221, 247,
    358, 365
Rosellini, Robert, 353–54,
    355, 377
Rosellini's Other Place, menu
    from January 1975, 353
rosin baked potatoes, 175–76
rum:
  balls, 257
  Bundt cake, 309
  Hawaiian punch, 282
  zombie, 274–76
rumaki, 282

salad(s), 2–14, 176, 326
  Alice Bradley's kitchenette
    valentine, 4–5
  banana, 2–4
  banana and popcorn, 5
  bird's nest, 4
  Caesar, 13–14
  candlestick, 5
  Chinese chicken, 109–10
  frozen, 9–13
    fruit, 12–13
    Fruit & Flower Mission
      cheese, 11–12
    tomato frappé, Pictorial
      Review, 12
  garden, California baked
    goat cheese with, 354–55
  gelatin-type, 7–9
  ginger ale, 8–9
  hearts of celery, working-
    gal tomato aspic rounds
    with, 188
  iceberg lettuce in, 6
  jewel, 8
  pasta, 398
    with olives, yellow toma-
      toes, and three peppers,
      398–99
  pear, 6
  pumpkins, 75
  spinach, with Cheddar
    cheese dressing, 326–27
  stuffed peach, 48
  tea room, 15
  three-bean, 176–77
  three p's, 7
  "topiary," 70
  water lily, 4
salad bars, 332–33
salsa, 417
  fresh (salsa cruda; pico de
    gallo), 379–80
  fresh peach, 417
  simple chicken soup with,
    379
sandwich(es), 15
  casserole, 344, 346
  cheese dreams, Procter &
    Gamble, 57

cream cheese and fig, 88
  grilled cheese (cheese
    dream), 56–58
  loaf, Betty Co-ed surprise,
    66–67
  loaves, checkerboard, 67
  marmalade, for ladies, 16
  tea
    date-nut bread for, 63
    olive and cheese, 62
    peanut butter, 62
    rolled (diplomas), 62–63
    taste-t bridge, 64
saté, shrimp, 276–77
sauces:
  barbecue, 170
    cowboy-type spicy, 171
    gourmet-type, 171–72
  beurre blanc, 369
  bourbon-pecan, 376–77
  chocolate, 413
  Grand Marnier chocolate,
    237
  hot dipping (nuoc cham),
    296–97
  lemon, for gingerbread
    waffles, 55
  Madeira, 233–34
  raspberry, 396
  salsa cruda (fresh salsa;
    pico de gallo), 379–80
  tempura dipping, 288
  tomato coulis, 352
sausage:
  French casserole of corn
    and, 156–57
  polenta with two cheeses
    with wild mushrooms
    and, 403–5
scallop(s):
  grilled, with watercress-
    lime beurre blanc,
    368–69
  vegetable terrine with
    tomato coulis, 351–52
Scandinavian food, 203–5, 319
  Swedish meatballs (kött-
    buller), 204–5
sea captain's special, 145

seafood:
  billi-bi, 243
  cioppino, 321–22
  crab and artichoke
    casserole, 248
  grilled scallops with
    watercress-lime beurre
    blanc, 368–69
  hot crab dip, 343–44
  *Kraft Music Hall* clam
    appetizer dip, 208
  lobster-asparagus mousse,
    343
  lobster in pineapple boats
    flambé, 224
  lobster thermidor,
    canopener gourmet-style,
    197
  lobster thermidor classique,
    197
  merry old sole (sole stuffed
    with crab and cheese),
    330–31
  scallop-vegetable terrine
    with tomato coulis,
    351–52
  shrimp saté, 276–77
  shrimp tempura pu-pus,
    283
  velvety crab and cheese
    soufflé, 185
  *see also* fish
Sea Legs, 290
Seventies, 300–355
  brunch in, 302–19
  foreign foods in, 319–27
  health food in, 335–41,
    351, 353
  nouvelle cuisine in, 350–55
  restaurants in, 329–34, 351
  silly names in, 300, 301,
    332
  suburban gourmet cooking
    in, 342–50, 351
shake, health, 260–61
sherbet, 391
  Canton lemon-ginger, 270
  lemon, with crème de
    menthe, 198

shrimp:
  cioppino, 321–22
  merry old sole (sole stuffed
    with crab and cheese),
    330–31
  saté, 276–77
  tempura pu-pus, 283
*Silver Palate Cookbook*, The
  (Lukins and Rosso), 365
Sixties, 217–67, 301
  Chinese cooking in, 103–6
  desserts in, 253–57
  entertaining in, 230–42,
    246–49
  flambéed food in, 220–25
  fondue in, 237–42
  foreign foods in, 244–46
  health food in, 258–62,
    335
  instant food in, 217–19
  Julia Child in, 225–28,
    226, 230
  soul food in, 263–65
sludge, or how to keep alive,
  128, 131
Smith, Jeff, 365
smoothee, strawberry-banana,
  339
smorgasbord buffet, 204
snow peas, 105–6
sole stuffed with crab and
  cheese (merry old sole),
  330–31
sorbet, 387, 391
  passion fruit, 387
soufflé:
  tomato spinach, cups
    elegante, 342
  velvety crab and cheese,
    185
Soulé, Henri, 155, 156
soul food, 263–65, 418
soup mixes, dried, 247
  pot roast à l'oignon (sweep
    steak), 247–48
soups, 77, 339
  baby borscht, 184
  billi-bi, 243
  boula, 78–79

chicken and coconut milk,
  297–98
cream Mongole, 78
cream of corn, with roasted
  red pepper cream and
  corn kernels, 362–63
crème vichyssoise, General
  Electric Institute,
  157–58
jellied gazpacho, 246
Mongole, 77–78
pumpkin-orange bisque,
  331
simple chicken, with salsa,
  379
split-second gourmet with
  a blender gazpacho, 245
soups, canned, 76, 182–83,
  247
  crab and artichoke
    casserole, 248
  elegant string bean
    casserole, 249
  golden gourmet chicken,
    248–49
  mystery cake, Campbell's
    soup, 76
southeast Asian foods, 293–99
Southern food, 377
Southwestern food, 378–84
spa cuisine, 406
spaghetti, 35
  carbonara, 322–23
  1924 Italian, 37
Spam, 189, 190–91
  fruit cocktail buffet party
    loaf, 190–91
  quick-cook stove-top
    special, 191
Spanish food, 31–35, 244, 245
  chili con carne, 58–61
  Henry Fonda's mother's
    rice, 32
spareribs, Chinese-style, 100
spinach:
  braised chicken luau with
    coconut milk and, 273
  feta quiche, latter-day,
    318–19

Joe's special, 306–7
salad with Cheddar cheese
dressing, 326–27
tomato soufflé cups
elegante, 342
spring rolls with hot dipping
sauce, Vietnamese, 295–96
starfruit (carambola), kiwi, and
raspberry tart, 385
steak, 173, 266, 407
170-degree, 407–8
planked, directions for, 82
ranchero, Arthur Froehlich,
170
steak houses, Japanese,
289–90, 291
Stern, Jane and Michael, 410
Stewart, Martha, 358, 359,
362
stews:
cioppino, 321–22
crockery chicken, with wine
and tarragon, 345
stir-fried bean curd (tofu) with
pork and vegetables, 104
strawberry(ies):
banana smoothee, 339
pie, glazed, 328
Romanoff, 163
à la mode americaine, 164
squares, 348–49
stroganoff, beef, 191–92
classic, 192
hamburger, 193
sugar, 146
tips for saving, 137
sukiyaki, 286–87
beef, 287
Sunday night supper, 44–61
of dreams, 58
surf and turf, 333
surimi, 290
sushi, 112, 290, 291–93
California roll, 292–93
Swedish food, 203–5
meatballs (köttbuller),
204–5

sweet potato(es):
marshmallows and, 42
marshmallow surprises, 43,
43
party kebabs, 178
pie, 265
roast possum with, 263–64
Swiss steak, 141–42
Szechwan food, 107–11, 112

tamale:
loaf, 1920s, 34
pie, 33, 34
1920s humble, 35
Tang, 259
pie, 259
tea, heavenly, 303
tapas, 373
tarragon:
chicken breasts with, Instant
Haute Cuisine, 218
crockery chicken stew with
wine and, 345
tart:
kiwi, carambola, and
raspberry, 385
shell, 385–86
tea, 64–65
afternoon, 362
parties, Thirties, 61–65
rooms, 15–17
television parties, 213–15
after-television intellectual
supper, 213
football menu, 214
tempura, 288
dipping sauce, 288
pu-pus, shrimp, 283
tenderloin tips, The Cattleman's of New York, 267
tequila sunrise, 302–3
teriyaki, 288–89
beef, 289
terrine, scallop-vegetable, with
tomato coulis, 351–52
Tex-Mex food, 378

Thai food, 293, 294, 297–99
chicken and coconut milk
soup, 297–98
chicken with basil or mint,
298–99
iced coffee, 299
Thirties, 41–84, 183
club luncheons in, 65–73
cocktail parties in, 82–84
Depression and, 40, 41–42,
44, 84, 139, 167, 190,
276
end of, 84
entertaining in, 73–77
formal dining in, 77–81
plank dining in, 81–82
Sunday night supper in,
44–61
tea parties in, 61–65
Thomas, Anna, 341
Thousand Recipe Chinese
Cookbook, The (Miller),
104–5
Tibetan food, 111, 112
tiramisù, Café Louis, 412–13
tofu (bean curd), stir-fried,
with pork and vegetables,
104
tomato(es):
aspic, 186, 230
finest, 186–87
rounds with hearts of celery salad, working-gal,
188
cioppino, 321–22
coulis, 352
scallop-vegetable terrine
with, 351–52
frappé, Pictorial Review, 12
Henry Fonda's mother's
Spanish (Mexican) rice,
32
jellied gazpacho, 246
salmon lomi, 272–73
spinach soufflé cups
elegante, 342

split-second gourmet with
a blender gazpacho, 245
Swiss steak, 141–42
water lily salad, 4
yellow, pasta salad with
olives, three peppers
and, 398–99
tongue, boiled, 132
"topiary" food, 69–71
torte:
Grand Marnier, 236–37
meringue, 72
angel pie, 73
tournedos, 202–3
Rossini, 203
Tower, Jeremiah, 358–62,
363, 370
Trader Vic (Victor Bergeron),
98–99, 100, 101, 113,
170, 188, 274, 275,
276, 277, 278, 279, 288
Trader Vic's, 98–99, 113, 275,
276, 277, 278, 279
Chinese dinner party menu,
1946, 99, 100
Trader Vic's Book of Food and
Drink (Bergeron), 99
Treet, 190
tropical food, 274–84
truffles, 394
dark chocolate, 394–95
Tryabita celery cereal, 260
TV mix, 214–15
nuts and bolts style, 215
Twenties, 1–40, 183
desserts in, 17–28
exotica craze in, 87–89
foreign cooking in, 31–40
Prohibition in, 29–30,
37, 40
salads in, 2–14
tea rooms in, 15–17

valentine pink-and-white
luncheon, 68

valentine salad, Alice Bradley's
kitchenette, 4–5
veal, 142–43
ham pinwheels from the
roaster, 47
mock drumsticks, 143
Orloff, 227–29
pastry party loaf, 74–75
patriotic pinwheel meat
roll, 122
vegetable(s), 80
curry cheese pie of the year
without the damn
crust, 341
pasta primavera, 323–24
scallop terrine with tomato
coulis, 351–52
stir-fried bean curd (tofu)
with pork and, 104
see also specific vegetables
Velveeta cheese, 185
and crab soufflé, velvety,
185
vichyssoise, crème, General
Electric Institute, 157–58
Vietnamese food, 293–95
spring rolls with hot
dipping sauce, 295–96
vodka sauce, penne with, 401

waffles, 52, 53–55
basic, 54
gingerbread, 55
walnut(s):
bourbon or rum balls, 257
date bread for tea
sandwiches, 63
linguine with caramelized
onions and, 366
maple angel food cake,
all-American, 137–38
maple cream filling, 138
watercress-lime beurre blanc,
grilled scallops with,
368–69

water lily salad, 4
Waters, Alice, 353, 354, 355,
358, 360, 363, 380
wedgies (bologna pie), 210–11
Welsh rabbit (rarebit), 46–49
absurd rictim chitti, 49
American, 48
West Coast Cook Book (Brown),
98
whiskey Bundt cake, 309
wild rice, 230
wine, 202
Buwei Yang Chao's wine
smothers meat slices, 97
cooking, 30
crockery chicken stew with
tarragon and, 345
Madeira sauce, 233–34
World War II, 114–39, 144,
146, 167
black market in, 122–23
Chinese-American food
after, 95
eating orgy after, 139–54
end of, 139, 140
entertaining and, 129–39
rationing and, see rationing
soldiers in, 124–26, 144,
155, 190, 285
candy consumed by, 135,
146
K rations for, 126
weddings and, 138–39

zabaglione, 161–62
zombie, 274–76
zucchini, 80
bread, 310
frittata with, 305–6